Raised on Christian Milk

Raised on Christian Milk

Food and the Formation of the Soul in Early Christianity

John David Penniman

Yale

UNIVERSITY PRESS

New Haven & London

Chapter 5 originally appeared as "Fed to Perfection: Mother's Milk, Roman Family Values, and the Transformation of the Soul in Gregory of Nyssa," *Church History* 84.3 (2015): 495–530. Reprinted with permission.

Yale University Press books may be purchased in quantity for educational, business, or promotional use. For information, please e-mail sales.press@yale.edu (U.S. office) or sales@yaleup.co.uk (U.K. office).

Set in Bulmer type by IDS Infotech, Ltd.

Printed in the United States of America.

Library of Congress Control Number: 2016950164

ISBN 978-0-300-22276-0 (hardcover : alk. paper)

A catalogue record for this book is available from the British Library.

This paper meets the requirements of ANSI/NISO Z39.48-1992 (Permanence of Paper).

10 9 8 7 6 5 4 3 2 1

To my family,
for teaching me to eat well

What is known of the moral effects of food? Is there a
philosophy of nourishment?

—Friedrich Nietzsche, *The Gay Science*

Contents

Preface   ix

Acknowledgments   xiii

INTRODUCTION

Same Essence, Same Food: Nourishment, Formation, and Education
in Early Christianity   1

ONE

The Symbolic Power of Food in the Greco-Roman World   23

TWO

Mother's Milk as Ethno-religious Essence in Ancient Judaism   52

THREE

Ruminating on Paul's Food in the Second Century   79

FOUR

Animal, Vegetable, Milk: Origen's Dietary System   109

FIVE

Gregory of Nyssa at the Breast of the Bridegroom   138

SIX

Milk Without Growth: Augustine and the Limits of Formation   165

Conclusion   201

Notes, with List of Abbreviations   211
Bibliography   279
Index of Subjects   313
Index of Ancient Sources   320

Preface

Each word has a life, its past, its ego, its self-esteem. It resists. It doesn't want to
leave all this to the mercy of foreign handling, however reverential.

—Kiki Dimoula, *The Brazen Plagiarist*

PINYTOS WAS HUNGRY. SO WAS HIS congregation. He had been
feeding his flock the same lessons for a while. Milk can nourish only for so
long. The folks on Knossos were growing restless, anxious for more substantial food. His teaching had become repetitive, uninteresting, weak. It seems
that some in the community were ready for stronger nourishment, a meal
that might enable them to progress toward deeper maturity in faith.

In book four of his *Ecclesiastical History,* Eusebius recounts the
exchange between Pinytos, the bishop of Knossos, and Dionysius, the
bishop of Corinth. For some reason, Dionysius had intervened in the affairs
of the church at Knossos, recommending that Pinytos "not place a heavy
burden concerning compulsory chastity upon his community, but rather
to set his sights on the weaknesses of the majority." It seems that the two
bishops differed on how best to read the apostle Paul's teaching regarding
marriage and chastity. Dionysius took the more flexible approach,
suggesting that Pinytos be lenient in his lessons so as not to alienate anyone
who shrinks from the rigors of chastity.

Pinytos became annoyed. A teacher ought not teach to the weakest
pupils. The bar should be set higher. He turned to the apostle Paul's first
letter to the Corinthians for support and found evidence there for the superiority of chastity over marriage. But Pinytos also discerned in Paul's writing a
method for distinguishing the weak of faith from the strong, and a curricular
paradigm for goading the former toward the latter. In his reply to the bishop
of Corinth, Pinytos summoned Paul's words about nourishment—words

about breast milk and solid food—in order to pressure his Corinthian correspondent into giving an advanced lesson. Eusebius narrates: "To [the letter
from Dionysius] Pinytos replied that he admired and welcomed Dionysius,
but petitioned him to distribute now already a more solid food, and to
nourish the people under him with another more perfect letter, so that they
might not be stuck feeding on milky words, and thus reach old age without
noticing that they are still living as infants."

It is telling that Dionysius is described as the preparer and distributor
of Paul's nourishment. When the apostle wrote to Corinth, he too had written in frustration. 1 Corinthians 3:1–3 attests to this. The Corinthians were
weak and fleshly infants. They could not stomach anything more than what
the apostle had already provided. His breast milk was the only food suitable
for such souls. But in the second century, it seems that the milk-drinking
infants of Corinth had finally outgrown their fleshly natures. And so Pinytos appealed to this legacy, seeking from Dionysius what the Corinthians
had received from Paul: a stronger food that had the power to transform the
one who eats it into the apostle's fully grown, spiritualized ideal.

This second-century exchange between Pinytos and Dionysius,
archived in the fourth century by Eusebius, is a window into the complex
afterlife of Paul's words about milk and solid food. It reveals one disagreement among many others that would follow concerning the movement from
milk to solid food and how best to understand the apostle's discussion of
growth from an infant faith to one of maturity. But it is interesting to me less
as an accurate historical record of an epistolary exchange than as evidence
for the enduring power of food to communicate the deepest values of
early Christians. In the centuries that followed his correspondence to the
Corinthians, Paul's reference to milk and solid food became an irresistible
symbol. The disagreement between Dionysius and Pinytos about chastity
being the higher teaching, the solid food, is merely one iteration of how that
symbol was put to work in structuring Christian communities and organizing the people within them. Their debate reflects deeper tensions within
early Christianity about the role of food in the proper formation of souls.

Words have weight, a density. They contain complex histories. The ghosts of their previous uses lurk behind the senses they acquire in the present. They function like oracles—invoking pasts and imagining futures. Words also inescapably conjure the social and cultural realities of embodied life that invest them with meaning and power. The common vocabulary, tropes, and phrases we use to make sense of our world are never neutral. They bear witness to the ideologies, tensions, and anxieties that animate human life together. Such words are not simply abstract, merely metaphoric. They carry a formative power to mold, structure, and give shape to reality. What follows is a story about the weight, the histories, and the symbolic power of milk and solid food in early Christianity.

Acknowledgments

MANY OF THE WORDS THAT FOLLOW WERE written and revised and rerevised while I sat under the headless gaze of Nike of Samothrace. A copy of the classic statue of Winged Victory towers over the tables in the Cohen Reading Room at Ohio State University library. There is a violent grace to her posture. Her wings fight against the prevailing winds; her robe clutches her legs and torso while she raises a missing arm to signal victory. Nike's sturdy stride elevates her, providing balance in spite of the unseen forces that would restrain her motion, as she steps forward to shout in jubilation. After sitting beneath her for weeks, I found it hard not to see Nike as somehow symbolic of completing this project.

Unlike Nike, however, I have had the fortune of favorable winds.

When I was an undergraduate at Elon University, Jeffrey Pugh first brought the world of ancient Christianity to life in my imagination. His lectures had an oracular power, conjuring the ghosts of church history, channeling the tensions and passions of their life and thought. From Jeff I learned to look at the past as a resource for asking better and better questions about the present. I consider it a great fortune to call him a friend today, some fifteen years after he unwisely let me into a senior-level course as a first-year student.

At Emory University, I found an ideal context to develop my interest in the history of Christianity. I sat in Ian McFarland's classrooms for four consecutive semesters of a two-year degree. With patience and characteristic precision, Ian always guided my unfocused and inarticulate historical grumblings into a more thoughtful and nuanced expression. I still sense his keen editorial gaze over my writing long after his ink has disappeared from my pages. I was fortunate to overlap in Atlanta for two years during Richard Valantasis's tenure at Emory. It was in his seminar on ancient contemplative practices that I first encountered Foucault. Richard was a nurturing presence at Emory for young scholars interested in ancient Christianity. With his trademark wit, encyclopedic knowledge, and an allergy to nonsense, Lewis Ayres shepherded me through a thesis on the theme of sorrow in Augustine's *Expositions of the Psalms*. From Lewis and his cabal of doctoral students (Mark DelCogliano, Adam Ployd, Andrew Radde-Gallwitz, Kate Wilkinson, and Ryan Woods), I received a crash course in the texts, questions, tensions, perils, and promises surrounding the study of early Christianity. I am grateful to have been at Emory at such a fruitful time for conversation about late antiquity, and Lewis was the center of gravity around which such conversations made their orbit.

I began doctoral work in Fordham's Department of Theology at a moment in which the study of ancient Christianity was undergoing a rapid expansion due to new faculty hires, course offerings, methodologies, and opportunities for collaboration in the New York City consortium. On the last point, I had the privilege of auditing a course taught by Virginia Burrus at Drew University in my second semester. This was, without question, a revelation that reshaped the questions and methods animating my research. Likewise, Raffaella Cribiore graciously welcomed me into her Education in Antiquity seminar at NYU during my fifth year—an experience that helped bring many of the bigger concerns of this project into focus. I also found at Drew and Union Seminary a dynamic group of friends and colleagues from whom I continue to receive much support and inspiration: Peter Anthony Mena, Jennifer Barry, Natalie Williams, Beatrice Marovich, Christy Cobb, and Brantley Dean. Maia Kotrosits, in particular, has been a resuscitating force. Her boundless creative energy always sends me back to work with a greater sense of urgency.

At Fordham there was no shortage of messmates. The doctoral students in theology there embodied the possibility of a table fellowship that endeavors to leave difference undigested and unassimilated: Eric Daryl Meyer, Daniel Reginald Soowoong Kim, Brendan McInerny, Ian Kinman, Matthew Lootens, Emily Cain, Lindsey Mercer, Kathryn Reinhard, Brianne Jacobs, Beth Pyne, Mike Azar, Zachary Smith, all the Jo(h)ns (Stanfill, Garza, Gleim), Andy Ballard, and Ashley Purpura. Almost immediately, Allan Georgia and I partnered in our doctoral work like two hobbits embarking together on a formidable journey. I have been strengthened by his expansive wisdom about the ancient world, his quick humor, his fondness for spirited drinks, and his tenacious friendship. Rather unexpectedly, and for quite different reasons, both Allan and I found ourselves in Ohio during the final stages of writing our dissertations. I was glad to celebrate the completion of our final steps in person, "here at the end of all things."

Among the faculty at Fordham, I received only enthusiasm, support, and the most constructive of criticism. With Brandon Bayne and Franklin Harkins, I commuted to and from Connecticut for over a year; I was glad to have their captive audience and nagged them with questions about research and pedagogy on a daily basis. Robert Davis has been a crucial conversation partner on questions about metaphor and helped me suss out Derrida's importance for this project. Bob's deep insight is surpassed only by his unparalleled kindness. Karina Martin Hogan and Sarit Kattan Gribetz both offered crucial guidance at the beginning and at the end of this project, respectively. Sarit voluntarily commented (in detail!) on the first 150 pages, although she was under no administrative obligation to do so. Her questions and critiques were sorely needed and made completion seem like a tangible possibility. She also provided herculean support and sage counsel on matters professional and otherwise. I arrived on campus at the same time as Michael Peppard. Those who know his work (and his personality) can readily identify his fingerprints across this project. For a time, we rode the subway together from the Bronx to the Upper West Side, and those commute conversations were always generative. It was in a directed reading under his supervision that I was prompted to grapple with the intersection of Roman social history and the language of nourishment in early Christianity. Michael's advice (or "Peppardisms," as Allan and I came to call them) lit the path between coursework and completion. Larry Welborn and George Demacopoulos have been stalwart advocates and tireless readers of my research since I began doctoral work. Larry's inexhaustible storehouse of energy, his profoundly pastoral disposition, and his Rolodex-like ability to cite primary and secondary sources from memory provided a constant source of momentum for this project. Likewise, George

has been for me a *magis Ecclesiasticus:* his sensitivity to the connection between historical questions and contemporary concerns is a model to which
I aspire.

Frustrated by a lifetime of disappointing teachers, Augustine asks in
his *Confessions*: "Qui doceat me?" (Who can teach me?) I have had no such
frustration. The greatest of fortunes afforded me during my time at Fordham
has been the opportunity to work with Benjamin Dunning. From matters of
method and theory, to those of writing style and structure, to the questions of
consequence and "So what?"—Ben has been an uncanny mentor, a trust-
worthy guide, an exemplum of the highest order, and a caring friend. The last
of those has been as crucial to the completion of this project as the rest. What
follows began in 2010 under the auspices of a summer research fellowship
that examined imitation in early Christianity—an ill-conceived and impossi-
bly broad subject. But it was through Ben's careful supervision, and the conversations that ensued over the next year, that the vexed relationship between
food and formation appeared as a potentially worthwhile avenue for further
research. Since that time, I scarcely typed a word that didn't receive Ben's
scrutiny. I am better for it. His unflinching commitment to clarity and coherence has been a touchstone, as has his theoretical sophistication. Whatever is
novel or persuasive in the pages that follow is as much Ben's as it is mine.
Whatever falls short of that belongs to me alone.

I am deeply grateful for the enthusiasm and support I have received
from my new colleagues in religious studies at Bucknell University. A special thanks goes to Karline McLain, who went above and beyond the call of
duty for a department chair in ensuring that my transition was a smooth
one. In the broader field of late antiquity and early Christianity, Andrew
Jacobs and Ellen Muehlberger have both shown this junior colleague the
very best of what academia can be. I am especially pleased to have this book
published in the Synkrisis series at Yale University Press. Dale Martin and
Larry Welborn have been generous series editors, and Heather Gold's careful editorial guidance has made the prospect of letting this project go after
six years a bit less terrifying.

The debts incurred during doctoral work—be they financial, emo-
tional, or relational—are mitigated only by a network of friends and family

willing to show grace, patience, and understanding beyond the normal human measures. I count myself among the lucky ones to have had such a network. Ryan Smyth, Kevin Bray, and the rest of the Oak House folk from Elon have been with me since before my curiosity about history had much content or form. I am grateful for their friendships and for the ways in which our differences have become opportunities for joyful communion rather than occasions of tension. Joshua Ralston has been a close confidant, intellectual sparring partner, and sounding board about life inside the academy and out since our first days together at Emory. His social awkwardness, a trait his friends know well and love deeply, pales in comparison to his generosity of spirit and his scholarly passion. The Keys family modeled a capacious approach to kinship. They welcomed me and supported me without reservation. For the past dozen years, Marsha, Bill, Lauren, and especially Erin buttressed my life. Without them I would have toppled over long ago.

This is dedicated, fittingly, to my family. They have been an unceasing source of encouragement, setting up bleachers to cheer me on at every turn. Whether at the dinner table or from afar, their love nourished my life and my vocational pursuits even when I felt a creeping sense of atrophy. From my earliest memories, they have embodied the possibility that difference can serve as a stronger bond than sameness. My two older sisters, Kara and Rachel, have played the parts of mother, father, tutor, and counselor at various stages. They were my teachers before I ever set foot in a school. They continue to teach me still with their unique wisdoms and passions. My parents, Charlotte and David, created a household energized by intellectual curiosity. Growing up in a home overflowing with books was like living inside a classroom. I can't think of a greater gift to give a child. If I have had favorable winds, those currents originate in large part from my mother and father. I don't think this book squares the debts between a son and his parents, but I hope it proves those debts to have been somehow worthwhile.

Raised on Christian Milk

Same Essence, Same Food: Nourishment, Formation, and Education in Early Christianity

"YOU ARE WHAT YOU EAT."

It is a phrase so worn down by use that its origin remains, for most, hidden beneath the dulling repetition of cliché. But every cliché has a past. And this particular cliché beckons us into the deep rabbit hole of history, into a story about the power of food to determine who we are as people.

It was Ludwig Feuerbach who insisted that "Man is what he eats."[1] And as a result he was mocked by his contemporaries, many of whom viewed the saying as evidence of an absurdly reductive materialism.[2] The full context of the quote draws out the force of its sense for Feuerbach: "From this we also see the ethical and political significance of the study of nourishment for society. Food turns into blood, blood turns into heart and brain, into thoughts and character. *Human food is the basis for human formation and for character.* If you want to improve society, give the people better food rather than declamations against sin. Man is what he eats."[3]

Precisely what Feuerbach intended with this observation is a matter of some debate.[4] Ten years later (1860), in "The Mystery of Sacrifice or Man Is What He Eats," he offered a defense and a clarification.[5] In that essay, Feuerbach turns to Greco-Roman antiquity in order to analyze the ways in which food functioned both as a cultural marker and as a mechanism for identity formation. His goal was to draw a straight line between gastronomy and theology and thereby to demonstrate the fundamental connection between nourishment, human self-understanding, and knowledge of the nature of the gods. It was significant to Feuerbach that the food and drink for which we hunger and thirst are identical to the food and drink that feeds the gods in ritual. The idea of a common nourishment suggested something deeper concerning a common nature shared between humans and gods: "the same essence, the same food, and vice versa."[6] If man is what he eats, and man eats what the gods eat, then the link that joins the human and the divine is knotted within the stomach. The prominent position of food in ritual sacrifice thus opened a window, for Feuerbach, into the material dimension of the human impulse toward transcendence.

That a shared food could imply a shared essence was readily observable, for Feuerbach, in the feeding of infants with mother's milk. He concludes the essay with an examination of breast-feeding and its significance in human formation:

> Our first, original nourishment is the obvious mystery, the corporeal concept of food. This takes the form of human blood in the womb of the mother—human blood in a specific and mediated form—thus, a liquid, but a liquid identical with the mother's essence and with our own essence. Because, at this stage, we are yet still liquid, aqueous, unformed, malleable beings. Thus, the nature of our essence is one with the nature of our nourishment. The individuality of the animal or human is one with the individuality of the authoritative, archetypal, and original food: Milk. Although the matter that comprises all milk is the same, each one is endowed with a different value, so that each animal species and even every woman has their own, individual milk. The child consumes his own mother. By sucking on her breast, it sucks in milk, the blood, the essence of the mother.
>
> "It is not prejudicial," says Moleschott in the *Lehre der Nahrungsmittel*, "that the essence of the mother is imparted to the child through the milk." In itself, [the child] is what it eats and eats what it is. It is therefore an anthropophagos [that is, a cannibal].[7]

Feuerbach goes on to suggest that this primordial, cannibalistic nourishment—in its power to transmit a shared essence—forms the basis for all ritualistic eating, especially that cannibalistic meal called the Eucharist, in which the flesh and blood of a god-man are offered in order to bring reconciliation between humanity and God.[8]

Feuerbach's famous aphorism that we become what we eat was, in fact, grounded in the assumption that milk mediates the substance of the mother (her person, her character, her very nature) into the pliable dough of the child. Her food is the material realization of her character and her culture, transferring her inward essence in the quotidian act of feeding.[9] This eccentric thesis regarding the connection between food and essence not only anticipates a burgeoning contemporary interest in food as a site for moral, philosophical, and theological reflection but also crucially reflects widespread traditions from antiquity surrounding nourishment and human formation. The provocative suggestion that our natures can be perfected by our food has roots that stretch back into the literature of Greco-Roman antiquity and is echoed within the writings of the early Christian communities who inherited and transformed that cultural legacy. In ways that even Feuerbach's suggestive hypothesis did not fully realize, the ancient worlds of Greece and Rome were deeply invested in the notion that humans become what they consume. And ancient Christians were no exception.

Human nourishment takes place at the intersection of biology and culture. A complex combination of creaturely instinct and social habit, the physical materials and social settings of our nourishment reveal much about our biological constitution and our cultural formation. Food implies both a state of being—we eat in order to survive—and a process of becoming—we eat (especially in earlier years) in order to grow into something more. At once fundamental to our nature and yet intricately involved in every stage of human social development, the relationship between food and formation slips easily between the literal and the symbolic.

In recent years, scholars of early Christianity have given increasing attention to the function of meals as markers of cultural identity or as the traversing of cultural identity.[10] Hal Taussig offers a clear account of this when he suggests that "specific foods were considered important in social experimentation around interethnicity at meals. What one ate (both at the community meals and most likely at other times) had come to represent by

the time of Acts' composition major social markers."[11] For Taussig, as
for many other scholars of meals in early Christianity, the sharing of food
offers a crucial site for tracing the formation of Christian identity in the
ancient world.

But what about food as more than a marker of social identity? That
is to say, what about food as a mechanism for cultivating and perfecting
human nature? To borrow from Feuerbach's framing, in what ways and to
what extent was shared nourishment imbued with the power to share essence? Echoes of this question can be heard in the apostle Paul's first letter
to the Corinthians. Paul's pronouncements about "the social effect of eating
particular foods" have long been a focal point of New Testament scholarship and, more recently, of interest in early Christian meals.[12] Paul's ambivalence about food and its impact on human transformation is best exemplified
in the juxtaposition of 1 Corinthians 8:8 ("Food will not draw you close to
God") and the emphatic language about nourishment and human growth
in 1 Corinthians 3:1–3: "I was not able to speak to you as people of the spirit
but rather as people of the flesh, as infants in Christ. I gave you milk to
drink, not solid food, for you were not able [to eat solid food]. In fact, even
now you are not able to eat, for you are fleshy people. Since there is quarreling and rivalry among you, are you not fleshy people who live in the manner
of people?" On the one hand, it would seem that 1 Corinthians 8 reflects
Paul's "literal" understanding of the essence of food and its relationship to
human nature, while 1 Corinthians 3 provides a "metaphoric" description
of spiritual maturity and immaturity that is symbolically mapped onto particular forms of nourishment. On the other hand, the direct appeal to the
nourishment of breast milk offered by the apostle himself seems to suggest
a more complex dynamic between symbolic language and the proper formation of human persons. As I will demonstrate, ancient theories of intellectual formation depended upon corresponding theories of the power of
material food to shape both body and mind. These theories show little investment in a stark distinction between literal and metaphoric nourishment.

Over the course of this introduction and throughout the chapters that follow, I will unpack this dynamic between literal and symbolic food within

ancient discussions of human formation. For the moment, however, I want to raise the possibility that Paul's milk is no mere metaphor but evokes a broad and pervasive strategy in antiquity whereby eating and feeding functioned as cultural markers and also, more crucially, as mechanisms for the production and transmission of that culture. Paul's appeal to his own milk imbues it with a formative power for the ongoing development of his Corinthian children. In this sense, milk carries within it the material stuff of legitimate identity. Food becomes here a means for perfecting the infantile state, a developmental process that they could not achieve on their own. From his breast milk, the Corinthians are made his children, even as he calls them "infants in Christ," and they are given the sustenance needed to grow. These "infants" are aqueous beings, shaped and molded by the milk they receive from their mother. The same essence. The same food.

In his distinction of milk and solid food, the apostle Paul appropriated the symbolic power of nourishment and breast-feeding that was already established within ancient theories of formation. The relationship between food and intellectual development implied in Paul's writing and made explicit in his later interpreters was, in fact, embedded within a broader discourse of formation that can be observed across a wide range of literature from Greek and Roman antiquity. This discourse acquired its force through a combination of social, medical, legal, and literary interventions that, instead of partitioning the growth of the body from that of the soul, bound the two ever closer together. It is in this context that we must understand Paul's reference to milk and solid food and the various early Christian interpretive traditions that developed around it. As we will see, breast-feeding—through its capacity to signify nurtured growth, a transferring of essential material, and a gradual intellectual attunement—figured prominently in theories about the formation of Christian identities. This has as much to do with actual food practices in antiquity as it does with the theoretical and theological functions that they acquired.

What do we mean when we talk about "eating well?" What social and ethical norms, what deeper concerns about self and society are embedded within this phrase? Despite its simple formulation, the notion of "eating well" implies a gastronomic regime. That is, discussions of proper nourishment are one of the most basic yet most potent ways of identifying, classifying, and organizing people. Food arrives on our plate and into our mouths already coded with cultural values. For those who came after the apostle Paul, food functioned as just this kind of regime. The trope of milk and solid food was a regulatory principle that enabled early Christian authors to designate boundaries between mature and immature, perfect and imperfect, wise and simple, orthodox and aberrant. More crucially, the trope of milk and solid food allowed such boundaries to appear natural, even biologically constituted. Thus, by foregrounding the reception and interpretation of 1 Corinthians 3:1–3 as part of a broader ancient discourse of formation, I will chart the ways in which early Christians theorized the transmission of true knowledge, orthodox faith, and legitimate identity as a process of eating and feeding.[13]

What is needed is a framework for understanding the symbolic power of food in early Christian accounts of human formation that does not rely on an overly simplistic dichotomy between physical food and intellectual or spiritual nourishment. To that end, this introduction aims to situate the relationship between food and formation in antiquity in three preliminary ways: First I will show how scholars have struggled to interpret symbolic language surrounding nourishment and education in antiquity without also relying upon modern binaries like "literal" and "metaphoric," or "nature" and "nurture." Second, through a brief examination of the conceptual slippage that attends the ancient vocabulary pertaining to food and formation, I will look at a few recent studies that have begun to destabilize the scholarly binaries in fruitful ways. And last, I will consider some theoretical resources for understanding "symbolic language" as distinct from this scholarly tendency in such a way that foregrounds the socially situated and irreducibly embodied nature of human speech—even when (indeed, perhaps *especially* when) that speech is figurative.

The Separation of Body and Soul in Scholarship on Ancient Education

The Greek notion of *paideia* is of singular importance for understanding the intersection of food and human formation in antiquity. For our purposes, when I speak of *paideia* I am referring to the constellation of social ideologies, medical traditions, and educational and curricular standards that contributed to the proper formation of the human person. Typically reserved only for the elite, *paideia* was not viewed simply as the highest form of intellectual training one could receive but, more emphatically, was understood as the perfection or consummation of one's nature.

In 1961, just prior to his death, Werner Jaeger published a small volume titled *Early Christianity and Greek Paideia.*[14] In the final chapter of that book, in which he examines the transformation of *paideia* in the work of Gregory of Nyssa, Jaeger observes that the core of Gregory's own educational theory is drawn from that ancient Greek ideal of *morphosis*—the conviction that human nature is plastic and susceptible to transformation. Jaeger viewed Gregory's blending of Christian theological and biblical commitments with ancient ideals about the transformative effect of education on the human person as the great achievement of his thought.

But the concept of formation articulated in the ancient ideal of *morphosis* carried with it a more complicated aspect, one that Jaeger readily identified and attempted to resolve: "The metaphor of the gradual growth of the human personality and its spiritual nature implies the analogy of man's physical nature; but it is specifically different from the development of the body, and the nourishment of the soul must be apportioned differently from the material food we consume. The spiritual process called education is not spontaneous in nature but requires constant care."[15] In this brief passage, Jaeger observes the striking yet convoluted relationship between physical nourishment and intellectual development. He concludes that bodily growth and spiritual development are distinct topoi, related only by way of analogy.[16] The former, he argues, unfolds along natural, predetermined pathways, while the latter requires "constant care" and calibration. If the two are related within the broader context of education, it is a purely linguistic relationship. My contention, however, is that a more focused analysis of early Christian language about food and formation, and the Greco-Roman traditions from which it emerges, undermines Jaeger's separation of material nourishment from its psychic corollary.

In the preface to *Early Christianity and Greek Paideia,* Jaeger notes that the book was meant to be "a kind of down payment" on a larger and more comprehensive treatment of the transformation of classical education in the early Christian era. Unfortunately, Jaeger died shortly after its publication. His unrealized goal was to publish an account of education within Greek Christianity that would serve as the capstone to his earlier three-volume magnum opus, *Paideia: The Ideals of Greek Culture*.[17] Thus readers are left with only the "main outlines" of what would have been his final effort of intellectual inquiry.

In the seventy-five years since Jaeger first published his magnum opus *Paideia*, education in Greco-Roman antiquity has received ever-increasing scholarly attention.[18] Yet among historians of Christianity it has only been in the last few decades that scholars have begun to expand upon the work initiated by Jaeger in *Early Christianity and Greek Paideia*. This delay can, to some degree, be attributed to the historical partitioning of academic disciplines—disciplines that have benefited recently from greater cross-fertilization.[19] Nonetheless, while some of the recent studies take up the issue of the transformation of classical education in an early Christian context directly, for most the topic is not at the center of analysis.[20]

Raised on Christian Milk

This partition between the growth of the body and that of the soul, and the food apportioned to each, is rendered increasingly porous upon closer examination. For early Christian engagement with the ideals of *paideia* involved complex appeals to nourishment and breast-feeding as a regulatory symbol—a symbol with such structuring power, such capaciousness of meaning, that it could be put to work on behalf of quite divergent configurations of social identity.[21] One crucial factor contributing to the vexed relationship between nourishment and education in antiquity is the terminology employed. The very grammar through which that relationship was articulated reveals a fundamental ambivalence or, at least, ambiguity of sense.

Both the Greek noun *paideia* and the Latin verb *educare* contain bodily as well as psychic resonances within their lexical scope. The rearing of children—of *paides*—did not simply imply physical nourishment by analogy. It required it by practical necessity. It is for this reason that Sophocles refers to a mother's "care of nourishment" (*paideios trophe*) in *Antigone*.[22] The correlation between nourishment and formation cannot be relegated to the realm of mere metaphor because the semantic slippage that the relationship implies necessarily entails a conceptual slippage. The proper education and formation of children was, throughout antiquity, wrapped up in the material provision of food and the ways in which that provision was theorized and regulated. To be well-born and well-bred and well-formed, one first and foremost had to be well-fed.

The extent of this semantic and conceptual slippage, especially within the context of early Christian literature, is revealed in a brief comment made by Tertullian in *To Scapula*. In a text that seeks to persuade a "pagan" audience against the persecution of Christians, Tertullian offers evidence for the positive contribution Christians have made to Roman society. As Geoffrey Dunn has observed, the treatise tries to demonstrate how "there are those, from pagan officials to the former emperor himself, who could attest the physical benefits Christians have brought them."[23] As a striking example of these benefits, Tertullian points to the emperor Severus's son Antoninus (Caracalla). Tertullian notes with pride that this man was "raised on Christian milk" (*lacte Christiano educatus*) by his attendants in the imperial court.[24] In light of Tertullian's rhetorical strategy, the implication of this phrase can be understood as both plainly literal and highly symbolic: Caracalla was nourished as an infant on the milk of a Christian wet nurse, but also benefited from the material-nurture and soul-formation provided by Christian child-minders in general. The two processes of nourishment and nurture are, in fact, collapsed within this one phrase: *lacte Christiano educatus*.[25]

From this historical vantage, easy modern dichotomies (nature and nurture, nourishment and education, literal and metaphoric food) begin to erode. Geraldine Hodgson—writing one of the first studies of the twentieth century on early Christian education—noted the significance of nourishment language within early Christian literature while silently passing over the social, cultural, and political implications of such language.[26] Hodgson has not been alone in overlooking the context within which this literature appealed to the symbol of nourishment. In most cases, scholars have either confirmed Jaeger's view of a dichotomous and strictly analogical relationship between bodily growth and spiritual formation or have simply omitted the issue outright. A few salient examples will suffice.

In a brief section of his *Education in Ancient Rome,* Stanley Bonner explores the important roles played by slaves in the rearing of young children—with special attention to the *paedagogus,* the *educator/educatrix,* and *nutrix/nutritor.*[27] The terms *educator/nutritor* and cognates often referred to one and the same person who would be expected "to raise" the child—both in the sense of supporting his most basic intellectual development and also including the provision of his food and administration of his feeding. This could entail chewing the food first to make it palatable, but also implied tasting it as a safeguard against poisoning.[28] But Bonner's analysis remains primarily a social history—a survey of the concrete social practices of nourishment and education. He does not trace how these practices, in turn, might have served as resources for theorizing *paideia* and the proper development of children.

Teresa Morgan, for her part, argues that there is no such thing as a "theory of remedial education" in the literature of antiquity.[29] Focusing on the educational handbooks, she has deduced two "contributing sets of factors [that] are determined as essential. The first is a series of tendencies innate to the pupil. The second is the information and the patterns of thought that are imposed on the pupil by the teacher. The pupil develops by means of a productive tension between the two—nature and nurture."[30] Morgan attempts to reverse engineer a theory of preliterate education through these two categories. Yet, tellingly, her own examination of the pedagogical significance of the care and nourishment provided by nurses and pedagogues is allocated under "nature"—a concession that speaks to the difficulty of coherently applying these modern categories to ancient theories of human formation.

What Morgan qualifies as "nurture" (that is, the process of instruction) is often dependent upon language, imagery, and social customs drawn from processes she designates as "nature" (that is, that which is innate within the pupil). Ancient theories of education and formation that employ symbolic language drawn from breast-feeding and nourishment destabilize the categories of nature and nurture. On some occasions, such language was utilized to describe innate tendencies and characteristics transmitted from one generation to the next. On other occasions, it referred to the techniques used to regulate comportment—the dispositions of body and mind— through which a person's wisdom and maturity was made evident. The symbol of nourishment in antiquity reveals that nature and nurture were related to one another as in a chiasma: each bound to the other, entwined in the ongoing production, transmission, and reshaping of traits and dispositions that constitute the well-formed human person.[31]

Recent studies have begun to push this conversation into more dynamic frames of analysis. Raffaella Cribiore, in *The School of Libanius in Late Antique Antioch,* draws upon the extensive correspondence of Libanius and offers a specific account of ancient pedagogical theory. She notes how "Inheritance of parental characteristics was not complete at birth" and therefore required someone who, like a foster parent, could provide ongoing nurture to ensure the inborn potential of the student was realized.[32] Likewise, W. Martin Bloomer has convincingly demonstrated that the handbooks of Plutarch and Quintilian both view the young child and pupil as a fundamentally vulnerable subject liable to contamination. Indeed, Bloomer explicitly argues that the perfecting of human nature in the process of nurture within educational theories was not simply a rhetorical flourish or literary embellishment, but rather evidence of a deep concern for how "injury to the body taints the soul."[33] Finally, drawing upon a wide array of texts and genres, Maud Gleason has given a compelling account of rhetoric as "the calisthenics of manhood"—a kind of "deportment training," which was the concern not just of the educational handbook but also of "physiognomical treatises, moral essays, [and] medical advice manuals."[34]

Despite increasing attention to the slippery relationship between nature and nurture in ancient education, there has not yet been a robust examination of this slippage as a historical problem in itself—one that indicates something crucial about theories of formation in antiquity. In most cases, the question raised by Jaeger's partitioning of "spiritual nourishment" from "material food" remains live. Beyond the recognition that nourishment and breast-feeding "played a role" in the social and historical reality of *paideia,* what is the significance of the link between food and formation within ancient education? And in what sense did food communicate essence?

Like their ancient counterparts, prominent modern scholars have also theorized education in ways that evoke the biological. In the ground-breaking studies of Jaeger and Marrou, for example, the content of *paideia*—that is, the "stuff" transmitted in education—is often described in static or essentialized terms. Thus, education is variously and broadly defined as the preservation of a culture's "true form,"[35] its "concentrated epitome,"[36] and its "type."[37] Such descriptions, while drawing upon ancient theories of education, fail to give an adequate account of the ways in which education inevitably entails the ongoing construction and renegotiation of individual and collective identity. Insofar as imitation constitutes the bed-rock of learning in the ancient world, this aspect has typically been articu-lated as simple repetition (that is, learning occurs primarily through being molded to the form of a model). Less attention has been given to the ways in which imitation allows or even necessitates innovation and improvisa-tion.[38] Do we always become what we eat, molded to the form of the one who feeds us? Or does nourishment open up surprising and unanticipated modes of transformation?

The tendency in scholarship on ancient education to accept the no-tion that *paideia* is the reception and replication of a static cultural essence misses, in my estimation, some important ways in which imitation and im-provisation were bound together.[39] In the precise places where education was naturalized through language of procreation and nurturance, there re-mained a space for play in the meaning of that language and the ends toward which it was employed. The rhetoric of transmission and imitation (so aptly exemplified in the trope of milk and solid food) was itself a site for working out the content of the culture being passed on.[40] My theoretical wager is that an intervention into how "metaphor" has been defined and understood will allow for a more complex and robust framework for analyzing milk, solid food, and their role in human formation.

Beneath the Metaphor of Milk and Solid Food

[W]hat is now in question is precisely the possibility of restoring or
reconstituting, beneath the metaphor which at once conceals and is concealed,
what was "originally represented."

—Jacques Derrida, "White Mythology"[41]

I am interested in excavating beneath the metaphor of milk and solid food,
not to retrieve "what Paul really meant," but rather to see what historical,
rhetorical, and ideological dynamics supplied it with the force to articulate
a program of identity formation—a force that early Christians readily and
regularly employed to realize a Christian cultural essence. Hans Conzelmann's landmark commentary on Paul's first epistle to the Corinthians is
unequivocal: "The idea of *paideia*, 'training,' suggests itself [in the distinction of milk and solid food]. But it remains only a suggestion. Paul's
concern is not with education and development, but with the antithesis
of the moment. *Nepios en Christo*, 'children in Christ,' here means no more
than that they are still beginners in the field of Christian knowledge. They
can make progress, but they must show it. The shift is plain. . . . Paul
explains *nepioi* in an expanded metaphor from the diatribe: they could—
and can—stomach only infant food. *This is immediately understandable*."[42]
Conzelmann's emphatic assertion that the sense of the metaphor is obvious
ought to give us pause.

First and foremost, the unqualified category referred to by Conzelmann as "Christian knowledge" presumes, on the one hand, that we can
readily agree upon a monolithic sociality called "Christian" (at least according to Paul and his interlocutors) and, on the other, that this sociality was
anchored by Paul to some coherently reified mode and body of learning. I
want to state here at the outset that although this study frequently uses
terms like "identity" and "identity formation," the content of those terms
remains necessarily ambiguous and undefined. Repeated reference to milk
and solid food was, in fact, an important way that the ancient authors sought
to establish a more fixed definition of what it means to be Christian in the
face of myriad other articulations. Put another way, talk of food and feeding
(even in highly figural or symbolic language) was an important strategy for

locating and defining the content, the essence, of an otherwise amorphous "identity."[43]

And so Conzelmann's argument about milk and solid food runs the risk of eliding or flattening the complex and historically contingent processes in which certain figures of speech gain their power. Recent trends within linguistic theory have called into question the idea that metaphors are "immediately understandable." The question of what lies beneath a metaphor, and the extent to which it can be excavated, rests at the heart of the present study. In contrast to Conzelmann, Paul's appeal to milk and solid food was more than just suggestive of *paideia* but was, in fact, structured by the conceptual framework, social or political sanctions, and embodied practices that made *paideia* an enduring cultural phenomenon in the ancient world. As such, later Christian citations of 1 Corinthians 3:1–3 specifically—and appeals to the symbol of nourishment and breast-feeding more broadly—reactivated and participated in the discourse of formation that was the very foundation of ancient education.

Let me first make explicit some of the theoretical orientations that guide my thinking in this project. While there has been much recent work on metaphor theory, I mostly avoid using the terminology of metaphor in the chapters that follow in order to resist the almost instinctive connection between metaphor and an obviousness of sense.[44] The commonplace phrase "mere metaphor" permits us to pass silently over complex legacies of certain habits of speech and their capacity to regulate individuals and structure social groups. What Conzelmann takes as the "plain" meaning in the distinction of milk and solid food is anything but plain. Paul's figure of speech is no simple turn of phrase but depends, in fact, upon broader cultural and historical valences. As a result, I prefer to draw upon Pierre Bourdieu's theory of the symbolic power of language. This approach allows for a more precise and potentially more capacious analysis of how nourishment acquired its force in early Christianity and, as a result, how it was strategically retooled for various models of identity formation and community formation.

Language, for Bourdieu, is fundamentally a means for clarifying and establishing social position. Language is the primary mode through which a person's relationship to the world is named and claimed. It is the verbal expression of one's situatedness in the world and of the dispositions that are cultivated as a result of this contingent social situation.[45] The weaving together of language and embodied reality within certain patterns of speech (for example, "I gave you milk") reveals a dynamic interplay between the individual, the materiality of life, and the culturally specific values that determine social location. As such, idioms are employed as strategies for negotiating and renegotiating position and status within the social field. Linguistic exchanges, for Bourdieu, are acts of power that structure what is thinkable, sayable, and doable between individuals.[46] To offer a robust account of Paul's reference to the feeding of infants and the power of breast milk in human formation requires situating his use of milk and solid food within its broader social and discursive framework—precisely as an act of defining and regulating social position.

From this foundation, Bourdieu concludes that "every speech act . . . is a conjuncture."[47] By conjuncture, he means that the words we use to make sense of the world are produced by an encounter between two dynamic forces: the "linguistic habitus," those socially inscribed dispositions toward certain forms of speech that reside within each person and that each person embodies as a second nature, and the "linguistic market," the broader network of social relations that sanctions, censors, and invests our speech with value and thus arranges us according to its own system of symbolic power. The linguistic market is not a repository of words and grammar—as if each person in a community were simply citing words from a static lexicon. Rather, it is the dynamic space in which discourses are exchanged and reshaped according to the goals or values of particular individuals and groups. This is to say, our use of language can never be abstracted from the embodied social spaces in which these discourses circulate, gather momentum, and undergo a process of sedimentation in meaning. Speech, for Bourdieu, is always bound up in the agonistic process of distinguishing one's social position from that of others. Returning again to the phrase "I gave you milk," we might consider how this simple locution encodes a complex set of relational values upon speaker and hearer and that the weight of these values sits most heavily on the word "milk."

Bourdieu's aim here is to correct what he views as an overly individu-
alistic, intellectualized account of how speech happens and what speech
does.[48] In contrast to other linguistic theorists who reduce the meaning of
speech to a verbal exchange between two isolated parties, Bourdieu prompts
us to look at "linguistic conventions as social phenomena, implicated in sets
of social relations, imbued with power and authority, embroiled in conflict
and struggle."[49] Authority comes to a figure of speech, and thus to the
speaker herself, from the outside.[50] He explains:

> [L]inguistic relations are always relations of symbolic power
> through which relations of force between the speakers and their
> respective groups are actualized in a transfigured form. Conse-
> quently, it is impossible to elucidate any act of communication
> within the compass of linguistic analysis alone. Even the sim-
> plest linguistic exchange brings into play a complex and ramify-
> ing web of historical power relations between the speaker,
> endowed with specific social authority, and an audience, which
> recognizes this authority to varying degrees, as well as between
> the groups to which they respectively belong. . . . A very impor-
> tant part of what goes on in verbal communication, even the
> content of the message itself, remains unintelligible as long as
> one does not take into account the totality of the structure of
> power relations that is present, yet invisible, in the exchange.[51]

To understand the meaning of a figure of speech such as that used by Paul
in 1 Corinthians 3, it is necessary to push beneath the metaphor. This means
taking stock of the "totality of the structure of power relations" that makes
the distinction between milk and solid food intelligible, endowing the one
who provides nourishment with "social authority."

Bourdieu refers to this authority as "symbolic power."[52] It is symbolic
because "symbols are the instruments . . . of social integration [and] make
it possible for there to be a consensus on the meaning of the social world, a
consensus which contributes fundamentally to the reproduction of the social order."[53] It is power because those symbols are representations of the

world and not the world as such; but in exploiting the definite relations that exist within the social order, symbols acquire the capacity to construct realities out of representation.[54] The symbolic power of language is demonstrated in its capacity to make historically contingent and culturally idiosyncratic notions of how the world works appear natural, unavoidable, universal, and even biological.[55] Bourdieu calls this an "embodied politics," a "somatization of the cultural arbitrary."[56]

What I am proposing, then, is not merely a re-situating of Paul's appeal to milk and solid food within a broader embodied politics of food, breast-feeding, and human formation in antiquity. In addition to that, I seek to chart the ways in which a variety of early Christian authors reactivated the sedimented meaning of food in order to fashion modalities of identity formation and social belonging.[57] In attending to the "movement" of meaning within the symbol of nourishment in early Christian literature, the very fact of that movement indicates shifting conceptions of how social relations could be articulated and regulated within these ancient communities.[58] I trace the various strategies whereby early Christians pulled the conventional meaning of nourishment from its culturally specific, early Roman educational context and repurposed the trope as a means for constructing and transmitting a Christian cultural essence. The embodied politic of feeding and being fed provided a potent symbolic resource for regulating proper growth and legitimate identity among those considered "infants in Christ." Yet, the symbolic power of nourishment was in no way deployed consistently. In the precise places where early Christians attempted to secure the transmission of "true" knowledge and "orthodox" faith at the level of biology, the movement from milk to solid food proved to be a malleable— and thus unstable—concept, thereby allowing for diverse understandings of legitimate Christian formation.

Scope of the Project

In emphasizing the symbolic power of nourishment in the shaping of Christian self-understanding, I am following the lead of recent work in early Christian studies that seeks to draw the methods of social history and rhetorical analysis closer together. Andrew Jacobs and Rebecca Krawiec, for instance, have suggested that historiography on "family ideology" and "real Christian families" need not be two separate modes of inquiry. While recognizing the difficulty of observing the family in late antiquity "as it really happened," Jacobs and Krawiec point to the power of "family discourses" to "construct Christian reality in antiquity."[59]

Following their model, and drawing upon Bourdieu's notion of language as conjuncture, I explore the movement of one prevalent trope derived from families (both real and rhetorical), its basis in the social and intellectual history of the ancient world, and the ways in which it was wielded by different early Christian authors as an index for proper intellectual growth and social legitimacy. Food—specifically breast milk and the maternal body from which it is derived—functioned as a volatile yet potent culture-shaping currency in the ancient world. In the hands of elite male authors, this currency was invested with the power to realize, sanction, and safeguard particular accounts of what makes a Christian, what makes a Christian "mature," and the precarious process through which one might grow from infancy to perfection. Indeed, in all the figures explored in this study, the logic of nourishment and its power to form the soul is consistent with the idea already voiced by Feuerbach: same essence, same food—and vice versa. Shared food, especially food derived from the body of another, offered ancient Christians a rich resource for thinking through the sharing of essential qualities. Insofar as these arguments appealed to and were often dependent upon the embodied practice of feeding and being fed, they are also a prime example of how language acquires its symbolic power through the conjuncture of social practices and intellectual or ideological traditions.

This project can be understood as a kind of reception history of 1 Corinthians 3:1–3. At the same time, I have avoided identifying it as such in order to guard against the idea that the figures and texts explored in these pages represent an exhaustive or even linear account of how the symbol of milk and solid food was understood, passed on, and utilized in early Christian discussions of formation and education. The apostle Paul is not the focal point of the entire book but rather a pivot point and a touchstone for later authors to sharpen their own use of nourishment's symbolic power.

The primary authors to be examined in this book are Irenaeus of Lyons, Clement of Alexandria, Origen, Gregory of Nyssa, and Augustine of Hippo. In each case we encounter a distinct mobilization of food's symbolic power for the Christian community.[60] It is by no means the case that these are the only authors who have recourse to such language in the literature of early Christianity.[61] Rather, the figures and texts selected are particularly illustrative of the ways that the symbol of breast-feeding and nourishment was wielded to produce diverse and at times conflicting accounts of Christian identity and its transmission.[62] Augustine, for example, will prove to be a "marginal" figure in his presentation of food and formation (at least as compared to the other authors examined). But this makes the pervasive emphasis on milk throughout his work all the more important, I think, as a case study for just how mobile the meaning given to milk and solid food was in the interim between the apostle Paul and Augustine.

In the first two chapters, I examine the complex history of food within the broader discourse surrounding human formation in Greco-Roman antiquity. I begin with an exploration of classical theories concerning the soul, the body, and the role that nourishment plays in their development. Here, I emphasize that food was long viewed as a powerful substance, penetrating through the matter of the body into the matter of the soul. Turning next to the Roman imperial era, I observe how breast milk was increasingly identified as a crucial site for the preservation and transmission of Rome's *imperium*. Following the lead of scholarship on the Roman family, I analyze various legal, moral, and medical texts—all of which establish the necessity of proper nourishment for the perfection of the child and, as a result, the stability of the empire.

In chapter 2, I read three sets of Greek texts from ancient Judaism (the Maccabean martyr narratives, Philo of Alexandria, and Paul of Tarsus), each produced within provincial Roman culture and utilizing this discourse of formation to realize a specific ethno-religious essence. In so doing, I demonstrate how ancient Jews, like other subjects of Rome, reshaped the symbolic power of nourishment to construct their own models of human formation but did so increasingly through the language and narratives supplied by scripture. It is in this specifically Jewish permutation of

Greco-Roman ideals about formation that Paul's language of milk and solid food must be situated.

From this framework, the following chapter examines the significant contribution of Irenaeus of Lyons and Clement of Alexandria. The exegetical battles of the second century—many of which circled around 1 Corinthians and Paul's use of nourishment—offer an important example of how controversies over biblical interpretation prompted early Christian thinkers to engage broader moral, medical, and philosophical traditions. Both Irenaeus and Clement amplify infancy and breast-feeding as legitimate and necessary modalities of identity in order to counteract "Gnostic" accounts that denigrated the milk-drinking Christians as inferior by nature. To that end, they couple biblical exegesis with complex anthropological and physiological paradigms in an attempt to make sense of the ambiguous and seemingly negative categories that Paul employed in 1 Corinthians 1–4. For Irenaeus and Clement, infancy was a necessary and praiseworthy status for Christians precisely because it was in the milk-drinking stage that the "stuff" of faith was transferred to the soul.

In the third century the intense exegetical battles faced by Irenaeus and Clement had largely diminished. In chapter 4, I turn to Origen of Alexandria and analyze his attempt to harmonize Paul's anthropological categories of carnal/soulish/spiritual with three Pauline "diets" of milk/vegetable/solid food—thus imagining a tiered structure for Christian development. However, the difficulty embedded within Paul's categories complicates Origen's efforts at a more coherent gastronomic regime. Even as he emphasizes the fundamental potential for transformation within human nature, and even as he recognizes the power of food within this process of transformation, Origen largely advocates a model that reifies Christian identity according to the type of food a person eats. Milk drinkers, it seems, rarely advance to the solid food. The problem for Origen is not whether there are Christians who are perfect, spiritual, solid-food eaters. The persistent question is whether those who are fed on milk can make any progress at all or if they must await the transformation of our bodily senses into the divine sense found within resurrected bodies.

In chapters 5 and 6, I turn to two figures from late antiquity that represent two divergent possibilities for understanding food and formation—possibilities that were already anticipated in Origen's struggle to harmonize the categories of 1 Corinthians. Following Werner Jaeger, I observe how Gregory of Nyssa amplifies Origen's account of human transformation, highlighting especially the ways in which food fundamentally represents a transfer of essential characteristics. Indeed, in Gregory we encounter a full expression of the ancient discourse of formation. In his *Homilies on the Song of Songs,* there is a profound optimism that all Christians can be formed to perfection if they eat well. As a result, Gregory reconfigures the Pauline trope of milk and solid food into a progressive model of spiritual development in which the church becomes an extensive nursery system of eaters and breast-feeders.

Augustine of Hippo's use of nourishment runs in the opposite direction. In chapter 6, I observe how his optimism about the role of food in human transformation wanes over the course of his career. As a result, while the North African bishop increasingly identifies the importance of breast milk as a symbol for transferring the Word and safeguarding orthodox faith among the faithful, he all but abandons the ideal of progress toward perfection upon which the symbol of milk had gained its power. That is, for the mature Augustine, the church is composed solely of infants suckling on milk—for it is only in this posture that humility before the mystery of God and obedience to the Word is sustained.

The conclusion queries the broader significance of nourishment in early Christianity and revisits some of the more enduring questions that were raised already in this introductory chapter. Here I reflect on the legacy of food to symbolize cultural belonging, the transfer of essences, and a program of formation. In so doing, I evaluate the stakes—theological, political, or otherwise—involved in rhetoric about milk, solid food, and the binding together or dividing of people based on similar gastronomic regimes. I end with a consideration of the imperative to "eat well" and question how this imperative might be put to work in more-just social configurations of feeders and eaters, teachers and students within a new Pauline gastronomy.

ONE

The Symbolic Power of Food in the Greco-Roman World

Meals are values quoted on the Stock Exchange of History.
—Roland Barthes, *How to Live Together*

IF MEALS INDEX A LARGER ECONOMY OF social values, the feeding of children is a particularly powerful ideological currency. This is as true today as it was in Greco-Roman antiquity. Food—and especially the milk of a mother—was a crucial site for the fleshing out of social identities as well as a singularly important mechanism for describing the transmission of that identity. It is my contention that the relationship between nourishment and human formation in the ancient world offers us a prime example of symbolic power in the sense that Bourdieu outlines in his linguistic theory. That is, throughout Greco-Roman antiquity, food and mother's milk acquired a formative force because they represented a *conjuncture* of embodied social practices, cultural ideologies, and philosophical traditions, the effect of which was to shape a social reality and collective identity out of the act of feeding and being fed.

In what follows, I highlight some of the foundational philosophical, medical, and moral texts that account for the power of nourishment within the formation of the human person. Focusing primarily on Hippocratic treatises, Plato, and Aristotle, I consider how classical anthropological theories about the relationship between body and soul broadly emphasized the importance of food in shaping human nature (both corporeally and intellectually). I then turn to the social and political context of the Roman Empire and its explicit program of family values within which breast-feeding and child-rearing were highly politicized—and thus highly theorized—activities.

In the next chapter, I expand this narrative by turning to Jewish texts and to the apostle Paul himself. Paul, I will argue, is situated squarely within this discursive framework by his reference to milk and solid food. However, the thinkers and texts examined in the following pages are not understood as the background from which his use of milk and solid food emerges. Rather, together they comprise the complex and sprawling discursive field within which Paul thought and wrote about the proper formation of his Corinthian children. I have chosen to situate thinkers and texts from a wide range of chronological and geographical settings—some of which come well before Paul, others well after—in order to accentuate the durable and pervasive interest in food and formation that can be observed throughout Greek and, especially, Roman antiquity.

There is, of course, a risk of anachronism in such a framing. However, I am not so much arguing for a direct causal relationship between these texts and the ones from early Christianity that I analyze. Rather, in emphasizing the discursive nature of the relationship between nourishment and education in antiquity, I propose that the movement from milk to solid food was part of a dynamic and constantly shifting argument about how a person might become "properly formed," both individually and socially. The question at the core of all this is: What does it mean to "eat well?" For when Paul's successors called upon 1 Corinthians 3, they inevitably pulled up with it the tangled web of associations and connotations about proper feeding and its effect on human formation.

In the pages that follow, specific discussions about nourishment and its impact on the soul are analyzed, compared, and contrasted. My contention is that these disparate texts and authors each contribute in some crucial way to the discourse of human formation. In each attempt to describe or theorize the power of food, such writings are located within a larger constellation, the result of which is what I more generally refer to as the symbolic power of nourishment. This produces a tension, or at least an ambiguity, between statements about actual nourishment and what it was specifically believed to do, on the one hand, and the symbol of nourishment as a nebulous cultural value, on the other. The boundary between actual nourishment and its symbolic power is necessarily ambiguous and that the two are inseparable. As authors and texts theorize food and formation, it is crucial to recognize these interventions as participating in and contributing to the wider currency of that symbol.

The Psychic Reach of Food in Ancient Theories of the Soul

The relationship between nourishment and the soul is a persistent theme in some of the earliest medical and philosophical texts of classical antiquity. Food is inextricably bound to the broader dilemma of the formation of the soul within the body in the ancient imagination. The power of food thus serves as an indicator for the porous boundary between physical growth and intellectual transformation. Texts ranging from the work of the Hippocratic corpus, Plato, Aristotle, and later culminating in Galen all contribute to the prominence of nourishment as a focal point within the discourse of human formation—a focal point wherein the proper growth of the body implicates and impacts the proper growth of the soul.[1]

"WHEN MIXED WITH ITS PROPER FOOD": HIPPOCRATES ON FEEDING THE SOUL

Within the curious Hippocratic writing called *On Nutriment*, at stake is not simply a discussion of food and its effects, but, more precisely, a greater appreciation for the porousness of human nature.[2] Although it is brief and aphoristic in structure, the treatise provides a complex and at times mystifying theoretical framework for understanding the physiological effects of nourishment. One recurring theme is the "power of nourishment" (*dynamis trophes*)—variously described as that which "increases, strengthens, clothes with flesh, makes like, makes unlike"[3] or also that which "reaches to bone and to all the parts of bone, to sinew, to vein, to artery, to muscle, to membrane, to flesh, fat, blood, phlegm, marrow, brain, spinal marrow, the intestines, and all their parts; it reaches also to heat, breath [*pneuma*], and moisture."[4] The transformative power of nourishment is here elevated beyond simple sustenance through its impact upon all aspects of the body—most crucially, its penetration into the *pneuma* and bodily humors.[5] And so we are told, "From the outside, nourishment travels through the external surface to the innermost parts."[6]

In his consideration of *pneuma* in Greco-Roman thought, Dale Martin notes that the concept refers to a ubiquitous and permeating "stuff" that vivifies and nourishes the whole human person. Drawing upon a wide array of genres and ancient authors, Martin concludes that "The *pneuma zotikon* [vital spirit] provides life to the different parts of the body and is itself further refined in order to nourish the *pneuma psychikon* [psychic spirit]. The body is a refinery for processing, among other things, *pneuma*."[7] For Martin, the processing of *pneuma* within the body clarifies a broader dynamic within ancient theories surrounding the relationship between body and soul: far from being neatly quarantined, concepts such as *soma* (body), *psyche* (soul), *physis* (nature), and *hyle* (matter) occupied distinct yet interrelated points on "a spectrum of essence."[8] *Pneuma*, along with the four humors, was thought to permeate all aspects of this spectrum—even the lofty intellect. In its fluid passage among the essences, *pneuma* comes to signify the aqueous quality of the body's most basic constitution.[9]

The Hippocratic text *On Nutriment* theorizes that the power of food is found in its capacity to "reach" (*aphikneomai*) through the body and impact all the elements that weave together human psychosomatic existence. The result of this is that the "power of nourishment," in its manipulation of the *pneuma* and the humors, spreads through the spectrum of essence all the way to the rational soul. Yet in the Hippocratic work *Regimen*, it is the soul itself that flows through the body. There, the soul is described as an elemental mixture of fire and water coursing through the body according to its own movement.[10] In this way, the body is conceived as a network of passages—a circuitry, even—through which the soul travels.[11] Maintaining the proper inner balance of fire and water through diet and physical activity is the first and most crucial step toward health and fertility.[12] Indeed, the psychic building blocks of fire and water are related to the balancing of masculine and feminine characteristics within each person. In *Regimen* 28, the author suggests that if parents want their "baby to become brilliant in soul and strong in body," both mother and father must undertake a diet that activates the "fire element."[13] This parental diet, prior to the child's conception, indicates a close correlation between the nourishment taken in by mother and father and the inchoate character of the child after conception. In order for the infant to become brilliant, the parents must regiment their food intake, even—perhaps *especially*—before conception.

The logic undergirding the recommendations in *Regimen* presumes that nourishment directly impacts a person's psychic vitality as well as the psychic vitality of any offspring produced. As such, in a section that advises on the proper diet required to produce a male or female child, the text concludes, "[T]he degree of manliness [in a child] depends upon the blending of the parts of water, and nourishment, education, and habits."[14] In order to give birth to a baby that is healthy, strong, and virtuous, *Regimen* proposes a method in which characteristics and behaviors that are usually quarantined as nature, on the one hand, and nurture, on the other, are here presented as a single process of feeding and formation. In a lengthy section on the proper diet for promoting intelligence, the text explains how each person's "soul is more stable when it is mixed with its appropriate food than when it lacks nourishment."[15] This curious statement suggests that there is a diet properly suited to the health and growth of the soul. If food travels "from the outside to the innermost parts," then one's diet must be structured such that whatever nourishment reaches the soul will produce only beauty and intelligence.

In all of its prescriptions regarding nourishment and the soul, the Hippocratic treatise on *Regimen* widely promotes the idea that one's diet can either help or hinder the health of the soul and, as a result, can greatly influence the psychic and bodily health of one's children. According to the author of *Regimen,* it is not just that we become what we eat. Children too become what their parents eat. Before an infant is born, before it is even conceived, the dietary practices of mothers and fathers impact the balance of vital essences within them that will contribute directly to the characteristics of the infant's nature. By this transfer of elemental substance, the nourishment consumed by the parents is transported through seed and womb into the very being of the child. It becomes the stuff from which the infant soul is made.

Theories about how parental likeness replicates itself in children were widespread and diverse in classical antiquity.[16] Some attributed this process of replication to the notion of pangenesis, in which the "seed emitted during

intercourse was drawn from all over the body" and thus the structural components of the body were prearranged in miniature form within the father's
seed.[17] Others rejected this idea of a tiny skeleton within the semen, favoring
instead an "organizing principle" in the seed.[18] While the emphasis in such
discussions is primarily focused on the seed of the father, it is clear in *Regimen* that nourishment functions similarly in the development of the child as
well. As the soul flows throughout the body, nourishment provides both
body and soul with stability, strength, and brilliance by bringing them into
their proper form.

In these Hippocratic texts, food has the power to produce likeness in
those who consume it. A person is transformed not only by the food he eats
and the nourishment given to him by others but also, crucially, by the food
his parents ate long before conception. Same food, same essence. Proper
nourishment ensures the proper formation of one's own soul as well as the
soul of one's offspring.[19] Early theories about the power of food were, in this
way, strategies for thinking about the porousness of the human body and
the ideal conditions for procreation.

PLATO, ARISTOTLE, AND THE PROPER NURTURE OF THE SOUL

In his study of the Hippocratic corpus, Jacques Jouanna has convincingly
demonstrated that the basic premise in *Regimen* is that proper observance
of its prescriptions "improves nature."[20] Further, Jouanna has charted the
points of convergence between *Regimen* and Plato's *Timaeus* concerning
the impact that sensations of the body have on the movement of the soul.[21]
Here too nourishment is emphasized as a crucial and constant factor in the
health and stability of the soul. Jouanna concludes, "the abundance of nutriment is, for Plato, an essential factor in the perturbations of intellect, not
only in the initial incarnation of the soul but also when plethora leads to
disturbances in the soul's rotations and troubles of thought such as forget-
fulness and ignorance."[22] Jouanna's brief comparison of Plato with the Hippocratic material on the topic of nourishment prompts further consideration
of how food was viewed to impact the soul in Plato and Aristotle.

Plato's *Timaeus* offers an etiology and anthropology for the embodiment of souls. The pre-embodied soul is characterized by its revolution—a movement Plato variously describes as harmony, proper ordering, and attunement.[23] Yet these natural revolutions are soon disrupted when the soul is deposited within a body. The fluctuations that characterize mortal, embodied life result in disorder and disharmony. The soul's movement loses its rhythm as it is jostled by the body's chaos.[24] This, for Plato, is why the soul lacks understanding and intelligence when it is initially placed within the physical confines of a body. In fact, for certain people, the irrationality caused by the disordered revolutions of the soul can last a lifetime if left unchecked.[25]

While it is because of the body that the soul's proper revolution is thrown into a confused spinning, it is through the body that the soul begins to settle and return to its original rotation. The proper application of nourishment to the body (and thus the soul) is the decisive element in balancing the two: "But eventually the stream of growth and nourishment (*trophe*) abates, and with the passage of time the circular motions regain tranquility and return to their proper courses, and things increasingly return to normal. From then on, as each of the rings regains its normal shape, their revolutions become less erratic, begin to identify difference and identity correctly, and make their possessor intelligent. Also, if proper nurture (*orthe trophe*) is supported by education, a person will become perfectly whole and healthy."[26] This passage demonstrates the complicated lexical range of the Greek word *trophe*. In the first instance, it seems clear that the text is referring to "literal" food, since the issue at hand is how the soul stabilizes at the same time that the body's nutritive care is properly regulated. The second reference (*orthe trophe*) functions ambiguously—indicating both the proper diet of food as well as the proper care that childhood and adolescence require. This enfolding of nourishment and nurture within the lexical range of *trophe* occurs regularly in Plato's writing, often in close proximity to discussions of education (*paideusis* or *paideia*). The power of nourishment is thus inextricably linked from the outset to education and child-rearing. The discussion of food, nurture, training, and instruction in Plato presupposes a messy interdependence between body and soul. Put simply, without *orthe trophe* there can be no *paideia*. At the lexical level, then, being well-fed and well-formed was bound together within *paideia*'s totalizing system.

In a different vein, Plato's *Republic* warns against the corrupting of children's souls through the immoral stories told by the nurse (*trophos*). For Plato, education begins in the lap and at the breast of the one who provides the earliest nourishment.[27] A little later, however, the relationship between nourishment and education becomes more explicit: the soul contains a "high-spirit," which is a naturally endowed counselor to reason that can be destroyed by evil nurture.[28] Likewise, in the *Laws,* "right nurture" (*orthe trophe*) is once again identified as a foundational element in the educational process that trains the soul of children to love what is good.[29] Plato's account of the relationship between *trophe* and *paideia* is aimed at the production of the most beautiful bodies and souls—which suggests that *trophe* refers to actual food as much as it refers to the general socialization and moral formation of the infant.[30] But the conceptual slippage is vexed throughout, sliding between *trophe*-as-food and *trophe*-as-formation.[31]

The widespread (if often ambiguous) link between *trophe* and *paideia* in Plato presents the reader with a problem: in the precise places where he seems to join the two together in a single process, Plato sometimes constructs a partition between them in which one (*paideia*) is apportioned to the soul and the other (*trophe*) to the body. There is a tendency within Plato to recognize and even attempt to quarantine the conceptual slippage between nourishment and education. For example, in the *Protagoras* (313c–d) and the *Sophist* (230c–d), nourishment and education are distinguished from one another by way of elaborate analogical models. These models are used to describe how the soul is fed on teachings in the same way that the body is fed on food.

This tendency to analogize the feeding of the body and the teaching of the soul has often been read (by Jaeger, for example) as the limit of any possible relationship between food and formation. However, the fact remains that the enfleshing, educating, and moral training of the soul nevertheless require a simultaneous administration of *trophe* and *paideia*.[32] The soul remains precariously dependent on the role that proper nourishment plays to prevent its slide into physical disorder, irrationality, and moral corruption.

Given this complex lexical and philosophical relationship, it is no simple metaphor to say that "instruction nourishes the soul." The analogical power of food to explain human intellectual formation is grounded in the intimate entanglement of nurture and nourishment at both practical and conceptual levels.[33] Thus, the ancient ideal of *morphosis*—of bringing the human person into a proper and perfect form—requires a more robust and integrated understanding of the relationship between *paideia* and *trophe*. To say that teachings are "like food for the soul" does not render absurd the notion that material nourishment impacts the soul. Rather, it is an analogy premised upon a more fundamental connection between food and formation—that is, a more fundamental belief that both foods and teachings travel from the outside into the innermost parts of the human person.

Aristotle's *On the Soul* describes the structural functioning of the soul with even greater detail. Of primary interest within this complex text is the discussion of the "nutritive soul," which is confined to the work of reproduction and nourishment.[34] These twin functions are presented by Aristotle as the means by which the nutritive soul sustains and strengthens its embodied life, and, ultimately, enables "each creature [to] produce another like itself."[35] Without food, the soul cannot grow, cannot share in life, and cannot be properly formed. To be alive is to hunger for food. Nourishment, for Aristotle, facilitates growth and reproduction and thus the replication of individual likeness.

In *On the Soul,* the functions of the nutritive soul are largely isolated from that of the rational soul above it. However, in *Parts of Animals,* Aristotle notes how nature placed a diaphragm between the nutritive soul and the sensory soul to serve as a partition wall and fence.[36] This partition is meant as a prophylactic for the upper divisions of the soul, preventing them from being "quickly overcome" by the excess of heat and air produced by digestion.[37] There is an inherent risk in this partitioning: on the one hand, the intake of food is absolutely necessary for sustaining and replicating life. On the other hand, if not administered properly, food threatens to destabilize and disrupt the soul's higher functions. The partition between lower and upper soul is unable to withstand the power of nourishment that reaches through the body and all its vital essences. This power either nurtures life—bringing strength, promoting vigor, and enabling virtue—or is destructive, sickening, and precipitates a loss of balance in body and character. In framing the nutritive soul as the gateway through which nourishment enters and impacts a person's higher rational faculties, Aristotle foregrounds the practical and daily relationship between food and the functioning of the mind. Humans, for Aristotle, neglect gastronomy to their own psychic peril.

Within this account of nourishment and its power, Aristotle theorizes that breast milk results from a process of transubstantiation that also includes menses and semen.[38] As the temperature of a woman's body fluctuates during pregnancy, it becomes a laboratory in which vital essences move from one region of the body to another and are transformed into sustenance for the infant. Lesley Dean-Jones has analyzed how "both the Hippocratics and Aristotle believed that a mother's milk was at its optimum around the time of parturition."[39] While the nutritive soul has as its goal nourishment and reproduction of likeness, it is through the mother's postnatal body that an infant receives it's most suitable food. Her milk is a meal produced by a precise concoction of physiological elements that are created during pregnancy and childbirth. The power of mother's milk, consequently, is found in its unique ability to stabilize the infant, causing it to grow properly and enabling the likeness of the parent to be fashioned within the child. Breast milk carries a powerful and transformative essence through the nutritive soul of the mother into that of her child.

In reading Aristotle's theory of the nutritive soul alongside his discussion of the production of breast milk, I am suggesting that adult nourishment, the rational functions of the soul, and the impact of a mother's milk upon her child all contributed to proper human formation in the classical tradition. The calibrating role that the nutritive soul plays in the higher orders of human reasoning also emphasizes nourishment as a transport of vital essences, a delivery system for psychic "stuff." Likewise, if the nutritive soul is understood as the site where human likeness is replicated, then the food a mother eats and the milk she subsequently provides to her child are linked in a single alchemical process. Breast milk, so construed, becomes a particularly potent form of nourishment insofar as the infant, quite literally for Aristotle, ingests the stuff from which the mother's own soul is made.

Hendrik Lorenz has recently explored the continuity between Plato and Aristotle concerning appetitive desire. Emphasizing the ways in which both figures describe the appetite (and even the spirit) within each human person as a kind of creature, Lorenz notes that this nature "is a brute, at least in part because it cannot itself engage in the distinctively human activity of reasoning about what is best. But it is a highly educable brute, and it can be *humanized* to a very considerable extent."[40] The humanizing of the creature within is, in a sense, the result of a gastronomic regimen. The taming of the appetitive soul is achieved not through stark abstention from nourishment but through greater consideration of its precise relationship to how the mind functions.

For the Hippocratics, Plato, and Aristotle, the power of nourishment in the growth and flourishing of the human person was a central theme— albeit in diverse and, at times, divergent ways. Each viewed eating as a mechanism for promoting intellectual development. Food was understood to stabilize the infant soul and transmit certain vital essences from parent to child. However, such theories about the power of food and its role in infant nurture underwent an intensification in the centuries that followed, especially in the context of the Roman Empire. Galen of Pergamum is an ideal point of contact between these different historical and cultural epochs. In his work, there is a kind of consummation of the classical intellectual traditions concerning food and formation. As a result, despite the fact that Galen arrives nearly one hundred years after the apostle Paul, he represents an especially potent moment in the discourse of formation during the Second Sophistic—a moment that has implications for how Paul's later interpreters inflect their own reading of milk and solid food within the dominant medical and moral terms of the Roman Empire.

"TO INCREASE YOUR POWERS OF REASONING": GALEN AND THE INTELLECTUAL DIET

In her persuasive studies on the physician Galen, Susan Mattern has detailed his role as an heir to the legacies of the traditions previously described.[41] A participant in that cultural foment known as the Second

Sophistic, Galen (b. 130 C E) presented himself as a "cultured man" (or a *pepaideumenos*) beholden to no single school of philosophy or medicine but rather a master of all. So intent on securing his place within the legacy of the ancients who came before him, Galen "worked to distinguish 'genuine' treatises in the corpus that circulated under Hippocrates' name from those of the great physician's rivals or imitators, and produced vast commentaries on several Hippocratic treatises."[42] Thus, Galen's smorgasbord approach to the traditions of Hippocrates, Plato, Aristotle, and the Stoics—along with the intellectual crucible of the epoch in which he lived—demonstrates that the link between food and the formation of the soul became a focal point within the medical and moral texts of the first centuries of the Roman Empire.[43] Galen takes the tantalizing yet underdeveloped claims of his classical forebears and amplifies them into a detailed program for the soul's nourishment.

In *The Capacities of the Soul Depend on the Mixtures of the Body*, Galen outlines a medical regimen "for anyone who wants to put their soul in order."[44] He ascribes to the rational soul a range of sensory functions such as taste and touch. Galen goes so far as to indicate a "desiring" faculty within the rational soul—a curious and potentially controversial description for the seat of reason.[45] Borrowing from Plato, Galen offers a taxonomy of the desires specific to each division of the soul: (1) the appetitive soul (seated in the liver) desires sex, food, rest; (2) the spirited soul (seated in the heart) desires freedom, victory, power; and (3) the rational soul (seated in the brain) desires knowledge and memory.[46] While Galen is quick to note that the rational soul does not, in itself, have the capacity to desire food or sex, it is nevertheless susceptible to the effects of food. That is to say, Galen's chief concern is with the relationship between dietary habits, intellectual capacities, and the ongoing growth of the soul.

The guiding question in *Capacities of the Soul,* then, is whether a medical/dietary regimen, in producing a change in the state of the body, can produce a correlative change in the state of the soul. Galen's answer is a clear affirmative. As Jouanna notes, "modifications in the humoral mixture of the body, and particularly of the organ in which the rational soul is situated, produce disturbance in these faculties."[47] Galen contends that when one is endowed with a gifted intellect, a proper dietary program will greatly enhance that which nature has set in place.

"So it would be wise of my opponents—those men who are unhappy at the idea that nourishment has this power to make men more or less temperate, more or less continent, brave or cowardly, soft and gentle or violent and quarrelsome—to come to me even now and receive instruction on their diet. They would derive enormous benefit from this in their command of ethics; and the improvement in their intellectual faculties, too, would have an effect on their virtue, as they acquired greater powers of understanding and memory."[48] The Hippocratic notion of the "power of nourishment" finds its consummation in Galen's medical regimen for the intellectual elite. The body is here depicted as an intricate ecological system of essences and faculties. Nutrition has the capacity to sustain and even improve or strengthen that balance. Negligence of nutrition can throw it into disarray. The rational soul sits atop this system and yet is dependent upon a precisely calibrated diet for its full attainment of wisdom and virtue.[49] Proper nourishment, in Galen's dietary program, increases one's powers of reasoning and improves one's character. Human gastronomy, for Galen, is a kind of soul-tuning—a process of psychic tweaking that produces optimal rational output.

At the outset of this section I observed that the "power of nourishment" was a central idea to classical theories of the development of the soul. Yet the function or meaning of this idea was in no way consistent. Galen, writing during the Roman imperial era, reflects this interest in food and intensifies its significance through proposing a regimen of intellectual nutrition. Elsewhere, in his treatise *On the Properties of Foodstuffs*,[50] Galen spends considerable time relative to other foods examining the power of milk: "about the power of milk, of which the greatest is this: it is perhaps the best and most conducive to good humors of all the foods we consume."[51] The power of milk is observed by Galen in its capacity to interact with the body's internal temperament and to assist in the balancing of its essences. When combined with his more thoroughgoing dietary regimen for the soul articulated in *Capacities of the Soul,* Galen's observation about milk's organizing function suggests that food intake and soul development are linked from very early on. The delicate mixture of humors that compose human nature is his primary concern. As with the Hippocratic text *On Nutriment,* Galen describes milk as a potent essence uniquely suited to the task of producing and maintaining the harmony of our internal chemistries.

By amplifying classical traditions concerning the power of nourishment, Galen provides a medical warrant for broader moral and political concerns about the impact of nourishment on an infant's soul within the literature of the Roman Empire. Galen's work on the power of nourishment in the health of the soul serves as a link between the intellectual traditions he inherited and the dominant ideologies of his own particular epoch. These ideologies stretched from the technical literature of medical and physiological theory into larger debates about proper child-rearing and education within elite families. Even as Galen's provocative dietary regimen offered in *Capacities of the Soul* can be read as an amplification of theories derived from his classical predecessors, it must also be placed within the broader context of the ideological system promulgated in the first centuries of the Roman Empire. In this way, Galen builds a bridge between the intellectual and physiological traditions of the classical world and the social and political concerns that characterized the Roman Empire in the first centuries CE.

"To Nourish and to Educate": Mother's Milk and Roman Imperial Family Values

Romulus offered milk to drink, not wine.

—Pliny the Elder, *Natural History*

The survival and reproduction of Rome's imperial system was sought, in part, through a program of "family values." Within the cultural program instigated by the reign of Augustus Caesar, two focal points were the institution of marriage and child-rearing among the elite.[52] The building blocks of the empire were to be carved out of the Roman family and the maintenance of its household. The health and strength of Rome's *imperium* would be hoisted upon the twin pillars of reproduction and education.[53] One result of this was that a concern for the proper nourishment and nurture of children proliferated widely throughout the literature and iconography of the period. For Augustus had ascended not during a period of stability but rather in the aftermath of a civil war among the Roman elite.

The early days of the Roman Empire, marked as they were by social upheaval, prompted increasing concern over a perceived shortage of "legitimate" male heirs. Historians have noted this dynamic, though explanations for its cause remain uncertain.[54] What is certain, however, is that this perceived shortage was largely viewed as evidence of a widespread deterioration of the social morals that had made Rome great in previous generations.[55] By staking the stability of the empire on the health of the Roman household, the regulation of child-rearing practices became a primary mechanism for achieving social unity in the aftermath of the civil wars of the late republic. Rome's mythic origin involved a story of infants being suckled and nurtured. Romulus—as the epigraph that opens this section notes—gave milk and not wine in his ritual libations. Inasmuch as it was present at the creation of the city, a mythos of milk was to serve as the foundation for Rome's future as well.[56]

The Ara Pacis (or Altar of Peace) given to Augustus by the Roman Senate in 13 BCE upon his return from a three-year military expedition in Spain and Gaul offers an entry point into this program of family values. Dedicated four years later, the altar was constructed on the boundary between Rome's domestic and military space.[57] From this in-between ground, the altar's ornate iconography demonstrates that the stability and power of Rome, its *imperium*, was secured not only through martial strength but also through domestic harmony. The two were inseparable: the peace that follows military victory abroad could not endure without moral vigilance at home (indeed, within the *domus*).[58] This ideal is found most clearly in the depiction of Tellus (or Mother Earth) on the southeast side of the altar.

Beryl Rawson has described the figure as a "fecund female variously interpreted, e.g. as Italia, or Pax (Peace), or Tellus (Earth). She nurses infants ready to suckle, surrounded by other symbols of her fertility."[59] The polysemic quality of this figure is typical of the altar's entire iconographic orientation.[60] Each image draws upon diverse histories, mythological traditions, and values in order to offer an elaborate pictorial account of Augustus's new imperial ideology. The "mother" sits between two half-robed women in an agrarian setting. Her own robe hangs delicately off her shoulders. She balances some fruit on her lap while gently holding two well-fed infants, who reach up toward her. Her gaze is fixed upon one of the children, who offers her a piece of fruit picked from her lap. There is a gentleness to her cradling. Her face is placid, almost resolute, expressing something between duty and care. The scene is a tactile evocation of the increasing importance of family, of child-rearing, and of the nourishment given to infants. This image of Tellus, situated as she is between *domus* and *imperium,* accentuates the politicizing of the Roman mother and her nurturing care.

But the Ara Pacis was merely one vivid tile in the elaborate mosaic of Roman family values.[61] The ideology that represented the Roman *familia* as a site for the maintenance of empire spread, like so many tentacles, throughout the legislation and literature of the Augustan age—persisting well into late antiquity.[62] In the past few decades, there has been a surge in scholarship on the Roman family attempting to clarify its social setting and ideological function.[63] Some of this work has shed new light on the role of nurture and nourishment in the *familia*—especially on the figure of the wet nurse.[64] Drawing upon this robust scholarly field, a host of literary materials from the early Roman Empire can be plotted within the broader imperial narrative that emphasized the power of nourishment in the formation of souls. This discourse promoted, theorized, and regulated certain kinds of nurturance in order to ensure the health and strength of the empire.

"FROM YOUR OWN BLOOD AND RACE AND SUBSTANCE": ROMAN LAW AND THE REPRODUCTION OF ELITE SOCIAL STATUS

At the end of his life, Augustus depicted himself as a "guardian of laws and morals."[65] Nothing exemplified this "custodial" role more than a series of stringent and unpopular laws enacted by Augustus in the final decades prior to the Common Era—laws aimed solely at stabilizing the Roman family and, through it, the future of the empire. Three laws in particular were issued with the aim of regulating marriage among the senatorial class: the

Lex Julia de Maritandis Ordinibus (18 BCE), the *Lex Julia de Adulteriis* (17 BCE), and the *Lex Papia Poppaea* (9 CE). Each was different in scope, but all can be read together within a broader concern for the vitality of those families in the highest social strata. From this concern, elite families were "strongly encouraged" to produce, nurture, and educate heirs who would lead the empire in the future.[66] These laws were "experimental" in nature.[67] Augustus, having defeated all other threats, sought to secure the empire by policing the family. In particular, this legislation primarily aimed to make marriage mandatory, to enact compulsory measures for remarriage among widows (following a grace period), to penalize those in the senatorial class who married below their status, to rein in extramarital affairs through stiff punishments (such as exile), and to revise inheritance laws to ensure proper transmission of nobility from one generation to the next within a given family.[68]

As Karl Galinsky has noted, the social and political ethos espoused within these laws demonstrated how, for Augustus, "Caring for a family exemplifies [the] highest, moral form of existence and makes a man a true citizen of the *res publica*. By contrast, refusal to have offspring is *impietas*."[69] A free man in Augustus's Rome was one who fulfilled his duty to the empire primarily through overseeing the nurture and growth of his *familia*.[70] This expectation is displayed forcefully in a speech to the senate, recounted by Dio Cassius, which was given by Augustus in response to outrage over his marriage laws. At its core, the speech is an exhortation concerning the function of the family in stabilizing the empire. Among the benefits of family life praised most, Augustus especially emphasizes "a wife who is chaste, domestic, a good house-keeper, a rearer of children [*paidotrophos*]"[71] and the blessing of "taking up into one's arms to nourish and to educate a child who shows the endowments of both parents—the physical and spiritual image of yourself."[72] This child, Augustus says, is "left behind as a successor and heir to the family, having been born from your own blood and race and from your substance."[73]

Far from an arbitrary tyrannical rule, the figure of the *paterfamilias* as found within the ideology of Roman family values appears to be just as fraught and precarious a role as any other in preserving civic virtue within the *domus*.[74] Likewise, according to Dio Cassius, it was incumbent upon the father to oversee the proper nourishing and rearing of his children into their rightful place within both *domus* and empire. While the mother—as *paido-trophos* (or child-nourisher)—was defined primarily by her body's putative function as site and source of this crucial sustenance, it was the father's duty to set his house in order and ensure that the children were "well-fed" and "well-raised." The father's supervision of this household ensures that the family's essence (its *ousia*) is instilled, preserved, and cultivated within the child. Supervising the transfer of the familial essence through nourishment and education is, according to Augustus, how a Roman man demonstrates his fidelity to the empire. Rome's *imperium* depended on elite children eating well.

The Roman *familia*, as Jane Gardner has observed, was not "an end in itself" but rather a "mechanism" through which the production and nurture of legitimate heirs secured the welfare of the state.[75] The laws that served to keep that mechanism functioning relied upon robust ideologies about gendered roles within the family. These roles were a barometer for the stability of the empire.[76] While it is true that the experimental character of the Augustan marriage laws produced new forms of "symbolic honor" for women in terms of civic responsibility, this honor was worked out through the policing of women's bodies, sexuality, fertility, and overall health.[77] As such, the health of the Roman matron indicated the health of the empire writ large.[78] Elaborate discourses focused on women's hygiene were, in large part, a way of talking about male eugenics. Which is to say, the development of detailed protocols surrounding the health of Roman women was symptomatic of anxieties about the proper formation of male infants. And so the matron's symbolic function meant that the proper nurture of children under her care became an index for broader societal concerns regarding growth, identity, and legitimacy within elite Roman families. The body of the *matrona*, often redirected to the body of the *nutrix*, was the instrument through which social legitimacy was birthed, nurtured, and sustained.[79] Women were viewed as natural resources that were to be quarried for the task of maintaining Rome's *imperium*. If Roman rule depended on Rome's children eating well, it was the mother and the wet nurse who carried, quite literally, the burden of that political ideology.[80]

MILK AND THE MAINTENANCE OF EMPIRE

The legal mechanism that sought to regulate gender roles within Roman families was one tactic in a broader discourse. "Augustan culture" could not be secured among Roman *familiae* solely through legislation. Propaganda cannot create a social ethic or realize a political ideology without participation.[81] Legal attention to the family as a symbol for the vitality of the empire required ratification from channels outside the official imperial apparatus. In the years following Augustus's reign, the discourse about proper nurture of children proliferated beyond the legal documents into popular medical wisdom, moral treatises, rhetorical handbooks, and other literature.

Children remained the focal point of this burgeoning discourse. As we have already seen in the works of the Hippocratic corpus and in Plato, child-rearing and feeding had long been viewed as a critical locus for ancient theories about the proper formation of the soul and the maintenance of social well-being. As Sarah Pomeroy notes, "The Greeks, in general, believed that offspring resemble their parents in physique, personality, and character. How these characteristics were transmitted, however, and the nature of the mother's contribution was much debated."[82] Likewise, in the Roman context, scholars have observed how "the role of children in the transmission of social memory [was] an instrument for the construction of social identities within the family."[83] One difference between the Greek and the Roman contexts is that within the latter the transmission of such characteristics was increasingly identified with the breast milk of the mother or her wet nurse.[84]

The social realities of life in Rome's *imperium* must have heightened the concern regarding children—not simply in their role as inheritors of a *familia* but also in their function as "bearers of a family tradition" and as an antidote against the potential disintegration of the whole empire.[85] Estimates suggest that, in the Roman Empire, 25 percent of all children died within the first year of life and another 25 percent would die before reaching the tenth birthday.[86] Malnourishment—compounded by inadequate sanitation and poor public health standards—would have been one of the primary causes for concern about children "at all levels of society."[87] With an astonishing mortality rate for children in the first decade of life, their vulnerability to sickness and death (especially among the elite) was a scale for measuring the vulnerability of Rome itself.

Those with the means to do so could acquire assistance in the nurture and feeding of their children.[88] Nurses and other child-minders became common figures in the Roman social landscape. Indeed, their place within the cultural imagination is most evident in the epitaphs and inscriptions that mention them throughout the city of Rome.[89] And while it is a matter of some debate as to what prompted families to hire wet nurses, it is probable that these *nutrices* were viewed primarily as a strategic resource for coping with the vulnerability of children.[90] Given the symbolic stakes of successful child-rearing, wet-nursing became a contentious practice within the ongoing association of family values with civic virtue.

It is within this precise historical moment of the early Roman Empire that physiological theories about the relationship between nourishment and human formation proliferated. The practice of public medical demonstrations during this time expanded the reach of technical medicine across the social landscape.[91] Physicians like Galen could ply their trade before a wider audience, and, as a result, their theories about health, illness, and human formation were integrated into the broader network of social ideologies upon which the early empire had staked its claim. Medicine, as Rebecca Flemming has observed, "is a site of social negotiation . . . a site of discursive production. . . . The making of medicine is thus inevitably bound up with the making of gender."[92] As with imperial-era legislation, the medical literature of the period also contributed to the construction of the family by focusing special attention on the nourishment of infants.

In this way, medical interventions into embodied practices like breast-feeding reveal that the discursive production of gender was, crucially, a site for clarifying and naturalizing social status as well. In its emphasis on the formative power of milk, Roman imperial-era medicine distinguished the Roman matron from her wet nurse through elaborate theories about the moral, intellectual, and even ethnic qualities contained in breast milk. The symbol of milk and the practice of breast-feeding were thus bound together in efforts to clarify distinction and difference, whether that difference was one of kinship, ethnicity, character, or some combination of these and other categories. We must not lose sight of the fact that the articulation of difference through theories about breast milk presumed the ubiquity but also the instability of Rome's slaveholding culture.[93] The power of milk to convey such status within the Roman family required corollary theories about the unstable quality of slave milk. As we will see, the logic of same essence, same food is reflected within such theorizing. It is expressed in the assumption that people from different levels of the social strata carry a different essence and so consume and produce a different food. As a result, the wet nurse and her milk received intense scrutiny.

This is most clearly demonstrated in the *Gynecology* of Soranus, written sometime in the late first or early second century. According to Ann Ellis Hanson, the "woman" found in Soranus's medical treatise is viewed primarily as a vehicle for reproduction: "The stance of the gynecologies is pronatalistic. Their intent is to protect women's fertility, and their concerns are 'product oriented.' . . . This concern with a product, an heir for the household who projects the family into the next generation, is common to medical writing."[94] The body of the *matrona* or her *nutrix*, and the milk produced by these women, served as a resource that was monitored, theorized, and moralized in order to provide the optimal nutritive output for the child. The fertile and nurturing woman found in Soranus, like the domesticated man in Augustan marriage legislation, was a cipher for the empire's vitality.

It is in this sense that we can see the rhetorical and symbolic force of Soranus's prescriptions regarding the proper nurture of infants by mothers and wet nurses in book 2 of his *Gynecology:* "If the circumstances allow a choice of women able to suckle the child, one must select the best and not necessarily the mother, unless she also shows the attributes characteristic of the best nurses. To be sure, other things being equal, it is better to feed the child with maternal milk; for this is more conformed to the infant's nature, and mothers become more sympathetic towards the offspring."[95] While the mother's milk is preferable to that of the nurse, Soranus's primary concern is not for the health of either woman as such, but rather for the quality of the milk produced on behalf of the infant. The maternal nourishment is "more conformed to the nature" (*oikeioteron*) of the child, and, as a happy result, the mother will become more affectionate toward her infant.

I'd like to pause here and emphasize the potential significance of the modifier that Soranus uses to describe the superiority of the mother's milk. The comparative form of the adjective *oikeios* is derived from the Greek word for "house," "home," or, by extension, "family." As such, the semantic link between the family/home (*oikos*), the mother's milk, and the infant's nature also suggests a conceptual link between the material food provided by the biological mother and the bonds of kinship borne by those of the same household. In Augustus Caesar's speech reported by Dio Cassius discussed earlier, the child becomes an image of and heir to the family through the proper administration of nourishment and education. There too *oikeios* is the operative term. And while Soranus is less emphatic in his rejection of wet-nursing as a general practice than other writers, he reflects the broader trend in viewing mother's milk as containing the bonding matter that connects the infant to its specifically familial nature. The infant is more suited to that food because it was born of the same stuff.

Nevertheless, should the mother prove incapable of providing the highest quality nourishment, or should she be unable to provide sufficient milk more generally, other means must be sought. The wet nurse, in Soranus's handbook, should not be chosen without serious consideration. He offers a litany of parameters for families to consider, including the woman's age (between twenty and forty years old), previous birthing experience (one who has already given birth two or three times), breast size, personal disposition and comportment, and even ethnicity.[96] On the last point, Soranus recommends a Greek woman whose beautiful speech and rich cultural heritage will compliment and fortify the high quality of her breast milk.[97] Yet despite the rigorous qualifications enumerated in his *Gynecology,* Soranus notes that it is preferable for a family to "provide several wet nurses" to ensure that the infant receives milk not only high in quality but also in sufficient quantity.[98] The wet nurse herself, however, recedes from view in Soranus's emphasis on the quality of her body's food and its effect on the one being fed.

The forced labor of the wet nurse, who was typically a slave, produced and reinforced the livelihood and social standing of her owners.[99] Even so, she also became a source of anxiety about the myriad corrupting influences that could deter the proper formation of the child placed under her care. This concern was not restricted to medical manuals. Tacitus amplifies this point in his *Dialogue on Oratory,* a work roughly contemporaneous with Soranus's *Gynecology.*[100] Pearl-clutching conservative that he was, Tacitus laments the fact that children are no longer reared in the mother's lap but, instead, are now "brought up in the tiny room of some slave-nurse."[101] What was once a "rigorous method of nurture" had lapsed, in Tacitus's estimation, and caused an epidemic of moral backsliding and social decay in his beloved Rome.[102] Fears concerning the health of the state that were implicit within the Augustan marriage laws are fully realized a century later in the *Dialogue.* According to Tacitus, improper nurture had spread like a disease from Rome throughout the entire empire—and in its wake the virtue and eloquence that gave Rome its strength had deteriorated.[103]

The correlation between nourishment, education, and the health of the empire was also readily perceived in prominent instruction handbooks from both Latin and Greek authors. Quintilian's *Institutes of Oratory,* written in the twilight of the first century CE, observes from the outset that the nature of a child is plastic, subject to shaping and reshaping. As a result, the child's inability to fulfill the expectations placed upon him or her is "due to the failure not of nature but of care."[104] The heightened concern for care and the role that nurture plays in long-term intellectual development leads Quintilian to offer his own suggestions for hiring a *nutrix:* "First of all, make sure the speech of the nurses is not vile. Chrysippus wished them, had it been possible, to be philosophers; failing that, he would have us choose the best that our circumstances allowed. No doubt the more important point is their character; but they should also speak correctly. These are the first people the child will hear, theirs are the words he will try to copy and pronounce."[105] Nurture is here depicted as either the enabler or corrupter of a generally good nature. A good birth can be undone by improper feeding and care, such that nurture becomes the arbiter of nature.[106] The two are, in fact, intimately intertwined.

While the *nutrix* functioned as a proto-educator for the infant (a theme found in Plato's *Republic* as well), Quintilian also depicts the teacher as a nurse for the student: "I would urge teachers too like nurses to be careful to provide softer food for still undeveloped minds and to suffer them to take their fill of the milk of the more attractive studies."[107] The weaning of children was a precarious process, and moving from milk to solid food too quickly "would undermine the child's health."[108] Proper nourishment required care, and this care was demonstrated through the strict regulation of diet and food intake, precisely calibrated to the capacity of the one being fed. This precariousness was so widely understood that it functioned as a typology among education theorists who believed, like Quintilian, that if a student moved thoughtlessly from rudimentary instruction to more challenging subjects, he could be permanently damaged. Soranus, for example, devotes an entire section to the weaning of infants.[109] There, a detailed regimen is prescribed for transitioning the infant from milk to solid food in a manner that will not cause it harm.[110] Thus, the physical weaning of the infant from milk, and the intellectual weaning of the student from elementary lessons, cannot be dismissed as a simple turn of phrase. Rather, the analogy of one's dietary capacity must be viewed within the complex interplay of eclectic traditions regarding the power of nourishment and the formation of the child's body and mind in a single developmental process.

In a treatise on the education of children attributed to Plutarch, the nobility of a child's birth presages the esteem in which the child will be held throughout adulthood.[111] Nobility of birth (*eugeneia*) is not, in this treatise, something one acquires simply by being born, but it is rather something that must be earned, cultivated, and demonstrated. Put another way, for Plutarch, noble birth was not simply a question of good "stock," but was, more precisely, the result of good nurture. For Plutarch, the goal of education is the development of a just disposition that is indicative of one's inward nobility. This outcome, in turn, depends upon the cultivation of three factors: nature (*physis*), reason (*logos*), and habit (*ethos*).[112] And after parentage, it is the child's *trophe* that helps secure his noble birth and earns acclaim for his character.[113]

As in the writing of Soranus and Quintilian, the intricate connection between food and formation is a key motif within Plutarch's text—so much so that it also offers counsel on the selection of milk providers for the child.[114] Mothers are here enjoined more vigorously to nurse and to feed the one whom they have birthed, as nature intended.[115] Greek women are again held up as the best alternative, and their nutritive care the most effective at shaping the infant's moldable (*euplastos*) and aqueous or pliant (*hygros*) nature. The nurse is both caregiver and proto-teacher. Her milk and her speech are simultaneously digested into the "soft soul" of the child.[116] The belief that a child's nature and, by implication, its soul were amorphous and aqueous was a fundamental component of these broader theories surrounding child-rearing.[117] The plastic soul of an infant, like the doughy composition of its newborn limbs, could be molded into perfect form through proper nourishment and nurture.

The literary crescendo of imperial-era ideology on the power of nourishment and breast-feeding is found in a curious anecdote about the sophist Favorinus within Aulus Gellius's *Attic Nights*.[118] While visiting a woman in a senatorial family who just gave birth to a boy, Favorinus is astonished to learn that the mother is not planning to breast-feed her own child. He draws upon the medical tradition that viewed the maternal milk as blood that was frothed up by the heat of the mother's postparturient body. As such, the quality of the nourishment received at the breast is, for Favorinus, just as potent as the father's seed in the transmission of physical and moral characteristics. Depriving a son of the "nourishment from his own familial and accustomed blood [*consueti atque cogniti sanguinis alimonia privare*]" is framed as an act of abandonment, no different, in Favorinus's view, from an abortion.[119] By ingesting the wet nurse's milk, the infant also consumes that nurse's family bloodline. In feeding from a wet nurse rather than from the biological mother, the child is not simply symbolically handed over to the care of another but quite literally becomes the product of another.

According to Favorinus, the maternal milk, just like paternal seed, carries within it the power to "form likenesses of body and mind" in the child.[120] Unlike his predecessors, Favorinus seems unwilling to make even an occasional allowance for the employment of a wet nurse, arguing that the nourishment she provides will be detrimental to the body and soul of the infant: "What evil, then, is the reason for corrupting the nobility of body and mind of a newly born human being, formed from gifted seeds, by the alien and degenerate nourishment of another's milk? Especially if she whom you employ to furnish the milk is either a slave or of servile origin and, as usually happens, of a foreign and barbarous nation, if she is dishonest, ugly, unchaste, and a drunk. . . . Shall we allow this child of ours to be infected with some dangerous contagion and to draw spirit into its mind and body from a body and mind of the worst character?"[121]

Although emphatic in tone, Favorinus's condemnation of the *matrona* is clearly engaged with the broader discourse of formation and its investment in the proper nourishment and nurture of children. His speech reflects the moral and medical dimensions attested to in other sources, amplifying the logic embedded within various traditions regarding the power of breast milk and its role in the development of the infant's moral and intellectual character. The woman's *spiritus* is carried within the breast milk and ingested by the infant at her side. Just as the Hippocratic text *On Nutriment* emphasized the power of food to produce likeness by reaching through the body's essences and attaching itself to *pneuma*, Favorinus views breast milk as pregnant with the *spiritus* of the woman who feeds the infant.[122] For Favorinus, milk is a carrier of maternal spirit, of familial blood, and of a broader social and cultural identity. Note especially the connection between the *spiritus* of the breast-feeding wet nurse, her "servile origin," and her "foreign" ethnicity. The proper formation of the elite Roman man is destabilized by the deficiencies and differences that Favorinus perceives within the breast milk of the slave.

And yet, as Erik Gunderson has noted, the "power of nourishment" in Favorinus's account of breast milk also functions on a secondary level for the audience of the *Attic Nights*. The discourse reaches its climax in a seeming non-sequitur comparison of two quotations from Homer and Virgil.[123] Beyond the biological claim that nature is transmitted from mother to son via breast milk, Favorinus has also situated his argument on a literary claim about intellectual parentage: "The original context of the discussion has been replaced in a new context: what was once a harangue addressed to a wife and mother by a Gaulish sophist is now food for thought for the readers of Gellius's miscellany. . . . Gellius all but describes Favorinus's prose style as having a *lactea ubertas*."[124] In this rich interplay between biological theory and literary criticism, nourishment—and specifically breast milk—is invested with the power to sustain or degrade personal character, familial nobility, and social stability as much as it indicates the broader transmission of an intellectual culture. The milk of the Roman *matrona* imparts character, virtue, health, and intellect in the same way that Favorinus's Greek words, transcribed into Latin by Gellius, impart the milk of literary wisdom. Gellius's highly figurative appropriation of the power of breast milk is situated explicitly upon the assumed power of breast milk in a literal or material sense. The figurative and the material senses are, in fact, bound together.

In this account, breast milk is a potent food that forms the body and mind, whether it is received from the breast of a mother or the mouth of a teacher. In both cases, it perfects nature, replicates identity, and secures legitimacy within the social order. In Gellius's depiction of Favorinus, becoming Roman required that one eat well. These interventions into the proper feeding of infants during the Roman imperial era created curious possibilities for complicating the more conservative family values they were designed to support: slave women were viewed with suspicion insofar as they held the power to usurp the father's primacy in forming the child; likewise, mother's milk educated a child by conveying kinship, social location, and moral character into the infant's nature at least as much as the father's seed; and in response, teachers like Quintilian invoked this power of nurturance and were, in a sense, "feminized" or "maternalized" in their efforts to nourish their students properly.[125]

Conclusion

In the third act of Shakespeare's tragedy *Coriolanus*, the title character has lost the favor of the Roman people and is chastised by his mother, Volumnia. A lifelong soldier, Coriolanus failed miserably as a politician seeking the consulship of Rome and has alienated the plebs. Volumnia urges him to

flatter the people in hopes of restoring their goodwill. But Coriolanus remains obstinate, so his mother tries a different tack. Volumnia argues that it
is more embarrassing for her, a noblewoman, to plead with her son to do
what is necessary than for him to plead with the plebs for their support. She
reminds Coriolanus that she is just as virtuous and courageous as he is. In
fact, she is the source of his nobility. In a climactic scene, she declares, "Thy
valiantness was mine, thou suck'st it from me."[126]

As it developed out of classical medical and philosophical discussions, the "power of nourishment" served to amplify broader ideologies at
the service of Roman family values. This was, after all, a sociopolitical system that had emphasized a mythos of milk at its very origins. And so the
transformative role that classical texts ascribed to nourishment within human psychic development was reactivated and reformulated with particular
force in the early centuries of the Roman Empire.[127] In that period, the
power assigned to food focused specifically on milk's capacity to transmit
the stuff of identity—be it biological, ethnic, social, moral, or pedagogical—
from one person to the next. At the intersection of these medical theories,
legal sanctions, moral prescriptions, and educational protocols, the quotidian act of breast-feeding was laden with symbolic freight at the service of
Roman imperial ideology. The breast-feeding woman—or, more precisely,
her body—became the arbiter of the child's familial identity, intellectual potential, and social legitimacy. Lactation, whether actual or figural, was used
to locate one's place in Rome's *imperium*. If meals are values quoted on the
stock exchange of history, then the currency of milk was significant enough
during the Roman Empire to designate a person as slave or free, subject or
elite, malformed or well-born.

The symbolic power given to the female body was employed by male
teachers, who were similarly tasked with the responsibility to feed, nurture,
raise, and mold their students. This ideological connection between a
mother's breast and a teacher's mouth was premised on the pervasive concern regarding the formation of children as the means for preserving the
empire. Indeed, the relationship between milk and instruction in the development of the soul can be thought of as a chiasma. The matter of nurture,
always composed of both food and instruction, was believed to attach itself

to the infant's malleable nature in order to produce beauty, intelligence, familial likeness, and social belonging. Any attempt to separate the intertwined strands of food and education introduces a conceptual distinction within a process that was not viewed as separate in any strict sense. Whether from the breast of the nursing woman or the mouth of the teacher, *romanitas* was passed from one generation to the next, as from Volumnia to Coriolanus, within the nourishing power of milk.

Same essence. Same food. And vice versa.

Mother's Milk as Ethno-religious Essence in Ancient Judaism

[M]others dissolve parts of themselves to feed their young.
—Katie Hinde, "Motherhood"

IN THE ROMAN WORLD, mother's milk carried significant ramifications for the social, political, and moral formation of the one being fed. Dio Cassius described how the food given to infants implants race, blood, and parental essence (*ousia*) in the newly born. Favorinus said that a woman's *spiritus* flows within her milk. And Soranus noted how the milk of a biological mother, unlike that of the wet nurse, is more conformed to the nature (*oikeioteron*) of the child. In these and other examples, specific parts of the woman were dissolved within her breast milk. Indeed, milk's capacity to transport the mother and her social, intellectual, and even ethnic characteristics in concentrated form reveals that this food was a resource of singular importance for identifying one's place within Rome. The scope and reach of this discourse can be traced to Jewish writings of the late republic and early empire. Indeed, some ancient Jewish texts drew upon the same strategies and assumptions we have encountered in Greek *paideia* and Roman family values in order to think through the very characteristics of their "Jewishness." In so doing, they devised similar gastronomic regimes out of milk and solid food. Yet something was also different in how food functioned in this literature as the material basis of a deeper religious bond.

The three sets of Jewish texts examined in this chapter indicate how the idioms, values, and embodied politics of Roman rule could be repurposed within a specific provincial culture. And they do so in such a way that emphasizes their own scriptural and philosophical commitments. This is not to say that other traditions concerning nourishment and breast-feeding did not exist among the varieties of Judaism thriving at this time. Rather, it is to suggest that certain Jewish texts and authors can be readily plotted within the nexus of Greek *paideia,* Roman rule, and Jewish cultural particularity. Precisely because they are written by authors familiar with classical *paideia* who were, to one degree or another, learned in its literary canon and cultural values, these texts share in *paideia*'s impulse toward imagining and realizing a specific cultural essence through protocols of formation. At the same time, that cultural essence takes on a strikingly ethno-religious specificity, as it is increasingly anchored to the words, traditions, and moral imagination derived from scripture.[1] And it is an essence that is located within the mother, dissolved in her milk, and fed to her children.

Unpacking Paul's enigmatic reference to milk and solid food within 1 Corinthians requires more than just tracing the intellectual lineages and social realities of milk's power within Roman family values. In addition to that, a robust account of how food functions in the apostle's letter requires that we also clarify more precisely the ways in which those family values were "subverted, absorbed, and manipulated" by provincial subcultures within Rome's *imperium.*[2] We've already encountered examples of prominent provincials who participated in Roman ideologies about milk in our examination of medical writers like Galen and Soranus, moralists like Plutarch, and historians like Dio Cassius. Each of those figures provides a window into the wide purchase of Roman imperial family values. Each reveals a more nuanced account of how quotidian expressions of Romanness (like those concerning food, feeding, and child-rearing) could be grafted onto other strategies of self-representation. In turning to Jewish texts from Greek-speaking provinces, we begin to see with greater clarity how the symbolic power of milk could be both absorbed and repurposed by Rome's subjects. For if certain ideals of *romanitas* could be mobilized toward different ends, evoked in different registers, then examining the symbolic power of nourishment in Judaism reveals an important modality in which Rome's rule could be simultaneously reinscribed and subverted.[3] That is, the "Jewishness" of some Greek-speaking provincials within Rome's *imperium* was framed as a matter of eating well.

Within the scholarship that helpfully articulates the relationship between food and formation in ancient Judaism, the intersection of Greek *paideia,* Roman family values, and child-rearing has received less attention.[4] In
what follows, this intersection will be analyzed in the stories surrounding the
Maccabean martyrs (in 2 Macc. 6–7 and 4 Macc.), in the writings of Philo of
Alexandria, and finally in the apostle Paul's first letter to the Corinthians. I
recognize up front the difficulties that attend this method of analysis. For
example, 2 Maccabees predates what I have been referring to as "Roman
imperial family values." Yet the text's emphasis on the symbolic power of
breast milk not only invokes long-standing theories about nourishment and
its impact on the soul but also anticipates the Roman imperial era's preoc-
cupation with breast milk as a carrier of cultural identity. As such, it provides
a critical bridge linking classical philosophical traditions, specific cultural
concerns of Judaism at the time, and the educational context of food's transformational power that was so central to Greek *paideia.* I will examine 2
Maccabees and 4 Maccabees in turn, noting how they compare and contrast
on the topic of food and nurturance. I am especially interested in how each
text encodes certain cultural values within the milk of the martyr-mother.
Turning toward Philo, I observe how these values take on greater scriptural
specificity as he inscribes the gastronomic regimes of Roman family values
into biblical passages about nurturance and nourishment. Thus, by framing
my reading of Philo and the apostle Paul with an analysis of the Maccabean
mother tradition, I am suggesting that the symbolic power of milk is fully at
work within these provincial texts as a strategy for realizing a Jewish essence
within—and sometimes over and against—the dominant *imperium.*

In so doing I seek to situate the apostle Paul's trope of milk and solid
food squarely within this broader discourse of formation, but also as
reflective of other Greek-speaking Jewish authors who used it to imagine a
specific ethno-religious essence. The reference to breast-feeding in 1 Corinthians 3 is no mere metaphor but rather a conjuncture of Greek philosophical traditions, Roman imperial ideology, and the available literary strategies
among Greek-speaking Jewish authors. Like Philo and the authors of the
Maccabean martyr narratives, Paul reflects the symbolic power of milk, manipulating it like other provincials according to his own cultural strategies.

Through it he gestures toward an inchoate model of social identity that would powerfully communicate the idea of "same essence, same food"—a model that becomes the structuring logic for how later writers attempt to think through a "Christian" cultural essence.

The Power of Milk in the Maccabean Martyr Tales and in Philo of Alexandria

"MILK FROM THE SAME FOUNTAINS": MARTYR'S MILK IN THE MACCABEAN TRADITION

Both 2 Maccabees 6–7 (ca. 124–63 BCE[5]) and 4 Maccabees (late first or early second century CE[6]) recount the gruesome death of an old man along with seven brothers and their mother at the hands of the Seleucid king Antiochus IV Epiphanes. The army of Antiochus had occupied Jerusalem and had begun a program of forced assimilation to Greek customs upon the Jews there (ca. 167 BCE). This assimilation included prohibitions of Sabbath observance, circumcision, and other purity laws. The deaths of the elderly man Eleazar, the mother, and her sons dramatize the cruelty of Antiochus's program and the piety of the Jews in Jerusalem who resisted it. The texts have a hortatory function, beckoning readers to locate themselves within the familial and religious framework embodied by the martyrs.[7]

In the narrative, each character is brought before Antiochus and instructed to eat pork.[8] Refusing, they are tortured and brutally killed one by one. The core theme of both narratives is the relationship between fidelity to the Law and piety toward family and "nation"—a fidelity consummated in each character's death. Scholarship on the Maccabean martyrs is extensive. Yet only in the past two decades has the character of the mother received more focused attention and critical analysis.[9] Specifically, recent scholarship has especially noted the mother's fulfillment of or resistance to her "natural maternal affection" as her sons were killed.[10] Drawing upon the insights of these studies, the following analysis foregrounds the mother's pregnancy, nurture, and breast-feeding of her boys in order to better understand the central role these themes play in the narratives of 2 Maccabees and 4 Maccabees.[11]

Throughout both texts, the mother's exemplary character is framed in explicitly androcentric terms.[12] This androcentric framework has led Jan Willem van Henten to argue that "disregard [for] her deep motherly affection for her sons" is represented in each text as a prerequisite for the noble death of the entire family.[13] Robin Darling Young has argued that the two accounts actually diverge on the mother and her orientation to parental affection: 2 Maccabees, Young suggests, demonstrates "the coherence of the Jewish families in death" while 4 Maccabees shows "how the family, although important for training in religious devotion, will be transcended into a kind of spiritual parentage."[14] Mary Rose D'Angelo, however, has suggested that 4 Maccabees presents the mother and her sons as the consummation of familial piety.[15] Yet the intersecting themes of pregnancy and nurturance in both texts makes it difficult to maintain a stark division between religious piety and familial piety. The authors of 2 Maccabees and 4 Maccabees construct the mother's maternity as an integral component of her noble character and, crucially, as the foundation for the noble character of her sons. Her maternity, D'Angelo argues, is not antithetical to martyrdom but is rather a complex literary device that enables the martyrdom of her sons and discloses the deeply ingrained quality of their virtue.

Turning to the specific discussions of the mother and the particular mode of her influence over the sons, each text reveals a shared concern about the milk and nurture provided. Yet that significance is inflected in different ways. In 2 Maccabees, for example, there is an explicitly theological explanation for the conception and formation of the children in the womb of the woman: "The mother was especially admirable and worthy of honorable memory. Although she saw her sons perish within a single day, she bore it with good courage because of her hope in the Lord. She encouraged each of them in the language of their ancestors. Filled with a noble spirit, she reinforced her woman's reasoning with a man's courage and said to them, 'I do not know how you came into being in my womb. It was not I who gave you life and breath, nor I who set in order the elements within each of you'" (2 Macc. 7:20–22).[16] The mother's words, given to her sons in their native tongue, establish the divine origin and providence of the children, a supernatural force that arranged their natures while she carried each one to term. The emphasis on ancestral speech is significant, as it amplifies the legitimacy of her children's nurturance.

Indeed, her speech is typical of ancient hortatory maneuvers and, as Susan Haber has observed, it also indicates "the mother's essential influence over her sons and her role in teaching them to live their lives in accordance with the Law."[17] But the "essential influence" of the mother goes deeper than words spoken in a native tongue. In the following passage, the mother enumerates the details of her nurturing care, pairing the power of ancestral tongue with her own milk: "But, leaning close to [her youngest son], she spoke in their native language as follows, deriding the cruel tyrant [that is, Antiochus IV]: 'My son, have pity on me. I carried you nine months in my womb, and nursed you (*thelasasan*) for three years and have reared you (*ekthrepsasan*) and brought you up (*agagousan*) to this point in your life and have taken care of you (*trophophoresasan*). I beg you, my child, to look at heaven and earth and see everything that is in them, and recognize that God did not make them out of things that existed. And in the same way the human race came into being. Do not fear this butcher, but prove worthy of your brothers'" (2 Macc. 7:27–29).

The mother's opening ("My son, have pity . . .") mimics the lament of the Trojan queen Hecuba as she sought to persuade her son Hector not to fight Achilles. Undoing her robe with one hand while holding out her bare breast with another, Hecuba cries out, "Hector, my child! Look— have some respect for *this*! Pity your mother too, if I ever gave you the breast to soothe your troubles, remember it now, dear boy!"[18] For the Maccabean mother, as for Hecuba, the essential bond formed through maternity and breast-feeding serves as the basis for persuasive speech.[19] Her milk is a material link between the child's familial background and his present actions. Yet the author of 2 Maccabees has inverted the purpose: rather than trying to protect her child from death to keep him within the family, as Hecuba had done, the Maccabean mother appeals to her nurturance of the boy so that he might endure pain, torture, and death. In dying for the Law, he will remain bound to the family, its ancestry, and its religious piety. His death will prove that her nursing was not, in fact, in vain.

But there is more to these passages than tropes of motherly persuasion. Haber has observed the close connection between breast-feeding as "providing physical nourishment for the child" and breast-feeding as "a metaphor for the imparting of knowledge."[20] It is here that we can trace the outline of Greek ideals concerning food and formation within the mother's climactic address: she shepherded the children through pregnancy and infancy, she reared them all identically at her breast, producing in them a likeness of mind, body, and soul. She was the site and source of their *paideia* under the Law. God works through the mother's body as through a conduit—instilling fidelity to the Law, the bond of brotherhood, and the ongoing formation of a noble character.[21] But it is the mother's milk, her care of nurturance, that brings this divine work to its noble completion. By dying in obedience to Law and fidelity to family, like his brothers before him, the youngest boy embodies the inward and material bond signified by the common milk that God provided each boy at the breast of his mother.

The string of verbs contained in this second passage accentuates the close connection between physical nourishment and intellectual formation. Haber observes how "Along with his mother's milk, the boy imbibed his first lessons in the Law."[22] Yet even the verbs that follow the mother's claim that she "suckled" (*thelazo*) her boy indicate a more intricate relationship between nurture and nourishment. Taken in sequence, the use of *trophophoreo* and *ektrepho* along with *ago* amplify the impact of the mother's milk in forming and raising her boys. The collecting of these terms in the space of a few short lines is meant to intensify the mother's dual role as nourisher and instructor. Her milk is their bond, connecting them back to their primordial source. The essential elements that God used to knit the boys together as individuals flow from one to the next through a common milk and thus a common *paideia*.

Turning to 4 Maccabees, we see a continuation of these same themes, yet now inflected through even more specific language about fidelity to family. Indeed, following Mary Rose D'Angelo, I think that the intensified familial piety of 4 Maccabees is best viewed as a provincial appropriation of the household values that were so central to Roman imperial ideology. Two examples bear this out forcefully, the first of which establishes the central role of the mother's milk as the materialization of that familial piety:

> You are not ignorant of the affection of family ties, which the divine and all-wise Providence has bequeathed through the fathers to their descendants and which was implanted in the mother's womb. There each of the brothers spent the same length of time and was shaped during the same period of time; growing from the same blood and through the same life, they were brought to the light of day. When they were born after an equal time of gestation, they drank milk from the same fountains. From such embraces brotherly-loving souls are nourished; and they grow stronger from this common nourishment and daily companionship, and from both general education and our discipline in the law of God. (4 Macc. 13:19–22)

The text foregrounds the central motif of familial piety, the affection of the brotherly bond (*ta tes adelphotetos philtra*). Like 2 Maccabees, God is identified as the source of the elements from which the boys were knit in their mother's womb. But here, divine providence isn't just the origin of those material elements but is also, emphatically, the origin of their familial ties. That brotherly affection takes on deeper material and spiritual connotations. Unlike the mother's speech in 2 Maccabees ("I carried you . . . nursed you . . . have reared you"), 4 Maccabees emphatically maintains the equal apportioning of the mother's nurture for each boy. The bond of the family is numinous, established by God's eternal wisdom, but that bond is also grounded in the common materiality of an unbroken genealogy and is revealed in the present moment by the common nourishment (*suntrophias*) consumed by the boys at the shared breast of their mother. Same essence, same food.

It is hard to miss the emphatic attention to the identical nurture of the children: same gestation time, same blood, same life, and same fountains of milk. The passage begins with a reference to familial piety, claiming God as the primordial origin of that piety, tracing it to the present through an

unbroken ancestral lineage, and finally dissolving that piety within the elemental sustenance of the mother's milk. It is within this growing connection
between milk and piety that the mother's faux speech three chapters later
makes the most sense: "If this woman, though a mother, had been faint-
hearted, she would have mourned over them and perhaps spoken as follows:
'O how wretched am I and many times unhappy! After bearing seven children, I am now the mother of none. O seven childbirths all in vain, seven
profitless pregnancies, fruitless nurturings, and wretched nursings! In vain,
my sons, I endured many birth pangs for you, and the more grievous anxieties of your upbringing'" (4 Macc. 16:5–8). This passage should not be read
as a rejection of motherly affection as such. Rather, in light of the previous
passage, 4 Maccabees makes explicit a contest between different kinds of
maternal affection. She nourished the boys from the same sources of milk,
providing a common nurture from which an education and discipline in the
Law would develop. The mother's acceptance of their deaths is not an abandonment of her maternal bond but rather its pious completion. The family's
sacred bond is not destroyed by the death of the brothers. It is fulfilled.

According to the logic of 2 Maccabees and 4 Maccabees, the mother
had fed and formed the boys for an end such as this. To be sure, a lower
form of maternal affection is rejected in 4 Maccabees 14:13 and 15:23 through
the use of terms like *storge* and *philoteknia*.[23] In contrast to this lower form
of affection, the mother's "devout reasoning" is emphasized (15:23): her
birthing, breast-feeding, rearing, and educating of the sons becomes a single, seamless philosophical curriculum forming them to the Law and to the
specific kind of reasoning (*logismos*) she carries within her. It is this power
of devout reasoning that the boys received from her while in the womb, at
her breast, and by her side. Through her common milk, they shared a common discipline in the Law. Feeding on the same milk that carries her *logismos* enables them to face the same death, demonstrating that they have
digested and been conformed to her devout reason.

Both 2 Maccabees and 4 Maccabees absorb and reactivate the symbolic power of nourishment as a resource for articulating a program of dis-
ciplined formation in the face of persecution and death. In 2 Maccabees we
see a more general application of the ideals surrounding food and formation

that were prominent within the educational protocols of Greek *paideia*. In 4 Maccabees we encounter a focusing of those protocols into a more robust familial piety, one that reflects the broader trends of Roman household ideologies. The brothers, having shared the same food when they were infants, were enabled to meet death as one family, materially bound to each other through the devout reasoning of Torah piety dissolved in their mother's milk. Her breast-feeding functions as a kind of prophylaxis, inoculating the boys against the temptation to eat the contaminating pork upon the king's altar. The body of the Maccabean mother and the food she provided for her sons establishes within them a virtuous, Law-observant, and unafraid character. They share these common traits because they also shared a common womb, a common breast, a common food.[24]

Of course, the mother herself recedes from view in the narrative after the youngest boy dies. Her death is not dramatically recounted in detail. Her character, like that of the Roman *matrona* and the *nutrix,* is attached primarily to her dutiful nurturing of the children under her care. In 4 Maccabees, the martyrs are "deemed worthy of a divine portion" (18:3), the inheritance of those who are counted among "the children of Abraham's seed" (18:1). The mother's significance is not in her own death but in her devotion to the proper nourishment and formation of her boys—her legacy displaced onto their achievement of manly virtue and pious reasoning. She has nourished them into their inheritance as Abraham's sons. With her sons honorably dispatched as rightful heirs of Abraham, and her reason for being fulfilled, the mother is pushed offstage. As a mother, her deeds are significant to the story. As a woman, her fate is troublingly inconsequential.

It is worth noting here that later rabbinic traditions related to the mother and her seven sons also highlight the act of nurturance as a central theme in the narrative, though toward quite different ends and with different concerns in mind. In Lamentations Rabbah, a rabbinic text that Martha Himmelfarb locates in fifth-century Palestine, the mother of the martyred boys doesn't just reference her breast-feeding.[25] In a dramatic scene with the youngest son, she actually breast-feeds him one final time just before he is killed. The text tells us that this was done "to fulfill what is said, 'Honey and milk are under thy tongue' (Song of Songs 4:11)."[26] After feeding him, the mother instructs the boy not to be afraid because he is going to join his brothers "in the bosom of Abraham." The discussion of the mother is framed here within a commentary on Lamentations 1:16 ("For these I weep"). In this way, the rabbis accentuated the importance of the mother's milk by having her give the boy a final meal from her flesh and connected this common feeding and common death to their common ancestry in Abraham, all at the service of illuminating a brief passage of scripture.[27]

The traditions surrounding the Maccabean mother readily invoke the discourse of formation with its emphasis on the power of food to realize, preserve, and transfer a cultural essence into the soul. Likewise, these traditions reflect the intimate association between nourishment and education that were central to both Greek *paideia* and Roman family values. Both 2 Maccabees and 4 Maccabees demonstrate the nascent theological potential of nourishment and infant-rearing within a Jewish worldview that found itself reoriented (however antagonistically) as a provincial subject of Greek and Roman rule. The mother is a conduit for an alternative *paideia* that flows from God. Through her body passes the stuff of divine wisdom, devotion to the Law, and thus the material bond of a kinship that can trace its lineage back through a holy ancestry into its divine origins.

"FOOD FROM A LEGITIMATE SOURCE": NOURISHING DIVINE WISDOM IN PHILO OF ALEXANDRIA

In addition to her analysis of Roman family values in the Maccabean literature, Mary Rose D'Angelo has also observed how "Philo's gender categories are plotted not only using the hierarchies of middle Platonism but also the moral propaganda of the Roman Empire. . . . [Philo] represents the moral demands of Judaism as meeting, and indeed exceeding, those of the imperial order. He thus assures both the Jews of Alexandria and their Roman masters that Jewish sexual probity, marital chastity and familial devotion are of such a high standard that the Jewish tradition can instruct the empire and its subjects in the piety, restraint, and manliness that enable rule of the world."[28] Likewise, Maren Niehoff has convincingly demonstrated the ways in which Philo "cared about the transmission of culture which would transform new-born children into authentic Jews."[29] The role of nourishment and breast-feeding in Philo's writing can be usefully plotted within this broader concern about the transmission of Jewish culture in the context of the Roman Empire. More than that, Philo develops the general Torah piety of the Maccabean use of food into a more specific exegetical method for approaching biblical texts. In this way, textual meaning and food symbols meld together as Philo blends elements of Greek *paideia* and Roman family values at the service of a Jewish cultural essence—an essence that is realized and articulated through the words of scripture.

In *On Flight*, Philo answers the question "What is it that nourished the soul?"[30] Commenting on the manna from heaven described in Exodus 16, he concludes that this soul food is a "divine word, from which flows all *paideia* and everlasting wisdom."[31] On this passage, Rosenblum has suggested, "Manna eaters have ingested their identity and as such are not only eligible for, but also apparently gastronomically predisposed toward, Torah study. Manna seemingly has all the essential vitamins and nutrients for Torah exegesis. After it is 'absorbed into their bodies,' manna ontologically changes the manna eaters. In this case, the notion of eating practices embodying tannaitic identity seems to be both figurative and literal."[32] Philo's correlation of God's Logos with the nourishing manna—a correlation that posits a metabolizing of scripture's words—offers a new theological register in which the sayings or teachings of God become food for those who read correctly.[33] This manna, then, is the purest form of food for the soul: the words of scripture contain a nutritional power, nourishing and forming the soul according to its wisdom. Philo presents the reading of scripture as a mode of trophic formation in which the wisdom on the page is consumed and digested like manna falling from the sky. But this is not the only form of nourishment Philo discusses.

Throughout his exegesis of scripture, Philo regularly comments upon the important role of mothers and fathers in the rearing and educating of children.[34] In *Who Is the Heir of Divine Things?* Philo interprets Genesis 15:16 (in which God tells Abraham that his descendants will not return from exile until the fourth generation) as an allegory for the maturation of the soul through successive ages. For Philo, the "first generation" is equivalent to the first seven years of life: "The infant from the day of its birth for the first seven years, that is through the age of childhood, possesses only the simplest elements of soul, a soul which closely resembles smooth wax and has not yet received any impressions of good or evil, for such marks as it appears to receive are smoothed over and confused by its fluidity."[35] The infant is once again depicted as a plastic and malleable being, liable to many impressions without much consequence. As we have seen in other texts, the "soul as wax" was a popular trope in antiquity.[36] Nevertheless, it is not until the "second generation" that the moldable soul receives the more lasting impressions of good and evil. Philo explains how, in this age, "instructors to sin are legion, [including] nurses and pedagogues and parents."[37] According to Philo, a child progresses from infantile innocence to childhood guilt largely due to his own weakness and the poor instruction of those who are charged with his care.[38] Only in subsequent "generations," it seems, can the child be formed to goodness and virtue.

Parents and nurses are primarily negative in their influence upon the formation of a child's soul. Philo's suspicion evokes Plato's *Republic* and the concern over immoral tales that children are told in the laps of mothers and nurses. Yet Philo also has much to say about how the proper nourishment and nurture of a child are vital to its ongoing development. In *On the Virtues,* Philo spends considerable time discussing the natural bond between a mother and her newborn and argues that Nature has ordained this bond through the feeding of the child by the mother. He describes breast milk as a "timely and most-gentle nourishment that forms all tender creatures. Milk is drink and food in one substance. As much as it is watery, it is milk, and as much as it grows thick, it is food."[39] Here, breast milk is once again figured as the material expression of a mother's bond with her children—a tender love that has as its sole purpose the formation of the infant through the powerful food provided by her body.[40] The nourishment of her body is both milk and food (*sition*)—a curious distinction, especially since the word Philo uses here for "food" typically refers to bread, corn, or grain-based victuals. But the point is clear: breast milk, regardless of its outward consistency, has an unchanging and powerful essence that forms the child.

Yet elsewhere Philo contrasts the father's influence upon the child (who provides "the masculine and perfect right-reason") from that of the mother ("the intermediate and general course of education").[41] The father's instruction comes from nature and imparts truth, while the mother represents a human *paideia* of the polis that embraces those things that only seem to be true.[42] Philo suggests that, while right reason (*orthos logos*) is embedded in the father's nature, the *paideia* of the mother's instruction is provisional, subject to error, and incomplete. Nevertheless, Philo's denigration of human *paideia* as a weaker, "feminized" mode of intellectual formation does not result in an outright rejection of maternal care or the system of education known as *enkyklios paideia* for the development of wisdom and virtue.[43] The naturally instilled reason and the culturally imposed education can, when properly paired, work together for the benefit of the child.

In *On Mating with the Preliminary Studies,* Philo expands the connection between maternity and *paideia:* using the narrative of Sarah and Hagar—Abraham's wife and her handmaid, both of whom gave him a child—he concludes that one cannot "mate" with Wisdom and give birth to virtue until he has first had intercourse with the handmaid of Wisdom. Hagar, the handmaid, is identified as *enkyklios paideia,* the preliminary course of formative instruction.[44] Philo then shifts from the allegory of "mating" to another image in order to describe this preparatory instruction: "Do you not see that our body is not first nourished on solid and costly foods before it is given the simple and milky nourishment needed during childhood? In the same manner, consider also how the nourishment of general education (and the knowledge within each of its subjects) prepares the childhood of the soul; since the virtues are [a food] for the fully-grown, suited to those who are truly men."[45]

Philo toggles between the language of sexual intercourse and that of infantile feeding to develop two modalities of proper formation based on the language and narratives of scripture. To "mate" with Hagar is to receive the basic and milky nutriment found within the general course of education.[46] Just as no one eats solid food before first being fed on milk, there is no intercourse with Wisdom (and thus no giving birth to virtue) without first joining with the course of instruction represented by Greek *paideia.*

Abraham, it seems, was not yet man enough for Sarah. Unskilled and immature, he required training and growth before he could receive her Wisdom. In this passage, the milk of Greek *paideia* is a prerequisite for the solid food of Jewish wisdom. Nourishment and procreation, nurturance and erotics are folded together in a single course of education. There can be no solid food prior to breast milk, no wife prior to the handmaid, and so no eternal wisdom prior to rudimentary instruction.

The trope of milk and solid food employed here by Philo is strikingly similar to that found in 1 Corinthians 3. It is this blending of food and formation that the apostle Paul evokes in order to distinguish his correspondents at Corinth. The slippage between figurative and literal senses allows Philo to outline a process of intellectual formation through an elaborate allegorizing of Abraham's coupling with Sarah and Hagar. In *On Mating*, one must be properly fed on a step-by-step curriculum of milky knowledge prior to receiving the denser sustenance of Wisdom.[47] There is a sequence of instruction, of feeding, and of procreating that must be followed to produce one who is "truly a man."

However, Philo elsewhere offers a model quite different from that found in *On Mating*. In *On Dreams,* he reads Genesis 21:8 ("The child grew and was weaned, and on the day Isaac was weaned Abraham held a great feast") as meaning that Isaac had no need of breast milk at all. That is to say, the immediate weaning (*apogalaktizo*) of Isaac indicates to Philo that the child "altogether rejected the feeble and milky nourishment required by infants and children" because he was self-taught.[48] From the time of childhood, Isaac had such strength of mind and character that he was able to eat the vigorous and perfect (*eutonos kai teleios*) food of the fully grown. In contrast to *On Mating*, in which Abraham symbolizes the need to be weaned on the preparatory milk of general education before receiving Wisdom, Isaac here offers an alternative approach. He requires no formal instruction and, thus, no breast milk at all. Some, it seems, are wise enough to skip the weaning process and move directly to feeding themselves on the perfect food of wisdom. To be self-fed at such a young age indicates an uncommon capacity for wisdom and an intimate connection to the Logos of God.

Read on the whole, Philo employs the trope of nourishment and breast-feeding pervasively, if not coherently, in various attempts to discuss the formation of the soul. First, in *On the Virtues,* he seems to demote the general course of education associated with Greek *paideia* as a feminine and weak substitute for masculine "right-reason." Next, in *On Mating,* both Wisdom and *paideia* are associated with feminine characters—the latter functioning as a kind of prerequisite for the former. Last, in *On Dreams,* the brevity of Isaac's suckling demonstrates not only his rapid physical growth but also his exceptional intellectual advancement. Philo makes use of breast milk in a variety of ways to think through human growth, intellectual formation, and the inculcation of social location and ethnic belonging.

Sharon Lea Mattila has commented upon this ambiguity in Philo's use of nourishment, breast-feeding, and the biological functions characterized as "feminine" or "maternal":

> [U]pon first inspection it would seem that at least in one respect Wisdom continues to play a "female" role with regard to humanity, and this is in her role as "mother of all things." The nourishment she provides from her breasts, however, is of the heavenly kind, which must be carefully distinguished from the material sustenance provided by Mother Earth and Nature. When elevated onto a spiritual plane, the one female role most clearly associated with a woman's biological function—that is, the role of motherhood, especially the processes of childbearing and breast-feeding—carries for Philo a certain ambiguity with respect to his gender categories. The qualities that Wisdom brings forth from her breasts and womb are spiritual and "male"; they are of the same kind as those which she "sows" and "begets" in the soul.[49]

Mattila rightly identifies the ways in which Philo uses maternity—especially childbearing and breast-feeding—as a resource for describing how humans are acclimated toward eternal wisdom. And this functions in a clearly allegorical mode in *On Mating* through a chain of symbolic relationships:

biblical characters are identified with particular modes of intellectual development, and those modes are then described as distinct forms of nourishment. The reader is placed within a process of masculinization as he or she moves from the childish milk of Hagar's general education to the manly solid food of Sarah's wisdom. Both women provide Philo with a scriptural analog for the dutiful Roman *matrona,* who properly births, rears, and instructs her male infants. The reader plays the part of both infant and husband in this pedagogical dance between feeding and procreating.

Yet Mattila's distinction between a "heavenly kind" of nourishment and "material sustenance" replicates the assumption that physical growth and intellectual development were separable in antiquity. The allegorical or spiritual function of nourishment within Philo's exegesis cannot be quarantined from the social ideology and moralistic idiom of his time, grounded as they were in the embodied realities of nurture and feeding. Philo's emphasis on the maternity of Hagar and Sarah in *On Mating*—and the construction of maternity in general throughout his writings—is only legible within a social and cultural backdrop in which the mother already functioned as a powerful site for the working out of familial devotion and the construction as well as transmission of its specific essence. Any symbolic discussion of the care and feeding of infants (even in highly allegorized terms) is necessarily implicated in the broader discourse of proper child formation that was so prominent in Philo's day and the long-standing view that nourishment was a potent element in the formation of the human person. The milk and solid food mentioned in *On Mating* carry an essence that molds the soul of the one who eats.

Perhaps the most provocative aspect of Philo's participation in this discourse of food and formation is how thoroughly he situates it within the lexicon and conceptual framework of scripture. Philo's exegesis therefore reactivates Roman family values in a variety of registers, imbuing the dominant ideologies regarding the nurturance of infants and the care provided by mothers and child-minders with theological significance. This is most evident in his *On the Life of Moses,* in which the nursing of Moses as an infant is given special attention. The narrative from which Philo's commentary is drawn occupies four brief verses from Exodus 2:7–10. Moses's birth mother has set him afloat down the river, and the daughter of the pharaoh finds him. Unsure of how to nurture the child, the pharaoh's daughter unwittingly hires the birth mother to serve as his wet nurse.[50] The biblical text says little about the mother's role as wet nurse to Moses other than that, when he had matured, he was returned to the pharaoh's daughter.

Philo fills in the gaps of this narrative with particular emphasis on what is transferred from mother to son through the clandestine use of his biological mother as a wet nurse. The mother is selected as the one from whom the child is to be fed on milk (*galaktotropheo*). This detail is significant for Philo: "By the foreknowledge of God, the very first nourishment given to the child was provided from a legitimate source."[51] The word for "legitimate" here is *gnesios* (γνήσιος). It carries with it significant lexical and rhetorical weight as a means of identifying something or someone as a genuine, natural, and lawful member of a broader social community and cultural identity.[52] Put within these terms, Philo is arguing that the breast milk given to Moses was provided from "a legitimate Hebrew woman." The proper nurturance of Moses at the breast of his biological mother secures his status among the Hebrews, nurturing him in his people's wisdom and transmitting to him the Law.

Whereas the biblical text only says that Moses was returned once he had matured (Exod. 2:10), Philo amplifies this process by describing how the infant was weaned more quickly than is normal for most children.[53] He was then brought back to the Pharaoh's daughter by his "mother and wet-nurse in one" because he no longer required the nourishment of milk.[54] The exceptional growth of a wise man was a common topos within ancient biography and hagiography. As Patricia Cox Miller has observed, statements about the prodigious development or innate wisdom of a child illustrate that "the point of [the wise man's] education seems primarily to be a kind of discipline, the fine tuning of an already overpowering intelligence."[55] In *On the Life of Moses*, as in his discussion of Isaac as self-fed and self-taught in *On Dreams*, Philo demonstrates the deeper legacy of this hagiographical theme by describing the uncanny wisdom of Moses through his abnormally quick progression from mother's milk to solid food. From her divinely ordained milk, the "well-born and graceful" nature of the child was made readily apparent.[56] Likewise, after being returned to Pharaoh's daughter,

Philo tells how Moses received "the nurture and care worthy of a king."[57] Philo provides a lengthy description of this kingly education: Moses had tutors and teachers from all over the world, but he surpassed them all in his capacity for wisdom. He notes especially that Moses was "given the *enkyklios paideia* by Greek teachers."[58] Yet despite this throng of educators who flocked to Moses, their instruction functions only as a proving ground for the wisdom that was already planted firmly within him—a wisdom that was nourished on the legitimate milk of his mother's breast.[59]

Here, as in the narratives of the Maccabean martyrs, mother's milk has a divine origin and is imbued with power to realize, stabilize, and transfer social identity. In this way, Jewish authors like Philo and the traditions surrounding the Maccabean martyrs used the dominant ideologies about food and the formation of infants to construct their own models of intellectual development and the preservation of a cultural identity. Set in this broader scope, it is inadequate to view the appeal to milk and solid food in *On Mating* 19 as merely an interesting parallel to 1 Corinthians 3. The striking similarity of these two passages must also be read within the exegetical contexts that prompted Philo to consider the power of food and its formation of character. That Moses's mother is explicitly framed as a "legitimate" source of milk speaks to the transfer of a material essence that binds infant and mother together as kin, as part of a people, similar in effect to the *logismos* found in the milk of the Maccabean mother. And so ancient Jewish texts dissolved certain values within the symbol of milk in order to develop a more robust articulation of their ethno-religious essence. It is within this discourse that we must read Paul's appeal to milk and solid food, attending to the specific qualities he attributes to the milk given to the Corinthian babes.

Pneumatic Atrophy: Paul's Milk and the Corinthian Infants

> [W]e have all been given one *pneuma* to drink.
>
> —1 Corinthians 12:13

Some forty years ago, E. A. Judge cautioned scholars of the New Testament against locating the apostle Paul within ancient philosophical schools or even positing that he was "influenced"—that most nebulous of historical categories—by one or another of them.[60] Judge concluded that "in a vital and mixed society [such as Paul's] one simply picks up and uses the vocabulary and technical ideas and fashionable notions of the time wherever they come from. If one is the kind of independent thinker that Paul is, one is simply building out freely from that, exploiting the material rather than subjecting oneself to it. The ways forward for historical research in this field . . . lie along the lines of studying this kind of popular intellectualism."[61] While recent studies have continued to trace the contours of certain philosophical orientations within Paul's letters, scholars have also increasingly pushed beyond either/or categories "to see Paul in the broad cultural context to which he belonged."[62] Paul's appeal to milk, solid food, and the power of nourishment to transform his Corinthian correspondents is best understood as embedded within the structuring logic of this discourse. As with 2 Maccabees, 4 Maccabees, and Philo, Paul's emphasis on food in 1 Corinthians 3:1-3 draws upon the symbolic power of breast milk to describe and sanction certain modalities of identity, intellectual growth, and social formation.[63] And like other Greek-speaking Jewish writers, Paul also retools this compelling symbol in light of the pressing concerns and needs of his particular community.

When Paul declares that the Corinthians were not ready for solid food and require his milk instead, he is making an argument about the presence of *pneuma* shared by the members of that community. Specifically, Paul is building upon 1 Corinthians 1-2, in which the absence of *pneuma* is identified as the source of division, discord, and quarreling among those at Corinth. A lack of *pneuma* has resulted in a lack of spiritual maturity and the breakdown of social unity.[64] To remedy this, Paul reminds the Corinthians of their common birth in the Gospel: the members of the community at Corinth can largely trace the origin of their faith to Paul's preaching (1 Cor. 1:17). In the intervening time, some had become disappointed with his lack of sophisticated speech. They wanted demonstrations of wisdom according to the conventions of rhetoric so prominent at that time. Yet Paul observes, "not many of you were wise according to the flesh, not many were powerful, not many were of noble birth" (1 Cor. 1:26).[65] The apostle argues that he did not bring them wisdom in the way the world perceives it, because they were in no position to receive it as such. Moreover, he states that God's wisdom does not appear in the same way as the "wisdom of the flesh." Rather, Paul's preaching offered the Corinthians wisdom in the form of *pneuma*. Had the Corinthians ingested the *pneuma* he provided, they would have become *pneumatikoi*—or spiritual people who can "discern spiritual things to those who are spiritual" (1 Cor. 2:13). All those who have the *pneuma* also have the mind of Christ (1 Cor. 2:16). There can be no strife, no factionalism when God's *pneuma* is shared.[66] While not all of the Corinthians were noble by birth, they could have been nurtured into nobility if only they had ingested this *pneuma*. Like Plutarch's *On the Education of Children*, there is in 1 Corinthians a subtle connection between a child's ongoing nourishment (*trophe*) and its embodiment of a noble birth (*eugeneia*).

The pressing problem for Paul is that the Corinthians have not been properly formed. As a result, they are in a state of atrophy—pneumatic malnourishment. They have lapsed toward a more "animal" or "natural" or "soulish" state.[67] Rather than being *pneumatikoi*, they have taken on the form of *psychikoi* (1 Cor. 2:14–15).[68] The discord and division among the Corinthians is, in Paul's view, symptomatic of the deeper and more troubling loss of *pneuma*. Without sharing in this *pneuma*, they could not share in the mind of Christ, they could not achieve unity as a community, and they could not grow as members of the *pneumatikoi*. Lacking the *pneuma*, the Corinthians regressed to a baser, fleshly existence.

Paul's prescription of more milk for the Corinthians is offered as a remedy for this pneumatic malnourishment. The nutritive power of his *pneuma*-laden milk is meant to staunch that atrophy and to promote proper growth once again. His milk is both a site of social unity and a carrier of the *pneuma* that will cause spiritual growth and concord to occur. The power of the apostle's milk reflects the pervasive tradition that viewed nourishment as essential to the work of human formation and to the bonds of kinship that create social stability. In this way, the trope of milk and solid food in 1 Corinthians 3 employs the logic of the discourse that has been traced in the preceding pages, evoking themes such as the Hippocratic concept of the power of nourishment, in which food permeates the body's essences (and especially *pneuma*) and, when properly administered, makes an infant brilliant in soul and mind; the ideology of Roman family values reflected in Favorinus, in which the mother's *spiritus* is absorbed by her infant's body and mind through breast milk; the Torah-centric familial piety of the Maccabean mother, in which her *logismos* is dissolved and transferred to her sons through breast-feeding; and the nourishment Moses received at his biological mother's breast, which Philo refers to as "legitimate" or even "natural" and thus a guarantor of Moses's divine wisdom. As with Plutarch or Quintilian after him, Paul sees his pupils, his Corinthian "infants in Christ," as moldable mounds of flesh (*sarkikoi*) needing a proper regimen for the ongoing formation of body and mind. That regimen begins with his milk and the divine *pneuma* contained within it.

The fact that Paul's pneumatic milk is transferred by either spoken or written word need not soften the power of his language regarding nourishment. As Troels Engberg-Pedersen has persuasively demonstrated, the transfer of both physical and cognitive essences via the *pneuma* is no less "literal" in Paul's epistolary practice than in actual breast-feeding: "Paul, it seems, is literally filled up with *pneuma*. . . . [*Pneuma*] literally streams out of Paul's mouth toward [the Corinthians]. . . . Paul is evidently trying to convey the *pneuma* (his *pneuma*) to the Corinthians through his literary practice itself."[69] Indeed, the apostle "saw his letter writing as a bodily practice through which the *pneuma* might (once more) be transmitted to his addressees."[70] The stark distinction between the literal and the figural is further destabilized by this materialist framing of Paul's epistolary practice. His milky words convey the essence of a material bond linking writer and recipients together as kin. To the extent that they are properly fed and formed by the *pneuma* within his words, they become one family, sharing in the mind of Christ. From Paul's body flows a stream of pneumatic words, reflecting the same formative power of the *spiritus*-carrying milk that flows from the breast of a mother.[71]

Nevertheless, the precise meaning Paul intends with his distinction between milk and solid food has vexed scholarship on 1 Corinthians for some time. The categories Paul deploys in 1 Corinthians 2–3 (carnal/soulish/

spiritual, infant/perfect, milk/solid food) represent a persistent and seemingly irresolvable exegetical problem. Conzelmann, as noted earlier, was emphatic that *paideia* "remains only a suggestion" and that "Paul's concern is not with education and development, but with the antithesis of the moment."[72] But this remains merely one option in an overwhelming array of scholarly interpretations. One alternative to Conzelmann's view argues that Paul's appeal to milk and solid food offers a distinction between infantile lessons and "deeper elements of the wisdom of God."[73] Others have concluded that "a different sort of curriculum is appropriate to each level of maturity,"[74] or, conversely, that the solid food is merely a "fuller elaboration of the truth about Christ" and not a different lesson as such.[75] Some have suggested that Paul is chastising those at Corinth "for failure to engage the moral conversion expected of Christians."[76] Still others have contended that this distinction relates to the Corinthian acceptance of "Paul's authority" more than to the "reader's intellectual progress."[77] And finally, in a monograph on Paul's use of maternal imagery, Beverly Gaventa has concluded that solid food indicates "a more profound understanding of the Gospel rather than some mystery tradition."[78] To be sure, Paul explicitly states that he did not offer any wisdom, any special mystery of God, other than Christ crucified (1 Cor. 2:1–2). This, combined with the letter's overall goal of removing discord and promoting unity, has resulted in a loose consensus that 1 Corinthians 3:1–3 does not propose a division between intellectuals and simpletons or between remedial and advanced content in instruction. Paul lumps the entire Corinthian community under the category of milk-drinking infants.[79] They must receive the milky matter of his pneumatic words before they can partake of a solid food that is, like in Philo, identical in essence if not in appearance.

Yet, contrary to Conzelmann, Paul's distinction between milk and solid food seems inextricable from a larger process of spiritual formation, intellectual development, and pneumatic growth that culminates in "having the mind of Christ." And while some scholars have cautioned that it is a "grave mistake" to view this passage as "warrant for ranking individuals within the church on a scale of spiritual advancement,"[80] such a reading became the inescapable temptation and dominant issue at stake throughout the text's early interpretation.[81] Paul's identification of his Corinthian infants with milk necessarily opens up a range of possibilities about what it means to be a mature, perfect, solid-food-eating "spiritual." Regardless of his original intentions, the kaleidoscopic array of identifying and distinguishing categories that Paul uses in 1 Corinthians 1–4 (infants, fully grown, carnal, spiritual, milk-drinking, solid-food-eating, and so on) readily suggested to Paul's earliest interpreters a progression of character formation, curricular advancement, and the means for preserving and transmitting a cultural essence.

In his appeal to familial roles of authority—mother/nurse, father, pedagogue—the apostle participates in the ideological system of Roman family values in order to unify the fractious and immature Corinthians. Paul's shift from the role of *materfamilias* (1 Cor. 3) to that of *paterfamilias* (1 Cor. 4) is part of a broad rhetorical strategy in which he assumes the identity of those Roman household figures endowed with the greatest capacity to create a likeness of themselves within others and, through that likeness, stabilize the social order.[82] The goal is mimetic, as Paul makes explicit in 1 Corinthians 4:16 ("Be imitators of me").[83] This was the highest aim of parenting in Roman ideology: to produce, nourish, and raise another who reflects your own strength of body, character, and soul resulting in a stable *domus* that is a microcosm of the empire at large.[84] Paul's exhortation that the Corinthians should imitate him as they would a father is not distinct from his self-identification as a nursing mother in 1 Corinthians 3. Milk and imitation, as we have already observed, were linked in the ancient imagination as constitutive elements within the formation of the human person. Breast milk was understood as the material from which the bonds of kinship were established and fortified. And it is these bonds that were thought to produce a likeness of bodies and minds among those who consumed a common nourishment. Imitation of the father is merely the next logical step in their progress toward a spiritual existence.

Given the widespread concern regarding the proper nurture of children, it is perhaps less shocking that Paul would apply to himself both maternal and paternal roles. While the goal of child-rearing in Roman ideology was a son whose character and appearance reflected the father, the mother was nevertheless emphasized as a crucial resource in this process.[85] It was also from her body that the "stuff" of moral character, intellect, and kinship was passed on to the infant. Improper nurture could result in a deformed nature. A mother's milk contributed significantly to the proper formation of the male heir. Parts of her character, her virtue, even her ethnic and cultural identity were dissolved in her milk and transferred to her son. As we have seen throughout the literature of antiquity, the modern binary of "nature versus nurture" is not a useful category in analyzing this phenomenon. The two were inextricable: birth, nourishment, and education were all components of a single, ongoing process of formation. Put another way, noble birth had to be worked out through the application of food and instruction, of instruction as food—or, in Tertullian's later phrasing, by being "raised on Christian milk." The administering of milk to the Corinthians by the apostle was the first step in a *pneuma*-centric *paideia*, the goal of which was growing together into the mind of Christ.

Conclusion

The formative power attributed to milk by Greek-speaking Jewish authors of the late republic and early empire reflects the suffusing reach of ideologies about food and formation that can be traced from the classical period into late antiquity. The traditions surrounding the mother of the Maccabean martyrs, the exegetical philosophy of Philo, and the writing of Paul to the community at Corinth should be located within this discursive framework as prime examples of how provincial subjects made use of Rome's family-values system to their own advantage. In each case, proper feeding and proper formation are intimately drawn together. Likewise, in each case breast milk is invested with the power to convey a particular cultural or social identity. It symbolizes a material bond that links people together as "a people." The trope of milk and solid food in 1 Corinthians 3 inscribes the dominant social practices and ideologies concerning the practice of breastfeeding that was also already being put to use by other Greek-speaking Jewish authors of the period. Here, the language and narratives of scripture increasingly contributed to the formation of an ethno-religious identity—

the essence of which was communicated in breast milk drawn from a "legitimate" source. Dissolved in Paul's milk was the *pneuma* so lacking in Corinth. To be properly formed according to this pneumatic identity, one had to eat well.

But situating Paul's categories of infant and perfect, breast milk and solid food within this framework is only the first, crucial step toward a more robust account of nourishment in early Christianity. For the compelling power of milk would extend from this ambient discourse through Paul's letter into the later Christian imagination with particular force. Indeed, those who followed Paul in the nascent Christian communities of the Roman world would turn, time and again, to the power of milk evoked in 1 Corinthians 3 in order to construct their own models of identity, education, and legitimacy. Some did so working explicitly from Paul's letter in the form of commentary and exegetical debate. Others did so less wedded to Paul's words while remaining nevertheless indebted—however implicitly—to the ways in which he used symbols of food to categorize and distinguish people. In what follows, the apostle will sometimes play a central role and at other times will recede from view. The fact that nourishment became a powerful and pervasive symbol in early Christianity should not only be credited to Paul. The movement from milk to solid food had been widely and increasingly invoked as a mode of social identification, as a process in which the deepest held values were encoded and retained within the body, and as a means for projecting those values into the next generation.

Nevertheless, this is not to downplay the significance of 1 Corinthians 3. "Why," Margaret Mitchell recently asked, "would the road to early Christian hermeneutics run through Corinth?"[86] She concludes, "Given the hermeneutical density of these letters (because so much was at stake and contested between Paul and the Corinthians, including the meaning and status of the letters themselves), they were naturally to furnish abundant interpretive axioms for later expounders, but we would miss that very point if we were to try only to see what they thought the text meant (in some abstract sense) rather than what they did with it. The Corinthian letters were not just received, but acted upon and with. They are not just the subject of hermeneutical inquiry, they are the agent of it."[87]

Paul's trope of milk and solid food is a particularly forceful example of how the Corinthian letters became "an agent" of hermeneutical inquiry within later Christian exegesis. The "density" behind these few verses, I would argue, speaks to the freight of milk as a symbol for locating oneself and one's group within Rome's *imperium*. When Paul's exegetes approached the trope of milk and solid food, they inevitably pulled up with it the tangled web of traditions associated with nourishment and the formation of the soul. The symbol of milk and solid food served as more than a potent axiom for Paul's successors. "What they did with it," to borrow from Mitchell's phrasing, was in fact authorized and made intelligible by the long-standing and complex discursive tradition about intellectual formation in which food functioned in both *literal* and *figurative* registers. Within a community whose goal was growing into the "mind of Christ," the two senses were easily conflated.

THREE

Ruminating on Paul's Food in the Second Century

> Breathing, eating, babbling, singing, and speaking make a puzzling continuum of experience; we are always at, or on, the oral stage wherever else we are. What kind of meals does the child make of words? They come out of his mouth, but in what sense do they go into his mouth, like food and air? Are words something spat out? How does the child digest both the language he is being offered and the language going on around him?
>
> —Adam Phillips, *The Beast in the Nursery*

WHAT KIND OF MEALS DID THE CHILDREN of Paul make of his words? Food, as we have seen, was encoded with the power to communicate and convey a cultural essence. This remained true in the generations following Paul's first letter to the Corinthians. Yet interpreters in no way received the apostle's milk as a single, coherent mode of "Christian knowledge" or "Christian identity." Indeed, the meals made of Paul's words reveal a startlingly divergent range of options for how one could be well-fed and well-formed in Christ.

According to 1 Corinthians 3, the community at Corinth was given milk from the same source. Paul employs breast-feeding to establish social unity and to diagnose levels of maturity—of growth in the *pneuma*—among his correspondents. In this way, the apostle stands within a long tradition of ancient authors who understood maternal milk as an inescapably political symbol. Aristotle, for example, explicitly links the formation of a sociopolitical community to the common milk upon which its people are fed: "But when several families are united, and the association aims at something more than the supply of daily needs, the first society to be formed is the village. And the most natural form of the village appears to be that of a colony from the family, composed of the children and grandchildren, who are said to be nursed 'with the same milk' [*homogalaktes*]."[1]

As I argued in the previous chapters, from classical Athens to the Roman Empire, the home was viewed as a microcosm of society at large. The bonds of kinship forged within the household strengthen the bonds of the state. It is for this reason that Aristotle opens his *Politics* with an examination of household management. A community of people linked by a shared milk nourishment also shares a more profound commitment to common goals and values. Establishing kinship is the first step toward a coherent mythology around which a community gathers. According to Aristotle, a social group composed of *homogalaktes* is the basis for a healthy and unified sociality.[2] Shared milk realizes that kinship at the material level and links individuals together as a people, a bound social group, through the transfer of this essence from one person to the next. In this way, shared milk is the origin not only of the family or the village but also of the city and all its people.

It has been my contention from the start that the words, phrases, and tropes that populate common language inevitably (and often unwittingly) invoke the complex historical, social, and political realities that provide structure to the world. When the apostle Paul reprimanded his Corinthian children for their lack of maturity, their lack of *pneuma*, he was perhaps so thoroughly enmeshed in the inescapable sprawl of Roman family ideology and its attendant discourse of formation that he could neither name it as such nor anticipate the ends to which his own idioms would be used. Such is the symbolic power of language. The first letter to the Corinthians witnesses to the concern that Paul himself had over his own legacy. But even in the second century, this legacy was far from settled. In the contentious exegetical battles that ensued, the argument for ownership of Paul emphatically relied upon the idea that common nourishment could establish one's kinship with the apostle and with a legitimate Christian sociality. That is to say, in the unsettled world of second-century Christianities, the appeal to a shared source of milk served a strategic function, insofar as it came to authorize certain arrangements of Christian social identities and relations over and against others.

The power of the connection between the apostle and his milk is vividly evoked in an apocryphal account of Paul's martyrdom (usually dated to
the mid- or late second century). In the climactic scene of his death, Paul
stretches out his neck for the executioner's sword and is decapitated. From
the top of his headless body spurts milk, not blood. All who witness this
event, even the executioner (whose clothes are soaked with Paul's milk), are
amazed and praise God.[3] At roughly the same time this story was written,
polemics surrounding the apostle's legacy intensified—especially those that
focused on the meaning of his milk and its significance for the structure of
the Christian community. The question of who was and who was not a true
child, raised on Paul's *pneuma* food, also entailed more specific conflicting
claims about direct descent from the apostle himself.

It seems the Valentinians made an especially strong case. Their
teacher, Valentinus, had been taught by Theudas, who was a direct disciple
of Paul.[4] Competing Pauline lineages were part and parcel of the more
general competing Paulinisms that circulated throughout the marketplace
of second-century Christianities. And within this context, the trope of milk
and solid food was a persistent exegetical problem, the resolution of which
provided the tantalizing possibility of a more unified Christian "family." But
the attempt to resolve the legacy of Paul inevitably demonstrated the more
fundamental problem contained within the system of symbols that Paul
employed in 1 Corinthians.

As Margaret Mitchell has persuasively argued, the various categories
Paul used to describe Christian identity in 1 Corinthians created an aporia
that the apostle left unresolved—an aporia bequeathed to later Christian
exegetes. Mitchell provides an excellent summary of this problem:

> [The apostle Paul was] not providing a hermeneutical map, but
> offering a provocative diagnosis, meant to prod the Corinthians
> by an insulting label flung out to change their behavior. Given
> that this is his rhetorical aim, Paul must certainly leave open the
> possibility for hermeneutical change and growth, even as in
> "systematic" terms there appears to be an ontological fixity.
> The lack of precise fit can be seen in the sheer mathematical

difficulty with mapping the duality mature/childish onto the triad spiritual/psychical/fleshly. And the reasons Paul gives or implies for theses statuses are at least theoretically different: one is spiritual by endowment ("but we received the Spirit which is from God"), but fleshly or psychical by nature, a condition subject to change either by spirit-infusion or by proper maturation. Furthermore, the literal-allegorical template is doubly confusing here, in terms of the reality Paul describes and the words he chooses to do it: are all three properly "real" states, or is the spiritual person no longer (allegorically? Literally?) also a person of flesh?[5]

The difficulty of mapping these categories (adult/infant, spiritual/psychical/fleshly, and allegorical/literal) onto one another is further compounded by the food categories of solid food/milk. As we will see later, some Christian authors, such as Origen, add a third category of food (vegetables) in an attempt to bring harmony and symmetry to what was an unharmonious and asymmetrical system of symbols.[6] But in the exegetical foment of the second century, harmonizing Pauline categories proved less pressing than establishing the fundamental sense in which those categories ought to be understood.

Nowhere is this urgency more evident than in the writings of two very different contemporaries, Irenaeus of Lyons and Clement of Alexandria. As John Behr has observed, the theological and exegetical positions of these two figures are useful for comparison because they were "developed in response to common opponents."[7] But a common enemy did not result in a common solution to the problem of Pauline categories inherited by later generations. Rather than solving the problem, Irenaeus and Clement only intensified the theological and anthropological issues generated by the troublesome categories of milk and solid food, as well as fleshly, soulish, and spiritual.[8] And in so doing, they opened an exegetical space capacious enough to allow rather divergent readings of the same terms long after the specter of Valentinian or Gnostic influence had begun to recede.[9] Indeed, as we will see, not only were Clement and Irenaeus not consistent with one another in their reading of Paul, but in fact Clement himself provided quite divergent readings of the milk and solid-food trope that are not easily reconciled. One of these proved strikingly similar to the position of opponents he had targeted elsewhere.

My argument in what follows, then, is that from very early on, these Pauline categories carried with them a host of cultural connotations about kinship bonds, the transmission of cultural identity or legitimacy, and the ongoing formation of a nascent social community. And Christians of the second century wielded those categories accordingly. To that end, I will begin by examining scholarly discussions that attempt to link Paul's original opponents in Corinth to so-called proto-Gnostics and then move on to the opponents of Irenaeus and Clement. At stake here is clarifying the complicated origins and legacies of Paul's terminology. Turning next to Irenaeus's and Clement's own writings, I will explore how two of the earliest and most evocative uses of the trope of nourishment attempt to construct a coherent vision of Christian formation.

Foregrounding the prominent emphasis on the church as composed of God's infant nurslings in both authors, I will argue that this trope was readily employed to articulate a shared lineage of Pauline Christianity. This was a lineage, so Irenaeus and Clement maintain, that did not denigrate milk as inferior but rather made it an identifying characteristic—in order that all Christians might be counted among the *homogalaktes* of a newly unified Christian community. Yet as we will see, even as these two prominent second-century authors staked a common ground in reconfiguring the connotations of Paul's milk, they did so toward different ends. And this difference resulted in not a single solution to the competing Paulinisms of the second century but rather an intensification of the problem itself.[10] In these writings we encounter just how quickly the meals made of Paul's words resulted in conflicting interpretations of milk, solid food, and the character of the people apportioned to each.

Corinthian Pneumatics, Valentinian Solid-Food Eaters, and Other Invisible Enemies

In his study of the conflict within Paul's Corinth, Walter Schmithals concluded that the apostle's opponents (the "Corinthian Pneumatics") represented a "well-defined Christian Gnosticism."[11] The problem between Paul and these pneumatics, for Schmithals, was one of a shared terminology but not a shared doctrine. Paul was compelled to use terms like *pneuma* and *gnosis*, as well as the categories of infancy/fully grown or fleshly/spiritual, even though he "had long since surrendered or had never held" these as specifically Gnostic distinctions.[12] Schmithals concludes that, for Paul, "all Christians are through faith *pneumatikoi*, even if the gifts of the Spirit are variously imparted."[13] Such a reading may initially seem compelling precisely because it reflects the received tradition of interpretation that later developed around this text. (Indeed, as we will see, Clement explicitly makes the argument that infant Christians are already perfect.) But its problems are manifold.

First, there is the issue of classifying Christians under the nebulous and historically fraught category of Gnosticism. Labeling a single group in Paul's own context "Gnostic" is, at best, an overly simplistic way of resolving the divergent understandings of categories shared by the apostle and his correspondents at Corinth. After all, Paul's opening volley in 1 Corinthians 1 does not reject *gnosis* out of hand but rather attempts to attach it directly to his preaching of Christ crucified. His *gnosis* is the "wisdom of God" (1 Cor. 1:21).[14] The problem, for Paul, is not wisdom as such but rather wisdom's source. Second, the claim that Paul identified all Christians as *pneumatikoi* is not demonstrated in the text. Indeed, if it was clear that Paul viewed all Christians as *pneumatikoi,* this fact not only eluded the "Gnostic" or "aberrant" readers of the text, but also eluded many of the interpreters whose work became the basis of later "orthodox" exegetical traditions.

Unfortunately, we do not have an exhaustive or even an adequate amount of material from Valentinus, his followers, or any other so-called Gnostics that speaks directly to these different readings of 1 Corinthians 3. And while it is a truism that those within the "Gnostic" tradition denigrated

the simple, fleshly infancy of milk mentioned by Paul in favor of the esoteric, pneumatic maturity of solid food, this is an argument that must be
made primarily from the writings polemically opposed to the tradition in
question. Independent examples are woefully lacking.[15] The most relevant
extant writings by Valentinus (and his star pupil, Heracleon) come to us
through citations in Clement of Alexandria and, later, Origen.

A paradigmatic example of how we have come to understand the Valentinian approach to these categories is found in Origen's *Commentary on
John*—a text, coincidentally, that was written for a former "Gnostic" pupil
named Ambrose: "But even now the heterodox, with a pretense of knowledge, are rising up against the holy church of Christ and are bringing com-
positions in many books, announcing an interpretation of the texts both of
the Gospels and of the apostles. If we are silent and do not set the true and
sound teachings down in opposition to them, they will prevail over inquisi-
tive souls which, in the lack of saving nourishment, hasten to foods that are
forbidden and truly unclean and abominable."[16] Implicit in this argument is
the truism mentioned earlier: that Gnostic or Valentinian groups advertised
themselves as the inheritors and purveyors of Paul's solid food. That these
groups apparently denigrated other modalities of Christian identity—especially the status of those with little or no intellectual training, those perceived to have a lower capacity for spiritual things—posed a significant
exegetical problem to second-century contemporaries of Valentinus and
Heracleon who preceded Origen.

In this brief account, we can begin to see the difficulty in reconstruct-
ing a robust account of Paul's Corinthian opponents as well as the direct
interlocutors against whom Irenaeus and Clement developed their own approach to milk and solid food. And yet it was through Irenaeus and Clement that the Gnostic/Valentinian exegetical method is most directly
addressed, rejected, but also repurposed toward other ends in the second
century. Both Irenaeus and Clement seek to rehabilitate infancy as a positive category for Christian identity. Achieving this rehabilitation required of
them no small feat of exegetical gymnastics. The result was not so much a
solution to the problem of Pauline categories but rather an intensification of
the problem itself.

Irenaeus, Human Infancy, and the Nursing God

THE INFANT CREATURE,
THE NOURISHING CREATOR

The cosmological scope of Irenaeus of Lyons's anthropology has occupied historians and theologians for quite some time. Tantalizing statements about infancy and development—often viewed as a kind of evolutionary theology of human spiritual growth through the ages—can be found throughout the bishop of Lyons's polemical magnum opus *Against Heresies*. In his popular study of theodicy, *Evil and the God of Love*, John Hick famously presented Irenaeus as the antidote and antithesis to Augustinian pessimism about the fallen condition of humanity after sin.[17] On Hick's reading of Irenaeus, Adam and Eve in the garden represent not so much a perfection irrevocably lost but rather the clumsy infancy from which human beings grow into a future perfection.

Such a reading is not entirely unwarranted. As other scholars of early Christianity have noted, Irenaeus was not interested in a "lost golden age of primordial perfection."[18] Rather, for him, humanity is but a recent creature—the most recent, in fact—and thus "appeared as a child in a world specially prepared for [its] nourishment and growth."[19] This much is evident from the opening of Irenaeus's treatise titled the *Demonstration of the Apostolic Preaching*: "[F]or each and every person, God is the nourisher. . . . But [at the time of creation] humanity was a young child, not yet having a perfect capacity for judgment."[20] Like their Edenic ancestors, all humans are brought into this life containing the latent, raw material out of which maturity and perfection will be formed. For Irenaeus, human perfection is the result of God's nursing, weaning, and reshaping the plastic material of human nature. God's role as nourisher of humanity—as *tropheus*—establishes a common source of food from which each individual might be rendered, in time, into the unifying likeness of God.[21]

This theme is developed at length in *Against Heresies*, where Irenaeus also depicts God as "our maker and nourisher" (*factor et nutritor nostrum*).[22] From the nursing God comes forth the human person, "a mixture of soul and flesh, who is formed according to the likeness of God and is molded by His hands, that is by the Son and Spirit, to whom he said 'let us make man.' "[23] The plastic materiality of human nature is the basis, the condition, of its infancy.[24] The human creature is not metaphorically infantile due to its lack of spiritual maturity. It is, quite literally for Irenaeus, an infant by its very nature as a material creature.[25] God's activity as a *nutritor/tropheus* is strikingly consistent with contemporaneous discussions of proper wet-nursing practices, like that found in Soranus and elsewhere. God feeds, swaddles, massages, and molds human nature, using the Son and Spirit as divine hands, so that this creature can arrive in time at its perfect adult form.

This, then, is the crucial strategy that informs Irenaeus's interpretation of Paul. Against readings that viewed the Corinthian "infants" as a designation of derision (that is, of individual and collective moral failing), Irenaeus makes infancy a universal anthropological category for the entire human species as it grows into the likeness of God. The paradigm of God-as-nurse/humanity-as-infant is the guiding strategy of Irenaeus's "genetic" approach to his opponents. According to Irenaeus, these opponents argue that they have achieved perfection and maturity—that is, they are the *pneumatikoi* mentioned in 1 Corinthians—because they contain within them the "seed of the Father." This seed planted knowledge and perfection within these select few.[26] They are the heirs of Paul's wisdom, carrying within themselves a genetic link to the apostle. Against such a claim, Irenaeus emphasizes nourishment, and specifically breast milk, as the guarantor of an authentic Pauline lineage. It is not the seed but rather the milk of God that proves one's legitimacy as a Christian.[27] Milk, for Irenaeus, functions first as a genetic bond knitting together the entire human race. But second, as we will see next, it also serves as a genealogical resource for tracing the lineages of particular social groups.[28]

"AT SOME FUTURE TIME . . . BROUGHT TO MATURITY"

One consequence of this shift from seed to milk is that, for Irenaeus, the growth and maturity of Christian infants is largely spoken of in collective terms. The bishop of Lyons depicts his opponents—those Gnostics carrying the seed of wisdom—as embarking on spiritual progress in isolation from others. For his opponents, one cannot cultivate the seed of *gnosis* in community, but rather must dive alone into the ocean of deities and "forever swim within the limitless abyss."[29] For Irenaeus, this model of spiritual progress cannot truly be called "progress" at all. The unfathomable depth of their cosmology is a ceaseless roll call of divinity. The ocean in which Irenaeus's "Gnostic" adversaries swim is gods all the way down. They continually yearn for a deeper deity, a more profound spiritual reality, "always seeking yet never finding God."[30]

This is one of the chief errors that Irenaeus perceives in those who claim to be Paul's *pneumatikoi:* they have mistaken maturity, progress, and perfection as an individual birthright of the seed carried within them. To refute this, Irenaeus offers an emphatic defense of immaturity, infancy, and imperfection as essential to human nature. And in so doing, he also situates God's nurturing of this imperfect creaturely nature as a communal, ecclesial process: "And so God determined all things for the perfecting of man, for his empowerment, and for the revelation of His work in history, so that goodness would be evident and righteousness brought to perfection and the Church molded to the form of His Son's image. And thus, at some future time, humanity may finally be brought to maturity."[31] Human materiality, our creaturely status, necessarily suggests a state of imperfect infancy. The church, for Irenaeus, is God's nursery. It is the space in which the as-yet-unformed material of human nature is nurtured into its proper shape.

The qualifier at the end of the previous quote is critical—"*at some future time,* humanity may finally be brought to maturity." While Adam and Eve were infants in the garden, the nature of all humanity remained in that same state of infancy, requiring the nurturing hands of God to mold it into perfection. As M. C. Steenberg has suggested, Irenaeus's use of Pauline categories is emphatically literalistic, even in the precise places where the bishop of Lyons deploys highly symbolic language.[32] Infancy, for Irenaeus, is not simply a metaphor for a lower level of moral or spiritual growth. It is an inescapable physiological fact. It is the essential condition of human existence: "Because humans are incomplete and created beings, for this very reason do they fail at being perfect. Insofar as they are made later, so are they considered infantile. For they are unaccustomed to and untrained in perfect discipline. Just as a mother is able to give perfect food to her infant, [she does not do this because] the child is not able to receive such hardy food. So too was it possible for God to make human nature perfect from the start, but humanity was not capable of this perfection: for it was, in fact, an infant."[33] Irenaeus's argument is simultaneously physiological and cosmological: human nature was not, from the start, acclimated to its creaturely status in relationship to God. There was need for a period of habituation and accommodation—a time in which human nature might grow up.

Impotent humanity (*homo impotens*), then, required a suitable food from God that could begin this process of acclimation and empowerment. Its nature could not yet contain the "perfect bread of the Father" (*panis perfectum Patris*). A simpler fare was needed. This, for Irenaeus, is the pedagogical basis of the Incarnation: human nature, "having been nourished, as it were, with the breast of [God's] flesh [in Christ], and by means of this milk-making [*lactationem/galaktourgias*], might as a result grow accustomed to eating and drinking the Word of God."[34] Jesus Christ is the milk offered by God to wean the infancy of human nature into adulthood. But the weaning phase, it seems, is still ongoing. The milk of God's breast, passed to humanity through the flesh of Christ, is the true food of all Christians past and present.

Irenaeus's blending of anthropology, physiology, and cosmology within a broader argument about human infancy sets up his climactic reading of 1 Corinthians 3 toward the end of book 4 in *Against Heresies*. While the apostle Paul had the power to give the Corinthians "meat" (*esca/broma*)—that is, "the Holy Spirit, who is the food of life" (*esca vitae/broma zoes*)—they were not able to receive such spiritual nourishment on account of their weak and untrained souls.[35] Since humanity, for Irenaeus, is only recently created (*nunc nuper factus*), the entire species remains unable to feed on the hearty meat of the Spirit. The soul implanted within human nature must be nurtured and nourished until it can contain the fullness of the Spirit. And so the milky Word of God was "conjoined in infancy" with us, "not for His own sake but for the sake of infant humanity."[36]

For Irenaeus, the Pauline categories of "infant" and "milk" are not read as a rebuke of moral or spiritual failing. Rather, they indicate the incomplete state of the human soul that requires a divine nurturer and nourisher to guide it toward perfection. And while, in the previous passage, Irenaeus had referred to the Holy Spirit as the "solid food," in a subsequent section he notes how God works cooperatively to bring about the divine image and likeness in human nature: "[T]he Father rightly plans and commands, the Son furnishes and gives shape, the Spirit nourishes and grows, and thus humanity is brought, little by little, to perfection and completion."[37] Those who refuse this infancy, "who do not anticipate the time of growth," Irenaeus calls "irrational."[38]

If we take the bishop of Lyons at his word, there were groups of Christians that identified themselves as the "perfect" ones. These "adults" claimed the capacity to eat Paul's solid food. They claimed to have become the spiritual ones that the Corinthians had failed to be. For Irenaeus, this posed several problems. First and foremost, there was an exegetical issue. How ought the Pauline binaries of infant/adult, carnal/spiritual, and milk/solid food be understood? For his opponents, it seems, the plain sense of the text was obvious: some people among the Corinthians were simply more spiritually mature than others and, as a result, were capable of deeper knowledge concerning God. But this interpretation, in turn, raised a second, anthropological issue: What precisely do these categories imply regarding human nature and, more specifically, the natures of those within the Christian community? Against the idea that there were deeper and deeper spiritual truths that could be plumbed by the *pneumatikoi*, Irenaeus insisted instead that all true Christians are fed on the same milk that flows from the breast of the Father's flesh. He asserts that all Christians are, by nature, infants suckling at God's breast. In this way, Irenaeus attempts to resolve the exegetical issue by expanding its scope to fit with his broader cosmological and anthropological arguments found throughout *Against Heresies*. From a God's-eye-view, there can be no distinction among Christians who, regardless of intellectual capacity, nevertheless belong to the same infant race.

The curious reader may find Irenaeus's response more evasive than descriptive. But the sleight of hand in Irenaeus's nonanswer—following, in some respects, the cagey precedent already set by Paul ("I only ever preached

Christ crucified!")—set the mold for many later interpretations of 1 Corinthians 3 and the meaning of its categories. As we will see, it became commonplace to say a lot about milk and solid food without ever describing precisely how Christians are located within those groups (much less how Christians can progress from one to the other). And out of this tendency, a third interpretive problem arose: Was the moral maturity and spiritual growth of one who eats solid food an individual achievement? Irenaeus depicts his opponents, despite grouping them within broad heresiological categories, as individual luminaries swimming alone in an abyss of *gnosis*. True Christians not only accept the infant state of their human nature but also gather together in the nursery of the church to be fed on the same milky food of God.

In this way, Irenaeus's reading of 1 Corinthians 3 in *Against Heresies* is at least as creative, expansive, and unprecedented as that of his much-maligned enemies. From a few short verses of the New Testament, the bishop of Lyons extrapolated both a cosmology and, within that universal framework, an anthropology. From Irenaeus's vantage, the only suitable nourishment for the Christian life is the milk found within the nursery of the church. Indeed, for Irenaeus, it is not entirely clear that humanity will grow up any time soon. He explicitly criticizes those who no longer anticipate the growth to come but presume a perfection already acheived. To expect spiritual progress, to yearn for it, even while being nourished on the milk diet of faith, is the closest Irenaeus comes to identifying Christian maturity in the current stage of human history.[39] Nevertheless, there is an eager optimism to Irenaeus's account of Christian infancy: perfection may not be at hand, but the milk that forms the soul into the likeness of God is yet doing its work. Only those held in the caressing hands of the nursing God will be made capable of consuming the Spirit. Whenever that time comes.

Clement, the "Milk-Fed" Among Men, and the Meat of God's Being

If Irenaeus primarily reads 1 Corinthians 3 in a cosmological framework, Clement's reading is, by contrast, framed in emphatically pedagogical terms.[40] Both authors emphasize the physiological implications of Paul's categories and that these implications have real consequences for how

Christians ought to understand human nature and its growth in relationship to God. And both emphasize a common nourishment as the basis for a legitimate Christian identity. But while Irenaeus worked within the burgeoning hierarchy of an infant church, Clement's role was, to borrow David Brakke's phrasing, more like that of a "teacher and a spiritual director."[41] From this orientation, the movement from milk to solid food—and from infancy to adulthood—suggested itself immediately (if not in an entirely coherent way) to Clement's work as an instructor of Christians.[42]

Clement readily recognized the challenge of implementing the Pauline categories of 1 Corinthians 3 within a paradigm of Christian identity and formation. Before diving into his tour-de-force reading of Paul in the *Paedagogus,* Clement offers a telling caveat: "A great difficulty emerges from the joining of these writings."[43] This disclaimer not only anticipates the vexed history of interpretation that would unfold around the trope of milk and solid food in the centuries following Paul, but more immediately it indicates Clement's own struggle to offer a coherent and consistent reading of the text throughout his writings.

The feature that most distinguishes Clement from Irenaeus is that, while both seek to overturn Valentinian or Gnostic interpretations of Paul, Clement explicitly appropriates the categories that he condemns. And so, unlike in Irenaeus's *Against Heresies,* Clement employs identifiers such as "gnostic" and ideas such as the "solid food of deeper wisdom" as positive categories in ways that would have been scandalous to his contemporary in Lyons. In addition, he amplifies the physiological and medical connotations contained within the "great difficulty" of Paul's language in order to support his case—an exegetical strategy that forcefully demonstrates the slippage between literal and figural interpretations of 1 Corinthians 3 that is characteristic of so much early Christian literature. It is as though Clement cannot decide whether he loves or hates the teaching of his opponents, and so, out of this ambivalence, he deploys both criticism for and appreciation of their exegetical strategies as it suits his pedagogical needs.

The different approaches that Clement provides to the symbols of milk and solid food must be viewed in light of his specific catechetical aims.

As Eric Osborn has outlined, "The divine movement from invitation (*Protrepticus*) through instruction (*Paedagogus*) to perfected humanity (*Stromateis*) is as decisive as are the earlier ages of the plan of salvation. Movement goes on in the new age, which has been inaugurated, as humans participate in the salvation which God offers and move from faith to the vision 'face to face.' "[44] Clement's work has rightly been described as one of the earliest attempts at a curriculum for Christian catechesis. Rather than a cosmological, universal account of human infancy, Clement offers instead a Christianized "course of instruction"—that is, a kind of Christian *enkyklios paideia*—that will guide his infant pupils from the milk of discipline into the solid food of a mature understanding of the Logos.[45]

But in contrast to Irenaeus's universalizing of infancy at the level of human nature, Clement employs the Pauline categories according to the needs of each individual pupil.[46] As a result, he offers several interpretations for Paul's categories of milk, solid food, infant, and adult—interpretations in which Clement mimics his opponents as often as he refutes them.[47] The catechetical curriculum loosely outlined in the *Protrepticus, Paedagogus,* and *Stromateis* does not ultimately provide a coherent and systematic method of Christian development. We find instead two separate readings of milk and solid food that cannot be harmonized. And this suggests, I would argue, two distinct responses by Clement to the question of spiritual, intellectual, and moral differences among those within the Christian community.

PROTREPTICUS: AN INITIATION INTO INFANCY

Clement's *Protrepticus* reads like a tabloid exposé of the salacious deeds done by initiates of various mystery cults. In an early passage, he emphatically states his purpose: "I proclaim openly the secret things you do, for I am not afraid to speak about the shameful things you worship."[48] For Clement, the goal of this treatise is to dispel the intrigue surrounding the mystery cults that had been attractive to members of his audience. In so doing, he intends to guide his readers from an irrational system of belief and practice to a rational one. One example of this is his treatment of the ancient mystery cult of the god Sabazios. He explains how those initiated into this cult partake in a ritual where a snake is drawn across their breast. The initiation is meant to invoke "the god within the breast."[49]

Crucial to Clement's exhortation is the argument that if his audience forsakes the deadly custom of the mysteries, they can then "return as youths to the fear of God and God will enroll you as innocent children."[50] Directed toward those not yet initiated into the Christian community, the *Protrepticus* calls on readers to abandon the foolish customs of their old age and be born anew in the truth, which is a "good nursing-mother."[51] Clement's emphasis on being made young again—transformed from old age to infancy and suckled by the truth—is likely an elaborate allusion to John 3 (in which Nicodemus asks Jesus, "How can an old man be born again?"). But Clement's sights are set higher than making simple exegetical connections within his broader protreptic goals. Interweaving scriptural ideas, references to classical sources, and refutation of mystery-cult practices and beliefs, Clement depicts the remedial stage of all Christian instruction as a return to infancy and nourishment through the milk diet of truth.[52]

In an earlier passage (drawing explicitly on John 3 and the language of being "born again"), Clement describes all Christians as being first-born sons that are breast-fed by God: "For this is the church of the first-born, which is composed of many good children. These are the first-born, the ones inscribed in heaven and the ones who attend the solemn assembly of innumerable angels. And we are these first-born children, we are God's nurslings, we who are the legitimate friends of the first-born—we who are the first of all humanity to know God."[53] The terminology employed by Clement in these few lines amplifies his deep investment in kinship rhetoric. The convoluted use of the term "first-born" (*prototokos*) on four separate occasions is especially emphatic: first, referring in general to all those within the church; second, drawing on Hebrews 12:23, referring more specifically to those who have been saved and counted among the angels; third, using the first-person plural, referring to all those who are nursed on God's milk; and last, alluding to Colossians 1:15 in which Christ is presented as the "first-born" of creation, Clement continues with the first-person plural to describe those who are "legitimate" (*gnesios*) friends of Christ. The word used by Clement to describe the legitimacy of these Christians explicitly

evokes relations of kinship and ethnicity. It is a term we have already encountered in Philo's reading of Moses's proper nurture at the breast of his
birth mother.[54]

Clement's description of the church as "God's nurslings" (*hoi trophi-
moi tou theou*) must be read within this more specific emphasis on kin and
social belonging. The milk received at the breast of God establishes the
genuine quality of newly born Christians, not only as "lawfully begotten"
but also, being first-born sons and "friends of the first-born," as rightful
heirs in a legal sense.[55] And although this reference does not explicitly comment on 1 Corinthians 3, it is nevertheless a direct allusion to the necessary
stage of milk-drinking infancy for those who trade the deadly customs of
the world for the nourishing truth of the church.

The invitation to Christianity that Clement offers in the *Protrepticus*
employs the "difficult" symbol of milk nourishment and childbirth to ex-
pound on the motif of being "born again"—a motif central to discussions of
Christian initiation. In Clement's hands, this general exhortation by Jesus
(recounted in the Gospel of John) is bolstered by references to ethnic, biological, and social belonging. To be born again in the church is to become a
first-born son, an heir, a nursling fed directly on the milk of God. The common milk shared by those initiated makes them legitimate in the eyes of
God and their fellow Christians. In contrast to the god within the breast of
Sabazian rites, Clement's new Christians are initiated into infancy at the
breast of God.

PAEDAGOGUS: OUR MOTHER, THE CHURCH; OUR NURSE, THE WORD

> Being called an infant does not make you a fool.
>
> —Clement of Alexandria, *Paedagogus*[56]

There is no more vivid and elaborate exposition of 1 Corinthians 3 in early
Christian literature than that which is found in Clement's *Paedagogus*
1.6. Clement readily admits that the meal of Paul's words is a great difficulty
to digest while also hazarding his most rigorous solution. The intricate

interweaving of physiological and theological arguments has exercised scholars for some time.[57] One study, seemingly exhausted by Clement's exegetical flourishes and squeamish at his prolonged emphasis on breast milk, concludes, "The whole of this difficult section is directed against Gnostic claims. We may not today find Clement's approach attractive or fruitful, but he is concerned about a real problem and a real distinction."[58] The "real" problem the *Paedagogus* attempts to solve—the problem that haunts all early Christian exegesis of the categories deployed in 1 Corinthians 2–3—is the categorical differences of development (intellectual, moral, spiritual) evident among those within the Christian community. If Paul's various symbols (soulish/spiritual, infant/adult, milk/solid food) are normative for developing a taxonomy of these differences, what are the implications of these identifiers for the structure of the church and the salvation of its members?

Accepting, for the moment, that the *Protrepticus* was first in Clement's curricular sequence preceding the *Paedagogus,* the invitation to infancy in the former is logically followed by a defense of infancy and milk drinking as a fundamental way of life for Christians in the latter. It has been widely noted that polemics guide Clement's reading of Pauline categories in the *Paedagogus.* In response to the stark categorical differences among Christians offered by his opponents, Clement prefaces his reading of 1 Corinthians 2–3 with an appeal to Galatians 3:28 and the erasure of all differences by those who are "one in Christ."[59] Pivoting from Galatians back to Corinthians, Clement observes, "there are not some who are gnostics and others who are soulish in the same Logos, but rather all who put aside the desires of the flesh are equal and spiritual before the Lord."[60] By combining Galatians 3:28 and 1 Corinthians 3, Clement sets the foundation for his argument that all Christians are already spiritual—that is, all are *pneumatikoi*—and, as a result, milk-drinking infants cannot be viewed as equivalent to "carnal" Christians. Rather, milk is the food of all Christians who "seek our mother, the church."[61]

Such an interpretation of 1 Corinthians 2–3 is nothing short of remarkable. Even the most open-minded reading of the biblical text does not easily lend itself to the conclusion that the milk-drinking Corinthian infants are already spiritual, already perfect. This is not necessarily to suggest that the opponents of Clement (or Irenaeus) more accurately ascertained "what Paul really meant." Rather, it is to assert that what became the "orthodox" reading of the Pauline text was a startling achievement of imaginative exegesis brought about through the coupling of polemical and pedagogical exigencies. For whatever Paul may have meant, identifying his correspondents at Corinth as "already spiritual" requires a reading that is, at the very least, swimming upstream against the flow of the apostle's argument.

Clement does not hide his struggle to bring coherence to the different possible senses of the Pauline text. In his first attempt, he concludes that "Childhood in Christ is perfection."[62] Initially invoking the voice of Paul, Clement explains the meaning of the apostle's distinction between infants and adults, milk and solid food as follows: "'Just as nurses nourish newborn children with milk, so also I [Paul] have nourished you with the milk of Christ the Word, instilling in you a spiritual nourishment.' Therefore, milk is perfect because it is perfect food. It leads those who are restless to perfection. And for this reason the same milk, with honey, is promised to them in the place of rest. . . . And even Homer prophesied this, calling the just among men 'milk-fed.'"[63] However, having called both the milk and the infants "perfect," Clement immediately doubles back on his own interpretation and offers a second reading: "It is possible to understand those newly-instructed, the infants in Christ, as carnal."[64] Here, Clement is aware that these two readings, offered in the space of a few short lines, would strike his readers as contradictory. To resolve the tension, he suggests that Paul's "solid food" might best be understood as "the full revelation, face to face, in the age to come."[65] Crucially, "milk is not understood as something other than solid food; they are identical in essence."[66]

Initially, Clement draws together the milk of 1 Corinthians 3 with the "land flowing with milk and honey" of Exodus 3:8 in order to demonstrate that milk will be present at the perfect end just as it was at the infant beginning. But what of the solid food? To answer this, he abandons the Exodus reference and turns instead to the carnal aspect of those who are still being weaned. To be sure, Clement admits that some are still being weaned on milk and cannot yet eat the solid food of seeing God face-to-face. This is a basic fact of instruction. But whether one consumes milk or meat, the food has the same essence (*ousia*). Dawn LaValle has convincingly argued that perfection, for Clement, is not so much "instantaneous knowledge" of all things divine but rather the disposition of "desiring perfection."[67] Nevertheless, the power of milk is marshaled by Clement to claim that both it and the infants who consume it ought to be identified as perfect.

It is worth pausing here to consider why Clement sets up a physiological account of milk with a comparative reading of 1 Corinthians 3 and Exodus 3. Read through the prism of the Promised Land, the Pauline milk is framed as the same food that will be consumed by those who have reached perfection. The land of milk and honey establishes at the textual level a connection between infant milk and the milk toward which human growth is progressing. The milk, the milk with honey, and the solid food are identical forms of nourishment—and they convey to each soul a common spiritual nourishment. The reference to milk and honey as a goal rather than a preliminary step allows Clement to bypass, for a moment at least, the problem of solid food. But the reference to Exodus 3 is also suggestive of a postbaptismal ritual practice that entailed drinking milk mixed with honey.

Edward Kilmartin has observed the "liturgical overtones" that echo throughout Clement's extensive analysis of milk.[68] Andrew McGowan, on the other hand, cautions against overstating a potential ritual context for *Paedagogus* 1.6 and argues that Clement's primary concerns are exegetical rather than sacramental.[69] Nevertheless, the tantalizing possibility that Clement had in mind a milk rite when channeling the voice of the apostle Paul in *Paedagogus* 1.36.5–6 only amplifies the symbolic stakes of the biological excursus that follows. Indeed, the ritual practice of binding a community together through a shared source of milk would not undermine his exegetical agenda but, instead, would dramatically situate it within the embodied actions of the liturgy. Likewise, a ritual context would further situate the Homeric reference in Christian practice, insofar as the "just" among Clement's community would have a mechanism for enacting their identity as "milk-fed" (*galaktophagos*).

Nevertheless, the possibility of a ritual context remains simply that—a possibility. The force of Clement's argument does not depend on it. For immediately after pairing 1 Corinthians 3 and Exodus 3 with a biological observation about the "essence" of food, he begins a lengthy excursus on the physiological similarity of milk, blood, and flesh (the basis of "solid food"). These elements undergo changes "according to quality, but not according to essence."[70] Milk, Clement concludes, "is like a liquid flesh." His logic runs as follows: flesh is formed by blood; blood becomes frothy when it interacts with *pneuma* inside the mother's body and is transformed into milk; Christians who drink breast milk are thus still consuming the same "blood" that is the essence of solid food, just in a different form.[71] The role of *pneuma,* following LaValle, is critical—an emphasis that links Clement's milk theory not only to the terminology of the Pauline text but also to Favorinus's assertion that breast milk carries the mother's *spiritus* and the notion that food attaches itself to *pneuma* in forming the human person in the Hippocratic source *On Nutriment.* The fundamental argument is that food, and especially breast milk, is a carrier of a powerful pneumatic essence—an essence that "pneumatizes" the one who eats it.

And so Clement observes that any food provided by "God the Nourisher and Father" (whether milk or meat) is identical in essence to the heavenly nourishment of the angels called manna.[72] Through the maternal church, the nourishing God breast-feeds all Christians on the pneumatic milk of the Logos: for the Word is "father, mother, educator and nurse in one."[73] Clement modifies Homer's identification of the just as "milk-fed" when he characterizes all those who are righteous in the eyes of God as being nourished at the "care-banishing breast of God the Father."[74]

Clement's elaborate intertwining of physiological analysis, figurative exegesis, and social observation demonstrates the extent to which Paul's symbols evoked a wide range of interpretive strategies whose complexity is not adequately explained through a hard-and-fast binary between literal and metaphoric language. For even at the close of his physiological analysis, Clement draws together biological arguments and pedagogical concerns into a single vision for the proper formation of Christian infants: "If the nourishment we digest turns into blood, and the blood in turn becomes milk, then blood is the source of milk. . . . And so, as soon as we are born we are nursed on milk, on the Lord's nourishment . . . and through the nourishment of milk we are instructed into heaven, nourished as citizens of heaven in the company of angels."[75] Here again, Clement's language is highly suggestive of a postbaptismal cup of milk that has the power to forge a material bond of kinship, linking all those who nurse at the breast of God the Father. Whether the milk is ingested through liturgical practice or pedagogical instruction or some combination of the two, the result is nevertheless the same: infant Christians consume the same food and thus share the same essence.

From start to finish, then, Clement's exegesis of 1 Corinthians 3 in the *Paedagogus* frames the instruction of Christians as a process of being biologically incorporated into the bonds of kinship shared by all the milk-fed children of God. The connection between shared nourishment and membership in the "polity" of heaven forcefully evokes Aristotle's description of the primary political community as composed of those "nursed on the same milk." The divine nourishment and education offered through the church are, for Clement, more essential than those characteristics that people usually call "hereditary."[76] This, I think, is the rhetorical force behind Clement's attempt to resolve the "great difficulty" of the symbols in 1 Corinthians. Drawing upon categories that so readily identify differences and distinctions among Christians, Clement collapses these categories at the level of nature in order to demonstrate that the shared milk of the Logos makes all Christians "*homogalaktes.*" Whether milk or meat, infant or full grown, all those nourished by God through the maternal church are, according to Clement, already perfect.

STROMATEIS: THE SOLID FOOD OF DEEPER CONTEMPLATION

Between the *Protrepticus* and the *Paedagogus,* we can observe that pedagogy, more than polemics, serves as the primary catalyst for Clement's writing.[77] If Clement's exegesis of 1 Corinthians 3 shifts according to the pedagogical needs of his presumed audiences, then his "advanced" course of instruction in the *Stromateis* reveals just how great the difficulty of Pauline symbols was for the Alexandrian. For in that text, his reading of milk and solid food is nearly identical to that of the *gnosis*-obsessed opponents he rebuked in the *Paedagogus.*

Judith Kovacs has cautioned against reading too much into the seemingly contradictory interpretations offered by Clement:

> On a quick reading one might think that Clement has abandoned the position he defended so vigorously in the *Paedagogus* and adopted that of his opponents. But the text must be read in the context of other parts of the *Stromateis,* for example an assertion at the beginning of book V that seems to have Valentinians in view. Once again defending the church's "faith" against the charge that it is inferior to *gnosis,* Clement makes the polemical claim that the "true gnostic" is found among "us" i.e. within the church. . . . Although Clement now agrees with the Valentinians that 1 Cor 3,2 speaks of two distinct teachings—elementary katechesis and gnosis—he disagrees about where that gnosis is to be found.[78]

Kovacs makes an important observation about the *Stromateis* that is worth unpacking in greater detail. Her argument is that Clement employs Valentinian exegetical strategies while nevertheless remaining critical of the Valentinian claim to possess *gnosis.* The conflict between Clement and the Valentinians in the *Stromateis,* then, is about who holds the *gnosis*—not whether there is a select group of *gnosis*-possessors as such. For Kovacs, the crucial disagreement is about salvation: against the idea of a two-tier account of salvation—a higher one for those with the *gnosis,* a lower one for those without—Clement reframes the two tiers as discrete yet connected steps in each individual's ascent toward contemplating God "face-to-face."[79] For Clement, the "gnostic" is the one who has made greater progress.[80] Nevertheless, Clement's exegesis in *Paedagogus* 1.6 cannot be easily squared with the overall outline of advanced instruction described in the *Stromateis.* Any attempt to harmonize his thought must confront the stark difference in terminology he employs throughout the latter.

Clement uses the word "gnostic" (*gnostikos*) roughly one hundred times in the *Stromateis.*[81] In many places, the reference is unambiguously positive: "Therefore the gnostic is the one who is 'in the image and likeness,' who is the imitator of God as much as possible."[82] Elsewhere: ". . . born from the truth, the gnostic loves the truth."[83] And again: "The gnostic is already making progress in the Gospel"[84] Those who demonstrate an excellence of instruction and willpower are identified by Clement as a *gnostikos*—such a person is granted a noble birth (*eugeneia*) by God, becoming an "heir" to the Kingdom and "a fellow-citizen" among the righteous of old.[85] Language concerning education and imitation is thus folded in with that of procreation and kinship. Progress in *gnosis,* for Clement, is the process whereby Christians are incorporated into their rightful place within the household of the Lord.[86]

Throughout the *Stromateis,* Clement alternates between language of begetting (of sowing and cultivating the seed of the Logos within the soul) and that of nurturance (of nourishing the soul on different foods) in order to describe this process of growing into "citizenship" within the household of the Lord. At the very opening of the text, Clement notes how "the Logos is sown and held deep within the soul of the student like a seed in the earth. This is pneumatic growth. . . . Everyone who is educated in obedience to the teacher becomes a son."[87] As Denise Kimber Buell has observed, Clement frames the teacher's lessons as the semen of a father and the soul of the student as the womb of a mother. Teachings are deposited like seed deep within the student.[88] But Clement also describes teaching as various foodstuffs apportioned to different types of human souls throughout the *Stromateis:* "There is a nourishment derived from grains and there is a nourishment derived from words. . . . For each soul has its own kind of nourishment, some grow by means of knowledge and understanding while others feed on Greek philosophy (though, as with nuts, not all of that is edible)."[89]

At one point in the *Paedagogus,* Clement equates preaching with milk and guided instruction as the process by which milk becomes solid food.[90] But in the *Stromateis,* he speaks to an audience with a greater aptitude for instruction. These are not the infants in Christ. They are the gnostics in Christ. And so Clement reverses his defense of infancy from the *Paedagogus:* "The philosophers are infants if they have not been brought to manhood by Christ."[91] Here an infant is understood as a person untrained in the Logos and unable to give an effective articulation of the faith.[92] Such persons are at a lower level of instruction than the gnostic, having not yet been nurtured to maturity in their *gnosis*. To become a legitimate son in the household of the Lord, one must first have proper parentage and proper nourishment under a teacher who fills both paternal and maternal roles. Procreation and nurturance represent twin strategies within Clement's naturalizing of proper Christian formation.

In this way, the brief and seemingly contradictory exegesis of 1 Corinthians 3 that Clement provides in the *Stromateis* supports his broader emphasis on growth in *gnosis* so prominent in that work. Unlike in the *Paedagogus*—where he explicitly rebukes the *gnosis*-obsessed, who insist that milk means the "first lessons" (*ta prota mathemata*) and meat "spiritual knowledge" (*tas pneumatikas epignoseis*)[93]—in book 5 of the *Stromateis* Clement's reading is articulated precisely in the terms he previously rejected. Drawing on the reference to milk and solid food, Clement concludes that not all have access to the solid food of deeper *gnosis*. They require instead the milk of "the first lessons" (again using *ta prota mathemata*).[94] He elaborates on this a few sections later: "Therefore, if milk is the nourishment of infants and solid food that of the perfect according to what is said by the Apostle, then milk, on the one hand, should be understood as the first nourishing instruction of the soul while solid food, on the other hand, is the deeper contemplation. . . . For eating and drinking the divine Word is the *gnosis* of God's essence."[95]

Clement describes the nourishment of the Logos as an ingestion of God's very being. The Eucharistic context is now rendered more explicit, as the passages preceding this quotation make clear. By combining Paul's food symbols with a sacramental account of consuming God's *ousia*, Clement frames Christian growth as a process of being weaned on the milk of basic instruction until one is capable of consuming the meat of gnosis—that is, the "deeper contemplation" of God's being made manifest in the Eucharistic elements. If Clement's Alexandrian community did practice a postbaptismal milk rite (which seems likely given these references), then the apparent rupture between *Paedagogus* 1.6 and *Stromateis* 5 might be an indication of how different rituals allowed participants at various stages of initiation to enact their different levels of instruction according to those stages. Indeed, it seems likely that ritual feeding and pedagogical feeding would have been mutually supportive within this larger symbolic system.

Yet the rupture between the two texts is deeper still. The *Stromateis* does not contain any traces of the physiological excursus so crucial to Clement's exegesis of 1 Corinthians 3 in the *Paedagogus*. Noticeably absent is his argument for the substantial relationship between blood, milk, and flesh. Nor does he collapse the distinct categories of infant and perfect, as he did previously. Rather, Clement connects the Eucharistic elements—the flesh and blood of the Word—exclusively with the solid food of 1 Corinthians. This meat is the "direct apprehension of the power and being of God."[96] And a little later he continues, "If it is logical for us that the *gnosis* is of the same quality as solid food—for 'blessed' is the one according to scripture 'who hungers and thirsts' for the truth—then blessed also is anyone filled on this eternal nourishment."[97] Whereas in the *Paedagogus* the milk and honey of the Promised Land allowed Clement to avoid categorical distinctions between the members of the community, in the *Stromateis* the Eucharistic elements offer meaty foods of deeper understanding. And it is only the Gnostic Christian who ingests the *gnosis* of God through the bread and the wine.

I do not think the pervasive and positive use of *gnosis* and "gnostic" throughout Clement's exegesis of 1 Corinthians 3 in the *Stromateis* can be reconciled with his praise of infancy and milk-drinking as "already perfect" in the *Paedagogus*. These are two different frameworks for understanding spiritual development written with two distinct audiences in mind. In the latter, infancy is explicitly framed as a synonym for perfection. Whereas in the former, infants are said to lack the capacity—characteristic of the gnostic—to consume God's essence. Likewise, milk, which was previously identified as a perfect food and heavenly nourishment, is in the *Stromateis* relegated to a position in which it signifies a remedial lesson. In Clement's use of Paul's categories, pedagogical necessity trumps polemical caution. And while I am hesitant to present too stark a dichotomy between the first two works of this trilogy and its finale, the lack of any internal bridgework (at least as explicitly constructed by Clement) between the former and the latter makes the task of harmonizing his thought all the more precarious.

Yet the sacramental context of the three works might help to situate the contours of Clement's differing exegetical strategies with a bit more precision. In the *Protrepticus* and *Paedagogus,* a positive appraisal of infancy is employed, in part, to support Christian initiation through baptism. These two works, being primarily addressed to the uninitiated or recently initiated, can be viewed as a diptych meant to provide a robust curricular structure for baptism and the earliest stages of Christian instruction. By contrast, in the *Stromateis* the full meaning of the Eucharist is accessible only to those who have been filled with the solid food of *gnosis.* In one sense, the *Stromateis* can be read as an elaborate explanation of Clement's earlier claim that the formation of a Christian begins with the milk of preaching, and then gradually solid food is introduced through guided instruction. But Clement does not explicitly articulate a progressive, stage-by-stage paradigm for Christian growth from milk to solid food. This must be inferred from the text. And so the question that remains is whether Clement viewed some Christians as ontologically different from others in their capacity for *gnosis,* thereby ensuring that only certain Christians could consume the solid food of deeper knowledge.

One motif, however, remains consistent throughout all three works examined here. Clement continually employs the rhetoric of nurturance, kinship, and procreation as a primary strategy for articulating how Christians are properly incorporated into the Kingdom of God. Language drawn from legal and biological contexts is used by the Alexandrian teacher to express a robust mechanism for establishing social and familial legitimacy. Whether through nourishment or insemination, the overarching aim in all three works is to establish a framework for identifying Christians who are well-born, properly nourished, and instructed under the guidance of an authorized teacher. What mattered most to Clement was, to borrow Buell's phrasing, the "material bond" of seed and nourishment that linked all Christians under a common, divine household.[98] All children in Christ are counted among the "first-born," the legitimate heirs, bred and fed in the same familial home. It is possible that, through this linking of kinship and nourishment, Clement's *Stromateis* may have also resisted the Gnostic two-tier model of salvation that he explicitly critiqued elsewhere.

It is, nevertheless, a halfhearted resistance. After all, every family has its favorites.

Conclusion

In his study of "marginally orthodox Christians" in the second and third centuries, Alain Le Boulluec concludes that "an esoteric 'Paulinism' and mysticism" were among the "elements which made for the originality of a movement born of the encounter between Gnosticism and Christianity."[99] While this is certainly true of the criticisms leveled against the so-called Valentinians by their proto-orthodox antagonists, it is also the case that a mode of Pauline esotericism and mysticism can be traced from the New Testament through Clement and into the later tradition that came to be called orthodox. The great problem of the anthropological categories found in 1 Corinthians 3 was not resolved in the conflict between Irenaeus and Clement, on the one hand, and the *gnosis*-obsessed adversaries that populate their works, on the other.

Instead in the second century there was an intensification of the problem surrounding milk and solid food, infancy and perfection. In Irenaeus and Clement we witness an amplification of the inherent ambiguities and antinomies within Paul's categories rather than their resolution. Far from settling the questions percolating within the divisions of milk/solid food, carnal/soulish/spiritual, and infant/perfect, the exegetical-polemical debates of the second century bequeathed to later thinkers a range of interpretive strategies—strategies that likewise enabled a variety of possibilities for how those in the Christian community might be identified, arranged, ranked, and instructed. Are all Christians, somehow, infants? Or do some arrive at faith already more mature? Can the infants be fed toward perfection? Or are some relegated to infancy until the resurrection? Is milk an inferior, rudimentary level of instruction, and solid food a deeper, secret knowledge of the being of God? Or are the two essentially the same, indicating grades of understanding within the same content of faith? Do the categories carnal, soulish, and spiritual indicate a kind of ontological fixity in a person's orientation to the divine? Or can a person be rendered less fleshly—literally or symbolically—in her intimacy with spiritual things?

Navigating these and other questions through the writings of Irenaeus and Clement reveals the multiple ways in which the symbolic power of milk cut across categories of kinship, ethnicity, gender, intellectual ability, and social belonging. Welding the family values of Rome's *imperium* to medical theories and speculative theology resulted in eclectic images of God as a nursing woman, Jesus as God's breast, and milk as the most suitable food for those seeking the material bond of the Christian *pneuma*. In both figures, we encounter a complex repurposing of ideologies about food and formation. Like Philo, these two writers working from a provincial context evoke Roman social categories that held specific connotations for making distinctions about family, gender, social status, and intellect. Like Philo, both Irenaeus and Clement subvert these categories. (It is hard not to imagine Paul, who specifically avoided referring to himself as a pedagogue in 1 Corinthians, sounding a disapproving cluck while Clement refers to Christ as a child-minding slave.) But far from being rigid, the symbolic power of nourishment enabled precisely this sort of creative and strategic retooling of Roman family values. Paul may have set a strong precedent for early Christian interaction with the broader ideologies of food and formation, but he could not anticipate how his terms would be used to realize other modalities of Christian social identity.

Irenaeus, for one, sought to overcome the negative connotations associated with the Corinthian infants by making infancy the inescapable and universal fact of human nature's material existence. In the *Paedagogus,* Clement elaborates a similar position, doubling down on human materiality through an extended physiological excursus. Both emphasize God's character as "nourisher," the source of all human sustenance. In this way, they both offer a vision of the Christian life as one characterized by being suckled toward perfection at the breast of God. This framing of Christians as milk-fed kin, as sharing a common source of milk, evoked a long-standing tradition in political and moral rhetoric that viewed one's source of nourishment as the essential element that binds people together as family in a large network of social relations. Milk unifies. But it is a unity born of distinction between those who have shared its nourishing power and those who have not. It is both food and boundary marker, sustenance and standardized vocabulary. Milk is laden with the content of pedagogical, moral, and even familial identity.

Yet the specter of esotericism—of an elite, hierarchical, even mystical mode of knowing—could not be so easily exorcised from the early Christian imagination. It did not fade away with the marginalizing of figures like Valentinus or Heracleon. Indeed, the appreciation and appropriation of these "heretical" exegetes by their detractors—first in Clement and then in Origen—allowed the vision of an "elite" Christian culture to continue in one form or another well beyond the polemics of the second century. For whenever later interpreters sought a positive appraisal of Paul's advanced categories (perfect, solid food, spiritual), they invariably reopened for consideration the question of difference among a social group that was meant to be, at least in principle, "one in Christ." Milk may unify, but the meals made of Paul's words in the second century reveal exegetical fault lines and contested models of formation more than establishing a coherent Christian program of formation.

FOUR

Animal, Vegetable, Milk

Origen's Dietary System

So I opened my mouth, and he gave me the scroll to eat. He said to me, "Mortal,
eat this scroll that I give you and fill your stomach with it."

—Ezekiel 3:2–3

The scripture is no easy food.

—Henri de Lubac, *Histoire et Esprit*

IN *PARADISE LOST*, the temptation of Eve by the serpent is more like
a dietary recommendation. The serpent tells Eve that the prohibited food of
the apple will, when consumed, change her into a spiritual being. That is,
the tantalizing power of the fruit's nourishment is its capacity to transform
her from a nature of flesh to one of spirit, enabling her to ascend to a godlike
status. In response, God sends the angel Raphael to warn the Edenic pair
against this misguided nutritional advice. Raphael, Adam, and Eve sit together at the couple's dinner table and discuss the difference between
earthly and heavenly foods. The angel explains, "Man's nourishment, by
gradual scale sublimed to vital spirits aspire, to animal, to intellectual, give
both life and sense, fancy and understanding, whence the soul reason receives" (5.483–87). Through the internal alchemy of digestion, material
food is refined into a source of life, processed from matter into spirit until it
becomes fuel for the power of reason. Raphael observes that human digestion takes the physical matter of nourishment and slowly converts it into a
spiritual substance.

Like an unprepared host, Adam becomes embarrassed by the fact that
he can serve only food of a human sort to the angel. Raphael tells the couple
not to be concerned, for an angelic body metabolizes lower forms of food

into a "proper substance" suitable to its own nature, just as the human body does. True angelic nourishment, however, is of a purer form: "[A] time may come when men with angels may participate, and find no inconvenient diet, nor too light fare: and from these corporal nutriments perhaps your bodies may at last turn all to spirit, improved by tract of time and winged ascend Ethereal, as we" (5.493–98).[1] Higher beings can eat lower material foods, it seems, but lower beings cannot do the same with spiritual foods. While Raphael can eat the physical matter that Adam and Eve consume, angels usually feed on a more celestial fare. Humans too will eat this spirit-food once their bodies have been fully transformed through digestion of the "corporal nutriments." From material nourishment, then, embodied souls are gradually altered into spiritual things. Gastronomy is divinization. But human nature is not yet ready for the apple's spiritual sustenance. Adam and Eve must first metabolize material food, gradually converting it to spirit, in order to acclimate themselves to the spiritual life that is yet to come.

This emphasis on the slow transformation of material bodies into spiritual beings—that is, of the passage from a corporeal to a noetic existence—is a persistent theme within Origen of Alexandria's thought. In his early work, the *Dialogue with Heraclides,* Origen offers the following exhortation: "I beg you, be transformed. Be willing to learn that within you resides the capacity to be transformed."[2] In the lines that follow, he recounts how God created humanity in two steps: the inner person, made immaterially and in the image of God, and the outer, constructed from the dust.[3] Nevertheless, the body parts of the outer man are also found within the inner man.[4] Origen enumerates all the outward body parts, with their sensorial functions, and relates them to their corresponding inward aspect.

Spiritual transformation, in this sense, is a process in which the distinct yet related natures of body and soul—with their distinct yet related senses—are slowly integrated and then elevated into a single nature of spirit. For Origen, the integration of these senses takes place in the mind (or *nous*). The word "noetic" (*noetikos*) indicates both a specific, terminological designation unique to Origen's theological lexicon, as well as a general methodological orientation to the interpretation of scripture and the impli-cations of this orientation for the life of the interpreter. The two are, in fact, inseparable.[5] Blossom Stefaniw describes "noetic exegesis" as a "broad in-terpretive project" that is "particularly concerned with applying and devel-oping the *nous*."[6] That is to say, proper interpretation of scripture is a mode of consuming the text, ingesting its noetic content, and in so doing feeding and nourishing and transforming the *nous* of the reader. To think on the text properly, one must first eat it. "The mouth," as Alexandra Kleeman has observed, "is a site of transformation at the boundary of inner and outer."[7] And so the mouth is scripture's best route into the mind.

Unlike his predecessors, Origen is less concerned with rehabilitating infancy and breast-feeding as useful categories for distinguishing Chris-tians. For him, the question is not *whether* these categories should function in the Christian community, but rather *how* they should function. While Clement and Irenaeus developed robust exegetical frameworks around the trope of milk and solid food found in 1 Corinthians 3 in order to wrest that text away from "aberrant" readings that denigrated Christian milk drinkers, Origen uses the Pauline food categories as a hermeneutical key to unlock the whole of scripture and its significance for the structure of the Christian life. Put another way, 1 Corinthians 3 is not contested ground in the same way that it was for his predecessors. In his hands, it becomes instead an in-terpretive tool that can be employed in the spadework of sifting through the fertile soil of scripture.[8] Origen employs the symbol of breast milk as one of several "diets" for those embodied souls undergoing the slow transforma-tion into a spiritual body. Crucially, Origen is the first to develop at length the relationship between the milk and solid food of 1 Corinthians and the "vegetables for the weak" found in Romans 14. The inclusion of vegetables enables Origen to harmonize Paul's threefold anthropology of fleshly, psychic, and pneumatic. As a result, he creates an elaborate taxonomy of souls—a dietary system for classifying the different statuses of souls among Christians.

In what follows, I will explore the complex and at times convoluted ways in which Origen harmonizes Pauline food categories and how this relates to the transformation of embodied souls into spiritual beings. By emphasizing the close relationship between his use of nourishment and his broader anthropology, I argue that, like Milton's Raphael, Origen understood human transformation in dietary terms. The text of scripture is thus rendered as a multifaceted meal, from which the material and noetic senses are brought into agreement by nourishment suited to the "proper substance" of the reader's soul. The dominant image of Origen's pedagogical theory is that of ingesting a text in order to become more like it. We eat the mystery of scripture so that we ourselves may pass into that mystery. The innate capacity for transformation within human nature is bound up with its metabolism of nutrients drawn from the material world and the material Word, until "from these corporal nutriments . . . bodies may at last turn all to spirit."

To that end, I will situate how food functions for Origen as an emphatic marker of social location but also as a symbol for the gradual metabolizing of body and soul into spirit. I will begin with an examination of Origen's anthropology as it is developed in *On First Principles*. I argue that nourishment is crucial to Origen's account of the spiritual transformation of human nature—or, what Peter Martens has called "the larger drama of embodied minds."[9] From this anthropological background, I then analyze how Origen uses Paul's food categories as a broad exegetical resource to make sense of varying levels of meaning in scripture and, thus, varying types of souls within the readers of scripture.

Just as Raphael could metabolize different forms of food into the "proper substance" suited to the angelic nature, so too do the readers of scripture consume the text and convert it to the nutrients appropriate to their souls' capacity. To derive meaning from scripture, its words must be metabolized so that body and soul might ascend together toward spirit. But, as we will see, this broad exegetical work results in an antinomy that Origen himself does not fully resolve: on the one hand, food sometimes indicates distinct classes to which Christians are relegated. On the other hand, it sometimes outlines progressive stages through which each Christian must pass. Despite his attempt to harmonize the great problem of Pauline categories, Origen's recognition that scripture is no easy food results in an irresolvable tension within his appeal to nourishment: there is, for some

Christians, a distinct possibility for attaining the solid food of perfection while, for others, the remedial subsistence of milk remains a permanent limitation of creaturely life.

"Nourished to a Whole and Perfect State": Feeding Embodied Souls in Origen's Anthropology

Toward the end of book 3 in *On First Principles,* Origen pauses and signals to the reader one of the overarching concerns of the entire work: "Therefore, the whole argument holds together on this point: that God has composed two general natures—a visible nature, one that is bodily, and an invisible nature, one that is incorporeal. These two natures receive different kinds of changes. The invisible, which is rational, is changed through the action of the soul and its manner of life according to the fact that it has been given the freedom of choice. . . . The bodily nature, however, is changed in its substance."[10] The distinction here between rational and bodily natures involves a parallel distinction between the ways in which those natures are changed. The bodily nature changes according to its substance, a kind of involuntary molding of its material form, while the rational nature is transformed voluntarily through the practice of the soul.[11]

In a similar vein, Origen elsewhere notes that bodily nature (*natura corporeae*) is subject to "every kind of transformation" (*in omnia transformari*).[12] Anticipating the distinction between rational and bodily transformation outlined in book 3, he observes here a connection between the change of bodily substance and the food that humans eat: "Do not also articles of food whether used by men or by animals, exhibit the same fact of change? For whatever it is that we take as food, it turns into the substance of our body."[13] The malleable essence of matter undergirds all bodily existence. This material, Origen argues, is the inescapable stuff of embodied life, liable to formation and re-formation—notably under the powerful influence of food.

Yet the link between nourishment and bodily change requires closer consideration. Origen recognizes the capacity of matter to consume, metabolize, and transform itself in relation to other matter. What a person eats is incorporated directly into the bodily substance. The matter that is consumed as food has the power to induce either degradation or transformation of human bodily nature. Crucially, Origen observes how this bodily substance can be mired in the muck of "lower beings" (*inferiores*) or raised up to the "splendor of celestial bodies" (*in fulgore caelestium corporum*).[14] But this raises the question: If bodily matter can be raised to the "splendor of celestial bodies," how is it also the case that changes in the body's substance that are induced by nourishment do not also impact human rational nature in some way? In other words, how is it that the ongoing formation of bodily nature through digestion and the ongoing formation of the rational nature through the action of the soul are unrelated?

In his 1932 study, Hal Koch observed that the origin of materiality—and of the human body in particular—represents "one of the most difficult questions in Origen's entire framework."[15] More recently, scholars have sought to clarify this "difficult question" of the body's origin and its relationship to the soul—some seeking to rehabilitate Origen's reputation as a dualist.[16] Anders Jacobsen, to take only one prominent example, has emphasized Origen's discussion of a bipartite nature in humanity—constituted by a split between the "inner" and the "outer" man described in 2 Corinthians 4:16.[17] The corporeality of the outer man is not subject to corruption, according to Jacobsen's reading. Rather, it is the very condition of corruptibility.[18] And while "only the inner man will be saved,"[19] the body is not a totally negative thing. Jacobsen provides a helpful diagnosis of the tensions within Origen's anthropology. But the question of just how the body and its corporeal nature are involved in the formation and redemption of the "inner man" remains murky. In his analysis of Origen, Jacobsen variously describes the body as a "vehicle" that moves the soul "toward perfection,"[20] the "necessary tools" for raising up "fallen rational beings,"[21] and the site at which the soul is educated and from which it ascends to God.[22] Despite his close reading of Origen from a variety of textual vantage points, Jacobsen nonetheless offers an opaque conclusion that the "outer man, the body, only interests Origen insofar as it *plays a role* for the inner man."[23] The specific role of the body in the soul's development requires closer attention.

From the opening of *On First Principles,* the mixture of rational and creaturely natures within the human person is a key focal point. Origen observes that "we men are animals, formed by a union of body and soul, and thus alone did it become possible for us to live on the earth."[24] This union, it seems, is the very condition, the mechanism through which earthly existence became habitable. The body is a lifesuit for the soul, sustaining its journey through an alien world of material existence. In making earthly life possible, the body and the soul are confined to grow and change in close proximity to one another, a relationship increasingly symbiotic in nature. Elsewhere, Origen rejects the overidentification of the soul with the body by those who locate the soul within the blood. In contrast, Origen simply notes that the soul is a mediator, placed between flesh and spirit (*inter carnem et spiritum*).[25] As such, the lifesuit of the flesh is, in a sense, organically integrated into the functioning of the soul and its elevation to spirit.

Ensconced within the body, the mind can't help but be constrained by the physical changes that take place around it. The union of body and soul that makes human life possible is, it seems, an uneasy one:

> Mind certainly needs intellectual magnitude, because it grows in an intellectual and not in a physical sense. For mind does not increase by physical additions at the same time as the body does until the twentieth or thirtieth year of its age, but by the employment of instructions and exercises a sharpening of the natural faculties is effected and the powers implanted within are roused to intelligence. Thus the capacity of the intellect is enlarged not by being increased with physical additions, but by being cultivated through exercises in learning. These it cannot receive immediately from birth or boyhood because the structure of the bodily parts which the mind uses as instruments for its own exercise is as yet weak and feeble, being neither able to endure the force of the mind's working nor sufficiently developed to display a capacity for receiving instruction.[26]

Origen simultaneously distinguishes the growth of the mind from that of the body ("mind does not increase by physical additions") while nevertheless admitting that this distinction does not totally hold together (the mind cannot receive instruction until "the structure of the bodily parts which the mind uses as instruments" has sufficiently grown). It turns out that the growth of the rational nature is dependent, at least in some important respect, upon the state of the bodily nature. The "structure of the bodily parts," as instruments for the formation of the mind, must be properly formed before the mind can put them to use. The instruments and the mind that uses them are not easily distinguishable. The lifesuit of the flesh is fused to the soul that operates it. Origen thus presents the human person as a hybrid creature, a cyborg fusion of the *nous* and the corporeal tools through which the mind uncovers the spiritual reality embedded within the material world.

Origen further complicates the uneasy coexistence of body and soul by comparing the "bodily senses" (*sensus corporalis*) to what he calls the "sense of mind" (*sensus mentis*).[27] Each bodily sense has a physical substance that is the object of its function (that is, taste is directed toward flavor). The sense of mind, however, is directed toward intellectual "substances" of a divine nature.[28] But what precisely is an intellectual substance? Is it not a contradiction in logic to suggest that the mind, which is immaterial, has as the object of its functioning a substance?[29] Origen does not identify these intellectual substances as such, but instead notes how somatic organs help us to make sense of the soul's faculties: "[W]e speak of [the soul] as using all the other bodily organs, which are transferred from their corporeal significance and applied to the faculties of the soul; as Solomon says, 'You will find a divine sense' (Prov. 2.5). For he knew that there were in us two kinds of senses, the one being mortal, corruptible and human, and the other immortal and intellectual, which here he calls 'divine.' By this divine sense, therefore, not of the eyes but of a pure heart, that is, the mind, God can be seen by those who are worthy."[30]

This "divine sense," enfleshed within the material world of bodily senses and substances, must learn to "see" and "touch" and "taste" God's immaterial substance through the matter that surrounds it. This transfer of sensorial power from the bodily organs to the mind elevates the soul out of its materiality through the very faculties required by that material, embodied existence. To taste wisdom with the mind, then, isn't simply a cute turn of phrase for Origen. Rather, it indicates a deeper mystery of how the corporeal world of flesh and matter and sensation is sifted and plumbed by the soul. And, if the bodily functions are properly integrated into the soul's functioning, they too can be elevated into a spiritual form. The divine sense, the *sensus mentis,* is both the site and the means for noetic transformation.

Curiously, Origen does not unpack how this transformation of bodily senses into a divinized sense of mind takes place. It is only in his discussion of the resurrected, "spiritual body" that he offers a more detailed discussion of this alteration. Origen insists that the so-called spiritual body of resurrected life (as outlined in 1 Corinthians 15) is only possible by way of the material body: "For it is from the creaturely body [*ex animali corpore*] that the very excellence and grace of the resurrection draws up the spiritual body [*spiritale corpus educit*]."[31] This spiritual body is nurtured, nourished, and raised up within the creaturely body. He likens human corporeality to a grain of corn: though the stalk will decay in the earth, it has a "*ratio* implanted within it, which contains the substance of the body."[32] Like the kernel buried deep inside the husk, the decaying human body carries within it a *ratio* that "restores and refashions" it in the life to come.[33]

To draw the spiritual body up through the creaturely involves a slow and gradual transformation of the *ratio*—the very process in which bodily senses are educated and transformed by the sense of mind. It is at this point in his discussion that Origen introduces a crucial argument about nourishment in the gradual ascent of the embodied soul into its spiritual form. He first rejects out of hand the belief that resurrected bodies will "eat and drink, in no way lacking the power to do all the things that pertain to flesh and blood."[34] This view of heavenly corporeality is unacceptable, according to Origen, because it allows for a variety of other spurious claims about marriage, sex, and procreation after the resurrection. While the body that is refashioned by its inner *ratio* may look like the corporeal one that preceded it, Origen argues, this spiritual body does not function in the same way.

Having rejected the idea that the resurrection will include a form of eating and drinking according to the flesh, Origen then admits that the spiritual, celestial body will receive its own kind of nourishment:

> Truly those who follow the interpretation of scripture embraced in the understanding of the apostles hope that the saints will eat: but they will eat the bread of life, which nourishes the soul and illumines the mind with the food of truth and wisdom. . . . The mind, when nourished by this food of wisdom to a whole and perfect state, as man was made from the beginning, will be restored to the image and likeness of God; so that, even if someone has departed from this life less educated, but should he have a record of commendable works, he can be instructed in that Jerusalem, the city of the saints, that is, he can be educated and informed and fashioned into a living stone.[35]

It is not wrong to hope that the saints will eat, Origen explains. Nevertheless, this food will be strictly the kind that feeds the soul—the bread of life on which the mind is nourished. In this resurrected state, eating is no longer a corporeal function. Rather, in its celestial form, food is a purely divinizing substance. The food of wisdom on which the resurrected body is nourished illumines the mind (*inluminet mentem*), returning to it the image and likeness of God (*ad imaginem dei ac similitudinem reparetur*). Whereas the union of body and soul had previously served to make earthly life habitable, the refashioned body and soul of the celestial life requires a similar process of acclimation. Origen likens this to a kind of heavenly feeding trough for the mind, where wisdom and truth are digested and slowly metabolized until the spiritual body has been properly formed.

This shift from a material to a noetic metabolism—from earthly feeding to the celestial mind trough—evokes the persistent connection in antiquity between education (*paideia*) and human transformation (*morphosis*). This is developed further as Origen depicts life in paradise as "a place of instruction and, so to speak, a lecture room or school for souls, in which [the resurrected] may be taught about all that they had seen on earth."[36] Not all refashioned minds are ready for the nourishment of wisdom and truth. Some remediation, some weaning, is required. This "school for souls" provides a kind of celestial *enkyklios paideia* that will strip the mind of its "carnal senses" so that it "will grow according to intellectual development" until it has "attained perfection."[37] Just as the creaturely body of earthly life grew incrementally, the resurrected body must also undergo a process of growth through food and formation. For some, it seems, this will be gradual and progressive, like being slowly introduced to a heartier diet.[38] Others "will make swifter progress and quickly ascend to the region of the air."[39] In both cases, the soul undergoes further formation after the resurrection as the bodily senses are subsumed within the power of the divine sense.

Like its creaturely counterpart, the spiritual body is a tactile thing. In the resurrected life there are spiritual substances that nevertheless require a sense of sight, smell, touch, sound, and, indeed, taste. What was an ambiguous relationship between bodily senses and the sense of the mind in the creaturely body will be fully integrated within this new, celestial body. At the nourishing trough of wisdom and truth, the raised soul is nursed into its newly spiritual form. This is a remedial course of instruction in which the bodily senses are gathered and transferred into their noetic dimension once and for all. Having fluctuated between the senses of flesh and the sense of mind during creaturely life, the refashioned soul now performs all the sensorial functions needed in the resurrected life. The saints do eat, Origen admits. Their souls hunger for wisdom, for the bread of life. And this will be all the food that the spiritual body requires. The drama of embodied souls is, then, the story of how a soul is nourished from the material confines of a creaturely body into its proper spiritual and noetic form. It is the transformation of bodily senses into the divine sense—as the angel Raphael described: "[F]rom these corporal nutriments perhaps your bodies may at last turn all to spirit, improved by tract of time and winged ascend Ethereal, as we."

This anthropological framework governs how Origen uses Paul's food categories as an interpretive tool for digging through the layers of scripture's meaning. In pairing the apostle's threefold division of fleshly, soulish, and spiritual to the nourishment of milk, vegetable, and solid food, Origen develops a system for classifying souls according to their differing

digestive capacities for the Word.[40] The trope of milk and solid food becomes for him a means of diagnosing the progress of the *nous* in its transformation of the bodily senses into the divine sense. To the extent that the
reader of scripture receives hearty noetic nourishment from the Word, they
have already begun the spiritual integration of their rational and creaturely
natures—that is, they have already begun to eat like the saints and angels of
the celestial life. But it is precisely at this point that the problem identified
at the outset emerges: when Origen employs the Pauline food categories to
classify different states of the soul, it becomes increasingly difficult to determine whether he thinks that these categories indicate progressive stages or
distinct classes.

"What Is More Nourishing than the Word?"
Origen's Noetic Gastronomy

EXEGESIS AS ANTHROPOLOGY IN *ON FIRST PRINCIPLES* AND THE *COMMENTARY ON 1 CORINTHIANS*

Origen's most well known discussion of scriptural exegesis is found at the
conclusion of *On First Principles*.[41] Crucially, the proposed exegetical
method in that section is integrated into the broader anthropological theory
that he had developed in the preceding sections. Drawing upon the Pauline
categories of fleshly, soulish, and spiritual, Origen presents levels of biblical
interpretation and the status of embodied souls as reflections of each other.
Insofar as the soul is tethered between spirit and flesh—between the sense
of mind and the bodily senses—readers of scripture approach the text according to the progress of their soul in the journey from the creaturely life
to the spiritual. To read the text a certain way is to be a certain kind of soul.
Those who are "more simple-minded may be built up by the flesh of the
text."[42] Scriptural reading is a kind of nutritional diet. Those who have
made some progress are formed to the soul of the text. Likewise, the
"perfect" are edified by scripture's spirit. The threefold organization
of scripture is a microcosm of the threefold constitution of each person.

Nevertheless, Origen's pairing of Paul's anthropological categories (flesh, soul, spirit) with the apostle's food categories (milk, vegetable, and solid food) results in a muddled paradigm for classifying souls according to the various layers of scripture's meaning.

Nearly every major study of Origen over the past sixty-five years has attempted to settle the aporia created by Origen's use of Paul's categories. On the one hand, Henri de Lubac argued in favor of the "progressive stage" model: "There are not, then two categories of Christians, separated by the power of their intelligence; there is not one popular preaching and a different, more refined teaching for intellectuals."[43] On the other, Jean Daniélou concluded that "The Christian community consists of a hierarchy in which every Christian has a place corresponding to the degree of spiritual perfection he has attained, and the role of the *didaskalos* is to explain the Scripture by giving each class of soul the nourishment that it needs."[44] Henri Crouzel, whose extensive work on Origen contains elements of both these positions, falls somewhere between de Lubac and Daniélou. Crouzel sometimes describes the symbols of milk and solid food as indicating a "progressive divinization."[45] The "pedagogy of the Word," for Crouzel, is located in its power to take on different forms of nourishment according to the different capacities of soul. Yet elsewhere Crouzel suggests that each soul is "destined" for its particular food.[46]

In more recent years, scholarship continues to wrestle with these two interpretations. Karen Jo Torjesen has observed how Origen organizes the Christian community into "three groups which simply represent the three distinct phases through which a soul passes on its way to perfection."[47] This passage toward perfection reflects the ongoing "disclosure" of the Word.[48] Judith Kovacs has expanded upon Torjesen's interpretation by suggesting that, for Origen, milk and solid food symbolize the transformative effect of scripture's divine pedagogy—that is, the process by which the hearer/reader of scripture is drawn upward, if incrementally, toward God.[49] In these studies, the logic of formation embedded within symbols of nourishment is brought to the foreground in order to explore the possibility for growth, maturity, and transformation by the food of the Word in Origen's thought.[50]

Other scholars, however, have followed Daniélou's position more closely, rejecting the notion that Origen viewed Pauline food symbols as progressive stages of growth. R. P. C. Hanson, for example, emphatically dismisses de Lubac's position:

> Origen's exegesis is not exclusively for intellectuals. We have seen that his sermons were intended partly for what we might call the average man in the pew. . . . But [de Lubac] is certainly going too far when he suggests that to Origen the difference between the intellectual and the simple believer is ultimately insignificant because both classes of Christian can be brought to the higher knowledge which is the greatest secret and reward of the Scriptures. *I know of no passage in Origen's works which suggests that the simple and uneducated believer can attain to the higher knowledge.* Origen, as an orthodox Christian, of course admits that such people can be saved and, as we shall see, is quite firm upon the point that even the most intellectual Christian must start where the simple believer starts and go with him through the preliminary stages of his way. But he believes that the intellectual will outstrip the uneducated believer in his spiritual progress, and, as far as I can see, outstrip him, at least in this world, permanently.[51]

It is worth noting that, for Hanson, the "intellectual" nevertheless must begin at the preliminary stage along with the "simple." Though he does not develop this point at length, the implication is that for the "intellectual" or "perfect" Christian, milk and solid food symbolize progressive stages of formation. But for the "simple" and "uneducated," milk and solid food symbolize a partition—a limitation within the Christian community that divides those who passively receive remedial care ("milk") from those actively progressing toward perfection and divinization ("solid food").[52]

This is most clearly articulated in fragment 12 of the *Commentary on 1 Corinthians*. For Origen, like Clement of Alexandria and Irenaeus before him, 1 Corinthians 3:1–3 is singularly useful as a means for identifying different kinds of Christians and mapping different grades of intellectual formation. Unlike his predecessors, however, Origen's concern is not primarily one of polemics. The vexed question of Christian infancy and milk drinking that had so troubled his predecessors does not trouble Origen in quite the same way. Rather, the question that prompts Origen's frequent consideration of 1 Corinthians 3 is how the Pauline categories of food might be harmonized, systematized, and put to use in the work of organizing, distinguishing, and instructing Christians. And while he has little reservation calling some Christians "perfect" or "full-grown" (*teleios*), he also observes, "Not all who believe in Christ are spiritual [*pneumatikos*]."[53]

In her reading of these fragments on 1 Corinthians, Judith Kovacs emphasizes the discussion of spiritual nourishment as a kind of "upward progression" (*anaphora*)—one that passes from milk through vegetables to meat, what Origen calls the true meat and solid nourishment that are the flesh of the word.[54] The infants are those "weaker in moral character"[55] who lack training in scripture and need inferior teachings instead.[56] By contrast, the more perfect can consume teachings concerning purity, chastity, and martyrdom as well as instruction in the "mystical doctrines about the Father and Son."[57] The fragment on 1 Corinthians 3:1–3 ends with a brief example drawn from Numbers 2:6–9 that demonstrates how one might read a single scriptural passage according to its "milky" sense in contrast to its "meaty" sense. Kovacs concludes that the whole thrust of Origen's *Commentary on 1 Corinthians*—and this passage specifically—is to identify and unpack "two levels of morality."[58]

Whatever may be meant by Origen's use of the word *anaphora* to describe the various kinds of nourishment, the fragment on 1 Corinthians 3 does not endorse (indeed, does not even explicitly indicate) that advancing from bodily toward spiritual things is possible for all Christians. Given the prominence of Paul's food categories throughout Origen's work, this fragment is disappointingly brief. Nonetheless, the distinction between milk and solid food not only indicates two levels of morality, but also identifies how the content of Christian teaching and the form of the Christian life operate on two levels as well. Indeed, the instructional content (*mathemata*) and character of life (*ethikos*) are indistinguishable for those who live as infants drinking milk.[59] The milk imparts to them the essential content that, in turn, forms the very nature of their infancy. It signifies who they are as believers, what they are capable of in terms of formation, and the suitable teaching delivered to them. Likewise for the perfect who eat meat. Scripture operates in each of these two dimensions, instructing and forming the Christian according to their character and their capacity. The food is fit to the one being fed. But it is also a reflection of their character, their status within the community, and their potential for certain kinds of knowledge about God and disciplinary commitments. Put simply, Christians are identified by and share in the "essence" of the specific food that they are able to eat.[60] For it is this nourishment of the Word that feeds their rational nature according to its present capacity.

The brief and fragmentary nature of the *Commentary* does not give a complete picture of this problem. In order to see how these interpretive strategies play out, it is necessary to examine his use of nourishment imagery found in other texts.[61] Cécile Blanc has observed that, for Origen, the material food we consume is but a "shadow" of the true nourishment we will receive in heaven.[62] What interests me, however, is what happens when Origen attempts to compare and contrast the heavenly, true nourishment from that which is corporeal, shadowy—and how the logic he applies to the latter governs his understanding of the former. Whether it is material or noetic, Origen views food as fuel for human transformation.

"FOOD FOR OUR BEING": *ON PRAYER* AND THE DIETS OF THE MIND

In his consideration of the "daily bread" (*artos epiousios*) mentioned in the Lord's Prayer, Origen asserts that the "true bread is He who nourishes the true Man, made in the image of God; and the one who has been nourished by it will come to be in the likeness of the One who created him. And what is more nourishing to the soul than the Word?"[63] Origen then observes the widespread use of the term *artos* for any food mentioned in scripture, noting that this single word reveals the extent to which "the nourishment of the Word is changeable and varied."[64] No matter its form, the essence of the

Word's food is the same. Thus, he argues, "not all people are able to be nourished on the firm and vigorous bread of divine teaching."[65] Those who pray for daily bread do not all pray for the same diet. The nourishment of the Word comes to them only in the form proper to their status, the growth of their soul, and their capacity for nourishment.

Origen connects the "daily bread" of the Lord's Prayer to Jesus's statements regarding his body and blood in John 6:51–57. Yet in discussing this passage, Origen notes from the outset that Jesus's identification of his flesh as "true food" is a designation of nourishment offered only to those "athletes" who are "more perfect."[66] While the Eucharistic connotations are hard to ignore here—"when we eat and drink him, he dwells in us. And when he is distributed . . ."—Origen's basic point seems to be that only the more perfect (*teleioteroi*) consume the flesh of Christ as their "daily bread."[67] The rest feed on a different kind of bread altogether. To push this distinction further, he turns abruptly from the flesh of Christ toward the milk offered by Paul to the Corinthians, and the vegetables that the "weak man" eats in Romans 14.[68] These simpler foods, however, can also be consumed by those who are more perfect, "in order that no one becomes sick from want of food for the soul."[69] In all cases, Origen's emphasis on ingesting the Logos through scriptural study evokes the same moral, physiological, and cultural connotations that we have been exploring throughout the previous chapters. To interpret scripture is to receive, from the outside, the divine Word into one's own being—a process mirrored in material form through Eucharistic eating. Here, as within *paideia* and the Roman household, intellectual formation is linked to physical nourishment, just as intellectual nourishment is linked to physical formation.

The implication of this—and, as with Clement, the text is only suggestive here—is that the childish and the weak drink milk and eat vegetables as their "daily bread," even when they are eating the actual bread of the Eucharist. They are receiving a simpler teaching that is less rigorous, less intellectually and morally demanding than that of their more perfect fellow Christians at the table.[70] The more advanced souls, however, partake of the Eucharistic elements as meat—that is, by eating the bread, they digest the *broma* of the Word's stronger teaching. In the ritual of eating and drinking bread and wine, Christians ritually enact their own location within Origen's dietary taxonomy of souls. Origen seems to suggest that noetic nourishment and the nourishment of the liturgy are folded together into a single spiritual sustenance. Christians, for Origen, are what they eat. And the Eucharistic meal is the site at which these distinct noetic diets are realized and reinforced.

In the following section of *On Prayer,* Origen turns his attention toward the identification of the bread as "daily" (*epiousios*). Offering a philological analysis, he concludes that it ought to be understood "with reference to 'being' [*ousia*]"—for "bread" refers to "being" in that it is both "profitable" to being, as well as something, like being, which "people dwell around and share in common."[71] Origen then digresses on different philosophical conceptions of *ousia* and whether it primarily refers to incorporeal or to corporeal things.[72] He concludes that, despite these different meanings, the bread mentioned in the Lord's Prayer is "noetic" (*noetos*) in nature.[73] Origen explains:

> It is necessary to perceive with the mind how "being" and "bread" are of the same kind, so that just as the corporeal bread delivered to the body of one nourished goes into his being, so also the "living bread" that came "down from heaven" is delivered to the mind and the soul and shares its power with the one who derives nourishment from it. And it is for this reason we ask for "daily bread" in the sense that it will be "for our being." And moreover, just as the person being nourished receives that power in different ways according to the quality of the food—some nourishment being solid and suitable for athletes while other forms of food are milky or like vegetables—so also it follows that the Word of God can be as milk suitable for children or as vegetables useful for the weak or as flesh given to those contending for a prize. And each person, of those that are being nourished in proportion to their capacity to share the power of the Word, is able to do different things and to become different things.[74]

The "daily bread" conveys its essence into the one who eats it—an essence that has been made suitable in proportion to a person's capacity for "the

power of the Word" contained within it. Those who eat the daily bread of
the Word partake of the same essence, though in different forms. Despite
transmitting one essence, the daily bread affects different people differently.
They are not all transformed in the same way. In sharing a common food,
Christians may share in a common divine *ousia*—but they are not all
changed the same way. Origen's discussion of the daily bread is premised
upon a broader understanding of the material properties and physiological
effects of food that is no less crucial to his argument, even if it is less explicit,
than that of Clement in *Paedagogus* 1.6.

"NOURISHED ACCORDING TO THE WORTH OF EACH": THE NOETIC DIET AT WORK IN ORIGEN'S EXEGESIS

As part of his broader commitment to the principle that food shares its
essence with the one who eats it, Origen regularly emphasizes how food
adapts according to the capacities of the one being fed.[75] This is articulated
clearly in *Against Celsus* 4.18. In that section, Origen is responding to the
claim that the Incarnation requires one to believe that God changes in
nature. Origen's counterargument rests on the notion that the Word is like
nourishment. It may take on various forms, but it does not change in its
power or in its nature:

> Concerning the nature of the Word, just as the quality of food
> changes in a mother into milk suitable for the nature of her
> infant, or is prepared by a physician with the intention of restor-
> ing a sick man to health, while it is prepared in a different way
> for a stronger man, who is more able to digest it in this form; so
> also God changes for men the power of the Word, whose nature
> it is to nourish the human soul, in accordance with the merits of
> each individual. To one he becomes "the rational milk which is
> without guile," as the Bible calls it; to another who is weaker he
> becomes like a "vegetable"; while to another who is perfect,
> "solid food" is given. Surely the Word is not false to his own

nature when he becomes nourishment for each man according
to his capacity to receive him.[76]

The logic of "same food, same essence" governs the whole analogy. Whether
as milk, vegetable, or solid food, it is the same essence that is consumed by
the soul. Only the power of the Word is changed, not the nature. The analogy is all the more striking given that the nourishment of the Word is precisely what Origen thinks will feed the soul in the celestial life. The journey
from a material to a noetic existence is, in some sense, a process of being
weaned from material foods to the food of the Word that will sustain life
after the resurrection of the body. But in the present creaturely life, many
lack the capacity for the Word's power. This is the basis of the milk, vegetable, and solid-food paradigm: there are souls that are still too creaturely to
be fed on a purely noetic food.

Origen elaborates on this paradigm in a preface to his twenty-seventh
Homily on Numbers—a homily in which he offers an interpretation of the
various stages of the journey out of Egypt.[77] He opens his analysis of the text
by appealing to the notion that "each individual, whether in accordance
with his age or his strength or the health of his body, looks for food suitable
for himself and fit for his strength."[78] Here Origen sets the stage for a corporeal and a noetic reading of scripture that will be nourishing for people of all
kinds. He notes that some will read the text as "milk"—"that is, the more
obvious and simpler teachings, as may usually be found in moral instruc-
tions and which is customarily given to those who are taking their first steps
in divine studies and receiving the abc's of rational instruction."[79] Obscure
and difficult texts, such as the one from Numbers currently under consideration, will be a "heavy and burdensome food" to some people and thus of
less benefit. Different kinds of people are likened to different species of animals, each with its own proper nourishment.[80] This diversity is to the glory
of God and not, it seems, evidence of delinquency. It is instead a notion
foundational to Origen's anthropology: scripture itself becomes "different
food according to the capacity of the souls" it feeds.[81] Reading scripture,
then, is how the mind is fed. Christians are themselves akin to different

animals, each soul needing its own diet, its own nutriment, and scripture is the noetic buffet that can support these various dietary needs.

The "milky" form of the Word is elsewhere described as "first moral instruction" (*prima moralis institutio*)—a phrasing reminiscent of Clement's emphasis on *ta prota mathemata,* mentioned earlier. Origen elaborates that milk is "the correction of morals, the amendment of discipline, and the first elements of religious life and simple faith."[82] This food "allots life and health to those progressing toward the good."[83] What he calls the *prima elementa*—or the *rudimenta*—are the basic forms of instruction that will at some point enable the student to receive "more perfect lessons from the Teacher himself."[84] The progress toward the good (*ad bonum proficiendi*) signified by the nourishment of the Word is not described here as immediate or even progressive. In fact, "progress toward the good" does not seem to indicate a specific curriculum of advancement in the educational sense at all. It is a tantalizing suggestion that is premised, I would argue, on the logic that nourishment must somehow be forming the one eating it. Thus, even though he agrees with the principle that eating is a transformative and divinizing act, Origen is circumspect about how this works for the milk-drinking infants still bound to a creaturely nature.

This is why in *Against Celsus* Origen argues that Christian teachers should offer instruction suited to the specific intellectual capacities of their audience. If the crowd is composed of "more simple-minded folk" (*aplousteroi*), the difficult teachings must remain hidden and undiscussed.[85] The mixed crowds of varying intellects and ages that were attracted to Christian preaching scandalized Origen's opponent Celsus. Origen defends the practice, arguing that Christians do, in fact, "want to educate all men with the Word of God" in the hopes that "young boys receive encouragement and slaves freedom of mind and a noble birth."[86] In fact, the entire composition of *Against Celsus* is framed from the outset as an attempt to nourish weak Christians—all those lacking proper formation in Christian instruction—who may have been persuaded by the criticisms of Celsus.[87] In Origen's rebuttal, the milk of the Word seems to democratize classical *paideia*—offering nourishing teaching to all manner of souls and enabling the formation of their rational nature, even by means of the simpler fare that is offered to the *aplousteroi*.

The milk of 1 Corinthians 3, it seems, allows plebs to engage in a kind of paideutic formation once restricted to the elite. But, as Hanson emphatically noted in his own analysis, it is not at all evident that Origen thinks the milky food of rudimentary instruction will lead these infants toward perfection in any direct sense. It is a saving food, but not a perfect or perfecting food, as it had been with Clement and Irenaeus. It is not clear, then, that the milk given to these simpleminded people produces a spiritual transformation at all. It seems more like subsistence. That is, the milk appears mostly as a food that sustains the soul in its creaturely state—not necessarily a food that will enable the *ratio* buried deep within the flesh to ascend toward the spirit.

Origen's insertion of Romans 14:2—"vegetables for the weak"— within the Pauline distinction between milk and solid food is idiosyncratic to his understanding of the diversity of Christians that compose the church.[88] I know of no other early Christian author who so consistently includes Romans 14:2 within an interpretation of Paul's milk and solid food paradigm. It seems that for Origen, these texts were inextricably connected—each form of food reflecting one of the various states of the soul among Christians according to the schema already implicit in Paul's anthropology. Through this third food category, he is able to align milk/fleshly, vegetable/soulish, and solid food/spiritual into a system of classification—a taxonomy of souls and their respective foods.

In his interpretation of the vegetables, Origen attempts to parse the difference between the infancy of those who drink milk, the weakness of those who eat vegetables, and the perfection of those who eat solid food. He concludes that Paul "calls one 'weak in faith' who is not perfected in his senses enough to accept every kind of nourishment from the Word of God."[89] Drawing upon Hebrews 5:14 and the notion of "training the senses," an idea already developed at length in *On First Principles,* the spiritual maturity and intellectual capacity of the Christian is once again characterized as a "sense." It is an inward, noetic sense, however—one that is honed and trained and, at some point, perfected in its ability to consume and digest the Word of God. The divine sense—this sense of mind—will ultimately supersede the bodily senses within the spiritual body. These vegetable-eating Christians are weak in their noetic sense, susceptible to poor judgment, and thus require a weaker food suited specifically to their tendency toward such lower senses.

In a curious turn of phrase, Origen notes that Paul is "not a teacher of palate or of throat," but rather is identifying the nutritive needs suitable to the "sense of mind" among those under his care.[90] Vegetables are therefore given to the weaker ones in order to sustain their spiritual health and prevent the deleterious effects of doubt. But here again, as with the milk for the simple, the vegetables for the weak do not seem to improve their noetic capacity.[91] It is a remedial food, not a strengthening one. The vegetable eaters are weak in that they recognize their own frailty, their own limited capacity, and this limitation can lead them to frustration. This is instructive, for Origen, insofar as these different food types can be used to provide a source of "unity in the church between the perfect and the imperfect" that allows each kind of soul to eat the food appropriate to their state, to its noetic sense, without judgment from the other.[92] While Origen recognizes that some will feel resentment when they see that others are more advanced, he does not take this as an opportunity to outline how the weak souls may, in time, grow into the solid food. He merely uses the vegetable diet to indicate that each soul has a type of food on which it feeds, and so each person should take comfort in the role or status within the community.

Origen's most detailed discussion of "weak" or "infantile" Christians is found in a later passage from *Against Celsus*. Responding to Celsus's argument that the basic tenets of the Christian community were said previously and more eloquently by Greeks, Origen replies with a defense of instruction for the "common people." His rebuttal is drawn "from a certain example concerning nourishment and its preparation."[93] This example emphasizes two things in particular: first, that the power of a given food is transferred to the one who eats it, and, second, that certain kinds of food identify distinct levels of status, indeed distinct classes, among people.[94] He explains:

Let it be granted that there is a solid food that is good for one's health, that implants strength within those who consume it, and that after being prepared in a certain way and seasoned with certain spices it is received not by those who have not learned how to eat such things—that is, the uneducated yokels who were brought up in the sticks and in poverty—but rather is only consumed by wealthy and luxurious people. And suppose that there are countless people who eat the same food, not prepared in the manner in which refined people eat it, but in the manner that the poor and the uncultured and the common folk have learned to eat it. Let us grant, then, that only those people called "refined" are strengthened by the first kind of food preparation, since none of the common folk are inclined toward such solid food, whereas the second kind of food will feed and strengthen the greater number of people. Which kind of food-preparer should we approve of more on account of the strength of the food shared in common? The one who prepares food only for the learned or the one who prepares it for the greater number of people? For while the same strength and health is imparted by the food whether it is prepared in this way or that, it is obvious that the one who is a lover of mankind and whose service is of greatest common benefit is the doctor who provides health for the masses rather than the one who provides it only for a few people.[95]

After this elaborate illustration, Origen then adds, "[I]f the example has been rightly apprehended by the mind, it must be altered so as to be made rational food for rational animals."[96] A teacher, in Origen's account, is a "food-preparer" (*skeuastes*) who must use expert knowledge of gastronomy to provide a suitable diet to the greatest number of people.[97] If the mouth is the best way into the mind, the teacher is the one who knows which foods will nourish and form the mind of the pupil. It is for this reason, Origen argues, that Jesus is superior to Plato. In this "example" Origen provides an extended analogy about food and the capacities of different souls, prompted by scriptural references to food, and concludes that this example is itself rational food to his readers.

While the milk/vegetable/solid-food trope is not explicitly mentioned in the previous quote, Origen's framing of *broma* and *trophe* as a classification system for different Christians does the same work here as it does, for instance, in his *Commentary on 1 Corinthians* or *On Prayer*. Here, however, Origen elevates the rhetorical stakes of how food types and soul types relate. The loaded description of those who are capable of consuming only the weaker nourishment (for example, *agroikoi, en epaulesin anatethrammenoi, penes*) accentuates Celsus's bafflement at the diversity of people who are instructed within the church. Origen readily accepts that Christianity welcomes ignorant and uncultured peasants into its lecture halls. He contends that this is what makes the food of the Word greater than that of the Greeks: it has the "greater common utility" (*koinophelesteron*). Only in the Christian community can the "country yokels" (*agroikoi*) and the "wealthy" (*plousioi*) come together and still receive a food specially suited to the needs and capacities of each.[98] In the Roman world, distinctions of food types clarified and reinforced distinctions of social status. And here Origen has taken it a step further to distinguish types of Christians, differentiating capacities of the soul.

In the precise moment that Origen defends the democratizing instruction found in the Christian community, he nevertheless reifies the very distinctions among the faithful that Celsus had mocked. By classifying Christians according to their differing capacities for nourishment, and inflecting these differences through the language of social status, Origen introduces into the symbols of milk, vegetable, and solid food an element of ontological fixity derived from differences within the social strata. Food, for Origen, may traverse social status, unifying diverse groups of people under the common essence of the Word. But it does not appear to enable every individual soul to transcend its particular status in this life. It seems not all people have the same capacity for transformation: they must eat the type of food most suitable to their status.

In his *Commentary on Romans,* Origen sought to demonstrate that food types promote unity in the church. Here his argument bends in the same direction, while nevertheless explicitly identifying the wide gap in intellectual acumen. It could be that Origen deploys terms like *agroikoi* with some sense of irony in order to exaggerate the criticism of Celsus. But the logic of Origen's distinction between various souls, as we have seen, nevertheless affirms the different social and intellectual statuses within the Christian community. The "refined" Christian—like the angel Raphael in *Paradise Lost*—can deign to eat among the plebs when required, for something can still be gained even from simple fare. But the true food of the *plousioi* resides elsewhere. The simpleton, it seems, has no such hope. And so the question remains: Does a milky, unseasoned meal enable growth from flesh to spirit among the *agroikoi?*[99] Can the peasant-soul be elevated to a higher status through good eating, transformed by the food apportioned to it?

Conclusion

In his catalog of heresies, the *Panarion,* Epiphanius of Salamis diagnoses the ills caused by Origen and those who followed his teaching too closely: "your mind [was] blinded by Greek *paideia,* you have vomited up poison for your followers and have yourself become a poisonous food to them."[100] It is a strange fate that Origen's teaching was later viewed by Epiphanius as tainted nourishment for anyone who consumed it. Indeed, the accusation that his mind was addled by Greek *paideia* reveals to us something about the unresolved tensions that Origen and Paul bequeathed to those who followed later. Of all the early Christian interpreters of Paul, Origen attempted the most thoroughgoing synthesis of anthropology and exegesis in a larger framework for spiritual transformation. Inflected through the categories of milk, vegetable, and solid food, Origen sought to harmonize levels of meaning within scripture and levels of maturity within the soul. In so doing, he took the schematic outline of Greek *paideia*—of the *enkyklios paideia*—and theorized a tiered curriculum of formation for embodied souls being nourished on the Word. But Origen described those tiers with a fixity that seems to preclude progress from one to the next.

The drama of embodied souls, for Origen, was a dietary matter. It was the mysterious transformation of a creaturely nature by means of noetic food. While the mouth may mark the boundary between outer and inner, for Origen it marked the threshold and contact point between the material and the noetic. Food traverses this boundary, crossing the threshold into the *nous* so as to grow the mind within the corporeal matter of the body. Even as the soul is pulled this way and that by its bodily senses, a healthy metabolism processes the Word within the divine sense and elevates the creaturely body into a spiritual one. Like Adam and Eve in *Paradise Lost,* all humans must be fed on a food properly suited to their bodily existence until, little by little, they can receive that purely noetic meal. Origen was clear that this spiritual nourishment will sustain the resurrected body, enabling the transformation of our sensate bodies into a spiritual state. What remains unclear, however, is how material and spiritual foods work together to sustain the corporeal life of the incorporeal soul. Indeed, what remains unresolved is whether the majority of souls will even begin this process of spiritual transformation prior to being raised in a spiritual body. Some souls, it seems, never progress from milk to vegetable to solid food. Relegated to the milky diet of a "country peasant," they cannot withstand the stronger, richer, more luxurious fare of the Word. They must await the resurrection for the food that will nourish them to a "whole and perfect state."

Irenaeus and Clement had sought to reclaim infancy and breast-feeding as positive categories for Christian identity—categories that were grounded both in Paul's ambiguous anthropological system as well as in the predominant physiological theories about food, breast milk, and human formation. This was, in many ways, a response to the inescapable appeal of esotericism and elitism among the highly educated men who employed their considerable intellectual training at the service of Christian instruction. From robust theories about food's substance and power, Irenaeus and Clement offered a defense of Christian milk-drinking that sought to reclaim it as a positive identifying category. But in the third century, Origen was less concerned with defending infancy and breast-feeding. He took these categories as a given, just as he carried forward the same physiological theories about the power of food to convey its essence into the one who eats it.

Origen located the "great problem" implicit within Paul's categories at the opposite end of the spectrum. If there are foods apportioned according to the capacities of each soul, then there must also be some who are capacious enough to receive the divine essence carried within the bread of life. While he focused more time accounting for the infantile and weak souls, Origen presumed that the Christian community contained people already able to eat the solid food of the Word. And these souls, it seems, did not need to be fed on milk or vegetables. Origen did not valorize infancy in the same manner as his predecessors did.

In this way, Hanson did not go far enough in his dismissal of the idea that Origen advocates for a model of progressive growth in his appeal to milk and solid food. Based on his anthropological framework—in which the divine sense slowly overtakes the bodily senses in its apprehension of "intellectual substances"—there are distinct classes among the rational souls being fed on the Word. These dietary statuses are reified along the social strata of Origen's cultural setting: some can eat like country peasants, others dine like the urbane. The two types of eaters are as far apart as Milton's Adam and Eve were from the angel Raphael. For Origen, meals materialized the blending of one's social status and spiritual capacity.

In the second century, interpretations of 1 Corinthians 3 emphasized the themes of infancy and breast milk, and sought to reclaim the troublesome category of infancy evoked within that text. In the third century, Origen, as much as Valentinus or Heracleon, bequeathed to later exegetes the problem of perfection, of fully grown souls, and of solid food. Interpreters of Paul who followed Irenaeus and Clement, on the one hand, and Origen, on the other, were caught between this Scylla and Charybdis of Pauline food symbols: either stressing milk to the detriment of those who would undergo more rigorous spiritual transformation here and now or, alternatively, stressing solid food to the exclusion of those who are not yet strong enough for hearty spiritual nourishment. Despite his emphatic claims about the innate capacity of humans for transformation, Origen sidestepped the question of how that transformation might take place for those souls feeding on the milky lessons of rudimentary faith. In so doing, he relegated a wide swath of Christian souls to the status of milk-drinking infancy and vegetable-eating weakness until, from those corporal nutriments, perhaps their bodies may at last turn all to spirit.

In what follows, I examine two attempts by fourth-century figures to resolve this difficulty. First, Gregory of Nyssa expands on Origen's Pauline diet, making explicit the transformative effect of all food. In Gregory, we encounter the consummation of the link between food and the formation of the soul insofar as the idea of a progressive nutritive development functions for him as a guiding principle. In so doing, he enables all Christians to be fed to perfection in a way Origen never quite articulated. Then, in turning to Augustine, I demonstrate how infancy and breast milk were not simply positive identifiers for the North African bishop but, rather, the only possible status of a healthy soul. Increasingly disillusioned with the human potential for progress in perfection, Augustine comes to view the entire Christian life as one of humble dependence on breast milk without the promise of growth. To leave the milk of the church, for him, became synonymous with being detached from the saving essence of God.

Gregory of Nyssa at the Breast of the Bridegroom

Salvation is first of all essentially subsistence.

—Michel Foucault, *Security, Territory, Population*

AT THE END OF HIS *Homilies on the Song of Songs*, Gregory of Nyssa makes the following observation about the power of food: "[T]he one being nourished is certainly formed according to the kind of nourishment consumed."[1] The link between the Song of Songs and theories of human transformation through food is a curious one. Gregory speaks here with clinical confidence. Although he is discussing the "good pastures" on which the soul feeds, he also evokes the dominant medical and moral wisdom of his day regarding nourishment and its role in the ongoing development of the human person. For Gregory, Christians are saved and perfected by what they eat and by the one who feeds them.

Virginia Burrus has noted how "[ancient] masculinity incorporated characteristics or stances traditionally marked as 'feminine'—from virginal modesty, retirement from the public sphere, and reluctance to challenge or compete on the one hand, to maternal fecundity and nurturance on the other."[2] Burrus specifically illuminates how late-ancient male authors such as Gregory employed the rhetoric of fecundity and procreation at the service of a nascent Christian "orthodoxy." Building on the work of Burrus, I examine a theme that has received less attention in the work of Gregory of Nyssa: the role of nurturance in the progressive perfection of the soul. Reflecting the social ideology of his time—in which breast-feeding functioned as an index for social legitimacy and the transfer of cultural identity—Gregory regularly emphasizes the symbolic power of nourishment in the

formation of the soul. Throughout his work, milk is described as a transformative meal—a form of subsistence that is the essence of salvation and the
way toward perfection.

I will begin with a comparison of Gregory's *Encomium on Saint Basil*
and the *Life of Moses* in order to demonstrate how these texts emphasize the
maternal food given to an infant as the foundation of and guarantor for later
intellectual prowess and social position. Turning next to the *Homilies on
the Song of Songs,* I will analyze the ways in which maternity, infancy, and
breast-feeding enable the various transformations of the soul that take place
throughout Gregory's reading of the Song of Songs. That is to say, Gregory
identifies the bride, bridegroom, and maidens at various points as infants
and mothers, food, and ones being fed. The Song of Songs is thus an itinerary of trophic mutations premised on the assumption that all food contains
an essence, a "being," which is shared with and assimilated by the one who
eats it. Throughout his writings, Gregory depicts human nourishment as a
mimetic process in which the eater becomes like that which she consumes.

Basil, Moses, and the Milk of *Paideia*

Within Gregory's understanding of the progressive transformation of the
human person, nourishment is a central motif. When seeking to make sense
of this complex theme in his thought, any stark analytical division between
"spiritual" and "physical" growth obscures more than it reveals. The symbolic logic of the former relies on the power derived from the embodied
social relations of the latter. Indeed, Gregory's broader understanding of
human nature precludes any clean division between the corporeal and incorporeal.[3] Soul and body are intertwined for him in the ongoing maturation of each person. Gregory views the journey toward God and toward
perfection as a protean movement characterized by unending transformations, mutations, and shifting identities. And throughout the various texts
in which he describes this movement, he regularly refers to various forms of
nourishment as the basis, the marker, or the catalyst for each new transformation. The crucial Gregorian concept of *epektasis*—the eternal stretching
and straining and expanding of human nature into the fathomless depths of

the divine—is built upon a fundamental connection between human *trophe* and the human *telos;* that is, between food and the ongoing perfection of the soul. This connection is crucial to understanding Gregory's account of the infancies of Basil (his older brother) and the biblical character Moses.

THE CHILDHOOD OF BASIL

In a brief letter without an addressee, Basil declares that although he has many friends and relatives and is a "father" to many others, he has but one foster brother (*suntrophos*).⁴ The translation is imprecise. Basil describes this singular man as "the son of the woman who nursed me."⁵ It is clear from the letter that Basil considers this family an extension of his own, a fact established by the language he employs: he refers to it as "the household in which I was brought up" and "the family in which I was nourished."⁶ In describing his relationship with this family, Basil's letter uses variations of the noun *trophe* or the verb *trepho* seven times. He references the food and nurture he received as a child as well as the resources by which he is presently nourished at the time of the letter.⁷ This family fed, nurtured, and reared the young Basil, and it seems that Basil had given them some slaves and a portion of the family estate in return. He insists that he remains indebted to his foster family—and to this man in particular—for his present sustenance as much as for his childhood upbringing.

Though the letter lacks an address, Basil is clearly leveraging his own episcopal status with the recipient in order to ensure that his foster family be allowed to manage the estate without any loss of value to the property. Basil's appeal hinges on the idea that the food and nurture he received from this family—food he received side by side with his *suntrophos*—helped him to become the man he is today. Implicit within Basil's logic is an argument that the food and formation he shared with his foster brother establishes the bona fides of both men, demonstrating their social and even legal legitimacy. They are uniquely and irrevocably tied to one another through a bond of kinship that, for Basil, is as strong as any biological relation. Indeed, his emphasis on *trophe* throughout the letter suggests that this common nourishment and nurture was tantamount to a biological relationship—just as it had been for the sons of the Maccabean mother.[8]

This anecdote provides an interesting contrast to the depiction of Basil's upbringing in Gregory of Nyssa's *Encomium on Saint Basil*. Late in the *Encomium*, Gregory breaks from the convention of panegyric and declares that his brother's homeland (*patris*) and birth (*genos*), and the nourishment received from his parents (*ten ek goneon anatrophen*) are all ancillary details—happy accidents unrelated to Basil's sanctity.[9] Gregory turns the Greek idea of "noble birth" (*eugeneia*) on its head, arguing that Basil's holiness is the product of individual choice (*prohairesis*) and not the result of birth and rearing and education.[10] At the moment when encomiastic style would require the author to praise the circumstances of his subject's nurture—and, presumably, describe his rearing in the family of his *suntrophos*—Gregory instead depicts his brother as an autodidact and an auto-*tropheus*, a self-nourisher.[11]

Basil's example as an auto-*tropheus* is elaborated in an earlier passage in which Gregory compares his brother to the prophet Elijah: both men are praised for their remarkable control of diet. Gregory observes that Basil was not fed by any other human, but rather received his nourishment from heaven as prepared by angels.[12] "Reason," Gregory concludes, "was the measure of his nourishment."[13] Gregory seems to minimize the circumstances of Basil's childhood, arguing that his nurture and nourishment as an infant were of little consequence. The *Encomium* focuses only on the man as he was in his full maturity—the self-made and self-fed man. In this way, Gregory largely ignores the conventions of genre that require some commentary on the childhood and upbringing of his subject in order to demonstrate that his brother's prowess was both evident from an early age and, at the same time, was not due to any human help. Basil's diet was reason, and his whole nature conformed to this nourishment.

Yet Gregory's disregard for rhetorical convention in the *Encomium* is not total. In his attempt to draw parallels between Basil and a panoply of biblical characters, he cannot resist reading his brother into the narrative of Moses's upbringing in Egypt: "An Egyptian princess, having adopted Moses, trained him in the *paideia* of her country. Yet he was not removed from the breast of his mother so long as his early age needed to be nursed by nourishment such as hers. And this is also true for our teacher [that is, Basil]. For although nourished by outside wisdom, he always held fast to the breast of the Church—growing and maturing his soul by way of the teachings drawn from that source."[14]

The analogy is a curious one. Gregory's aim is not to compare the infancy and childhood of the two men. Rather, it is to connect the breastfeeding of Moses by his biological mother and his education under the Egyptians to the fact that Basil never abandoned the teaching of the church (here construed as the "breast" of Basil's "biological mother"), even though Basil was trained by "outsiders" in a "foreign" country. The logic of the analogy, however, appeals to pervasive notions of the power of breast milk to establish and safeguard identity. Just as the milk Moses received from his biological mother guaranteed his intellectual and religious prowess, so too does the breast of the church prove Basil's quality.

Is it possible that under the constraints of encomiastic literature, Basil's childhood upbringing in the home of his wet nurse and subsequent departure for training in Greek *paideia* required just such a figural explanation in order to prove the unbroken legitimacy of his nurture and training? For no matter how steadfastly Basil clung to the breast of the church, it is unlikely he spent much of his childhood among his own venerable biological family—at least compared to his younger brother and their sister Macrina.[15] Indeed, it is unlikely he was ever nursed and nourished in his own home. The milk of the church, in Gregory's *Encomium*, inoculates Basil against the charge that he was the product of a wholly foreign *trophe* and an unchristian *paideia*. Despite presenting Basil as a self-fed man, Gregory is at great pains to demonstrate that his brother was nevertheless raised on Christian milk.

THE CHILDHOOD OF MOSES

The comparison of Basil's upbringing to that of Moses in the *Encomium* serves as a kind of first draft for Gregory's *Life of Moses*.[16] Many of the themes touched on in the *Encomium* are expanded upon and amplified in the *Life*. Especially prominent in the latter text is Gregory's emphasis on the role that nurture and nourishment played in Moses's education— and the importance of these events in understanding how the life of Moses offers a blueprint to Christians for attaining the "perfect life."[17] Through the upbringing of Moses, Gregory is able to emphasize the link between *trophe* and *telos*—between the food Christians eat and the perfection they seek.

From the beginning of the treatise, Gregory defines growth as the *conditio sine qua non* of the perfect life. He deploys a variety of terms to unpack this theme, none more important than the verb *epekteino*—a concept Gregory pulls from Philippians 3:13 ("straining forward") and expands into an entire paradigm for the development of the soul.[18] Starting from this emphasis on progressive growth at the outset of the treatise, Gregory then delves into the particular historical events of Moses's life before offering his interpretation of them.

As I have outlined in detail in chapter 2, the Jewish philosopher and exegete Philo of Alexandria expanded in a similar way upon the biblical account of Moses found in Exodus, giving particular attention to Moses's breast-feeding and early education in Egypt. For Philo, God had devised that Moses would be breast-fed by his biological mother so that "the child's first food be prepared from a legitimate source."[19] The legitimacy (*gnesios*) of the breast milk Moses received secured his place among his people, ensuring his connection to its Wisdom and Law. Given how brief the discussion of Moses's upbringing is in the biblical account, Philo's use of *gnesios* is a significant amplification of the text. Philo was keenly aware of—and thoroughly enmeshed in—the broader ideological system of Roman imperial family values.[20] His emphasis on the legitimacy of Moses's infantile nourishment is but one facet of this broader appropriation of Roman morality for articulating his own account of a Jewish ethno-religious essence.

Gregory conjures Philo's exegetical precedent as well as the Roman imperial ideology undergirding it when he also highlights the fact that Moses was nurtured by his birth mother.[21] Gregory glosses the text, suggesting that the princess plucked the infant from the Nile because she was struck by the grace that shined through him.[22] He then adds the following observation: "But when [Moses] naturally refused a foreign nipple, he was nursed at the breast of his mother through the planning of his biological family."[23] This rendering, like that of Philo, takes liberties with the canonical account in order to spotlight the importance of Moses's first nourishment being derived from his own mother.[24] Why does Moses "naturally" (*physikos*) refuse the breast of a foreigner? Why would Gregory frame the narrative in this way when, in his own day, wet-nursing had become so widespread that even his own brother spent the better part of his youth in the home of a nurse? Echoing the perspective of Favorinus in the *Attic Nights,* here the instinctive refusal of a foreign woman's breast milk establishes a deeper intellectual, social, and even ethnic legitimacy for Moses through his source of maternal care.

Immediately following the previous passage, Gregory describes the development of Moses: "After he had departed from the age of childhood and was educated in the culture of foreigners during his royal nurturance . . . he returned to his natural mother and joined with those of his own race."[25] There is a logical symmetry at work in Gregory's narrative: Moses first refused a "foreign" (*allophulos*) nipple and was breast-fed by his biological mother; he was then educated in that same "foreign culture" (*paideutheis ten eksothen paideusin*), and eventually integrated back into his own race.[26] Because the character of Moses was grounded in the proper (that is, biological rather than foreign) breast milk he received from his mother, the kingly nurture that he was given later in the court of the pharaoh was no impediment to his growth and development in wisdom among the Hebrews. In this way, Gregory again accentuates the "biological" or "natural" nourishment Moses received at his mother's breast as the foundation of his intellectual development. Mother's milk takes on a strikingly elemental significance, protecting Moses's religious and ethnic identity while also suggesting the means by which that identity was initially implanted within him. Biological milk precedes and overrides the time of his royal nourishment (*en basilike te trophe*), giving him mastery over worldly wisdom while also establishing his access to divine wisdom as a kind of birthright.

This stands in stark contrast to the narrative of events offered for Basil's childhood in the *Encomium*—or, rather, the explicit erasure of Basil's childhood nurture from Gregory's hagiography. Indeed, in praising

Basil, Gregory had argued that one's birth, family, and homeland were ir-
relevant details. Yet for Moses these serve as evidence of his deep-seated
virtue and wisdom among his own people. Nourishment functions as a
regulatory symbol, ensuring the proper development of Moses's character
and the replication of his family's culture at the level of biology. And while
Gregory minimizes the significance of Basil's actual infancy and nurture—
presumably because he was not breast-fed in a manner similar to Moses—
he does so by heightening the symbolic power of the "food" his brother
received.

One reason for this contrast between the *Encomium* and the *Life of
Moses* is that Gregory's primary objective in the latter is to demonstrate how
it remains possible to imitate the life of Moses even when the details of one's
birth, parentage, nurturance, and education are unremarkable. Maternal
provision of material sustenance during Moses's infancy becomes an archetype for all Christian infantile nurturance. The ever-expanding familial
bonds of the church must have its own kind of nursery system in which the
proper nourishment of its most vulnerable members can be achieved. For
Gregory, the slippage between "literal" and "rhetorical" family—like the
slippage between material and spiritual nourishment—grew out of the intricate and expansive web of kinship relations that composed the Christian
community of the fourth century.[27]

One way that Gregory, among other early Christian thinkers, worked
within this slippage was by appropriating the power of maternal nourishment to transform infants. In the *Encomium,* he simultaneously downplays
his brother's actual nurture as an infant while retaining and even heightening the symbolic power of nurturance as such. Whether figural or literal,
breast milk was invested with the power to establish bonds of kinship, legitimate social identity, and intellectual potential. In this way the capaciousness of the Christian family, when coupled with imperial-era values
concerning the formative power of milk, manipulated the basic gender roles
upon which the idea of the Roman family was built. The basic pastoral
work of the church, for Gregory, was one of nurturance. The implication of
this, as we will see in greater detail to come, is that bishops and teachers are
maternalized—transformed into vessels of nurturance and breast-feeders of

others. And through these vessels the food of right belief, the sustenance that forms humanity toward perfection, is distributed.

This much is clear when, in the opening of the second section of the *Life,* Gregory asks, "How then are we to imitate the circumstances of this man's birth through our own choice?"[28] Gregory contends that anyone can imitate the noble birth and rearing of Moses if, like Basil, they choose to cling to the breast of the church—if they all become *suntrophoi* through Christian milk. Gregory explains that the primary function of free choice is to "give birth to ourselves"[29] in virtue and "to nourish this offspring with the food proper to it."[30] "Free choice" is, in this sense, how wise men give birth to, breast-feed, and educate themselves. The milk Christians draw from the breast of the church and the milk Moses drew from the breast of his mother contain the same transformative power.

When he comes "to uncover the hidden meaning of the history"[31] of Moses's breast-feeding, Gregory emphasizes the point that Moses was never separated from his "natural mother."[32] He explains, "It seems to me this teaches that, if we should interact with foreign teachings during the time of our education, we should not separate ourselves from being nourished on the church's milk. This means the laws and the customs of the church, by which the soul is fed and strengthened."[33] The historical account of Moses being breast-fed by his natural mother while being educated by his adopted parents is a structuring paradigm for the growth and nurture of Christians who, like Basil, choose to cling to the breast of the church even while they participate in outside education. The milk of the church functions identically to that of Moses's mother and becomes a kind of prophylactic against the world's vices, a guarantor of access to divine wisdom, and a marker of legitimacy within the Christian community—especially for those who engaged in the "Rumspringa" that was Greek *paideia.* Just as Moses became the man he was because of the woman from whom he received his nourishment, so too do all Christians grow toward perfection because of the maternal food given to them—whether that food comes from the body of an actual mother, from the milk of the church, or some combination of both. The figural rendering of breast-feeding found in the *Life of Moses,* as in the *Encomium,* draws its sense and rhetorical force from a set of cultural assumptions about character, knowledge, and social/ethnic identity being contained in the potent milk of a biological mother and subsequently transferred by such means directly to her infant.

In both the *Encomium for Saint Basil* and the *Life of Moses,* nourishment is a marker of one's identity—either as foreigner or as kin. Indeed, nourishment is the very mechanism by which that identity is realized, secured, and transmitted. Likewise, the milk received in infancy is figured as the foundation for future wisdom, access to divinity, and growth in perfection. While the *Encomium* allegorizes Basil's upbringing in order to demonstrate his quality as a self-made, self-fed, and self-educated man of the church, Basil himself remained forever grateful for the "foreign" nourishment he received at the breast of his wet nurse and viewed his *suntrophos* as a uniquely important bond of kinship. Gregory may not have viewed this period of Basil's upbringing as theologically significant, but in Basil's *Letters*, letter 37 demonstrates just how powerful the relationship could be between a wet nurse, her family, and the child placed under her care. As we have seen, interrogating the source of infant nourishment—whether deemed legitimate or illegitimate, kin or foreign—was a primary strategy for working out social identity in the Roman world. In the *Encomium* Gregory views the milk of a "natural" mother in terms similar to that of Favorinus: that is, as the only sure means of preserving and passing on familial identity. He merely had a more capacious understanding of what qualified as a person's "natural family" than the sophist did.

When viewed alongside the *Life of Moses,* however, Gregory's suggestion that Basil remained fixed to the breast of the church even while educated outside its walls provides a model of formation for people from diverse backgrounds of nurturance and instruction. Anyone can achieve the perfection exemplified by Moses if they but choose to be fed on the milk of the church, regardless of the circumstances of their birth, nurture, and education. Perfection, for Gregory, is not simply progressive in an abstract sense. It is a kind of dietary regimen that requires vigilance about the source and quality of food ingested at every stage. And since the Logos is the food on which Christians are fed, there can be no satiety, no stasis in Gregory's trophic theory of spiritual transformation. Proper nourishment constantly expands the capacity of one's mind and its desire for God.[34] In this way, Basil's sense of kinship with his foster family was not so radical after all: in the Christian community of the fourth century, one's "natural mother" was a role that could be filled by a surprisingly wide range of social relations. What mattered most was whether those who filled this role had ever been separated from the milk of the church.

MILK AND MORPHOSIS IN GREGORY'S *HOMILIES ON THE SONG OF SONGS*

The church as a site of endless feeding and formation is also a thematic focal point of Gregory's magnum opus, the *Homilies on the Song of Songs*.[35] Behind all his references to nurture and nourishment within the *Homilies* lurks the idea that humans are transformed in accordance with the food they consume. Gregory's close association of material forms of nourishment with human spiritual transformation is as much an indication of his complex anthropology as it is of his exegetical method. As with Origen, exegesis and anthropology are mutually supportive: human nature is both flesh and spirit and requires food that can preserve and strengthen both aspects. The nutritive process, however, functions in the same way for each: we become in body and mind whatever we eat. Indeed, Gregory's theory of progressive perfection has at its foundation the Pauline categories of "fleshly" and "spiritual" Christians who must be properly fed so as to mature from one to the other.

THE MILK OF THE BRIDEGROOM

In the preface to the *Homilies*, Gregory tells his correspondent, Olympias, that the goal of these writings is not to assist her in "in the conduct of [her] life."[36] Rather, Gregory wants to offer "some assistance to the more fleshly people for the sake of the spiritual and immaterial state of their soul."[37] In this way, he frames the *Homilies* specifically in terms of the Pauline diagnosis of nurturing and guiding "more fleshly people" (*sarkodesteroi*) toward a spiritual existence—a task that Gregory describes as preparing the "divinely inspired words of scripture" in the same way one would prepare grain by making it edible and nutritional to human beings. In fact, Gregory argues that when these words are left "unprepared," they remain a food unfit for rational human consumption.[38] Unprocessed, the nourishment of scriptural teaching in the Song of Songs is suitable only for beasts.[39] The food of the Song must be prepared in such a way that it can assist Christians in their development from flesh to spirit.

Gregory's purpose in the *Homilies* can be understood in two ways: first, as a broader methodological argument for why scripture ought to be processed or digested by an authority in order for it to nourish more fleshly people, and, second, as a specific digestion of the Song of Songs into palatable bites for the women under Olympias's supervision.[40] In his preface, Gregory is proposing to "work over" (*katergazomai*) the text of the Song—cultivating, kneading, peeling, shucking, and chewing until its words are fit to feed the rational mind of carnal Christians. But, more generally, he is also arguing that all scripture must be prepared as food in order to assist the progress of Christians at various stages of perfection. While Origen had sketched an elaborate illustration for understanding Christian teachers as "food preparers," Gregory adopts this motif and applies it to himself and to all exegetes of scripture with one crucial modification: the interpreter of scripture must not only prepare the text for others but must also chew on it, digest it, and through his own body offer that text in a more refined form. Gregory returns throughout the *Homilies* to the theme of feeding and the power of food to transform the fleshly into something more spiritual, something more perfect.[41]

In his first homily, Gregory follows the paradigm established by Origen in which the works attributed to Solomon (Proverbs, Ecclesiastes, Song of Songs) offer their own model of *paideia*—a model that leads the initiate from moral exhortation to philosophical speculation.[42] For Gregory, the Song of Songs is a mystagogical itinerary. It is a road map, scrawled in secret signs, guiding the soul further into the fathomless depths of God. The terminology of ancient mystery cults permeates the opening homily, including references to "secret rites" (*mysteria*),[43] "mystical vision" (*mystikos theoria*),[44] and "initiation" (*mystagogia/mystagogeo*).[45] This is not a text to be handled by children whose souls are "still tender and malleable."[46] Indeed, Gregory observes that those who gain entry into the divine mystery of the Song "have been transformed in their nature into something more divine by the teaching of the Lord."[47] The carnal and erotic words cannot hinder such a person whose "nature is no longer composed of flesh and blood."[48]

The Solomonic classroom is, in this sense, not simply a paradigm for training Christians in a certain method of reading scripture or even in a particular way of life.[49] More drastically, as Gregory argues, it is a laboratory in which human natures are purified and reconfigured so that they may stretch themselves further into God's mystery. The sustenance of the scriptural Logos, for Gregory, contains the power to reconstitute milk-drinking carnal Christians into solid-food-eating spirituals. Does Gregory believe such Christians who follow his dietary regimen are no longer flesh and blood in some literal, physiological, or otherwise materialistic sense? Like Paul, Clement, Irenaeus, and Origen before him, Gregory seems ultimately uninterested in such questions. The guiding principle for him throughout is simply that we become what we eat. The perfection of human nature from a corporeal state to an incorporeal one is, first and foremost, a nutritive process. It is the weaning of the soul from flesh to spirit.

Having established the need to purify the words of scripture as well as the nature of the reader, Gregory then turns to the opening verse of the Song of Songs: "Let him kiss me with the kisses of his mouth, for your breasts are better than wine." The mystagogical metamorphosis is instigated by a kiss from the lips of the bridegroom that cleanses the fleshiness of human nature. Gregory observes, "For this kiss purifies all filth."[50] The Song's emphasis on the lips and breasts of the bridegroom evokes, for Gregory, not an erotic union but rather the transfer of divine power through breast milk:

> And the soul that has been purified, not covered over by leprosy
> of the flesh, gazes on the treasure house of good things. The
> treasure house is called the heart and from it the abundance of
> divine milk flows to the breasts—the same breasts on which the

> soul is nourished according to its proportion of faith as it drinks
> in grace. This is why it says "Your breasts are better than wine,"
> for the location of the breast indicates the heart. And certainly
> someone who thinks of the heart as the hidden and mysterious
> power of divinity will not be wrong. Likewise, someone might
> reasonably think of the breasts as the good activities of the di-
> vine power on our behalf. By these breasts God suckles the life
> of each person, giving the nourishment that is best suited to
> each of those who receive it.[51]

The categories of "power" (*dynamis*) and "activity" (*energeia*) are central to
Gregory's theological lexicon.[52] The basic schema of this distinction is that,
for humanity, the "power" of God is typically inaccessible and inexpressible
unless mediated to us through divine "activity." For those newly purified
infants, the wisdom of God is imparted first through the divine milk that
flows from the breast of God. And this breast is identified specifically with
the bridegroom of the Song in homily 1.[53]

Gregory redirects the highly erotic content of the Song of Songs'
opening by transforming the bridegroom into a mother, the bride into an
infant.[54] The bride's body becomes the malleable material through which
the powerful milk of God is drawn into the soul. Hers is a body that is always reconstituting itself, while the soul within expands and stretches further into God's mystery. Likewise, the morphing body of the bridegroom
marks a shift from nuptial bedroom to nursery. This shift is possible, according to Gregory, because "There is a certain correspondence between
the actions of the soul and the faculties of the body."[55] The image of kissing
lips and lingering eyes initiates a chain of signification, an index of body
parts and their putative social or biological functions, which leads the
reader through the intimate desire shared between husband and wife into
the deeper significance of maternal nurture and the nourishment of human
souls.

The erotic connotations of lips and breasts symbolize, for Gregory,
nurturance and the transmission of knowledge, character, and social legitimacy that takes place for an infant at the breast of the mother. The charged

sexual longing of the bride is registered here as the pangs of infantile hunger: "For what is produced by the breasts is milk, and milk is the food of infants."[56] Gregory observes that the "milk of the divine breasts" is the "simpler nourishment of the divine teachings"—teachings that nevertheless exceed "all human wisdom."[57]

While commentators have noted the bridegroom's maternal transformation, there has been little attempt to observe why this transformation would resonate so readily for Gregory and his audience.[58] It is not simply that the bridegroom, Christ, or Wisdom might be understood as a breast-feeding mother because of passages from scripture that use similar language—though this was no doubt in Gregory's mind as well. The force of Gregory's argument about food and its impact on the transformation of the bride's body and soul also resonates with the dominant social values concerning the family and child-rearing in the Roman Empire. Gregory's reconfiguring of the bridegroom into a mother who breast-feeds infants on divine milk buttresses his theory of human transformation—a theory in which bodies and minds are shaped and reshaped because of the food they receive. The binding together of bridegroom and bride through the sharing of breast milk as a link of kinship—simultaneously biological and spiritual—is consistent with Favorinus's argument that a woman's *spiritus* is implanted within an infant's body and soul through her breast milk.

The first step, then, in the protean movement toward perfection is a return to infancy. Unlike in 1 Corinthians, where Paul used infancy as a derogatory designation for stunted pneumatic development, Gregory suggests that the growth of the soul and the purification of the mind are possible only insofar as one reverts to a childlike state free from the stain of erotic desire. Expanding on this point, Gregory shifts from the encounter of bride and bridegroom toward the relationship between the bride and her maidens. He notes that "the erotic desire for material things does not grip those who are infants (for infancy does not allow this passion)."[59] Following their bride, the maidens "stretch themselves out" toward the virtues of the bridegroom.[60] Gregory reconfigures the relationships found in the Song of Songs, identifying maidens and bride alike as infants seeking mother's milk. He thus views infancy as a state of dispassionate receptivity.[61] The growth and transformation of the bride and her maidens begins at the breast. Infancy is the state in which the mind is purified of sexual passion, enabling it to imbibe the deeper meaning of the Song's erotic content and be transformed by it from the inside out.

There is a cyclical, mimetic aspect to the process of transformation described in the first homily. The bride, who Gregory considers "the more perfect soul,"[62] was "the first to come face to face with the Word, having been filled with good things, and was deemed worthy of hidden mysteries."[63] Within a few short verses, this bride has morphed from virgin to infant to mother. The food she receives at the breast of the bridegroom begins a process of *morphosis* that culminates in her offering to others the same milk she once received at his side. The maidens praise her accordingly: "Just as you love the breasts of the Word more than wine, so too let us imitate you and love your breasts, through which the infants in Christ are given milk to drink."[64] Not everyone, it seems, is able to drink divine milk directly from the bridegroom. The maidens must receive the simple nourishment of divine instruction from the breast of another.

The progression of human transformation outlined by Gregory in homily 1 provides a blueprint for the themes that occupy the rest of the *Homilies*. Indeed, the importance of the bridegroom's breasts at the opening becomes a textual anchor for any reference to nourishment, children, and instruction that Gregory perceives throughout the Song of Songs. But even as the bride remains a source of maternal nurturance, she continues to be reshaped into new forms. Gregory identifies her as "the teacher" whose primary concern is the progress of "learning souls."[65] These souls are eager for "the grace that flows from her rational breasts."[66] The bride is an "example" to the little ones in her care, a model in being made beautiful by the bridegroom's milk.[67]

THE MILK OF THE BRIDE

In Gregory's reading, the content covered in homilies 1 and 2 is merely an introduction to the Song of Songs as a whole. These opening verses contain a "power of purification" that prepares novices for the pure power offered in the later homilies.[68] Gregory marks this transition in homily 3 where the Word of God speaks "in his own voice" to the bride. As a Lenten sermon series, then, Gregory says that his first two homilies were meant to purify both the text and the souls of his audience. The words of the Song are like the filth that attaches to the flesh and must be rinsed off and washed away so that the Logos contained within can be encountered directly.[69] Yet this brief review offered by Gregory at the opening of homily 3 is more than just an outline of the previous sermons. In another sense, Gregory has inserted himself into the interpretation being offered: he has assumed the role of the bride, digesting what he has received from the bridegroom in order to pass it on to the infants under his care. And he has sent the *Homilies* to Olympias so that she might do the same. In this way, the later homilies provide a schematic outline for how "mature" Christians become milk providers to their infantile brothers and sisters.

In homily 6, Gregory returns to the bride's function as nurturer. She does not rest in her own progress, but wears Christ "between her rational breasts, which gush with divine teachings."[70] The bride moves from perfection to perfection through a process of transfiguration. Gregory accounts for her transformation from virgin to infant to mother by drawing a comparison to the changing appearances of actors in the theater, where the same person may be seen as a slave or a soldier or a king: "In the same way, because of their desire for higher things, those who make progress in virtue do not remain in the same character while they are being transformed from glory to glory."[71] Her maidens, having watched the bride's *morphosis* in awe, now praise the marriage bed. Gregory is referring to Song of Songs 3:7–8 ("Behold Solomon's bed: sixty mighty men surround it out of the mighty men of Israel. They all bear a sword, being instructed in war; each man has a sword on his thigh"). He offers a variety of ways to interpret this passage, but concludes by connecting it to Luke 11:7 ("The door is already shut and the children are with me in the bed"). The soldiers with swords girded on their thighs suggest, to Gregory, a presexual and dispassionate character typical of young children.

The bridal chamber again takes the form of a nursery, but this time with the newly maternal bride and the infantile maidens sharing the bed.

The maidens have become like infants, specifically male infants with "swords girded," who repose on the bed where the bride may feed them God's instruction from her rational breasts. (With its reference to "rational breasts," homily 6 here echoes Gregory's phrasing in homily 2: *ek ton logikon mazon*.) As the bride is transformed by the bridegroom's milk, so too do the maidens transform from young women to infants because of the bride's milk. Bridegroom, bride, and maidens are all linked to one another through a common food that is passed between them. Nourishment instigates the bodily alterations of all involved. Same essence, same food.

Gregory elaborates on the relationship between imitation, nourishment, and spiritual transformation in homilies 7–10 through reference to the church as composed of various body parts (following 1 Corinthians 12). He observes that "it is possible to find in the common body of the church lips and teeth and tongue, breasts and womb and neck and, as Paul says, also those members of the body that seem shameful."[72] The spiritualizing of body parts transmutes the erotics of praise found throughout the Song of Songs, enabling a paradigm of Christian formation that nevertheless follows the Song's litany of body parts and the social or biological functions associated with them. This is no simple allegory. It is an amplification of cultural values encoded upon the female body—values that had already emphasized the power of milk and the formation of infant souls. In the laboratory of Solomonic education, human nature is formed in accordance with the food it is given by mothers and nurses in infancy.[73]

The spiritual function of the breast is derived specifically from its putative biological purpose: "[F]or this reason, the text refers to the person who, after the likeness of the great Paul, becomes a breast for the infants and nourishes the newborns of the church with milk like two breasts that are created at the same time like twin fawns of the deer . . . [H]e [that is, the one who becomes a breast] does not lock up grace within himself but offers the nipple of the Word to those bound to him."[74] In response to the bridegroom's praise of the bride's breasts, Gregory amplifies the maternal function of the female body in nurturing and rearing children. This is surely an aspect of the "corporeal person," but its deeper meaning is readily applied to the process of spiritual formation Gregory has been outlining throughout the *Homilies*. The incorporeal, rational, and spiritual power of breasts, it turns out, is identical in form and function to that of the maternal, bodily power. For Gregory, breast milk signifies the raw material through which intellectual potential and cultural identity are passed from one person to the next.

This point is developed at length in Gregory's reading of Song of Songs 4:10 ("How your breasts have been made beautiful, my sister bride! How your breasts have been made beautiful from wine!"). Gregory exhorts his audience to listen to the words of scripture "as those already separated from flesh and blood, and as those whose basic composition has been transformed into a spiritual nature."[75] The bride, who at the opening of the Song of Songs praised her groom's breasts, now receives a similar praise from him. These words are no "simple compliment," but rather have a talismanic quality.[76] They are, for Gregory, the means by which the bridegroom beautifies the bride in proportion to her good works. The increase of her beauty is directly identified with "her fountains of good doctrine" (*en tais ton agathon didagmaton pegais*), which were the result of her nurture at the breast of the bridegroom. Thus the bridegroom "is explaining the reason why the bride's breasts have been altered for the better and made more perfect, no longer pouring forth milk-nourishment for infants, but well-up with uncontaminated wine to the delight of the more perfect."[77] Whatever the bridegroom says in praise to the bride becomes her reality. She is augmented and beautified, first by his milk and then by his words. In turn, she becomes a source of nourishment and a model in virtue to others.[78] The composition of her body is altered—Gregory says it has been "enhanced"—so as to become the optimal maternal vessel carrying divine nourishment and "good doctrine" for all; that is, for infants and fully grown alike.

Through the bridegroom's nourishing milk, the bride is transformed into his likeness. She is changed into a maternal body that dispenses God's mystery and feeds infants so that they too may become like her as she has become like the bridegroom. Bride and maidens are all molded into that which they consume. In fact, in response to Song of Songs 5:13 ("His belly is an ivory tablet . . ."), Gregory envisions the whole church as a giant "belly" (*koilia*) for divine nourishment. He notes that scripture uses the term *koilia* to refer "to the intellectual and rational part of the soul, in which the divine teachings are deposited."[79] Precisely how Gregory understands the deepest part of the rational soul as its "gut" or its "bowels" is unclear. Yet we have already seen how readily Gregory draws on the idea that food has the power to produce likeness of bodies and minds. The idea of "spiritual bowels," then, is merely the logical extension of his belief that spiritual food reconstitutes our material bodies into their perfect, spiritual form, freed from the carnal constraints of flesh and blood.

The spiritualizing of human digestion in homily 14 illuminates Gregory's claim about the power of food that opened this chapter: "[T]he one being nourished is certainly formed according to the kind of nourishment consumed."[80] In context, Gregory is discussing how those within the flock of the bridegroom graze among the lilies (Song of Songs 6:2–3) and, as a result, become beautiful like the lilies. This, for Gregory, is how the virtues function in the Christian life. A person must be guided to them, as to good pasture, and ingest them into the belly of the soul. Gregory's notion that the soul has a belly is, then, a robust application of ancient theories regarding the power of food to transform the one who eats from the inside out. The soul ingests, digests, and is remade by the nourishment it consumes. Food, maternity, and infancy all serve Gregory's exegetical project to purify the carnal character of the Song of Songs while also providing a model of transformation, leading individual Christians from a nature of flesh to one of spirit.

Following Gregory's earlier examples of Moses and Basil, the infancy of the bride and her maidens becomes a scriptural space in which Christians from any family background might locate themselves as infants to be breast-fed and reared by their "natural mother." There is no "foreign milk" in the model of formation described by Gregory. He offers the protean formation of the bride at the breast of the bridegroom as a paradigm for Solomon's *paideia,* refracted through the Pauline terminology of growth from flesh to spirit, from milk to solid food. As a result, the bride's identity, her access to divine knowledge, and her status within the community are all secured through the source of her milk. Likewise, the maidens who are fed by the bride share in her knowledge of God, her authority, and her very essence as she nourishes them. Gregory's *Homilies* provide a regimen of Christian nourishment aimed at transforming and enhancing a person's intellectual powers and moral character. All Christians are fed to perfection at the breast of the bridegroom or those who have been molded to his nourishing likeness.

In the *Homilies on the Song of Songs,* Gregory combines the ideal of *morphosis* that was so central to Greek *paideia* with a complex account of how food instigates this transformation. Werner Jaeger's partition between the development of the soul and the growth of the body misses the full force of this combination. In his discussion of food and formation in Gregory of Nyssa, Jaeger argues that "the nourishment of the soul must be apportioned differently from the material food we consume" and that "the spiritual process called education is not spontaneous in nature but requires constant care."[81] In framing Gregory's thought in this way, Jaeger does not account for the ways in which the material food we consume might also be a spiritual process, requiring constant maternal care. Indeed, to conclude that spiritual nourishment lacks any robust connection to its material corollary overlooks the pervasive and intricate role that food—especially the feeding of infants—played in ancient theories of intellectual formation and the ways in which food was understood to impact the development of the soul.

Conclusion

Commenting on the prolific reproduction of holiness that took place within the biological family of Basil and Gregory, John Henry Newman once observed, "Basil's family circle ... was a nursery of bishops and saints."[82] Newman's language unwittingly touches upon the prominence of nurturance, maternity, and especially breast-feeding in Gregory of Nyssa's theory of Christian formation. Emphasis on proper nourishment and the role of breast milk in intellectual development was, for Gregory, a way of creating, safeguarding, and replicating the kind of Christian cultural identity he found exemplified in the Song of Songs.[83] More than any other late-ancient Christian author, Gregory achieved a remarkable synthesis of Greek *paid-*

eia and Roman family values—including their attendant theories of human development—with the language and imaginative landscape of scripture. Gregory's Solomonic version of *paideia* found its true archetype in his sister, Macrina. If the family of Basil and Gregory was a nursery for saints and bishops, Macrina was the nurse, the midwife, the mother, and even the father presiding over it.[84]

Throughout the *Life of Macrina,* Gregory consistently links nurture, rearing, and breast-feeding to his sister's exemplary character and to the care and instruction she offered to others—including to Gregory himself. Early on, he notes how Macrina was exceptional among her siblings in that she alone was nursed by her biological mother: "So the child was nourished, breastfed primarily in the hands of her own mother, despite having her own nurse."[85] The inclusion of this detail at the outset of his hagiography is all the more striking when compared to the *Encomium on Saint Basil,* in which Gregory passes over the rearing and childhood of his brother in total silence. In fact, Macrina seems in this instance a more direct parallel to Moses than Basil, having been nurtured by her biological mother and not by some "foreign milk." Gregory's emphasis on Macrina's nurture at the breast of her mother also suggests that the nobility of his family lineage—nobility demonstrated in the renowned spirituality of his maternal grandmother and mother—was passed matrilineally from mother to daughter through the breast milk.

Gregory then tells us that Macrina's mother educated her exclusively on Solomon's wisdom and that the girl demonstrated an unprecedented aptitude because of this rearing. Unlike Basil, the "tender and moldable" nature of Macrina's childhood soul was not subjected to the risky content of Greek *paideia*. In the *Encomium,* Basil's nurture is considered an insignificant detail while, in the *Life of Macrina,* Gregory explicitly describes how his sister never left the breast of her biological mother. Macrina was the archetype for Solomonic transformation—morphing from infant to mother, from one being fed to the one feeding others. Basil may have been a self-fed man, never leaving the breast of the church, but Macrina was raised solely on the Christian milk of her natural mother and instructed exclusively through the tutelage of Solomon. From this perspective, Basil begins to look like the black sheep of the family: fed and educated by "foreigners," he overcame his unorthodox nurturance only through sheer force of will by fixing himself to the breast of the church.

Even Peter, Macrina's youngest brother, is said to have benefited from the nourishment received under her care. Gregory recounts how Macrina "tore [Peter] away from the breast of the one nursing him and nurtured him on her own, and led him to the whole higher education. . . . She became all things to the little one: father, teacher, guardian, mother, adviser in every good thing."[86] Once again, the distinction between material food and spiritual nourishment is blurred. In snatching Peter from the breast of his nurse, Macrina assumed the role of food provider and caregiver to her brother. The food and instruction offered to Peter results in a man of exceptional intellectual prowess—a man who, "without any guidance achieved a completely accurate knowledge of everything that ordinary people learn by time and trouble."[87] Not only does Macrina nourish her brother in his infancy, she also continues to nourish him on her deep wisdom of scripture as he grew. She plays the bride to Peter's maiden, just as it seems she had done earlier with Gregory. Indeed, according to Gregory, many of the women who lived with Macrina at the end of her life had been rescued from starvation and nurtured to health by her while they were still children. These women called her both "mother and nurse" because Macrina "had nursed and reared" them.[88]

It seems likely, then, that as Gregory edited his *Homilies on the Song of Songs* for Olympias and the women in her care, he had in mind his own sister—a woman who was first and foremost a nourisher of others. Like the bride of the Song of Songs, there was in Macrina a "divine and pure *eros* for the unseen bridegroom, on which she had been nourished in the secret depths of her soul."[89] Because the Song shifts abruptly from imagery of the erotic to that of nurturance and, later, to the pastoral, those who follow the Song's trophic itinerary must also undergo a parallel transformation from bride to infant until, at last, they can become a mothering shepherd to others. Nourishment is, in this way, a regulatory symbol in Gregory's reading of the Song of Songs. It signifies milky subsistence, good pasture, safe doctrine, ecclesial belonging, and proper formation. It is the means by which progress in perfection is charted in the Christian life. For Gregory, one is identified as a Christian not by birth but rather by nourishment.

In a series of lectures titled *Security, Territory, Population,* Michel Foucault set out to describe "bio-power"—a concept that he had first introduced in the opening volume of his *History of Sexuality.* In the lectures, he defines bio-power as "the set of mechanisms through which the basic biological features of the human species became the object of a political strategy, of a general strategy of power."[90] Foucault was primarily interested in the "technologies of security" that are exercised over a population through the governance and management of bodies—both individual and collective. He wanted to observe the ways in which bodies and their parts functioned as a site for social control and the reproduction of social order. While Foucault primarily viewed this phenomenon as emerging in the eighteenth century, he traces its origin back to early Christianity and, specifically, to the development of pastoral care.

The office of the pastor, for Foucault, was a mechanism for exerting social power over the body of the "flock" in the form of care—that is, benevolent concern for the well-being of the whole group as well as for each individual.[91] Foucault explains, "Salvation is first of all essentially subsistence. The means of subsistence provided, the food assured, is good pasture. The shepherd is someone who feeds and who feeds directly, or at any rate, he is someone who feeds the flock first by leading it to good pastures, and then by making sure that the animals eat and are properly fed. Pastoral power is the power of care."[92] In Gregory's discussion of progressive perfection, his pervasive appeal to nourishment and breast-feeding suggests this pastoral appropriation of the basic biological features of the human body—especially the features and supposed functions of the female body. The important role of the mother and wet nurse within Roman family values opened a charged symbolic space for early Christians to theorize the preservation and transmission of the essential material of the faith. Pastoral power, then, is built upon a similar nexus of feminine, maternal, and biological characteristics concerning food and formation, transferring these characteristics into the institution of the church and upon those vested with its authority.

But this social and ideological background does not in itself explain why an ascetic male author like Gregory would so prominently situate nurturance within his program of Christian formation. On the one hand, it is possible Gregory believed that incorporating one of the most regulated of "feminine" qualities within Roman political ideology could somehow overcome the temporal constraints of gender. The potential fluidity of coded household roles and biological functions might be construed as an indication of the evanescence of gender among the spiritualized bodies of the Christian household. Nevertheless, the prominent presence of actual women—Macrina and Olympias, for example—complicates such a conclusion. Even as he figures himself as the mothering virgin of the Song of Songs, Gregory is unable to match his sister's maternal virtuosity. The female body was, in this way, a quarry that early Christian writers mined for essential characteristics that could be put to work at the service of the church.

On the other hand, it is possible that Gregory found nurturance more useful than, say, the language of "planting a seed"—though such imagery was certainly not uncommon in discussions of education and intellectual formation.[93] The idea of regular insemination was, for Gregory perhaps, poorly suited as a model for the ongoing work of pastoral care among chaste men and women. Nevertheless, it is not immediately obvious why the intimate relational encounter symbolized by mother's milk would not conjure any erotic or sexual associations at all. Breast-feeding is an outcome of sexual coupling—with all of its attendant desires. Likewise, it is also an action in which complex, often unspoken pleasures and longings are shared between mother and child.[94] The fact that early Christians looked to the Song of Songs as a paradigm for teacher-student relations—and that Gregory amplified the themes of maternity and nourishment within that paradigm—destabilizes the notion that breast-feeding necessarily bypasses the erotics of the text. For an intensity of desire made the text generative in the early Christian imagination in the first place. The purified eros that compels the bride toward the bridegroom is not so easily quarantined from those less tidy desires that drive lovers to embrace or that bind mother and child together in the mutual give-and-take of nurturance. In this way, Gregory's model of food and formation retains the seductive energy of the Song of Songs, perhaps opening a space for unanticipated relational orientations and outcomes between feeder and eater alike.

Virginia Burrus has insightfully observed how Gregory uses his sister's nurturance of others "to reimagine the erotics of male receptivity, via performed reversal of gender. Allowing Macrina to take the lead as teacher, parent, and lover, Gregory turns the traditionally feminine necessity to submit into a desirable masculine virtue. In so doing, he decisively queers the family values conveyed beyond the ascetic household."[95] If Gregory queered the family values of his day, he nevertheless retained and, I would argue, amplified the ideology of nurturance that was at the bedrock of those values. Indeed, one place in which male receptivity was not viewed as socially taboo was within the proper breast-feeding of infants. One could be a male and an infant—submissive, receptive, and under the nurturing care of another—without necessarily sliding into effeminacy.

What is striking, however, is that Gregory frames the characteristically "feminine" biological function of breast-feeding, of offering milk from one's own body for the benefit of others, as the *telos* of all Christian growth. Unlike the Pauline paradigm in which "mature" Christians are identified by the capacity to eat solid food independently, Gregory's account of progressive Christian perfection emphasizes the milk. Maturity is found not in the food one eats alone but in the food one provides to others. While Gregory subtly foregrounds himself as a bride at the breast of the bridegroom, it is Macrina who emerges as a model for how the infant soul ought to be fed, the maternal form of the mature Christian, and the proper provision of sustenance to others in need. The biopower of the nursing body, best exemplified by Macrina, is put to work by Gregory as a mechanism for the perfection of the whole church.

As within the Roman household, kinship, moral character, and intellectual prowess were not granted as a birthright within the Christian "family"—even in venerable households like that of Gregory, Macrina, and Basil. One had to be nurtured into such things. As a basic human biological function, breast-feeding was a site of significant cultural debate in Gregory's time and, as such, was a structuring symbol for social relations within the Christian community. If we become what we eat, then those who nurse us as infants have a surprising amount of power over our future, our minds, and our souls. Gregory appeals to this cultural trope when he reconfigures all Christian growth in perfection as a movement from infancy to maternity, as a process of being nursed, weaned, and then nursing others. The Christian community is fed to perfection at the breast of the bridegroom or, at any rate, at the breast of those who have already been transformed by his nourishing care. Salvation is, in this sense, the subsistence of a mother's milk.

SIX

Milk Without Growth

Augustine and the Limits of Formation

We should drink, not think.

—Augustine, Sermon 119

You are neither a child of the gods, nor born from divine blood, you
faithless one; you were brought forth from the uneven crags of a rock,
and wild tigers raised you on the milk of their breasts.

—Virgil, *Aeneid*

ROME'S FIRST HERO was no poster child for the family values that
later defined the empire. In the *Aeneid,* Virgil dramatizes the moment
Aeneas leaves Dido, recounting the curse that the queen hurls at her be-
trayer. Having been unjustly abandoned by Aeneas, Dido declares that such
a dishonorable man could not have been born or nourished by noble parents. No virtuous, well-born man would behave this way, she seethes. He
must have been reared in the wild, birthed from the cleft of a mountain,
suckled by wild beasts. As with the twins Romulus and Remus, the great
hero of Rome must have been a feral child.

The link between Aeneas's deficient character and the savage milk on
which he was nursed evokes, albeit with literary subtlety, the discourse I
have been analyzing that surrounded the role of proper nourishment in the
formation of children in the early Roman Empire. The subtlety of this
theme, however, is drawn out explicitly some four hundred years later in
Macrobius's *Saturnalia.*[1] Composed in the form of a quirky repository of
Roman culture, the *Saturnalia* is presented as a dialogue in which the interlocutors are "enthusiasts of old learning, anxious to keep alive the old
traditions."[2] Whether or to what extent Macrobius was himself invested in

a project of cultural retrieval is unclear. But the archival quality of his work has the effect of foregrounding crucial elements of *romanitas* that had persevered into "the long fifth century."[3]

The image of Aeneas being suckled by tigers prompts Macrobius to consider the importance of breast milk in crafting a person's character. In so doing, the *Saturnalia* catalogs the enduring power of nourishment that had been crucial to the ideology of the early empire:

> [I]n implanting one's character a large role is generally played by the qualities of one's nurse and the nature of the milk received, which enters the tender babe and mingles with the parents' seed when it is still fresh, as the two-fold mixture shapes a single nature. That is why a provident nature caused the capacity of nursing to coincide with the delivery itself, so that the very act of nurturing would make children and parents resemble each other. For after the blood, like a craftsman, has shaped the body's every nook and cranny and fed it, the same blood rises to the upper regions of the mother's body as the delivery approaches and takes on the nature of white milk, so that it might nurture the new-born as it had previously crafted it. That is why it is correctly believed that milk's innate properties have the same capacity as seed's natural force to produce a likeness of body and minds.[4]

Dido's reference to the tiger's milk suggests, to Macrobius, the need for parents to ensure that the nature of the milk (*natura lactis*) is of the highest quality. From the combination of mother's milk and parental seed, the child's single innate character is molded into a solid form (*ex hac gemini concretione unam indolem cofigurat*). Like the theorists who preceded him, Macrobius observes the substantial relationship between blood and breast milk. Blood—which previously had behaved like a craftsman (*artifex*), shaping the whole body—turns white in the mother, becoming a nourisher (*altor*) of the child's inward nature, "molding it into a likeness of body and soul" (*fingendas corporis atque animi similitudines*). This, then, is the power of milk's essential properties (*lactis ingenia et proprietates*): to nurture a child's nature into its perfect form.

In previous generations, the power of breast milk had been amplified within the ideological system of Roman family values and incorporated into an enduring concern about human formation produced through Greek *paideia*. Authors like Aulus Gellius, Plutarch, Soranus, and Quintilian attest to the early Roman emphasis on milk in perfecting a child's nature. In Macrobius's fifth century, those venerable Roman institutions of family and education were increasingly absorbed by and refracted through the Christian imagination that had exerted increasing influence upon the social landscape.

As H. I. Marrou has observed, "Christian education, in the sacred, transcendent meaning of the word, could not be given at school like any other kind of education, but only in and through the Church on the one hand and the family on the other. . . . The natural environment for the development of the Christian soul was the Christian family. As the mainspring of all education is imitation, the most important thing was a good example."[5] From the materials supplied to it by classical *paideia* and Roman family values, the Christian community of late antiquity forged its own expansive system of kinship and education. Absent the teacher, the grammarian, or the rhetor, new models of instruction and imitation were needed and new molds had to be cut for the work of forming souls.[6]

Kate Cooper has demonstrated how, "at the end of antiquity . . . the older vision of Roman family life based on the legal powers of the *paterfamilias* gave way to a new ideal, in which the *paterfamilias* had essentially ceded to the Christian bishop his role of arbiter in matters of piety and justice."[7] By the late fourth and early fifth centuries, the role of the Roman *familia* as a microcosm of imperial vitality had been transferred in a significant sense into the scaffolding of a newly erected institutional church. The capacious Christian "household," described in Ephesians 2:19, was to be a place in which disparate peoples gathered under one roof as kin and were there made "one in Christ." As in the Roman *domus,* the household of God also found in the symbol of breast milk a means for safeguarding and transferring essential qualities, characteristics, and familial identity from one generation to the next.[8]

Augustine of Hippo is a striking example of the late-ancient transformation of Roman family values and classical education in the Christian imagination.[9] Crucially, Augustine refers to Christian formation as taking place in both "the household of God" (*domus Dei*)[10] and "the school of Christ" (*schola Christi*).[11] As observed in chapter 1 of this book, the "*domus*" was a complex and powerful symbol in the social world of the Roman Empire. It signified status, prestige, and lineage. It referred to a physical presence (as in the structural household) as well as an intricate web of relations (be they linked by a common descent or, more broadly, in service to the *paterfamilias*). While the *domus* increased in symbolic significance in the imperial era, the *familia*—which had often referred to the nobility of patrilineal ancestry—decreased in significance. The new reality of social power dynamics in the empire was worked out more through networks of friendship, patronage, and these networks were routed through the expansive space of the *domus*. And so, as the Christian bishop came to wield authority over the conceptual space of the *domus,* traditionally reserved for the *paterfamilias,* he had at his disposal all the symbolic resources of Roman family values with which an ideology about the Christian family might be constructed. This is the context in which Augustine's use of *domus* must be set.[12]

Increasingly suspicious about the efficacy of human authority, Augustine came to view the possibility of graduating through traditional stages of formation as inconsistent with the character of the Christian life he found described in scripture. In this way, he amplifies the symbolic function of the Roman *domus* and the maternal milk within it to safeguard and transmit his own account of Christian familial identity. However, he largely abandons the original *telos* of these symbols and the transformational role of milk in bringing the child, however slowly, into a perfect form.[13] The nature of milk for Augustine, as for Macrobius, carries within it the substance of familial character and identity. But, by the end of his career, the bishop of Hippo had largely emptied milk of its forming power. That is, for Augustine, the nourishment offered within the household of God was milk without growth.

Developing a coherent account of Augustine's approach to the power of milk inevitably raises a host of other questions and considerations, some of which have vexed scholars for decades. Looming above all these attendant issues is the dramatic shift in Augustine's approach to human formation that can be observed across his writing career. Indeed, this shift reveals in Augustine a lifelong attempt to incorporate elements of Roman values about the proper feeding and formation of souls within a late-ancient Christian context—an attempt that collapses, in the end, under the weight of its own exhaustion and disappointment. Scholars have traced some of the interlocking themes that are implicated in this shift, such as Augustine's approach to esotericism, the central role of humility in the Christian life, and the theological significance of maternal imagery. In each case, we see one piece of the picture but not quite the whole of it. A few examples will help to clarify this point.

From the earliest readings of 1 Corinthians 3, the specter of esotericism already cast a long shadow over the Pauline text that extends even into modern commentaries on the text. We have already seen how figures like Clement and Origen wrestled with its almost unavoidably elitist categories, and this shadow hovers above Augustine's own appeals to milk and solid food. It is, in fact, a persistent problem to which he returns time and again. In an essay from 1930, D. B. Capelle drew a stark division between Augustine's interpretation of the milk and solid-food trope and that of his Alexandrian forebears.[14] The guiding question for Capelle is whether Augustine's frequent citation of milk and solid food suggests a strand of Christian "esoteric doctrine" within the bishop of Hippo's thought.[15] According to Capelle, Augustine differs from his predecessors (especially from those like the Cappadocians, who were "influenced by Origen") insofar as he emphasizes different stages of understanding rather than different stages of doctrine.[16] Put another way, there is not one kind of remedial teaching for the uninstructed and another, more advanced kind for the well-educated. All Christian teaching is the same: the difference, argues Capelle, is the degree of intellectual "assimilation."[17] For Capelle, the only distinction among Christians observed by Augustine was the extent to which the food given to them had been properly digested.

Augustine's increasing attention to the theme of humility offers scholars another avenue of approach for thinking about his frequent references to breast milk. Tarsicius van Bavel has emphasized the function of milk as a metaphor for the humility of God in the person of Jesus.[18] This reading notes that, for Augustine, all Christians live in a state of infantile dependence as they emulate Christ's humility.[19] Despite the easy parallelism of milk-as-humility, van Bavel makes an important observation early on in the essay that reveals why this theme continues to generate commentary and analysis. He notes, "[P]roblems arise only when Augustine claims that a person must graduate from this [milk] stage and reach for the nourishment of adults."[20] Yet these "problems" have received little scholarly interrogation despite indicating a significant crisis in Augustine's understanding of Christian formation. For in what sense can Christians be said to mature if the *telos* of their growth in this life is a return to (and perhaps stasis within) the infantile milk diet on which their formation began?

Last, the broader metaphor of motherhood has become an important site for feminist intervention into Augustine's thought. Scholars such as Margaret Miles, Marsha Dutton, and Felecia McDuffie have provided illuminating studies on the pervasive presence of maternity and breast-feeding throughout Augustine's body of work.[21] Employing quite different methodologies, they have each demonstrated the bishop's ambivalence toward "feminine" embodiment and its contribution to the process of formation. While Augustine disavows the maternal as ultimately (that is, eschatologically) unnecessary, he never fully abandons the symbolic power of breast-feeding as a basic mechanism for sussing out Christian identity in the here and now. Once again the persistent problem of formation—of moving from milk to solid food—is identified. But the broader implications of that problem remain.

In each of these thematic considerations—esotericism, humility, and maternity—the deeper significances of milk and solid food in Augustine have been explored. In each case, a host of unresolved interpretive issues emerge surrounding the relationship between food and formation. Does Augustine endorse a deeper, mystical doctrine accessible only to an elite few? Can Christians, in his view, make progress to the solid food of maturity while remaining imitators of Christ's humility? And just how do

Augustine's references to maternity in general and breast-feeding specifically ground his developing understanding of Christian identity?

It is my contention that the picture remains piecemeal and incomplete. To see the full force of how the trope of milk and solid food functioned for Augustine, we must attend to its shifting strategic uses across a wider range of sources and periods of the bishop's life. Rather than analyzing these and other themes produced by his appeals to milk and solid food, I propose that we approach it the other way around. By focusing our attention specifically on the trope itself and how Augustine puts it to work in quite disparate ways over his career, my wager is that a widening rupture becomes evident. This is not just a rupture in how Augustine comes to view formation in the Christian life; it also reveals, as a result, a rupture in the entire discourse of formation we have been exploring.

The sections to come analyze how Augustine's approach to milk and solid food shifted according to these and other concerns. I begin first with his writings from 386 to 395 in order to demonstrate his early optimism about growth from milk to solid food, tinged as it is by lingering concerns about food from his Manichaean days. I then turn to the *Confessions* (ca. 396) and situate his reflections on the role of nurture and breast-feeding in his own formation. Lastly, I offer a reading of Augustine's later exegetical work (from the early 400s) in order to unpack his mature use of the trope of milk and solid food.

A word is necessary about dividing Augustine's literary output into these periods. Scholars have long noted the distinct change in Augustine's understanding of the Christian life before and after 396—often situating *Ad Simplicianum* as the boundary marker indicating his radical emphasis on grace and "the fall" that would occupy him for the rest of his life. I am by no means the first to perceive a rupture in Augustine's thinking when viewed over the full scope of his career. In a chapter titled "The Lost Future" from his landmark study of Augustine, Peter Brown popularized the notion of Augustine reaching an epistemic tipping point from which he never returns.[22] More recently, Carol Harrison has cautioned against overly dramatic renderings of the break between Augustine's earlier and later writings, which fail to recognize strong elements of continuity between them.[23] I have attempted to heed Harrison's warning in the pages that follow while still demonstrating the remarkable shift in tone, vocabulary, and conceptual orientation within Augustine's appeals to the symbolic power of nourishment and the progress from milk to solid food. As Augustine came to identify Christ as both milk and solid food, the value of human models of authority for instruction or for imitation—indeed the value of education as it had been conventionally and classically construed—declined precipitously for him. As a result, so too did the value of progressing from faith to understanding, from ₊ilk to solid food.

Reason, Authority, and the Growth of the Soul in Augustine's Early Writings

One of the crucial themes within Augustine's earliest writings, as Catherine Conybeare has helpfully illustrated, is the notion that a commitment to Christianity involves a decentering of reason as the defining pursuit of one's life.[24] The Cassiciacum dialogues are the earliest of Augustine's writings that have survived and were written while he was on a monthlong retreat with his mother, Monica, and a group of friends in the autumn of 386. The retreat to Cassiciacum followed Augustine's "conversion" in Milan and preceded his baptism. They mark a crucial pivot in Augustine's life, as he broke from the path of classical *paideia* on which he had been set. Conybeare observes how these early writings "serve as the forum in which [Augustine] works through intellectually the consequences of conversion."[25] This limiting of reason's power was one such consequence. In the education of Christians, reason is chastened by authority and, unlike in classical education, authority is not found in the teacher but rather is found in Christ alone.[26] It is telling, then, that although Augustine himself leads the Cassiciacum dialogues, he recuses himself from the role of the *dux*. He is reluctant to identify himself as a teaching authority.

Augustine's refusal to become a *magister* in the dialogues is complicated by the fact that these writings, taken on the whole, are a systematic attempt to reconsider the classical liberal-arts curriculum—a curriculum that was historically anchored by the authority of one's teacher.[27] It is possible, as Frederick van Fleteren has argued, that the irresolvable tension between authority and reason in Augustine's thought may be symptomatic of his time among the Manichaeans. The teachings of the Cassiciacum dialogues indicate an ongoing rectification and reversal of his Manichaean experience: "[N]ow Augustine asks for the acceptance of authority before an attempt at rational understanding."[28] In response to Manichaean *ratio,* Augustine asserts that authority takes temporal precedence because the Christian is formed primarily through humility, obedience to ecclesial teaching, and not through independent reasoning.

In a text from the same period that is aimed at refuting the Manichaeans, Augustine elaborates on this point through the language of nourishment. In *On the Catholic Way of Life* (387), Augustine points out the foolishness of the Manichaeans who go against the proper order of formation (*contra ordinem*) by thinking that reason can precede authority.[29] The authority of the church is presented as the prerequisite for any future growth. Yet, in this nascent phase of Augustine's thinking, he displays a marked optimism about the potential for progress from authority to rational understanding in this life: "And so, those whom the breasts of the catholic church sustain like wailing infants, if they are not pulled away by heretics, are nourished, each according to their own comprehension and strength, and are guided, one in this way, another in that. Thus, they arrive first at perfect manhood, then maturity and the old age of wisdom, so that to the extent that they are willing, they may live—and live most happily."[30] At this point, Augustine appeals to the symbolic power of infant nourishment in order to describe a process of Christian formation suited to all members of the Christian community and capable of leading each person toward a "perfect manhood" (*virum perfectum*). Here, Augustine's account of food and formation closely follows that of Roman family values. Nourishment properly received within the church promotes growth toward rational understanding, perfection, and beatitude.

This developmental scheme—in which the milk of the church guides the formation of her infants and allows for their maturation—reflects an abiding hope on the part of Augustine in the potential for growth from dependence on authority to independent reason. The church, in this sense, has taken over the role of the "good Roman mother" who carefully nurtures and nourishes her children. And just as the milk of the Roman mother was thought of as crucial to the proper formation of the child, so too does the milk of the church—its teaching authority—occupy a central role in the formation of the Christians under its care.[31] Even in his earliest writing, we can perceive in Augustine elements of the bio-power explored earlier. From the start, the maternal characteristic of breast milk is put to work at the service of the ecclesial institution. By foregrounding the symbol of milk, Augustine is here able to account for the fact of differing intellectual capacities among Christians while nevertheless maintaining the possibility that all Christians might grow from milk to solid food if they only learn to eat well.

The milk of the church is prescribed as an antidote to miseducation, a corrective to the overinflated *ratio* of the Manichaeans.[32] Milk and solid food thus indicate a Christian curriculum suited to the widest range of students, enabling each one's progress toward the *virum perfectum*. Augustine develops this notion further in his dialogue *On the Greatness of the Soul* (387–388 C E), where he considers "the greatness of the soul, not in terms of its spatial or temporal expanse, but rather its strength and capacity."[33] At one point, Augustine offers an explanation of the seven levels of the soul's greatness. These levels, like rungs of a ladder, lead the Christian from a corporeal to an incorporeal existence, from carnal life to spiritual vision, and from milk to solid food.[34] Reason is displaced by the capacity to digest the food of the church.

The seventh and final level of the soul's greatness is less like a stage (*gradus*) than a dwelling place (*mansio*) of perfect rest.[35] Here again, the trope of milk and solid food is employed to illuminate proper Christian formation: "Only then [that is, in the final stage] will we realize how true are the things we have been commanded to believe, and how we have been nourished to perfect wholeness by mother church through the milk [*saluberrime apud matrem ecclesiam nutriti fuerimus*]—which the apostle Paul spoke of as the potent drink he gave to little ones. To receive such a food when nourished by a mother is perfect wholeness [*quod alimentum accipere cum quis matre nutritur, saluberrimum*]. To receive it when one is already grown is shameful."[36]

Here, the potent milk of "mother church" is a catalyst for the growth of the soul through its seven stages. But upon reaching the seventh stage, the soul's increased capacity makes milk nourishment an inappropriate fare. It has outgrown the need for milk. But whether the seventh stage is temporally possible or only available in some eschatological future remains unclear. Augustine does not specify, but given his optimism that perfection and solid food can be attained temporally in other work from this period, it seems possible that he maintained a similar view here as well.

Augustine returns to the question of intellectual progress in *On True Religion* (390), where he offers a more complex theory of Christian growth. There, he contrasts the five stages of formation found in natural development and learning (*nascentis natura et eruditio*) to the seven stages of formation found in spiritual ages (*spiritales aetates*)—the former apportioned to the "old man" of Ephesians 4:22–24, the latter to the "new man." According to Augustine, the stages of natural growth proceed from infancy (*infantia:* devoted entirely to bodily nourishment), to childhood (*pueritia:* in which memories are first formed), adolescence (*adolescentia:* when fatherhood and the reproduction of offspring is possible), youth (*iuventus:* the age in which public office is held), and finally "the peace of old age" (*pax senioris:* which Augustine rather grimly associates with infirmity and death).[37]

The spiritual ages, by contrast, proceed as follows: first, in our infancy, the "useful breasts of history nourish with examples."[38] Second, human affairs are forgotten in favor of divine things and the bosom of human authority is abandoned for the unchangeable laws of reason.[39] Third, the strength of reason (*rationis robore*) begins to replace fleshly desires (*carnalem appetitum*).[40] Fourth, this *ratio* is put into action and the "perfect man (*virum perfectum*)" emerges, capable of enduring all the hardships of the world.[41] In the fifth, peace and tranquility are found by living in the midst of unspeakable wisdom. By the sixth spiritual age, the temporal world passes away and life reaches its "perfect form in the image and likeness of God (*perfecta forma, quae facta est ad imaginem et similitudinem dei*)."[42] The final age is marked by perpetual happiness.[43]

In the second stage of spiritual formation, human authority is quickly cast aside and milk is no longer required. As in *On the Catholic Way of Life,*

in *On True Religion* Augustine presents the *virum perfectum* as an achiev-
able goal within the temporal process of Christian growth. This is not without qualification, however, and in the following chapter he seems to suggest
that such "perfect men" have historically been a rare class of people:

> If any earthly person at any time had the merit of reaching illumi-
> nation of the inward man, he offered assistance, in the manner
> suitable to his age, relating through prophecy whatever was not
> required for clear presentation. Just as the patriarchs and proph-
> ets discovered from them, who did not behave as children, but
> piously and diligently handled the good and great secret of
> divine and human things. In our own times, I see that this has
> been handled with utmost care by great and spiritual men of the
> catholic church for its nurslings. They do not speak in common
> language what is not yet appropriate for the time, so that when
> speeches are given the multitudes understand. They urgently
> pour out a plentiful nourishment of milk to the eager masses.
> Those few who are stronger in wisdom are fed on solid food.
> [The spiritual men] speak wisdom among the perfect, but to the
> carnal and psychic (though they are considered "new men"),
> some things are concealed because these ones are still children.[44]

While no one is excluded from the growth that leads from milk to solid food,
On True Religion depicts a tiered Christian community, divided between the
"wise and spiritual men of the catholic church" (*mages et spiritales viri ecclesiae catholicae*) and the "nurslings" (*alumni*). This is a system in which only
a select few advance. The spiritual men are identified as those who assist in
suckling the infants beneath them. The distinction between the two categories is firm but not intractable, suggesting a loose commitment on the part of
Augustine to the existence of esoteric knowledge—of a special solid food—
within the church. In this passage the existence of a *virum perfectum* reflects
Augustine's shifting awareness of the intellectual gap between those called to
serve the *domus Dei* and those simply seeking sustenance under its roof.[45]

To be sure, Augustine's use of nourishment language in this earlier phase of his writing is highly figurative. While the symbol of milk is widely employed and elaborately developed, there does not seem to be much contact with "actual eating." However, it must be kept in mind that this period of Augustine's life is closest in proximity to his time among the Manichaeans. As an auditor among this group, Augustine would have been acquainted with their alimentary rites and, as his own writing regularly attests, would also have been familiar with the rationales behind them.[46] Elizabeth Clark perceptively noted thirty years ago how "there were remnants in Augustine's work that still breathed his Manichaean past."[47] More recently, it has been argued that Augustine's familiarity with Manichaeism was "astonishingly intimate."[48] And so it seems likely that the persistence with which Augustine returns to food as a site of theological reflection—and the notable emphasis on spiritual food over and against actual eating—reveals that he never fully exorcised the ghost of Manichaean meal rites as his default frame of reference on the matter.

Augustine admits in the *Confessions* that, during his Manichaean time, he believed God was contained within the food eaten during their rituals.[49] Jason BeDuhn helpfully explains this crucial aspect of Augustine's background:

> With its place as the daily centerpiece of Manichaean life, the sights, sounds, acts, and ideology of the ritual meal permeated Manichaean identity. Augustine appears to play off the rhetoric of the ritual meal with a bit of self-conscious irony in the part of the *Confessions* where he relates his experiences as a Manichaean. The entire section is riddled with gustatory imagery and word-play. Augustine refers again and again to his hunger and thirst for God, and to the teachings "served up" by the Manichaeans as "dishes" that failed to satisfy. Although as an auditor Augustine could not eat of the actual ritual offerings, he uses the setting of the meal as a rhetorical trope for his "gulping down" of the Manichaean teachings.[50]

For the Manichaeans, the consumption and metabolizing of material food was the process in which the body refines matter into its purest, spiritual parts. This ritualized digestion is the "one inescapable contact between the human body and the divine substance diffused in the world."[51] The stuff of food contains within its physical material a deeper spiritual deposit. As Augustine encountered these alimentary rites firsthand, food and the spectacle of its ritualized consumption would have become fodder for thinking about the interplay between nourishment, growth, and the communion between God and humanity in created matter.

Even as an auditor excluded from the ritual table of the Manichaean elect, Augustine was no doubt intimately aware of this characteristic practice. Indeed, in a certain sense, his struggles with the categories of milk/ solid food and infant/perfect throughout his career are likely symptoms of the Manichaean specter that loomed over his thinking long after he had abandoned their teaching. It is hard to imagine that, as Augustine approached Paul's categories, he did not also hear echoes of these dietary practices and gastronomic regimes—inflected as they were through complex medical and physiological theories—as well as the stark distinction between hearers and elect that were fundamental to his Manichaean indoctrination. As we will see, although Augustine does indicate a connection between the symbolic nourishment of milk and the ritual practice of Eucharistic eating in later writing, such connections were strongly colored by the perceived danger of conflating more "orthodox" meal practices with that of the Manichaeans.

This dynamic is readily apparent in the *Confessions*—a text so brimming with food imagery that the reader is hard-pressed to view Augustine's enduring interest in the power of nourishment as anything but an extended reaction to his time among the Manichaeans. Book 3, especially, reveals the tension between competing foods: on the one hand, he laments the outward, material nourishment fed to him in the sumptuous feasts held by the Manichaeans of his youth. On the other, he praises the inward, spiritual food that God had unceasingly prepared for him. The section opens with his sense of regret at having starved himself of God's "inward food" because he was "lacking desire for incorruptible nourishment."[52] His failure to eat this inner food resulted only in malnourishment and nausea. His starved condition, we are told, was exacerbated by the outward food given to him by the Manichaeans, which was nothing but a dazzling illusion. Their meals were merely the unsatisfying stuff of fever dreams, a diet that left him not sated but panged by exhaustion.[53]

And so even in both the early writings and in the *Confessions,* we witness a crucial reversal. Outer, material foods are impotent and empty, while inner, spiritual foods are wholesome and filling. If it seems that his references to food become exceedingly symbolic, stretching so far into the figural as to raise doubts about whether a connection to actual food and feeding can be sustained, we must bear in mind that he has come to view spiritual nourishment itself as our only real food in this life. From this vantage, the significance of outward, material foods appears tainted by his exposure to Manichaean meal rites. Where once he sought God's presence buried deep in the foods on the Manichaean menu, now he seeks sustenance only through immaterial nourishment. In comparison to all the sources previously examined, the Manichaeans alone took the theological significance of human gastronomy to its literal limits. But even as Augustine distanced himself from the group in later life, that theological significance remained for him. And so, even in his reversal of inner and outer nourishment, the Manichaeans continued to exercise his thinking about the role of food in forming Christian identity. This reversal helps make sense of Augustine's increasing emphasis on milk as the true food of the Christian life from the *Confessions* onward, to which we now turn.

Human Milk and the Milk of Christ in the *Confessions* and *On Christian Teaching*

In the *Confessions,* Augustine recounts the prominent role that infant food (*alimentum infantiae*) played in his own formation. In an early passage, he explains how he encountered God's comforting compassion in the "consolations of human milk" (*consolationes lactis humani*).[54] Breast milk is, for Augustine, the first evidence of God's providence. But Augustine clarifies that neither his mother nor his nurses were the original source of milk's nourishing and comforting power. It is God alone who gives food to infants through the "arrangement and riches that are appointed throughout the natural order."[55] Thus, the maternal body is figured as a conduit for the outpouring of God's grace—a subtle theological point that has large implications for how Augustine will refer to the milk of the church elsewhere. By making God the source of all breast milk, Augustine neutralizes (or at least sidesteps) the issue of wet-nursing and the risk of ingesting a woman's deficient characteristics. The firm faith and character that is passed to him through his mother's milk is supplemented, not degraded, by the comfort and nurture he received from God through his *nutrices*.[56]

Similar to his contemporary Macrobius, Augustine suggests that mother's milk nourishes the inward nature of the infant, transferring a powerful essence into the child. For Augustine, the essence within Monica's breast milk was the name of Christ: "By your mercy, Lord, my infant heart had piously drunk in the name of my savior, your son, with my mother's milk and retained it deep within."[57] The maternal food, for Augustine, was not simply a palpable presence of God's care. It was also the material form through which faith in Christ was transferred from adult to child. It is, in a sense, the physical implanting of that inward and spiritual food from which God feeds the soul throughout life. In Monica's milk, the name of Christ took up residence deep within Augustine's nature so that no other knowledge, no literature or wisdom, could captivate him unless it mentioned Christ.[58] So powerful was his infant food that the adult Augustine exclaims to God, "[W]hen all is well with me, what am I doing other than sucking your milk and taking pleasure in you (*fruens te*), food that is incorruptible?"[59] Students of Augustine know that the bishop only uses the verb *frui* restrictively in reference to God, given its erotic connotations. But here those resonances become all the more jarring given that it was only a few short passages prior that Augustine had been describing the Christ-carrying milk derived from his mother's consoling body.[60]

Crucially, in book 7 Augustine refers to the prologue of John's Gospel as a solid food (*cibus*) that he was unable to consume due to his own human frailty.[61] This frailty is equated to infancy (*infantia*): Augustine could not consume the solid food of God's eternal wisdom, and thus required the milky diet of humble faith.[62] Those unable to speak are not yet mature enough to consume the solid food of the Word. They must be fed, nurtured, and molded by the words and by the example of the more advanced. The progress of the Christian pilgrim is, in fact, a regression to infancy and to the pleasure of sucking God's milk. Gone is the stage-by-stage growth outlined in his earlier writings. In the *Confessions,* Christian formation occurs by retreating from an adulthood besieged by unrestrained desires and arrogant claims of wisdom toward a mute infancy of perfect obedience and humility.[63]

Augustine recognizes that the infancy of obedience raises the problem of human authority once again. Under whose nurturing care is the Christian infant placed? Whose milk does he drink? For even within the maternal arms of mother church there must nevertheless be models for the infants to imitate, "breasts" from which they might be fed within the Christian community. Early in the *Confessions,* Augustine asks, "Who can teach me [*Qui doceat me*]?"[64] The question is implicit throughout the narrative of his own education. It is a rot eating at the core of his waning commitment to the traditional structures of intellectual formation. In comparison to the milky instruction drawn from his mother's body, Augustine finds only dissatisfaction and disappointment in every teacher he encounters. His intellectual development was simply a long sequence of encounters with bad pedagogical examples: be it the hypocritical fervor for entertainment among parents and teachers (*Conf.* 1.9.15); the libidinous posturing and bro-ish one-upmanship among his adolescent peers (2.3.7, 2.9.17); the unrestrained passions of actors who co-opt the audience's emotions and incite an unhealthy love of misery (3.2.4); the dizzying desire for approval evoked by the esteemed orator Hierius (4.14.21–23); the disappointing ignorance of Faustus, the Manichaean master (5.6.11–7.12); or even the unapproachable demeanor of the Milanese bishop Ambrose, which frustrated Augustine's desperate need for spiritual counsel (6.3.3).

Of course, Augustine never declares that Ambrose was a bad teacher. But the reader of the *Confessions* can't help but sense in Augustine a restrained disenchantment directed toward his ecclesial mentor. Augustine, the anxious and eager pupil, finds Ambrose to be largely inaccessible, even aloof to the needs of those in his care—or, at least aloof toward Augustine specifically. At the same time, Augustine refers to some in Ambrose's circle as being *sub Ambrosio nutritore*—"under Ambrose the nourisher," or, more emphatically, "breastfed by Ambrose" (*Conf.* 8.6.14). Augustine, it seems, was never among those considered *sub Ambrosio nutritore*. Indeed, despite his extensive education, the only person whom Augustine spent significant time with *sub nutritore* was his mother, Monica. After a life of searching for other sources of formative nourishment, Augustine (perhaps begrudgingly?) returns to the infantile state whence he had first been fed the name of Christ. It is little wonder, then, that from his disenchantment with the master-disciple model so central to classical education, Augustine developed an abiding suspicion about the value of imitating living examples—especially one's teacher—and the central role of imitation in human transformation.[65]

This disillusionment with living teachers clarifies why, in recounting the events of his garden conversion, Augustine turns to the instructive words of Simplicianus and Ponticianus. In both cases, the counsel he receives deflects his attention away from the one speaking—that is, away from the living, breathing, embodied person sitting next to him. He is given instead words about Antony, a man no longer living, whose virtue is now rendered as a still life—as if, in death, the monk's life had frozen in place, like a tableau depicting how the scriptural words about Christ and his apostles ought to be put into action. The instructional value of Christian *exempla* such as Antony, then, is that through the still life of their virtue, the reader is inevitably led back to the words of scripture, placing themselves within that story.

The authority of the *exempla* in Augustine's curriculum is a misdirection: we think we are looking at a teacher only to find that the teacher has vanished behind the words of scripture. The question that nagged Augustine—"*Qui doceat me?*"—is abandoned in book 8 of the *Confessions,* where Lady Continence beckons Augustine with an outstretched hand filled with good examples, none of whom are named or described in detail. It seems that the only good examples for the Christian life are dead ones. For only the dead can be trusted to remain unwavering in virtue and unsullied by the inconstancy of the flesh. Their lives have been rendered into words and, as such, can be affixed to the words of scripture.

It is telling, then, that the phrase "a living example" (*exemplum vivendi*) is restrictively used in Augustine's *On Christian Teaching* in reference to scripture's words about Christ.[66] As Mark Jordan has observed, both *On Christian Teaching* and the *Confessions* follow an inverted incarnational logic that moves the reader from flesh to words.[67] He notes:

> You put on Jesus when you read Paul rightly. Right reading is your incarnation. . . . In the garden, Augustine turns from the page, he assures us, because he becomes it, passes through its signs to the thing it teaches. He is able to do this only after an arduous education affixes his reader's desire to the bodiless figure of Continence. Having chosen her, he can at last put on a verse about the body of Jesus. Writing *Confessions,* Augustine tries both to recapitulate and to enact that education for his readers. You came expecting to hear the scandalous past of this unlikely bishop? You'll get no pornography here. You want a miraculous appearance by Jesus at the moment of his conversion? No theophany either. *Confessions* elicits readers' desires, attracts them to itself, only to step out of the way in favor of the scriptures—but the scriptures as plain letter. You will see only examples. You will touch only the stylus.[68]

This crucial bait and switch is how the *Confessions,* despite its pervasively self-referential content, only teases at presenting its author as an exemplary model worthy of imitation.[69] The quality Augustine most wants to emphasize throughout the text—his humility—is achieved primarily by obscuring himself behind the words of scripture. Unlike the untrustworthy words of flesh-and-blood teachers, the instruction of the Word made text never changes. Its nourishment does not fail to satisfy.

In contrast to the tentative optimism of his earlier writings, in the *Confessions* and *On Christian Teaching* Augustine views all models of formation that depend on the mimetic play between student and teacher as unstable, misleading, and deforming. The pedagogical process of dialogue has been abandoned for the security of the divinely written word.[70] Thus in *On Christian Teaching*, literacy is presented as a critical skill for Christians because it enables access to the instruction of scripture's words. Crucially, Augustine develops this point in reference to Isaiah 7:9—a text he employs regularly in order to distinguish temporal faith from eschatological under-standing: "[In] one version it is translated, 'Unless you believe, you will not understand.' Another interpretation is, 'Unless you believe, you will not en-dure.' Unless one reads the original languages, it is unclear which of these words should follow. But to those skilled in reading, both versions suggest something powerful. . . . Therefore, since understanding is vision of eternal life, we are nourished on milk while we are infants in the cradle of this tem-poral life [*fides vero in rerum temporalium quibusdam cunabulis quasi lacte alit parvulos*]. For now we walk by means of faith, not by means of sight."[71]

Temporal faith, the product of right reading, is a milky and provi-sional nourishment that sustains Christians in the meantime, while they await the perfect understanding of the life to come. And so, at the precise moment when Augustine turns away from living models toward textual ones in the *Confessions*, he hears God say to him, "I am the food of the fully grown, grow and you will feed on me" (*Cibus sum grandium; cresce et man-ducabis me*).[72] The eternal wisdom of God, as solid food, comes to all Chris-tians through the flesh of the incarnate Word. But that Word is accessible, in the meantime, only through the milk of scripture's words. In the "cradle of this life," milk remains the surest form of sustenance for those who walk by faith and not by sight.

From Monica's breast, the name of Christ was planted deep within Augustine so that no other teacher, no other school of thought, not even the ornate menus and rationales of Manichaean feasts could slake his thirst for knowledge. The simple pedagogy of his mother's milk surpassed the com-plex wisdom of all the sages he encountered. In *On the Teacher*, Augustine had already established that the instruction of the "inner teacher" (that is, Christ), residing within the soul of each person, supplants all living teachers. This inner teacher, it seems, had entered the infant Augustine's soul through Monica's milk, becoming also his inner food. From his disappointment over the unsatisfying nourishment of living teachers, Augustine abandons his tiered model of spiritual progress from the earlier writings, preferring instead a return to the cradle of infancy and the Christ-bearing milk of his mother as all the instruction, all the food he ever needed. From Monica's actual milk, Augustine derived a powerful symbol for Christian pedagogy that would continue to shape his thought on the formation of the soul.

Given his suspicion about living models, it is not surprising that Augustine never refers to himself as breast-feeding the Christian "infants" in his care. Nevertheless, this did not stop his admirers from attributing to Augustine the same nourishing power that he attributed to his mother, to his nurses, and to God. Paulinus of Nola opens a letter admonishing his recipient to "hear the law of your father . . . and not reject the counsel of your mother." He was referring to Augustine, who was the source of the recipient's "first milk" and who, according to Paulinus, remained "eager to nurse and nourish [the recipient] with spiritual breasts."[73] Likewise, in a letter directed to Augustine, Severus rather vividly describes how he draws nourishment from the bishop of Hippo: "Attaching myself to you and receiving your overflowing breasts, I gather as much strength as I am able so that I might press and squeeze them. Thus, whatever is held in secret and inaccessible to me, as hidden by flesh, let those breasts pour out your innermost thoughts to me, the one sucking your milk."[74] Despite all his cautioning to the contrary, it seems that even Augustine's closest colleagues could not help but view him as a living model of maternal fecundity. In their description, he is figured as a kind of "Monica" from whose breasts they might draw in the mysteries of Christ, the inward food, and store it deep within their soul for continued sustenance.

Infancy Without Weaning in Augustine's Later Writing

From the tutelage of the Christ-carrying milk he derived from his mother and nurses to the disappointing meals—both literal and figurative—he received from the teachers of his youth, Augustine's later writing as both exegete and preacher further develops his emphasis on the Christian community as composed primarily of infants in need of milk. Here, Augustine's suspicion about the efficacy of living models deepens. At the same time, there is an increasing awareness that, for the vast majority of Christians, instruction will come not through their own literacy but rather through listening to sermons. In this phase, then, Augustine's use of milk and solid food indicates a pervasive reluctance to grant progress from milk to solid food as a general paradigm for the Christian community. Suggestive links between the Eucharistic meal and the Pauline category of milk indicate that, for him, the priests and bishops are the incarnate form of the church's breast—feeding the masses on the milk of Christ's body and blood. But crucially, in this period Augustine also begins to view the very notion of weaning as a practice primarily associated with heretics who grasp too quickly at solid food while they are still in need of milk.

SUCKLING ON THE MILK OF SALVATION: INFANTS, PROGRESS, AND THE SACRAMENTS

An example of Augustine's reluctance about being weaned from milk to solid food can be found in homily 7 of his *Homilies on the Gospel of John.* What begins as a meditation on Jacob's ladder (Genesis 28) becomes an extended discussion of "good preachers" (*boni praedicatores*).[75] Following the example of the apostle Paul, who both ascended the ladder (in being "carried off to the third heaven," 2 Corinthians 12) and descended the ladder (in giving milk to infants, 1 Corinthians 3), the good preacher is like a mother or a nurse who provides milk to little ones no matter how far they have progressed.[76] Paul is thus the archetype for the good preacher, whose work consists primarily in descending the ladder to breast-feed others rather than in ascending on his own journey. This interpretation builds upon the depiction of clergy as the ones who most commonly achieve perfect manhood in *On True Religion* (28.50). But here Augustine minimizes the intellectual ascent of Christian leaders in favor of the nurturing care they provide the masses.

It would seem that Augustine is suggesting—as in his earlier works— that some Christians have access to hidden, mystical wisdom not available

to the broader Christian community. Yet, in homilies 96–98 on the Gospel
of John, in which Augustine interprets John 16:12–13 ("I still have many
things to say to you, but you cannot bear them now"), he evokes the milk
and solid-food motif in an explicit attempt to undermine Christian esotericism.[77] In homily 96, Augustine admits that there are some within the
church who can understand the things that Christ withheld from the disci-
ples.[78] These things, he conjectures, include grasping the prologue of John
and the mystery of the Trinity it contains.[79] The following homily explicitly
connects the "many things" Christ withheld to the solid food of 1 Corinthians 3:1–3. Yet Augustine's tone is less descriptive than cautionary. Here, he
is more concerned with warning his audience against the poisoned solid
food of "wicked teachers" (*nefarii doctores*) than he is with providing a
blueprint for proper growth from milk to solid food.[80] The implication of
Augustine's admonition is that many (perhaps most) of those who proclaim
access to the solid food of understanding will only lead the infants of the
church to ruin.[81]

Milk and solid food are most prevalent in homily 98. There, Augustine pairs understanding and belief to the symbols of milk and solid food,
suggesting that the "spiritual" consume solid food through their understanding while the "carnal" must drink the milk of belief.[82] However,
Augustine curiously includes a reference to Hebrews 5:12–14 in order to
better distinguish the milk-drinking *parvuli* from the "perfect"—an exegetical move that is not common within his other writings that appeal to the
symbol of nourishment.[83] This is one of the rare occasions in his later writings in which "spiritual," "perfect," and "solid-food-eating" Christians are
specifically accounted for in descriptions of the Christian community.[84]
Nonetheless, Augustine does not use this verse to provide a more robust
account of progress toward perfection but rather speaks directly about the
parvuli: "[T]hey should neither be breastfed [*lactandi sunt*] in such a way
that they never understand Christ as Creator, nor should they be weaned
[*ablactandi*] in such a way that they ever abandon Christ as Mediator." The
idea of weaning is here associated with the temptations of independent reason, a risk closely associated with those who seduce infant Christians with
the lure of deeper truths and the promise of spiritual perfection.[85]

Augustine's growing concern for the infants is further elaborated in a provocative connection to the nourishment of the sacraments in the *Homilies on the First Epistle of John* (ca. 407). Interpreting 1 John 2:18 ("Children, it is the last hour"), Augustine concludes that the passage is exhorting all Christian children (*pueri*) to "grow up with haste" (*festinent crescere*).[86] The passage is an extended exhortation for his audience "to make progress" (*proficere*) in the growth of their souls. This raises, for Augustine, a question about why Christians are called *pueri* at all:

> Whoever has been born should know that he is a child and an infant. Let his mouth gape hungrily toward the breast of his mother and he will soon grow. Now his mother is the church and her breasts are the two testaments of divine scriptures. From this source the milk of all the temporal sacraments is sucked for the sake of our eternal salvation, so that in being breastfed and physically strengthened he might arrive at the solid food that is eaten—namely, "In the beginning was the Word, and the Word was with God, and the Word was God." Our milk is the humility of Christ. Our solid food is the same Christ, equal to the Father. He breastfeeds you with milk and he nourishes you with bread.[87]

The interweaving of highly symbolic language about the growth of the soul with direct references to the physical act of sacramental eating demonstrates the slippage in register so common in early Christian discussions of food and the formation. Augustine claims here that all who are born are, by nature, infants. Therefore, they ought to behave like infants by gaping their mouths toward the breasts of the church, sucking on its sacraments. The breasts of the church, described as the two testaments, flow with the milk of the Eucharistic elements. Those who nurse receive a foretaste of eternal salvation and grow, in due time, toward the solid food of deeper understanding.

In these passages, we can see Augustine struggling to navigate around the question of esoteric knowledge within the Christian community. He seems keenly aware that the notion of being weaned from milk raises tricky questions about categorical distinctions between infants and adults. Similar to Gregory of Nyssa, Augustine tries to identify the fully grown or the "perfect" primarily by the milk nourishment they offer to the others. Unlike the Cappadocian, Augustine avoids describing in detail any deeper mystical insights accessed by those who have made progress, much less the instructional routes by which they have progressed. And so, while Gregory associates breast-feeding with those individuals (himself, Macrina, Olympias) who had already undergone for themselves a mystagogical transformation, having been weaned at the breast of the bridegroom, Augustine transfers the work of nurturance almost entirely onto the abstracted institutional body of the church. This move is reinforced by an explicit reference to preaching, scripture, and the sacraments as the breasts from which infants receive milk. Unlike the Manichaean food rites that reify the division between elect and hearer, communicating divine truth to the former but never the latter, Augustine reimagines his liturgy as a form of nourishing breast milk suitable for all. Whatever optimism about growth he expresses here is subordinate to his insistence on nursing as the primary activity of the church. Turning toward his *Expositions of the Psalms,* we see that Augustine's interest in prolonging the phase of infancy only intensifies.

PERPETUAL INFANCY AND DEFERRED FORMATION
IN THE *EXPOSITIONS OF THE PSALMS*

Throughout the *Expositions of the Psalms,* Augustine regularly returns to his concern for protecting infantile Christians.[88] In the "Exposition of Psalm 8," an earlier commentary dated to the first period of his literary output examined previously, Augustine connects the psalm in question to Matthew 21:16 ("Out of the mouths of infants and nurslings you have perfected your praise").[89] This passage offers Augustine an opportunity to explore the distinction between Christians who are milk-drinking infants (*parvuli in lacte*) and those who are solid-food-eating youths (*iuvenes in cibo*).[90] The *parvuli,* Augustine explains, are those who follow closely behind Christ. Nonetheless, "there are some within the Church who no longer drink milk but eat solid food instead."[91] The observation seems almost perfunctory—necessitated by the apostle Paul's description of the "perfect" (*perfecti*) with whom he spoke wisdom (mentioned in 1 Cor. 2:6). Augustine adopts Paul's language of the perfect here, curiously applying to it the term "youth" (*iuvenes*), and also seems to address the infants with optimism about their potential for growing into maturity.[92] This orientation is consistent with the dating of this particular exposition to the earlier period of the bishop's literary output. And we can perceive in it traces of the same progressive, stage-by-stage paradigm of Christian formation that is found there.

Nevertheless, even here Augustine is ambivalent toward those who are deemed "perfect" within the church: "But churches are not made perfect through these [that is, the *perfecti*] alone. For, if it were only through them, then there would be no attention to the human race. Yet there is attention given to those who, although lacking the capacity to understand spiritual and eternal things, are breastfed by means of faith in temporal history."[93] The perfection of the church is not identified restrictively with the *perfecti*—but also includes those who have been suckled on faith, through their participation in the sacraments, and thus have recognized the authority of Christ.

This connection between perfection and the process of weaning noticeably fades in the later expositions—a shift made evident in a series of homilies on Psalm 30. Glossing a verse in which the psalmist prays, "you will be my leader and you will nourish me" (*tuum dux mihi eris, et enutries me*), Augustine explains how the "*et enutries me*" indicates the "motherly mercy" of God, who gives us food in a form fitted to our capacity. Since human weakness lacked the capacity to consume the food of heaven (*caelestem cibum*), the wisdom of God put on flesh and came in the palatable form of milk passing through the body of Christ.[94] For Augustine, the only suitable posture of the entire Christian community is that it perpetually prays to God, "you will nourish me."[95] Unlike in the "Exposition of Psalm 8," there is no consideration of those who have graduated from this infantile desire for the nurture of God. In the *Confessions,* Augustine had admitted to God that he is at his best only when he is but an infant suckling at the divine breast. Now, in his reading of Psalm 30, that prayer shapes his entire ecclesiology: the whole church is at its best when it prays to God, *et enutries me.*

In his next sermon on Psalm 30, Augustine turns his attention to the role of *exempla* in a church composed primarily of infants clamoring for God's milk. He observes that the enemies of the church (*inimici ecclesiae*) are neither pagans nor Jews but rather bad Christians (*mali Christiani*).[96] The church is teeming with bad examples.[97] Better to stay fixed to the institutional milk than reach for the solid food of a teacher. Augustine then anticipates a complaint from his congregation: With bad Christians lurking in every corner, who are the infants, these *parvuli in lacte,* supposed to emulate? Where are the *perfecti,* where are the *iuvenes in cibo* who are worthy of imitation?[98] Augustine tells his imagined interlocutors that they ought to "be done with imitation altogether" (*tolle imitationem hanc*). Those who rely on teachers as *exempla* will only be disappointed when their human models inevitably fail. Augustine continues, "If you are still stretching toward some man, and seeking to imitate him and to hang from him, then you are still wishing to be breastfed on milk. If so, you will become a *mammothreptus*—as children are called who suck at the breast a long time, which is bad for them. And, indeed, to enjoy milk to that extent is to want your solid food passed through the flesh of another. This is to live through another person. . . . Be made fit to eat at the table!"[99]

Having extolled the humble posture of milk-drinking at length, Augustine returns to the connection between breast-feeding and the master-disciple relationship of classical education. He argues that imitation of a living teacher is nothing but an absurdly protracted suckling that only harms the one being fed. Augustine's use of the uncommon word *mammothreptus* is significant here, as it indicates a child of questionable legitimacy who is overly attached to the breast of another and, as a result, is stunted in spiritual growth.[100] Human models of authority are frail and unreliable.[101] Their milk is weak and addictive, and lacks the power to form the soul properly. Only God can suckle a person on milk in such a way that he will be able to consume the solid food of the table.

By identifying all those who seek out the nourishment of living teachers as *mammothrepti,* Augustine has amplified the rhetorical force of his nourishment language. The legitimate children within the *domus Dei,* the best students of the *schola Christi,* are those who refuse to seek heartier food from other sources.[102] They do not grasp at solid food but are content with the saving milk of the church in front of them. In his "Exposition of Psalm 130," Augustine spends significant time considering verses 1–2: "O Lord, my heart is not lifted up, my eyes are not raised too high; I do not occupy myself with things too great and too marvelous for me. But I have calmed and quieted my soul, like a weaned child with its mother; my soul is like the weaned child that is with me."[103] Here again he anticipates a hypothetical complaint from his audience: "How am I to grow up on milk" (*Quomodo . . . cresco de lacte*)? In response, he argues that the infants of the church must simply believe that the milk they receive—namely, scripture's words about Christ—is of the same essence as the bread of angels. It is merely offered in a form more suited to their weak constitution.[104] Augustine seems to suggest that any person within earshot of the sermon belongs among those "not fit for strong food."

Indeed, as he continues, Augustine heightens his depiction of the church as a community of *parvuli in lacte* who should actively resist the temptation to grow up. He proceeds to offer two divergent readings of this passage, both of which are refracted through the trope of milk and solid food. In the first reading of the passage, he cautions that grasping for solid food before one is capable of eating it is a behavior typical of heretics:

> Therefore, our Lord Jesus Christ is bread, but made himself milk for us by taking on flesh and appearing as a mortal man so that in him death might be brought to an end. And believing in the flesh which the Word became, we would not stray from the Word. Let us grow from this place, being breastfed with this very milk. Until we are strong enough to grasp the Word, let us not withdraw from the milk of our faith. However, there are those heretics who desire to debate what they are not able to grasp. They say that the Son is less than the Father, and they say that the Holy Spirit is less than the Son. And they make divisions, hurling the notion of "three gods" into the church. For they cannot deny that the Father is God, nor can they deny that the Son is God and that the Holy Spirit is God. But if all three

are God they are unequal, not of the same substance, not one
God, but three gods. Therefore, disputing things which they
are not able to grasp, they puff themselves up with pride, and
become what the psalmist said: "If I was not humble in understanding, but exalted my own soul, as one in its mother's arms
who is snatched from its milk, so may I be repaid in my soul."
The mother is the church of God. These heretics have been
separated from her. They should have been breastfed and nourished there, so that they might grow up and grasp that the Word
is God with God, in the form of God and equal to the Father.[105]

In the arms of mother church and through her milk, the infant Christian is
inoculated against heretical speculations. Augustine offers the cautionary
injunction, "Let us not withdraw from the milk of our faith," as a prescription against the temptations of growth. This first reading views the movement from milk to solid food as an activity characteristic of those who are
not ready for it.[106]

Augustine then considers "another meaning, and another understanding of these words."[107] He does not identify the source of this second interpretation of the psalm. The most likely candidate is Hilary of Poitiers, who
advocates for a *via media* between humility and intellectual effort in his commentary on Psalm 130.[108] Hilary concludes, "to no longer require milk is the
greatest progress" for the Christian.[109] Whether or not he is directly refuting
Hilary, this is the basic argument presented by Augustine in the second reading: that failure to progress from milk to solid food indicates spiritual atrophy.

Further describing this second position, Augustine observes that
there are some who, upon hearing that they should be humble, "remain
fixed on the nourishment of milk alone."[110] Perhaps paraphrasing Hilary's
position, Augustine continues, "God wants us to be breastfed on milk, but
not to be stuck on that diet forever. But growing by means of milk, we will
come to eat solid food."[111] There is a clear progression of growth in this
model: "Suck milk and you will be nourished. Be nourished and you will
grow. Grow and you will eat bread. When you begin to eat bread, you will
be weaned—that is, you will not need milk anymore, but solid food."[112] By

this argument, Christians are to remain infants in wickedness, not infantile in intellect.[113] Growth from milk to solid food, honing the powers of one's own reason, is required for a healthy soul.

Augustine specifically rejects this second interpretation. He does not think the psalm is an exhortation toward progress from milk to solid food but rather, as with the first interpretation, takes the psalm to mean that only in being fed on the milk of the church can the soul be protected from false teachings and heretical teachers. Presuming for the moment that Augustine has Hilary's interpretation in mind, the difference between the two positions is revealed explicitly in their different citations of the psalm itself. Augustine's version reads, *Quemadmodum qui ablatus est a lacte super matrem suam, sic retributio in animam meam.* Hilary's, by contrast, is *Sicut ablactatum super matrem suam, ita retribues in animam meam.* Augustine's version uses the phrase *ablatus est a lacte* (is snatched from its milk) instead of the verb *ablactare* (to wean from milk) found in Hilary's version. The sense is changed dramatically with this alteration and heightens the force of Augustine's warnings about leaving the mother's arms too soon. As such, he reads the noun *retributio* as wholly negative (perhaps as "punishment"), while Hilary's version seems to view the verb *retribues* as wholly positive (perhaps as "reward"). This textual variance escalates Augustine's suspicion about Christians who are anxious for weaning and formation, and anchors those suspicions within the lexicon of the scriptural text as presented by him.

Unlike Hilary, Augustine views the weaning from milk to solid food as an indication that one has fallen away from proper faith. He is concerned that too many infant souls will be snatched from the saving milk of the church by some attractive new teaching or by some charismatic teacher who promises a deeper and more profound knowledge of God. The middle way between humility and exaltation is too precarious for most. The key to making sense of this psalm, for Augustine, is in the particularly negative rendering of the text that he has offered. It could rightly be translated, "as one in its mother's arms who is torn from its milk, so may I be punished in my soul."[114] Weaning, in this sense, is not a positive development but rather a falling away from the true faith—a departure from the saving milk of the mother. Those who are so snatched will face spiritual retribution.

Augustine then offers an elaborate defense of this kind of nondevelopmental view of infancy and breast-feeding. He observes a difference between infants and children, indicating that those within the church remain infantile in this life: "[I]nfants are not the ones who are weaned, but rather it is a child who is fairly well-grown. Moreover, because it is feeble, a nursling in early infancy—that is, real infancy—remains in its mother's arms. If it is torn from its milk, it dies."[115] The primary concern for Augustine here, as elsewhere, is the detrimental effect of being pulled from the breast. The *parvuli in lacte* that make up the Christian community must "find satisfaction in the command to be humble. . . . Let it believe in Christ, so that it may come to understand Christ. It is not able to see the Word, it is not able to grasp the equality of the Word with the Father or the equality of the Holy Spirit with the Father and the Word. Let it merely believe this, and let it suck its milk [*credat hoc, et sugat*]."[116]

The last line of that passage is a précis for Augustine's later thinking with regard to Christian formation, spiritual growth, and the progress from milk to solid food: *credat hoc, et sugat.* There is no need for striving and straining and grasping when all the food one could ever need is available in the milk of the church's liturgy. One can be nursed on the milk of preaching and the Eucharist, and derive spiritual benefit therein, without ever needing to contemplate the relationship between the Father, Son, and Spirit. True humility is becoming an infant at the breast, being content with that food alone, and never presuming to deserve a heartier meal until one can understand the nature of God face-to-face.

As he brings this commentary on Psalm 130 to a close, Augustine elaborates on the eschatological deferral of solid food: "You must not be separated from milk as long as you are in your mother's arms, or else you will starve to death before you are capable of eating bread. Grow up. Your strength will improve and you will see what you were not able to see and grasp what you were not able to grasp. What then? When I see what I am unable to see, and grasp what I am unable to grasp, will I be safe? Will I be perfect? No, not as long as you are in this life. Humility itself is our perfection. . . . So continue sucking milk, in order that you might grow toward solid food. When you arrive at your homeland, you will rejoice."[117]

Perfection, in this temporal life, is the embodiment of humility found among the *parvuli in lacte*. The "problem" of progress from milk to solid food, for Augustine, is one that can only be solved in the maturity and full vision of eternity. In the meantime, the Christian infant drinks the milk of faith as a prophylactic against bad teachers and false teachings, not as a means of attaining the solid food that is the knowledge of God. The saving nourishment of mother church is milk, but milk without growth—that is, a food that sustains souls but does not seem to transform.

Conclusion

And nourishment was seen as the central role of the mother.
—Brent Shaw, "The Family in Late Antiquity"

In a sermon delivered on Easter, probably after 409, Augustine offers a reading of John 1:1—a text that, as we have seen, he regularly associates with Paul's solid food. However, in this sermon Augustine is primarily interested in addressing the recently baptized *infantes* who would have been dressed in white and featured prominently in the liturgy for the day:

> Our reading of the gospel urges us toward a great and sacred mystery. Saint John belched up this opening to his gospel, which he had drunk in from the breast of the Lord. In fact, re-member what was read to you recently—that this same Saint John the Evangelist reclined in the lap of the Lord. Wanting to explain clearly, he says, "upon the bosom of the Lord" so that we might understand what he meant by "in the lap of the Lord." What are we to think that this one, reclining upon the bosom of the Lord, was drinking? We should not think. Rather, we should drink instead (*non putemus, sed potemus*).[118]

Augustine uses the rest of the sermon to articulate the "great and sacred mystery" into which these infants have just been inducted. They are the ones newly born from the "womb of their mother, the water of baptism" (*vulva matris, aqua baptismatis*). They are the new members of the *domus Dei,* counted among the children of God (*filii Dei*).[119] Contemplation on scripture's hidden mystery is no child's play. Thought cannot penetrate such depth. In the face of this inaccessible wisdom, Augustine tells his Easter Day congregation that the church should drink the milk of the text—of God's wisdom—rather than contemplate it. It is sufficient enough to be a babe at the breast of the church that has brought you forth from her womb. Here too we see a reversal of his Manichaean experience. The initiated are not inducted into elite, esoteric wisdoms through elaborate meal rites. Rather, they join all their brothers and sisters as hearers who nurse on the spiritual milk of the liturgy. Don't think, Augustine tells his congregation. Just drink. It is enough.

The dating of this sermon to the Easter service is significant for another reason. Canon 37 from the Council of Carthage (ca. 419) stipulates that the newly baptized are to receive a taste of milk during the liturgy, "as is custom in the mystery of the infants." While the council took place after the date of the sermon just mentioned, milk rites were a familiar practice in North African Christianity at least as far back as Tertullian.[120] It seems likely, then, that when Augustine preached on the prologue to John that morning, commanding his hearers to drink the milk of the words rather than contemplate the mystery of the Word, the ones clothed in white would have also ritually enacted their bishop's exhortation. In this way, the baptized *infantes,* the *parvuli in lacte,* embodied Augustine's figurative rendering of the entire Christian life as suckling on the breasts of mother church by ingesting the inward and incorruptible food that will sustain them.

In a rigorous examination of the family in Augustine's writing, Brent Shaw considers the role of breast-feeding and weaning:

> The process of weaning from the mother's/nurse's breasts also marked a further stage in the child's life. While attached to the mother, the child was seen as dependent and weak (*infirmus*), still a "mummy's boy" (*filius matris*). When he graduated he became a *filius patris.* The conscious attitudes to breastfeeding

by mothers and wet-nurses seems ambiguous, perhaps confused, in Augustine's reportage. On the one hand, he placed a
high premium on the willingness of mothers to feed their own
children; he saw the willingness of mothers to feed their own
children; he saw the unwillingness of those who disliked the
duty as symptomatic of a negative attitude to children that led to
the ruin of households (*ruinosa est domus*). Yet the implication
of some of these passages is that mothers shunt infants off the
breast in order that they might be able to give birth more
frequently. And nourishment was seen as the central role of the
mother, as much as domination was that of the father.[121]

Hearkening back to Dido's epithet from the *Aeneid*—"and wild tigers raised
you on the milk of their breasts"—Shaw observes in Augustine the dominant thread that has connected all the authors examined throughout this
study. In the family values of the Roman Empire, the nourishment given to
an infant conveyed a powerful essence into the child, shaping and forming
its nature, its character, and its soul. This basic belief was absorbed, reshaped, and then put to work in early Christian models of instruction and
soul formation. By the time of Augustine, the ideological system in which
the vitality of Roman children functioned as a barometer for imperial vitality had been overtaken by what Kate Cooper has called the "Christianiza-
tion of the household."[122] Augustine signals the eclipse of the Roman *domus*
by the *domus Dei*. In place of the *paterfamilias* and *materfamilias* who
long served as the arbiters of *romanitas* and physical sources for the material bonds of kinship, Augustine puts forth the church with its bishops and
priests as a many-breasted body through which saving faith and safe teaching are imparted into the gaping mouths of its infants. In so doing, Augustine transformed Paul's rebuke of the fleshy and immature Corinthians into
the only true form of the Christian life.

Ever since Henri Marrou published *Saint Augustin et la fin de la culture antique* in 1938—and the revised conclusion that followed a decade
later—much ink has been spilled in various attempts to situate the precise
nature of Augustine's relationship to the "end of ancient culture." Indeed,

surveying the scholarship of the last seventy-five years or so, one gets the impression that Augustine spent his life ending various aspects of antiquity. Charles Norris Cochrane concluded that Augustine represents the end of classical education *tout court*.[123] Likewise, in his landmark biography, Peter Brown refers to Augustine's "lost future"—an abandonment of the "classical ideal of perfection" to which he had devoted much of his life (including his early years postconversion).[124] Robert Markus charts Augustine's role in bringing about "the end of ancient Christianity." This epochal closure was, for Markus, prompted by Augustine's defense of a "Christian mediocrity," the result of an "epistemological crisis" that occurred when the bishop was disabused of his belief that human effort could attain its final goals.[125] More recently, Guy Stroumsa concluded that Augustine signals the "end of ancient esotericism."[126] There could be no "higher knowledge" than what is found in the words of scripture. The Christian reading program of *On Christian Teaching,* for Stroumsa, was a pin that let the air out of ancient mystery traditions. Augustine replaced the deep wisdom of the secret and the unseen with an infantile faith, a milky meal of scripture's words. And so the consensus view has been that Augustine's hope in human perfectibility dimmed, and with it the ultimate efficacy of education and formation. And tracing the sources as I have done here, with special attention to his use of milk and solid food, it is hard not to agree.

Weaning, maturity, and the ongoing development of one's intellectual diet all come to symbolize for Augustine the false promise of classical education. As Neil McLynn has quipped, "[I]t says something about late antique education that we never see Augustine graduate."[127] From his own admission, Augustine's education was one of fits and starts and of constant disappointment. The question "Who can teach me?" reverberates throughout his writing. Augustine already knew the answer before he had asked it. No one. No one can teach save that inward teacher. And yet, in a very real sense, Augustine had already admitted there was one living teacher, of flesh and blood, from whose body he had received the instructive milk that carried the name of Christ—the only lesson he ever needed. This nourishment was stronger teaching than any food he received among the Neoplatonists or the Manichaeans. For it was from Monica's body and the consolations of her human milk that Augustine developed his account of the nourishing power of mother church. Perfection, as he admitted to himself in the *Confessions,* was merely a reversion to that consolatory meal: a sucking and taking pleasure in milk, as infants are wont to do.

In this way, growth from milk to solid food was not simply a conceptual problem for Augustine. Unlike in the fraternal workshop of the Cassiciacum dialogues, the bishop Augustine came to view the weaning of Christians as too risky a practice to implement as a catechetical program in the church at large. In doing so, he placed himself in opposition to both Latin (Hilary) and Greek (Gregory of Nyssa) accounts of how milk and solid food might structure models of progressive Christian formation. Augustine's legacy in the history of this Pauline trope is singular in its radical emphasis on the unchanging infantile status of all Christians before God.

True growth was, for Augustine, regression out of the arrogances of adulthood and stasis within the milk nourishment of infancy—a food that transfers, sustains, and strengthens the proper form of faith in the Christian community. Augustine imagines a bodiless, many-breasted church suckling her children until the final days, when reason will no longer slide into hubris or desire into lust. Bishops and priests become here the provisional embodiment of that heavenly breast. In serving the cup of milk, the Eucharistic bread, and the milk of the preached Word, they incarnate the maternal body of the church and protect its children from those who would snatch them from its arms. Why would anyone want to leave this ecclesial Neverland, where nothing goes wrong so long as you never grow up?

"Give us solid food," Augustine seems to pray. "But not just yet."

Conclusion

"One must eat well" does not mean above all taking and grasping in itself, but learning and giving to eat, learning-to-give-the-other-to-eat. One never eats entirely on one's own.

—Jacques Derrida, " 'Eating Well' "

Let me suggest, then, parting bites that might nourish mortal companion species who cannot and must not assimilate one another but who must learn to eat well, or at least well enough that care, respect, and difference can flourish in the open.

—Donna Haraway, "Parting Bites"

WHAT BECAME OF Pinytos's hunger?

Eusebius tells us that Pinytos sought a "more perfect letter" from Dionysius—a teaching that might nourish into maturity those under his care. But we do not know if Dionysius ever relented, preparing the solid food of more rigorous instruction. Pinytos feared that his flock might live out its days feeding solely on "milky words" and never grow beyond infancy. This is where the record of the correspondence ends: a community stuck between the insufficient meal of milky words and the belief that perfection might come from the meat of a more advanced teaching.[1] And so this fragment of a conversation about how to be properly fed and formed is a keyhole view into the history that I have been exploring in the previous pages—a history of words about food, a history of how food was believed to transform bodies and minds, and a history of the ways in which meals were thought to produce and preserve particular ways of being in the world. It is also, more broadly, a history of how language is derived from the body, injected with the power of specific social and cultural values, and then reinscribed upon that body.

I began this history suggesting that, when we push beneath the metaphor of milk and solid food, we do not encounter some stable linguistic meaning or an obviousness of sense. Rather, we find an entanglement of social realities, political ideologies, and philosophical traditions. Judith Butler has described the complex interplay between word and body with particular force: "If language acts upon the body in some way—if we want to speak, for instance, of a bodily inscription, as so much cultural theory does—it might be worth considering whether language literally acts on a body and whether that body is an exterior surface for such action, or whether these are figures that we mobilize when we seek to establish the efficacy of language."[2] In the texts and figures at the heart of this study, language about food issues from the body, from specific embodied practices such as nursing, eating, and educating, but is then projected back upon the body as an organizing principle. Food becomes a lens through which the body is seen and understood, a mechanism for making sense of the body's place in the world. Our words cannot escape their embodied origins. And our bodies cannot escape the language used to encode meaning upon them.

Gastronomic regimes are built from language about food, and they perform precisely this kind of meaning-making work derived from and mapped upon the body. Gastronomy is a specific way of speaking about material foods and certain modes of eating in order to determine what is "good for the body"—whether that body be individual, collective, or a combination of the two. What else is Paul saying in the phrase "I gave you milk" but that the Corinthians must first eat well if they wish to be well? According to the figures examined in this study, the notion of "eating well" evoked a process of being physically formed, intellectually molded, and socially situated according to a particular set of transcendent values. The pervasive appeal of food as a symbol was derived from the fact that eating realizes a biologically bounded sociality. And within that network of relations, food items materialize the essential characteristics required to incorporate a person into that social system.

The power of nourishment among ancient Christian writers was premised upon two enduring and related ideas: First, that food consumption was a socializing act that marks the eater within particular modes of identity (mature or immature, perfect or newly formed, adult or infant, and so on). Second, that the physiological processes involved in human digestion have the power to shape the inner psychic life of the eater, implanting those modes of identity so deep as to make them appear natural. When paired with Paul's trope of milk and solid food, these two aspects provided a potent system for identity formation and instruction within early Christian thought. This combination of food-as-marker-of-identity and food-as-transfer-of-essence was a prime strategy among early Christians in articulating distinct visions of education, growth toward perfection, and social belonging.[3] And within these twin strategies, milk was uniquely employed to flesh out the essence of what made someone properly Christian.

The authors surveyed throughout the previous pages did not all wield this symbolic power in the same way or toward the same ends. Each chapter demonstrates the iterable nature of milk and solid food as a structuring paradigm. Precisely what made the symbol of milk "Christian" in essence was a matter of surprising flexibility. It could be readily employed to reclaim infancy as a positive status; it could be expanded to harmonize Paul's broader anthropological categories, thus providing a system of classification for various dietary capacities of the soul; it could serve to chart the soul's ongoing progress in perfection through an extended network of feeders and eaters; and, lastly, it could be used to prevent the arrogances of perfection, promoting instead a humbler vision of the Christian life as one of perpetual suckling. Eating well, moving from milk to solid food, thus took on a surprisingly eclectic range of meanings among early exegetes. Indeed, as we have seen, Paul's categories could be stretched to fit quite disparate modalities for understanding how one became "Christian" through regimens of feeding and being formed.

The use of breast-feeding and nurturance by ascetic males was, as I have argued, a form of "bio-power" (to borrow Foucault's phrase) or an "embodied politic" (to borrow Bourdieu's). As such, the frequent and evocative uses of breast milk by these authors do not provide evidence for an increasingly positive valuation of women in antiquity. Elizabeth Clark has noted that while asceticism "offered [women] a mode of life other than that of domesticity and childbearing," ascetic leaders "stood to benefit from the renunciations of their sheep."[4] Thus, even as women (Macrina, Olympias, and Monica come to mind) adopted ascetic practices that freed them from the burden of birthing and nurturing children, their male counterparts nevertheless found within the features and putative biological functions of their bodies a tactile symbol for the construction and transmission of a Christian cultural essence—an essence that could realize material bonds of kinship, processes of proper formation, and a means for safeguarding "orthodox" faith. In this way, the power ascribed to the female body in Roman family values was largely co-opted and displaced onto the abstract body of mother church and the ascetic bodies of male clerics.

As with the rhetoric of the body, rhetoric about the family is never neutral. In the midst of tectonic shifts that took place within the structure of Roman society between the first and the fifth centuries, appeals to the figure of the fecund female who dutifully nourishes her infants remained a primary strategy in the production, maintenance, and transmission of a Christian social identity. Like Tellus cradling her infants upon the Ara Pacis of Augustus Caesar, Christian authors articulated distinct visions of a well-fed, properly formed, and harmonious family system. Such systems were realized through the language of gastronomy. As Aristotle had observed long before Paul's letter to Corinth, the bond among foster brothers, the bond among those fed on the same milk, was tantamount to kinship. Milk made the family. It also made the *polis*. By expanding the sense in which Christians might share "milk from a legitimate source"—regardless of how literal or figurative that source may have been—early Christian authors bound together as kin under one household a sprawling network of nonbiological relations. And through that milk bond, they imagined Christian instruction in gastronomic terms. From Paul's words concerning milk and solid food, Christian catechesis was largely construed as an alimentary process. Growth "in Christ" required that one eat well.

Of course, the symbolic power of nourishment could be traced along other historical trajectories. Medieval monastic spirituality conjured maternity and nurturance in order to demonstrate, for example, the pious disposition of the abbot toward his monks.[5] Moving further afield, a provocative history surrounds "milk kinship" in Islamic literature. For example, in Sura

4:23 the Quran forbids marriage to milk mothers and milk sisters. In the Hadith—the traditions about the life of the prophet Muhammad—there is a story about how the prophet was forced to cancel marriage plans because it was discovered that the woman in question was his sister, having shared milk from the same breast.[6] And so complex arguments arose in Islamic law regarding the concept of "sire's milk"—a term referring to the legal relationship between a wet nurse's husband and the child she breast-feeds. One prominent strand of this legal tradition posited that, because it is the husband's semen that causes the milk production within his wife, any child she suckles falls under her husband's paternity.[7]

Much later, in eighteenth-century France, moral reformers sought to renew a decaying society by policing how women nurtured their children. In the age of the Enlightenment, over a millennium after the figures examined throughout this book, these moralists also emphasized the unique and "natural" power of biological milk to transfer moral character, social status, and intellectual attributes from mother to child. The figure of the wet nurse was once again viewed as a threat to social stability.[8] And indeed these ideological traditions persist well into contemporary American society. In a recent important book, Joan B. Wolf has discussed the "high stakes of motherhood," observing that "the proliferation and moral elevation of science meant that mothers became subject to a reign of expertise in areas that long had been considered somewhat mundane."[9] I hope to have shown here that motherhood and nurturance have rarely been considered "mundane" by prevailing social ideologies, and that this subjection of women's bodies to a reign of expertise has a long and violent lineage.

Despite these parallels, the force of Paul's reference to milk and solid food was produced by a specific conjuncture of social practices, intellectual traditions, and political ideologies bound up with Greek *paideia* and Roman family values. In the centuries that followed, Paul's successors appealed to nourishment in their varying attempts to frame the essential characteristics of the Christian life—that is, to frame what was thinkable, knowable, and doable within the household of God. These writers drew upon Paul's words about milk and solid food readily, if not coherently, in order to amplify claims about social legitimacy, scriptural interpretation, and proper spiritual development. As we have seen, the symbolic power of nourishment could be put to use toward a variety of ends. Authors writing from apologetic, polemical, exegetical, and speculative orientations premised their arguments on the idea that eating well and being well were essentially the same.

In the introduction to this book, I indicated that the project as a whole was prompted by a curious phrase in Tertullian's *To Scapula:* Tertullian had argued that even the emperor's son had benefited from the nurture of Christ followers. The boy, he says, had been "raised on Christian milk." What was, for Tertullian, an apologetic strategy that proved the positive influence of Christians on Roman society became later, for Jerome, evidence of autobiographical *bona fides*. Exhausted by accusations that he was a divisive and hostile thorn lodged in the flesh of the church, Jerome wrote, "I neither split the church nor separate myself from the communion of the fathers. From my very cradle I have been nourished on catholic milk. There is no wiser man of the church than the one who has never been a heretic."[10] It is not possible to be the cause of discord, Jerome countered, since he was properly nourished on the milk of orthodoxy from his infancy.

Jerome could not be in the wrong. He had always eaten well.

The imperative "to eat well" has been an undercurrent, a connecting thread, linking together disparate arguments about food and formation within the figures and texts explored in this study. Gastronomy inevitably carries with it a set of social, physiological, and intellectual valences regarding the power of nourishment in human development. If we become what we eat, better to eat well! The simplicity of the phrase "eat well" obscures the complex of ideologies in which a community gathers and to which its individuals are held accountable. The phrase thus evokes a process of growth and development, at once essentially materialistic and profoundly symbolic. What else is gastronomy, then, but a kind of socializing curriculum, a system for incorporating ambient cultural values into one's own person? A meal materializes the porous boundary between our individual bodies and the social body in which we participate. For the authors examined in this study, the trope of milk and solid food helped to realize such values about the essence and structure of the Christian community—including its ritual practices, its understanding of scripture, and the potential for transformation and unity among its diverse people. The symbolic power of food made these values tangible insofar as it conjured the embodied practices and lived reality of eating and feeding to which all people are bound.

What would an account of "eating well" look like in which the differences among those feeding and being formed are left, at least to some degree, unassimilated? How might the trope of milk and solid food be repurposed in such a way that it serves to weave together eclectic configurations of bodies, intellectual orientations, and relationships of care without trying to bring these into some kind of essentialized harmony of thought and expression? What about, as Catherine Keller has proposed, "the possibility that a mother's embrace could encode thought and not only feeling, that a woman's breast could bring to mind the circumambient embrace of 'reality,' good and bad, global and local, political and private, social and ecological, pumping its in/fluency into our prediscursive beings and demanding the continuous reinterpretation of our own discourses"?[11] While the history analyzed here readily recognized the possibility that a mother's embrace could encode thought or transfer reality, nurture was not framed as an act of mutual vulnerability in which caregivers and care receivers easily swap roles. Rather, as we have seen, gastronomic regimes appealed to breast-feeding in order to define, regulate, protect, and instill a particular cultural essence. Using the symbol of nourishment and nurture in this way, late-ancient authors largely foreclosed the possibility that the thought encoded or the reality transferred in nurturance might be open to revision, to reinterpretation, to an unending discursive exchange between eaters and feeders, learners and teachers.

The reopening of that possibility would require, I think, a shift away from the logic of "same essence, same food." For, as we have seen, this logic structured thinking about nourishment throughout the ancient worlds of Greece and Rome. An account of "eating well" might, in this sense, be predicated on the vulnerability and hospitality that is necessarily involved in all human nourishment and formation. There is scarcely a more vulnerable and relational act in the quotidian life of humans than feeding and being fed. This is most obvious in infancy and old age. But the precarious communion between eaters and feeders occurs in ways large and small at every meal. To "eat well," as Derrida suggests, is "a maxim whose modalities and contents need only be varied, *ad infinitum.*" How might Paul's trope of milk and solid food be used to imagine new ways of being in the world that reject the erasure of difference as a condition of human table fellowship—whether that "table" is found near a kitchen, in a place of worship, or in a classroom? If we take seriously the notion that "One never eats entirely on one's own," then food retains the potential to open up a greater space for difference, for vulnerable encounter, within the cliché that we become what we eat.

The first step toward a more capacious view of food and formation is already indicated in the constantly reconfigured family structures of the Roman *domus* and the early Christian "family." To be sure, both used the maternal body as a natural resource from which an enclosed and increasingly homogeneous institutional identity might be forged. Likewise, both the Roman *domus* and the Christian household reinscribed the violently asymmetrical relations of a profoundly patriarchal slaveholding society, arguing for the superiority of "legitimate" or biological milk over and against that of outsiders and foreigners. At the same time, pedagogical and kinship networks were being arranged and rearranged with surprising ease. This was true for Macrina (who readily played the part of mother, father, nurse, and teacher) as much as it was for Augustine (from whose breast, perhaps against his own wishes, Paulinus and Severus sought a nourishing milk of instruction). These expansive and malleable social configurations suggest an inchoate program of surrogacy, that is, a program of nourishment and education conducted outside of its "proper" place according to societal norms.[12]

In the Roman *domus,* this program of surrogacy was increasingly viewed as a threat to the stability of the empire. Asymmetrical relations between caregiving slaves and the children of their owners raised questions about the impact of eating food derived from sources beneath one's social location. After all, violent modes of surrogacy have long been the purview of both colonial and capitalist biopolitics.[13] And of course, the subversion and transformation of Roman institutions by the church would later become the norm as both the Roman family and the system of classical *paideia* slowly gave way. Nevertheless, in the early Christian imagination, answering the question "Who can teach me?" or "Who can feed me?" did not require the conventional institutions of education and kinship aimed at proper formation, even while the answers to these questions inscribed new categorical distinctions of social status and intellectual capacity. Yet from the apostle Paul through the first four centuries of Christianity, the proper nurture of infant souls was in fact a responsibility incumbent, in varying degrees, upon a broad network of surrogacy housed within the *domus dei*.

To eat well, in early Christianity, involved an openness to a range of people who might fill the role of mother, father, nurse, or teacher. And while this surrogacy most certainly played out as a discourse among elite men who employed the biological functions of the female body for the purposes of their own pastoral or theological projects, it could yet be put to use otherwise. We might find that the symbol of milk and solid food, derived as it is from these ancient shifting relational configurations, remains liable to still further reworking and transfiguration—what Judith Butler calls the insurrectionary moments that happen when the conventional relationship between words and bodies is broken open, making possible new embodied realities derived from old words.[14] We might find, then, that the shifty relational configurations essential to surrogacy enable us to queer certain ideas and expectations about nourishing and being nourished by others and that, in so doing, the logic of "same essence, same food" is replaced by a gastronomy of nurtured difference.

Donna Haraway has suggested that the ethical imperative to "eat well" requires that, in eating and learning together, we "nourish indigestion." Both food and education entail an opening up of the self to transformation. The result of this openness, the outcome of this formative process, cannot be known in advance. It requires an attentive witness to the differences we encounter and traverse at the table. What made the connection between food and formation such an anxiously regulated discourse in antiquity was the vulnerability inherent within it. Greater emphasis on this vulnerability would not result in the complete erasure of asymmetrical relations, since all human relationships involve, to some degree, shifting power dynamics. Yet to nourish indigestion entails a kind of gastronomic flexibility in which those dynamics are approached with greater care, consideration, and appreciation for the mysterious give-and-take that is essential to the work of feeding and eating, teaching and learning.

What is also needed is a better accounting of the ways in which nurturance is not "women's work," despite being affixed to women throughout history as though it were a biological fact.[15] Remaining conscious of the embodied realities of nurturance that are particular to women who are mothers, I wonder if the symbolic power of nourishment might be redirected from its function within a long-standing misogynistic framework in such a way that it comes to signify something many women who are mothers have written about and reflected on extensively: feeding, nurturing, and forming others is premised on a radical vulnerability, on the fundamental porousness of inside and outside that takes place in the sharing of food. This is work that involves openness to change and to peculiar, unexpected, yet welcome discoveries among those involved. It is a process that is also, at times, toilsome, painful, and exhausting. That we live in a world where we must give to one another and take from one another in order to become who we are, in order to flourish, is fraught with the possibility of harm. Nurture is, in this way, a profoundly political act. We are all participating in it, whether we see it or not. And so "eating well" might just be the open commitment to a space of mutual care in which eclectic arrangements of bodies and identities are bound together in the gentle economy of giving and receiving, of forming and being formed. This kind of nurture would not necessarily do away with the movement from milk to solid food as a powerful trope, bound as it is to troubled and complicated histories. Rather it would expand the scope of what is thinkable, sayable, and doable for both feeder and eater alike within the phrase "I gave you milk." To leave such differences undigested and unassimilated, indeed to nurture these very differences—and in so doing, to resist certain violences embedded in the history of moving from milk to solid food—would be, I think, a promising start toward a new Pauline gastronomy.

Notes

Abbreviations

ACW	Ancient Christian Writers
BA	Bibliothèque Augustinienne
CCSL	Corpus Christianorum Series Latina
CMG	Corpus Medicorum Graecorum
CSEL	Corpus Scriptorum Ecclesiasticorum Latinorum
CWS	Classics of Western Spirituality
FOC	Fathers of the Church
GCS	Die Griechischen Christlichen Schriftsteller
HTR	*Harvard Theological Review*
JBL	*Journal of Biblical Literature*
JECS	*Journal of Early Christian Studies*
JTS	*Journal of Theological Studies*
LCC	Library of Christian Classics
LCL	Loeb Classical Library
LSJ	Liddell-Scott-Jones Greek/English Lexicon
PL	Patrologia Latina
SC	Sources Chrétiennes
VC	*Vigiliae Christianae*
VCSup	*Vigiliae Christianae Supplements*
WGRW	Writings from the Greco-Roman World (Society of Biblical Literature)
WSA	Works of Saint Augustine

Introduction

1. Ludwig Feuerbach, "Die Naturwissenschaft und die Revolution" [Natural Science and the Revolution] Sämtliche Werke (SW) X, 22. All translations are my own unless otherwise noted. I have listed relevant English translations when used, and the "Ancient Texts and Translations" section of the bibliography provides a comprehensive list of critical editions and translations consulted. For Bible translations, I have usually rendered my own translation while working with the New Revised Standard Version (NRSV). I have indicated in the notes the places where I am quoting the NRSV directly.

2. On the context of Feuerbach's phrase, see especially Melvin Cherno, "A Rectification," 397–406.

3. *SW* X, 22, emphasis added.

4. For a nonliteralist interpretation, see Cherno, "A Rectification," 401–3.

5. Ludwig Feuerbach, "Das Geheimnis des Opfers oder Der Mensch ist, was
er isst" [The Mystery of Sacrifice or Man Is What He Eats], *SW* X, 41–64.

6. In German, "gleiches Wesen, gleiche Speise und umgekehrt." Ibid., 45–46.

7. Ibid., 63.

8. Ibid., 64.

9. A century after Feuerbach, Alexander Schmemann opened his study of sacramental theology in *For the Life of the World* with an appeal that "we are what we
eat." For Schmemann, however, the truth of this observation reaches all the way
back to Genesis and the creation of the world "as the 'matter,' the material of
one all-embracing Eucharist." See Schmemann, *For the Life of the World,* 15.
Schmemann construes the entire world as nourishment for humanity—not
simply as material food but also as that which was given by God as symbolic of
the spiritual communion between humanity and God. We are what we eat, for
Schmemann, because our matter, like the material of our food, is all a gift from
God.

10. See Jason König, *Saints and Symposiasts;* Dennis E. Smith and Hal Taussig,
Meals in the Early Christian World; Hal Taussig, *In the Beginning Was the
Meal;* Dennis E. Smith, *From Symposium to Eucharist;* Andrew McGowan,
Ascetic Eucharists; Matthias Klinghardt, *Gemeinschaftsmahl und Mahlgemein-
schaft.*

11. Taussig, *In the Beginning Was the Meal,* 170.

12. See ibid., 168, and especially Dale B. Martin, *The Corinthian Body.*

13. While commentaries on Paul's letters—especially his letter to the Corinthians—continue to fell forests, scholarship on the legacy of Paul's milk and solid-
food trope has been sporadic. Denise Kimber Buell's *Making Christians* is,
perhaps, the most thoroughgoing account of how nourishment functioned in
one early Christian author. For other examples, see also Judith Kovacs, "Echoes
of Valentinian Exegesis," 317–29, and Guy Stroumsa, *Hidden Wisdom.* I will
engage these more fully in the chapters that follow.

14. Werner Jaeger, *Early Christianity and Greek Paideia* was a revision of the Carl
Newell Jackson Lectures in 1960. More will be said on the semantic and
conceptual range of the Greek word *paideia.*

15. Ibid., 87.

16. I use the phrasing "bodily growth" and "intellectual/spiritual development" in
order to emphasize Jaeger's dichotomous presentation of these processes

while, at the same time, calling that very dichotomy into question. As I will demonstrate, this construal fails to account for the ways in which early Christian references to nourishment and breast-feeding resist such clean distinctions.

17. Jaeger, *Paideia: The Ideals of Greek Culture* was first published in 1939. It was originally titled *Paideia, Die Formung des griechischen Menschen*. The German word *Formung* reveals Jaeger's deep sense that education was a force aimed at transforming a person into something better, something more perfect.

18. Outside of Jaeger, the French historian H. I. Marrou's study *Histoire de l'éducation dans l'Antiquité* remains a classic. For studies on education in antiquity since Jaeger and Marrou, see also W. Martin Bloomer, *The School of Rome;* W. A. Johnson, *Readers and Reading Culture in the High Roman Empire;* Jean Ducat, *Spartan Education;* Rafaella Cribiore, *Gymnastics of the Mind;* Barbara Borg, *Paideia: The World of the Second Sophistic;* Yun Lee Too, *Education in Greek and Roman Antiquity;* Konrad Vössing, *Schule und Bildung im Nordafrika der Römischen Kaiserzeit;* Teresa Morgan, *Literate Education in the Hellenistic and Roman Worlds;* Kevin Robb, *Literacy and Paideia in Ancient Greece;* Joachim Dingel, *Scholastica materia;* Robert A. Kaster, *Guardians of Language;* Henry Teloh, *Socratic Education in Plato's Early Dialogues;* Alan Mendelson, *Secular Education in Philo of Alexandria;* Carnes Lord, *Education and Culture in the Political Thought of Aristotle;* Stanley Bonner, *Education in Ancient Rome;* J. P. Lynch, *Aristotle's School;* M. L. Clarke, *Higher Education in the Ancient World;* G. W. Bowersock, *Greek Sophists in the Roman Empire;* Donald Lemen Clark, *Rhetoric in Greco-Roman Education.*

19. A long-standing interest in ancient education among classicists did not directly result in an immediate and corollary interest on the part of early church historians or historians of what has come to be called "late antiquity." This gap has been slowly closing in recent years. To take but one example, the Transformation of the Classical Heritage series published by the University of California Press has proven to be one of the richest sites for cross-fertilization between what were traditionally two discrete disciplines: classics and early Christian studies.

20. For studies on the interaction between Christianity, late antiquity, and classical education, see, e.g., Lieve Van Hoof, "Performing Paideia," 387–406; Catherine Chin, *Grammar and Christianity in the Late Roman Empire;* Edward Watts, *City and School in Late Antique Athens and Alexandria;* J. W. Trigg, "God's Marvelous *Oikonomia*," 27–52; Kim Paffenroth and Kevin L. Hughes, *Augustine and Liberal Education;* Annewies van den Hoek, "The 'Catechetical' School of Early Christian Alexandria," 59–87; R. M. van den Berg, "The Christian 'School' of Alexandria in the Second and Third Centuries," 39–47;

C. Scholten, "Die alexandrinische Katencheteschule," 16–37; E. A. Judge, "Reaction Against Classical Education in the New Testament," 166–74; E. A. Judge, "The Interaction of Biblical and Classical Education in the Fourth Century," 31–37; Geraldine Hodgson, *Primitive Christian Education.*

21. Throughout this study, I will treat the motifs of nourishment, breast-feeding, and childrearing as part of a single rhetorical symbol, rather than separate (if interrelated) themes. This decision is meant to foreground a fundamental and inextricable relationship between what children are fed and how they develop into fully formed, perfect adults.

22. Sophocles, *Antigone* 918 (LCL 20:384). The Loeb translation curiously renders the phrase as "the joys of motherhood."

23. Geoffrey D. Dunn, "Rhetorical Structure in Tertullian's 'Ad Scapulam,'" 54.

24. Tertullian, *To Scapula* IV.5 (CCSL II.2:1130–31). In retrospect, Caracalla was perhaps not the best example of the positive effects of Christian milk. In *On Monogamy* 11.9 (CSEL 76:66–67), Tertullian employs the same combination of "*lac*" and "*educare*" in reference to Paul: ". . . the youth of a fresh and newborn church, which [the apostle] was raising on milk [*quam lacte scilicet educabat*], not yet the solid food of stronger doctrine."

25. Throughout this study, the partition between nourishment (often presumed to be a biological act) and nurture (conversely presumed to be a social act)—like the broader categories of bodily growth and spiritual formation discussed previously—is called into question. Again, this relationship is one in which the processes of feeding and of forming children not only imply one another analogically but require one another practically. Thus, in his *Institutes of Oratory (Inst.)*, Quintilian follows a lengthy discussion concerning the proper care needed in selecting a wet nurse for one's child with a consideration of how the child will then progress in his education: ". . . but studies also have their infancy. Just as the rearing of the body which leads to perfect strength begins with the milk of infancy, so too with the one who will become a most eloquent speaker, who was first crying and speaking with a wavering voice." *Inst.* 1.1.21 (LCL 124:30). I am suggesting that this analogy gains its force precisely because it is inextricable from the regulatory practices of child nourishment and child care implied in the selection of wet nurses to which Quintilian earlier referred.

26. Hodgson, *Primitive Christian Education,* 39.

27. Bonner, *Education in Ancient Rome,* 41.

28. Such poisoning was perceived to be a real threat, if we take Tacitus at his word in *The Annals* 13.15. See ibid., 42. More will be said on the social history of the *nutrix/nutritor* to follow.

29. Morgan, *Literate Education,* 242.

30. Ibid., 243–44.

31. Discussions in contemporary science surrounding epigenetics and human plasticity offer a provocative corollary to the chiastic structure I am suggesting here. For an interesting parallel from evolutionary developmental psychology, see David F. Bjorklund, "Mother Knows Best," 213–42. Bjorklund helpfully summarizes: "Development occurs as the result of the continuous and bidirectional interaction between various components of developmental systems—including but not limited to genetic activity, structural maturation, activity emanating from structures (or function), and the environment, broadly construed. Genes are not given special privilege, but are viewed as an integral part of the developmental system" (216). In turning to "maternal effects," Bjorklund observes how mothers comprise—materially, emotionally, spatially—the child's immediate environment. Given the plasticity of children and the ways in which mothers mediate the world to them, he hypothesizes that changes in these "maternal effects" influence evolution as well (235).

32. Raffaella Cribiore, *The School of Libanius,* 137.

33. Bloomer, *The School of Rome,* 64; see also 65–71, 100–107.

34. Maud W. Gleason, *Making Men,* xxii, xxvi. See also 143 for a discussion of the "psychophysical components that must be continually fostered" in order to produce and maintain nobility.

35. Marrou, *Education in Antiquity,* xiv.

36. Ibid., xx.

37. Jaeger, *Paideia,* xiii.

38. For studies that emphasize the mimetic core within ancient education, see Bloomer, *The School of Rome,* 95–98; George A. Kennedy, *Classical Rhetoric and Its Christian and Secular Tradition;* George A. Kennedy, *A New History of Classical Rhetoric;* Jaeger, *Paideia,* vol. 1, 34; Bonner, *Education in Ancient Rome,* 199; Aubrey Gwynn, *Roman Education from Cicero to Quintilian,* 14; Marrou, *Education in Antiquity,* 236; Bernard Bosanquet, *The Education of the Young in the Republic of Plato,* 2.

39. An important example of scholarship on mimesis-as-repetition is Elizabeth Castelli's *Imitating Paul,* 86: "[M]imesis is constituted through a hierarchy in which the model is imbued with perfection and wholeness, and the copy represents an attempt to reclaim that perfection[;] . . . the model has authority to which the copy submits. Finally, sameness is valued above difference. . . . The copy aims at sameness, but can never attain that sameness because of the hierarchical nature of its relation to the model. . . . Sameness and unity and harmony have positive value while, by implication, difference is associated with disunity and discord. This treatment of difference has profound implications

for processes of social formation, because it suggests that difference must be subversive of unity, harmony, and order." Noting the significant contribution of Castelli to our reading of power dynamics in the apostle Paul, Denise Kimber Buell has also helpfully developed the connection between imitative and pro-creative language. See Buell, *Making Christians,* 13. While building on these two illuminating studies, I'd also like to suggest that the twining of procreative and imitative language was both thoroughly invested in programs of cultural replication while also remaining inherently vulnerable to improvisation and reformulation. Indeed, scholars of the so-called second sophistic have identified improvisation as a crucial characteristic of the era. See, e.g., Tim Whitmarsh, *The Second Sophistic.*

40. Ancient authors of the first century CE explicitly commented upon the imitative impulse within education while also allowing for—indeed praising—the role of improvisation. Epictetus, on the one hand, uses the imagery of digestion and regurgitation to call attention to students who have not yet become wise. Those who merely vomit up the food they eat (that is, simply repeat and recite their teachers) have not yet begun the work of philosophy that requires the student to digest old material and transform it to something new (Epictetus, *Enchei-ridion* 46). Quintilian, on the other hand, concludes that "the greatest talents of an orator are inimitable" (*Inst.* 10.2.13), and thus he encourages each orator to improve upon the models in his own unique way (*Inst.* 10.3.27–28). These references serve as an important reminder that no matter how stable the pre-sentation of doctrinal instruction was, there was always a risk or potential (de-pending on perspective) for education to create something new. Contemporary scholars such as Raffaella Cribiore, Edward Watts, and Catherine Chin have begun to offer dynamic appraisals of the ways in which education can be con-servative as well as constructive, repetitive as well as innovative. See especially Cribiore's discussion of imitation of and departure from literary models in *Gymnastics of the Mind,* 220–44. More directly, I am following the brief inter-vention offered by Frances M. Young in the essay "Paideia and the Myth of Static Dogma," 265–83. I envision the current project as expanding upon this insightful essay.

41. Jacques Derrida, "White Mythology," 8.

42. Hans Conzelmann, *1 Corinthians,* 71–72 (emphasis added).

43. I am indebted to Maia Kotrosits for continually pushing me on this point. I am sure I have not gone far enough to satisfy her concern that any reference to "Christian identity," no matter how qualified, "blinds" us to other messier par-ticularities embedded within the histories we are trying to tell. I hope the pages that follow demonstrate my own sensitivity to the messiness of whatever we

mean when we talk about "identity." See Kotrosits, *Rethinking Christian Identity*, esp. 32–45.

44. For an example of a more complex approach to metaphor, see Derrida, "White Mythology."

45. Pierre Bourdieu, *Language and Symbolic Power*, 86.

46. Pierre Bourdieu, *The Logic of Practice*, 69; Pierre Bourdieu and Loïc J. D. Wacquant, *An Invitation to Reflexive Sociology*, 145.

47. Bourdieu and Wacquant, *Invitation*, 145, and Bourdieu, *Language*, 37.

48. Bourdieu's argument is primarily aimed at the linguistic theories offered by Ferdinand de Saussure in his *Course in General Linguistics* and by J. L. Austin in *How to Do Things with Words*. But in using Bourdieu I am also seeking to intervene in conversations on metaphor theory within New Testament and early Christian studies that have been preoccupied with cognitive approaches (typically in conversation with George Lakoff and Mark Johnson's popular book *Metaphors We Live By*). One relevant example of this approach is Jennifer Houston McNeel's recent book *Paul as Infant and Nursing Mother*.

49. Bourdieu, *Language*, 9.

50. This may seem like a rather banal observation. However, it is worth noting that Bourdieu sees himself as intervening in the dominant trend in linguistics with his approach to language as a socially constructed exchange of power that, consequently, has the power to validate or transform those structures. Likewise, Conzelmann's suggestion that the meaning of Paul's metaphor is obvious rehearses the tacit assumption that we can know what a particular figure of speech means without rigorously attending to the broader social dynamics and exchanges of power to which such speech would have been bound.

51. Bourdieu and Wacquant, *Invitation*, 142–43.

52. Bourdieu, *Language*, 164–70, and Bourdieu and Wacquant, *Invitation*, 148.

53. Bourdieu, *Language*, 166.

54. Bourdieu and Wacquant, *Invitation*, 148, and Bourdieu, *Language*, 170.

55. One way that this process has been articulated by theorists is through the idea of "linguistic" or "cultural sedimentation." The term "sedimentation" has a technical history in the philosophy of language. Edmund Husserl, in his essay "The Origin of Geometry"—found in *Husserliana*, VI—describes the concept as follows: ". . . [H]istory is from the start nothing other than the living movement of the coexistence and interweaving of original formations of meaning and the ongoing sedimentations of meaning" (380). For Husserl, sedimented traditions (*sedimentierten Traditionen*) are the product of an accumulation of truth-meaning (*Wahrheitsinnes*) within a given proposition (*Satz*). Put another way, sedimentation speaks to the "mobility of use" (*Beweglichkeit*) in which the

meaning of certain words and phrases is received, worked over, handed down, and then reshaped (377–78). Sedimentation is a particularly apt image for our purposes because it evokes both a "settledness" of meaning that, nevertheless, can be sifted, turned over, and shaken up. The idea of linguistic, historical, or cultural sedimentation also figures prominently in the theories of Jacques Derrida and Judith Butler, to name only the most prominent.

56. Bourdieu and Wacquant, *Invitation*, 172. While I am critiquing the dichotomy presumed in binary couples like figurative/literal, spiritual/material, etc., I do not think the solution is to be done with such terms altogether. In emphasizing the words "symbol" and "symbolic" in this study, I aim to identify the slippage within such binaries in order to analyze the ways in which that slippage opens new interpretive possibilities.

57. In *Excitable Speech,* Judith Butler critiques Bourdieu's emphasis on the social setting of symbolic power as unintentionally reifying social norms and thus presenting a picture of language that "forecloses the possibility of an agency that emerges from the margins of power" (156). That is to say, if authority is granted to speech and its speaker solely from the social field, then this precludes powerful speech from those outside the status quo. By contrast, Butler introduces the "performative" dimension of language as the site at which its socially produced meaning is made available to appropriation or misappropriation by social agents from a variety of positions. Butler wants to account for the ways in which the power of language not only precedes its present usage but also becomes liable to "insurrectionary" moments that break away from past meaning in order to imagine something new (159). It is unlikely that the early Christian appropriation of nourishment as a symbol can be thought of as insurrectionary in the sense that Butler suggests. Nevertheless, as a historian of antiquity, I find in Butler's account of language a source of optimism. We may never be rid of words and tropes that have historically been used to categorize and arrange people within profoundly unjust social systems. But if language is vulnerable to reactivation and to performative reappropriation, then there remains the possibility that such words and tropes might be wrested from the force of convention and put to work in building communities that are more just. I will return to this possibility at the conclusion of the book.

58. Husserl's notion of meaning's mobility (*Beweglichkeit*) informs Derrida's concept of the iterability of language found in "Signature, Event, Context" and in *Writing and Difference.* Derrida imagines linguistic (particularly written) signs as "a kind of machine that is in turn productive"—a machine that can then "engender infinitely new contexts." Derrida, "Signature," 316, 320–21. Butler draws upon these ideas when she suggests that linguistic symbols come to us

through a "chain of signification"—a chain from which we cannot extricate ourselves. See her *Bodies That Matter,* 219–20. She refers to the possibility for this chain of signification to undergo an interruption of meaning or break from traditional usage as the "phantasmatic promise" of all language. Ibid., 220. For a helpful assessment of these themes, see Amy Hollywood, "Performativity, Citationality, Ritualization," 93–115.

59. Andrew Jacobs and Rebecca Krawiec, "Fathers Know Best?" 261–62.

60. I mean "distinct" in a rather loose sense, as will be made clear. These authors and their exegetical strategies do not happen in a vacuum. Gregory of Nyssa's *Homilies on the Song of Songs,* e.g., can be rightly situated within an interpretive tradition traceable to Origen's own commentary on that text. So, while largely avoiding the historical category of "influence," I have tried to note the relevant places of overlap as much as I have the places of divergence.

61. In *Against Jovinian* 37, for instance, after observing that chastity is God's will (*voluntas Dei*) and marriage is God's indulgence (*indulgentia*), Jerome cites 1 Cor. 3. He appeals to Paul's categories of carnal and spiritual as well as to milk and solid food as indications of Paul's (and God's) attitude toward marriage: "The one who is a beast [*qui animalis est*] does not receive those things that are of the Spirit of God. . . . [S]uch a person is not nourished on the perfect food of chastity, but rather is nurtured on the coarse milk of marriage [*iste non perfectae castitatis cibo, sed rudi nuptiarum lacte nutritur*]" (PL 23:0263B). In *Letters* 122.4, Jerome amplifies this argument by scolding a man who has refused to follow his wife's example in chastity: "It would be fair for me to identify your soul (within which there is no sexual difference) as the daughter of your wife's soul—and because you are as it were a child, an infant being breastfed who is not yet strong enough to accept solid food, [your wife] invites you to the milk of infancy and offers to you the nourishment of a wet-nurse" (PL 22:1046). Tertullian makes a similar argument connecting the superiority of chastity to Paul's solid food in *On Monogamy* 11.9 (CSEL 76:66–67).

62. One road not taken in the current project is an account of how milk was employed in early Christian ritual. I had initially intended to include a study of this as a stand-alone chapter or an appendix, but it soon became clear that such a project would be too unwieldy and required a thoroughgoing analysis in its own right. (My next project will consider this more directly.) I have foregrounded the moments throughout this project where the symbolic power of nourishment is connected to Eucharistic/postbaptismal eating and drinking by the authors analyzed to come. Nevertheless, given the slippage between figurative and literal speech that is pervasive in this literature, ritual resonances are often implicit rather than explicit.

Chapter 1. The Symbolic Power of Food in the Greco-Roman World

1. There are, of course, entire libraries devoted to analyzing theories of the soul in Plato and Aristotle. I cannot hope to contribute to this expansive field of ancient philosophy. In this section, I will explore some of the intriguing ways that nourishment enters into these classical discussions of the soul and its embodied state. For a recent account of "appetitive desire" in these authors, see especially Hendrik Lorenz, *The Brute Within.*

2. Discussions around the dating and authorship of this text, like much of the Hippocratic corpus, are vexed. There is little support for the view that it is authentic to Hippocrates, but scholars have dated it anywhere from the late fifth to the early third century BCE. The latter date is gaining favor, following scholars such as Jacques Jouanna, who assert a Stoic influence. See his *Greek Medicine from Hippocrates to Galen,* 306.

3. On *Nutriment (Nut.)* 2 (LCL 147:342).

4. *Nut.* 7 (LCL 147:344).

5. That the treatise mentions *pneuma* along with heat and moisture is no coincidence. These latter two elements were related to the four humors, which, when properly harmonized, helped to keep the body's physical and psychic disposition in balance. Nourishment was widely thought to have a significant impact on the humors and could, in immoderate intake, result in psychosomatic chaos. In this way the humors and the pneuma can be viewed as the fabrics from which the various essences of the human person are woven together. Only through proper portioning and calibrating of these essences can a healthy mind, body, and soul be produced.

6. *Nut.* 22 (LCL 147:348).

7. Dale Martin, *The Corinthian Body,* 22.

8. Ibid., 7 and 12.

9. For more on the *pneuma* in ancient thought, see R. J. Hankinson, "Philosophy of Nature," esp. 228–29.

10. Hippocrates, *Regimen (Reg.)* 25 and 35 (LCL 150:262 and 282).

11. *Reg.* 35 (LCL 150:284).

12. *Reg.* 26–28 (LCL 150:262–68).

13. *Reg.* 28 (LCL 150:266).

14. *Reg.* 28 (LCL 150:268).

15. *Reg.* 35 (LCL 150:290).

16. See the discussion on this issue, with special reference to the Hippocratics, in Lesley Ann Dean-Jones, *Women's Bodies in Classical Greek Science,* 162–66.

17. Ibid., 162.

18. Ibid., 164–65.

19. In a section of *On the Nature of the Child* examining the process in which breast milk is produced, Hippocrates describes the power of mother's nourishment in forming her child: "The food and the growth of the child is produced by that which moves from the mother to her womb; and whatever be the mother's health or weakness, the child will have the same" (LCL 520:60–62).

20. Jouanna, *Greek Medicine,* 202.

21. See especially the textual parallels listed ibid., 220–21.

22. Ibid., 223.

23. Plato, *Timaeus* (*Tim.*) 47d (LCL 234:108). Anthropology and cosmology are bound together in the *Timaeus.* The human person is constructed out of the elements of the cosmos and thus the movement of essences within human bodies mimics the movements of heavenly bodies. See *Tim.* 41e–43e.

24. *Tim.* 43a (LCL 234:94).

25. *Tim.* 44a–b (LCL 234:96–98).

26. *Tim.* 44b–c (LCL 234:98).

27. Plato, *Republic* (*Rep.*) 376e–377c (LCL 237:174–76). The influence of the nurse upon the infant was taken so seriously throughout antiquity that, in the Theodosian Code, the misconduct of a nurse toward her charge is an offense punishable by having molten lead poured down her throat (9.24.1.1).

28. *Rep.* 441a (LCL 237:404).

29. Plato, *Laws* 643c–d (LCL 187:62–64).

30. *Laws* 788c (LCL 192:4).

31. In some places, *trophe* is strictly apportioned to the body. See *Laws* 807d (LCL 192:66).

32. There is an interesting discussion of the connection between the verbs *trepho* (and cognates) and *paideuo* in the ancient sources by W. C. van Unnik, *Tarsus or Jerusalem,* 29–45 and 59–72. Van Unnik concludes, " 'To feed' in its original meaning, a meaning that always remained closely associated with the verb, is to lay the basis of child-life, but the word also covers all that is bound up with the initial stages of upbringing. The meaning moves very much in the physical sphere, as is understandable at this stage of development; but it does not remain limited to giving suck and supplying food" (33). This general definition is a helpful starting point, though van Unnik proposes too stark a distinction between the various cognates of "feed" and "educate" when he argues that they ought to be understood as discrete stages or levels of human development. This is certainly true in some cases, but the slippage of meaning between the two remains constant and not coherently divided into discrete categories by the source material.

33. Analogizing bodily processes with intellectual ones is a crucial motif throughout Plato's dialogues. As David D. Leitao has observed, the close connection
between bodily reproduction in procreation and the reproduction of the mind
in education reveals the extent to which Plato situated his account of psychic
development within the terms set by medical theories of pregnancy: "Plato is
inviting us, perhaps not without some ambivalence, to understand not parturition but the very state of being pregnant itself as the ultimate goal of philosophy.
This hypothesis compliments the findings of other scholars. David Halperin,
in developing his reading of Diotima's speech, identifies an important distinction within Greek thought between male and female desire: male desire is oriented toward acquisition, female desire toward creation. And Lesley
Dean-Jones has shown, in a study of Greek medical texts, that a woman's creative impulse is focused not so much on generating a product (the child) as on
maintaining a healthy ecology of fluids within her own body. It is likely that
Plato is thinking in similar terms. A man's reproductive energies are geared
toward production—in the physical realm, this means producing children who
will maintain his *oikos* and his tomb cult; in the intellectual realm, this might
entail producing poems, laws, *logoi,* and *dianoemata.* These are reproductive
activities described, literally or metaphorically, by the verb γεννάω." Leitao,
The Pregnant Male as Myth and Metaphor in Classical Greek Literature, 224.
This context gives greater contour to the seemingly dualistic claim that
Socrates, the son of a midwife, was himself a midwife of the male soul (Plato,
Theaetetus 148e–151d). I am proposing that the connection of *trophe* and *paid-
eia* in nurturance functions in similarly ambiguous ways.

34. Aristotle, *On the Soul* 415a (LCL 288:84). For an excellent account of the nutritive soul in Aristotle, see Thomas Kjeller Johansen, *The Powers of Aristotle's
Soul,* 116–27; esp. 119: "I want to hold on to the insight that the nutritive soul
plays a special role in relation to the definition of soul which leads Aristotle to
devote his first chapter on the capacities of the soul to nutrition. . . . Aristotle
gives priority to nutritive soul in his account of the soul because nutrition
serves as a paradigm of how the soul works as the nature of living beings. The
nutritive soul thus has a special status among the capacities of the soul by il-
lustrating how the soul works to bring about life. It is of course of great importance that the nutritive soul is the one that all living beings have. But the
paradigmatic status of the nutritive soul lies in the extendibility of the causal
analysis to the other capacities."

35. *On the Soul* 415a (LCL 288:86).

36. *Parts of Animals (Part. An.)* 672b8–23 (LCL 323:278).

37. *Part. An.* 672b8–23 (LCL 323:278).

38. *Part. An.* 650a8. See also Helen King, *Hippocrates' Woman,* 34–35.

39. Dean-Jones, *Women's Bodies,* 222.

40. Lorenz, *The Brute Within,* 2.

41. Susan Mattern, *Galen and the Rhetoric of Healing,* 8–9, and Susan Mattern, *The Prince of Medicine,* 36–80.

42. Mattern, *Galen and the Rhetoric of Healing,* 8. Simon Swain calls Galen "one of the most accomplished intellectuals of the second century, a man of standing in his own time and hugely influential afterwards" (Swain, *Hellenism and Empire,* 357). Swain also emphasizes the importance of Galen's residence at Rome, which offers a unique vantage on Greek attitudes toward Roman rule.

43. While Jouanna provides a robust account of Galen's debt to the Hippocratic and Platonic traditions, for the Aristotelian and Stoic strands of his thought see, Rebecca Flemming, "Demiurge and Emperor in Galen's World of Knowledge," 59–84; Philip J. van der Eijk, "'Aristotle! What a Thing for You to Say!'" 261–82; and Teun Tieleman, "Galen and the Stoics," 282–99. In turning to Galen here, my intent is to indicate the ways in which pre-Roman theories of the relationship between the growth of the soul and physical nourishment became a fixture in the broader family ideology of the Roman Empire—an ideology I will explore at length in the following section.

44. Galen, *The Capacities of the Soul Depend on the Mixtures of the Body* (*Capacities of the Soul*) 1 (Kuhn 4:767). I have consulted the translation found in Singer's *Galen: Selected Works,* 150–76. See also Jacques Jouanna, "Does Galen Have a Programme for Intellectuals and the Faculties of the Intellect?" 190–205.

45. *Capacities of the Soul* 2 (Kuhn 4:771; translation, Singer, 151).

46. *Capacities of the Soul* 2 (Kuhn 4:772; translation, Singer, 152).

47. Jouanna, "Does Galen Have a Programme for Intellectuals," 196–97.

48. *Capacities of the Soul* 9 (Kuhn 4:808; translation, Singer, 169).

49. Mattern only provides a brief analysis of *Capacities of the Soul* with the observation that, for Galen, "some faults in character can be corrected with the proper diet" (Mattern, *The Prince of Medicine,* 269). But the full force of that quote seems to suggest more than that, emphasizing the role played by the "vegetative" soul in the ongoing formation of the rational mind.

50. Galen, *On the Properties of Foodstuffs* (Kuhn 6:681–89). It is worth noting here that the title of the treatise is a Latin translation derived from the first line of the Greek: τῶν ἐν ταῖς τροφαῖς δυνάμεων ("On the powers of nourishment").

51. *On the Properties of Foodstuffs* (Kuhn 6:685).

52. In his landmark study, Ronald Syme isolates marriage and child-rearing as particularly important elements in the "revolution." See Syme, *The Roman Revolution,* 443–46.

53. The phrase "family values" immediately draws together the piety enjoined upon the Roman *familia* and the moralizing found in much of contemporary social and political commentary about the family. This is not to suggest a straight line of continuity between past and present, but rather to gesture at the ways in which discourses—especially those about family, reproduction, and nurturance—undergo a process of sedimentation that is both durable and transformable. For Roman "family values" in this sense, see Richard Saller, "Family Values in Ancient Rome."

54. For further discussion of the shortage of heirs in the Roman Empire, see also Jane Gardner, *Family and* Familia *in Roman Law and Life,* 28, 210–11; Kristina Milnor, *Gender, Domesticity, and the Age of Augustus,* 140–41; Richard Saller, *Patriarchy, Property and Death,* 162; Beth Severy, *Augustus and the Family,* 50–52.

55. In his *Res Gestae* (*R.G.*) Augustus Caesar explains, "By new laws passed on my initiative I brought back into use many exemplary practices of our ancestors [*multa exempla maiorum*] that were disappearing [*exolescentia*] in our time." *R.G.* 8.5, 67. In "Family Values in Ancient Rome," Saller convincingly criticizes the ideal of a "golden age" in Rome's archaic past. He notes how "even the earliest Latin authors" were already "deploring the moral decline of their own time." This does not necessarily account for lack of heirs in the early imperial era, but it does illuminate how the moral status of the family—and the methods used to regulate it—remained a constant concern throughout Roman history.

56. In the literary imagination of writers throughout the empire, nourishment (specifically milk) functioned at the level of etiology. It was the nursing of Romulus and Remus by the *lupa* that saved the two boys who would later found Rome. Hence, Plutarch, in his discussion of Romulus in *Lives* 4–6 (LCL 46:99–103), speculates about the mythic milk at the beginning of Rome: "Some say that the name of the children's nurse, by its ambiguity, deflected the story into the realm of the fabulous. For the Latins not only called she-wolves 'lupae,' but also women of loose character. . . . As for the babes . . . we are told that they were named, from 'ruma,' the Latin word for teat, Romulus and Romus (or Remus), because they were seen sucking the wild beast." A couple generations later, Porphyry explores the mythic etymology of the word galaxy (γαλαξίας), noting that it is so called because souls are fed there on milk prior to receiving a body—and thus receive milk immediately after birth in order to ease the transition to embodied life (*On the Cave Nymphs* 28). At the origins of both Rome and its people resides a mythos of milk nourishment that was both cosmic and personal in scope.

57. For more on the Ara Pacis, see Karl Galinsky, *Augustan Culture,* 141–55.

58. Ibid., 150.

59. Beryl Rawson, "Iconography of Roman Childhood," 214.

60. Genevieve Lively has pointed toward a seductive quality in the figure of "Mother Earth"—with her robe slipping down over her shoulder—to suggest that the pairing of nurture and eroticism within such imagery destabilized them as representative of "good Augustan motherhood." See *"Mater Amoris:* Mothers and Lovers in Augustan Rome," 187.

61. The connection between Roman mothers and goddesses was a common motif in the material culture of the imperial era. Laura Nasrallah has examined the ways in which Roman women (especially mothers) were depicted in the form of Knidian Aphrodite. Nasrallah notes especially the curious interplay between modesty and erotics in this rendering of the Roman matron. See Nasrallah, *Christian Responses to Art and Architecture,* 249–68.

62. In using the term "ideology," I do not have in mind some external power imposed upon asymmetrical relations from the top down. Rather, I follow the lead of other scholars of Roman antiquity who have viewed imperial ideology as a system of symbols, a semiotics that is sanctioned and strategically used to determine what is thinkable, doable. This is a process that requires "participation" (to use Karl Galinsky's phrase) or "consensus" (to use Clifford Ando's). The symbolic power of nourishment in the Roman Empire, and the ideology of family values through which it was made intelligible, was not achieved by the fiat of Augustus or his successors on their own. It was the product of a broader discourse about the mechanics of proper human formation—a discourse that involved a wide array of interlocutors seeking representation, recognition, and legitimacy within a broader cultural script. Such participation allows for, indeed necessitates, the possibility that a given ideology will be reactivated in ways both conventional and innovative. The next chapter will explore this kind of participation in greater detail. For ideology in this sense, see Dale Martin, *The Corinthian Body,* xiv–xv; Galinsky, *Augustan Culture,* 8–9; Clifford Ando, *Imperial Ideology and Provincial Loyalty,* 19–48.

63. E.g., see Kate Cooper, *The Fall of the Roman Household;* Kristina Sessa, *The Formation of Papal Authority in Late Antique Italy;* Véronique Dasen and Thomas Späth, *Children, Memory, and Family Identity in Roman Culture;* Eve D'Ambra, *Roman Women;* Milnor, *Gender, Domesticity, and the Age of Augustus;* Severy, *Augustus and the Family;* Rebecca Flemming, *Medicine and the Making of Roman Women;* Geoffrey S. Nathan, *The Family in Late Antiquity;* Gardner, *Family and* Familia; Beryl Rawson and Paul Weaver, *The Roman Family in Italy;* Saller, *Patriarchy, Property and Death;* Emiel Eyben, *Restless Youth in Ancient Rome;* David Kertzer and Richard Saller, *The Family in Italy;*

Suzanne Dixon, *The Roman Family;* Keith R. Bradley, *Discovering the Roman Family;* Thomas Wiedemann, *Adults and Children in the Roman Empire;* Beryl Rawson, *The Family in Ancient Rome.*

64. Tim Parkin, "The Demography of Infancy," 50–57; Janet McWilliam, "The Socialization of Roman Children," 264–85; Patricia Salzman-Mitchell, "Tenderness or Taboo," 141–64; Peter Garnsey, *Cities, Peasants, and Food;* Peter Garnsey, "Child Rearing in Ancient Italy," 48–65; Valerie Fildes, *Wet-Nursing,* 1–31; Keith R. Bradley, "Wet-Nursing at Rome," 201–29; Sandra R. Joshel, "Nurturing the Master's Child," 3–22; Keith R. Bradley, "Sexual Regulations in Wet-Nursing Contracts," 321–25.

65. *R.G.* 6.1 (in Cooley, *Res Gestae Divi Augusti,* 64): *curator legum et morum.*

66. In her book *Family and* Familia, Jane Gardner helpfully delineates between *familia*—which was a legal category with an exclusive patrilineal membership—and what we refer to more generally as "family"—an expansive and adaptable collection of relatives and other members of the same *domus* (1). As I will demonstrate, it was the intrusion of outside influence into the *familia* (often in the form of wet nurses and other child-minders) which would cause such consternation among moralists of the period. For a detailed examination of the different meanings (legal, social, etc.) behind terms such as *familia* and *domus* in the Roman world, see also Richard P. Saller "Familia, Domus, and the Roman Conception of the Family," 336–55. Saller concludes that *familia* was used to indicate agnatic relationship (or kinship via paternal lines), while *domus* encompassed "the wider kinship group" and provided "a central symbol of social status under the Republic [that] was easily adapted to serve as status symbol in the new political conditions of the Principate which saw a rapid turnover of senatorial families" (337).

67. Galinsky, *Augustan Culture,* 130.

68. See Syme, *Roman Revolution,* 443–47.

69. Galinsky, *Augustan Culture,* 132.

70. There is little sense of how these laws were observed on the ground or the extent to which they were successful. It was typical throughout Roman history to call upon a prior golden age of family values. We must approach their apocalyptic depictions with more suspicion than did, say, Jerome Carcopino, who concluded, "It is obvious that unhappy marriages must have been innumerable [in Ancient Rome]." See Carcopino, *Daily Life in Ancient Rome,* 94. My concern is not with the extent to which legislation was an accurate diagnosis of real social crises. Rather, my interest is in the extent to which legal promulgations contributed to a larger symbolic discourse regarding family, nurture, and social well-being. On this point, see Antti Arjava, *Women and Law in Late Antiquity,*

78: "The practical operation of the Augustan laws is not particularly well documented, and their success is debatable. They may have had an effect on nuptiality if not on fertility. In any case they continued to be enforced up to the early fourth century. The restrictions on inheritance undoubtedly caused inconvenience among the upper classes."

71. Dio Cassius, *Roman History,* 56.3.3 (LCL 175:6).

72. *Roman History,* 56.3.4 (LCL 175:6).

73. *Roman History,* 56.3.5 (LCL 175:6–8). With a different historical moment in mind, Kathryn Lofton has observed how "constructions of the parent are almost always in service to a conservative politics of nurture." In this way, ideologies surrounding food and formation are recursive in momentum: the social values identified with the materials of familial nourishment are digested by the infant being nurtured and encoded upon the bodies of the ones doing the nurturing. See Lofton, "Religion and the Authority in American Parenting."

74. See Gardner, *Family and* Familia, 233.

75. Ibid., 279.

76. Milnor, in *Gender, Domesticity, and the Age of Augustus,* refers to this ideology as a "gendered Augustanism" (3–5). That is to say, the "Augustan age" both produced and was produced by social norms regarding gender roles within the family as the basic building blocks of civic virtue.

77. Ibid., 153.

78. For further reflection on this point, see Severy, *Augustus and the Family,* 52.

79. Crucial to the overall argument of this study is how the female body functioned as a site for the preservation and promotion of social identity. To the extent that this family ideology everywhere served a male-authored and male-oriented sociality, our sources perpetually elide the lived *realia* of women. As Sandra Joshel and Sheila Murnaghan have noted, "[W]hile we will always have special trouble recovering the subjectivities of ancient women and slaves, the differential equations of slavery and gender can teach us to relinquish the pseudo-subjectivities constructed in ancient male and masterly texts and practices. At the very least, we can resist the totalizing visions of Greek and Roman law and literature and avoid making them our own." Joshel and Murnaghan, *Women and Slaves in Greco-Roman Culture,* 21. It is my hope that the analysis offered throughout this book has likewise resisted the "totalizing visions" of how women and their bodies function in the promotion of social organizations that are interested almost exclusively in men as their presumed audience and subject. As Peter Garnsey has observed, "The guiding principle of the cultural explanation of food allocation is that food behavior reflects the social hierarchy and social relationships." Garnsey, *Food and Society in Classical Antiquity,* 108.

In Roman family values, the allocation of food and the instrumentalizing of the female body in that allocation exemplifies this point. Women not only occupied an inferior status in the provision of food within the family, their bodies were made food for those children who would later occupy a higher status.

80. On women's bodies as natural/national resources, recall Offred, the narrator of Margaret Atwood's feminist dystopian novel *The Handmaid's Tale*, who understands her entire existence under the new regime as a site from which the material of Gilead's future is mined.

81. I have in mind here Ando's account of "consensus" as "the product of a complex conversation between center and periphery." Imperial ideology is more accurately viewed as a constellation of sanctioned symbols open to disparate but related engagement rather than a unitary, monolithic culture tyrannically imposed. See Ando, *Imperial Ideology*, xiii.

82. Sarah Pomeroy, *Families in Classical and Hellenistic Greece*, 95.

83. Dasen and Späth, *Children, Memory, and Family Identity*, "Introduction," 9.

84. For more on the wet nurse, see also Véronique Dasen, "Childbirth and Infancy in Greek and Roman Antiquity," 307–10.

85. Dasen and Späth, *Children, Memory, and Family Identity*, 9.

86. For discussion of these estimates, see Tim Parkin, "The Demography of Infancy and Early Childhood in the Ancient World," 46–50; Richard Saller, "The Roman Family as Productive Unit," 119; Garnsey, "Child Rearing in Ancient Italy," 51; and D'Ambra, *Roman Women*, 66.

87. Keith Bradley, "The Roman Child in Sickness and in Health," 80. For more on malnourishment, especially among children, see Garnsey, *Food and Society*, 43–61.

88. In his essay "Wet-Nursing at Rome," Bradley cites an inscription from a freedman who claims with pride that his wife "reared her children with her very own breast milk [*quae filios suos propriis uberibus educavit*]" (222n3). Bradley views this inscription as evidence that wet-nursing may have been more common even among "the servile classes" (201–2) than previously thought and that scholars have too long been fixated upon the literature regarding wet-nursing that was aimed specifically at the upper classes of the empire. If Bradley is accurate on this point, then it is possible to situate the suffusion of an ideology regarding the family, nourishment, and child formation across an even wider swath of Roman society.

89. Bradley rightly notes that these women were first and foremost subjects of the ruling class. However intimate the depiction of the relationship between a *nutrix* and her *familia* may be in the inscriptional evidence, we must not forget that she and other child-minders were typically slaves whose bodies and lives

were viewed primarily as resources at the family's disposal. Bradley, "Wet-Nursing at Rome," 222. For a rigorous assessment of the asymmetrical relationship between nurse and the family that employed or owned her, see especially Joshel, "Nurturing the Master's Child."

90. Many hypotheses have been put forth regarding the decision to use a wet nurse during this period. Some have suggested that breast-feeding was a domestic task understood to be beneath the honor of a Roman matron (see Bradley, "Wet-Nursing at Rome," 216) or that the high mortality rate of the infant (or even the mother during birth) may have prompted a period of separation (Bradley, *Discovering the Roman Family,* 51–61, or Garnsey, "Child Rearing in Ancient Italy," 61). As we will see, some moralists of the imperial period viewed wet-nursing as an indication of female vanity—because the mother cared more about her physical appearance than the physical and psychic well-being of her child.

91. For an excellent recent study on the impact of public medical demonstrations, see Jared Secord, "Medicine and Sophistry," 217–24.

92. Flemming, *Medicine and the Making of Roman Women,* 25.

93. Though it was published late in my own research, I am especially grateful to Chris L. de Wet for his conversation and sharing his research on the structuring logic of slavery. See especially his discussion of "the slave as nurse" in chap. 4 of *Preaching Bondage,* 127–69.

94. Ann Ellis Hanson, "The Medical Writer's Woman," 316.

95. Soranus, *Gynecology (Gyn.)* 2.18.4 (CMG 4:65; translation, Temkin, 89–90).

96. *Gyn.* 2.19 (CMG 4:68).

97. *Gyn.* 2.19.15 (CMG 4:68). For more on the Greek nurses at Rome, see Véronique Dasen, "Des nourrices grecques à Rome?" 699–713.

98. *Gyn.* 2.20 (CMG 4:68–69). The practicality of such a recommendation seems limited, at best, since few families had the resources for even one wet nurse.

99. Sandra R. Joshel, *Slavery in the Roman World,* 214.

100. For an overview of this text, including debates concerning its genre and authorship, see Steven H. Rutledge, "Tacitus' *Dialogus de Oratoribus,*" 62–83. Tacitus also briefly discusses child-rearing in *Germanica* 20.

101. Tacitus, *Dialogue on Oratory (Dial.)* 28.4 (LCL 35:306).

102. *Dial.* 28.3 (LCL 35:306).

103. *Dial.* 29 (LCL 35:306–8).

104. Quintilian, *Institutes of Oratory (Inst.)* 1.1.2 (LCL 124:64–66): *non naturam defecisse sed curam.* This curious phrase, placed as it is at the very beginning of Quintilian's curriculum on education, indicates the extent to which care was viewed to perfect nature, to bring it to completion.

105. *Inst.* 1.1.4–5 (LCL 124:66).

106. Cicero makes a similar point in his *Tusculan Disputations* 3.1–3 (LCL 141:224–26).

107. *Inst.* 2.4.5 (LCL 124:282).

108. Garnsey, *Cities, Peasants, and Food*, 267.

109. *Gyn.* 2.46–48 (CMG 4:85–87).

110. *Gyn.* 2.47.2 (CMG 4:86).

111. Plutarch, *On the Education of Children* (*On Ed.*) 1 (LCL 197:4). I follow Bradley ("Wet-Nursing at Rome," 222 n. 1) in his observation that the questionable authorship of the text is not decisive for its relevance, as it depicts themes resonant with Plutarch's views espoused elsewhere and corroborates opinions found within many of the texts we have examined from this general period (i.e. late first and early second century CE).

112. *On Ed.* 2 (LCL 197:8).

113. *On Ed.* 3 (LCL 197:12). Among the treatises within Plutarch's *Moralia* no longer extant, there is one tantalizingly titled "The Wetnurse"; see his *Fragments* (LCL 429:18).

114. The author uses the Greek words τίτθη and τροφός interchangeably.

115. *On Ed.* 3 (LCL 197:15–16). On the supposed "naturalness" of maternal nourishment, see also Salzman-Mitchell, "Tenderness or Taboo."

116. *On Ed.* 3 (LCL 197:16).

117. On this theme, see Susan R. Holman, "Molded as Wax." Holman aptly notes how ancient authors widely utilized the images of wax and food within child-rearing as "formative tools—[which] similarly evoke the deliberate physical formation of a good social or spiritual character" (81). The malleable quality of the infant extended to both body and soul.

118. For the character of Favorinus, see especially Maud W. Gleason, *Making Men*. For his depiction in Aulus Gellius, see Leofranc Holford-Strevens, *Aulus Gellius*, 98–130; and Erik Gunderson, *Nox Philologiae*, 170–73. Favorinus and Plutarch were apparently well acquainted with one another. Favorinus's depiction of Roman motherhood and the proper nourishment of infants suggests a basic agreement with (if also an intensification of) what is presented in *Education of Children* attributed to Plutarch.

119. Aulus Gellius, *Attic Nights* 12.1.9 (LCL 200:354). Gunderson examines this scene with vivid analysis in *Nox Philologiae*, 225–28.

120. *Attic Nights* 12.1.14 (LCL 200:356).

121. *Attic Nights* 12.1.17–18 (LCL 200:356–58).

122. Thus, Holford-Strevens understates the case in concluding simply that "we may discern, as elsewhere in that age, a high valuation on familial ties." *Aulus Gellius*, 115.

123. *Attic Nights* 12.1.20–24 (LCL 200:358–60).

124. Gunderson, *Nox Philologiae*, 227–28. There is, of course, some irony that Favorinus would be the mouthpiece of an ideology of nurturance that is solely aimed at the production of legitimate male heirs within a thoroughly masculine framework. As Gunderson wryly jokes, "masculine authority is not exactly native to Favorinus's body." Ibid., 172. However, Maud Gleason has persuasively suggested that Favorinus's intellectual prowess demonstrates the extent to which manliness and rhetorical skill were the prizes of a social competition, not innate characteristics. She prefers "to see Favorinus' audacious self-fashioning as the conceptual equivalent to the exception that proves the rule: the fact that he could aspire to fill the roles of sophist and philosopher without the necessary anatomical prerequisites . . . and the fact that he succeeded, provide convincing evidence that in his culture gender roles were constructed by the interplay of individual effort and social expectations; a male could not claim title to them by the mere fact of biological sex." Gleason, *Making Men*, 162.

125. While it is important not to equate all lactating bodies with maternal bodies, my argument here and throughout is that the symbolic power of nourishment—and specifically breast milk—ascribed a parallel symbolic significance to the maternal body. And so, just as Favorinus demanded that milk must be given to an infant from its proper (read: biological-maternal) source to ensure kinship and status, so too did male authors develop notions of a legitimate intellectual maternity.

126. *Coriolanus* 3.2.131. Plutarch's *Lives*, which serves as Shakespeare's source for the tragedy, also emphasizes Volumnia's maternity as the basis of her son's courage and nobility.

127. A final and striking example is found in Artemidorus's roughly contemporaneous *Interpretation of Dreams*. At one point, Artemidorus considers the meaning of dreams involving breast-feeding, noting their power to signify a variety of peculiar fates. If a man whose wife is pregnant dreams he is being breast-fed, the dream presages that he will have a son who will resemble him and be nourished similarly. Thus, the man receives assurance that his likeness has been properly transmitted and will be properly nourished and reared in his newborn son (1.16). In the same section, Artemidorus states that dreams of breast-feeding also signal sickness, for "children who are still at the milk stage are weak. Indeed grown men rely upon milk when they are sick and unable to take nourishment." See also White's translation of *The Interpretation of Dreams*, 24–25.

Chapter 2. Mother's Milk as Ethno-religious Essence in Ancient Judaism

Epigraph: The epigraph to this chapter comes from a brief essay, "Motherhood," by Katie Hinde, an evolutionary biologist at Harvard's Comparative Lactation Laboratory. Hinde's work explores the organizational power of mother's milk and its impact on "infant outcomes." Hinde has been researching the effects of this food upon the neurological, immunological, and behavioral formation of the newly born. I am grateful to her for being a generous conversation partner open to inter-disciplinary connection and for writing extensively on her research in public online venues.

1. I use the term "ethno-religious" in this chapter to clarify the ways in which ancient Jewish authors developed Roman family values about eating and feed-ing well with a special emphasis on Torah piety, scriptural narrative, and the divine sources of mother's milk. Of course, one could easily say that the previ-ously examined discussions of proper nurture, like that of Aulus Gellius, also convey their own kind of ethno-religious essence. I would not argue that point. My emphasis here is that the particular ways in which mother's milk was en-coded with "Jewish character" takes on greater ethnic and religious specificity.

2. My approach here is shaped by the method described in Annette Yoshiko Reed and Natalie B. Dohrmann's introduction to *Jews, Christians, and the Roman Empire*, 1-21.

3. Mary Rose D'Angelo has helpfully mapped out some of the ways in which Roman family values were reflected within Jewish literature and has suggested that "Roman imperial politics must be taken into account in reckoning the de-velopment of both early Christian and Jewish sexual politics." See D'Angelo, "Early Christian Sexual Politics," 31. See also her illuminating discussion in "Gender and Geopolitics," 63-88, and "*Eusebeia*," 139-65.

4. Sources that touch on this subject in various ways include Jordan D. Rosen-blum, *Food and Identity in Early Rabbinic Judaism;* Gwynn Kessler, *Conceiv-ing Israel*, 77; Marc Hirshman, *The Stabilization of Rabbinic Culture*, 57-58 and 113; Martin Jaffee, *Torah in the Mouth;* Sacha Stern, *Jewish Identity in Early Rabbinic Writings*, 56-59.

5. This is the dating range found in Susan Haber, "Living and Dying for the Law," 75. Haber follows the lead of Jan Willem van Henten in *The Maccabean Mar-tyrs*. Both propose that the text is best located toward the beginning of this range. Robert Doran considers the significance of Eupolemus, the Jewish dip-lomat to Rome mentioned in 2 Macc. 4:11, in dating the text as a whole (2 Macc., 14-15). This offers no surer footing for the date, but does indicate that it was written between the Jewish appeal to Rome for support against the Seleucids

and the Roman conquest of Jerusalem by Pompey. That is to say, its date is reflective of an increasing awareness of Roman rule and, as a result, Roman social ideology.

6. The dating of 4 Macc. is notoriously contentious. While it is not crucial to the present argument whether it is located in the first or second century, I find recent attempts to situate it literarily within the Second Sophistic convincing. See, e.g., Jan Willem van Henten, "Datierung und Herknuft des Vierten Makkabäerbuches," 137–45.

7. Jan Willem van Henten has argued that the martyrs offer more than just an exemplary model of Jewish piety. Their deaths were "significant from a political perspective" in that they remained faithful to and thus preserved a specifically Jewish way of life. From this perspective, the mother's role becomes even more pronounced as a foundation and source of that Jewish identity for her sons. See van Henten, *The Maccabean Martyrs*, 187–269.

8. There is an interesting corollary here between the nourishment that is rejected (the Greek-offered pork) as foreign, polluted, and contrary to Jewish identity and that which is praised (the mother's milk) as the bond of brotherly love and the basis of their Jewish piety.

9. See especially Jan Willem van Henten, "The *Passio Perpetuae* and Jewish Martyrdom," 118–33; Robert Doran, *2 Maccabees*, 166; Susan Haber, "Living and Dying for the Law, 75–92; D'Angelo, *"Eusebeia"*; Stephen D. Moore and Janice Capel Anderson, "Taking It Like a Man," 249–73; David A. deSilva, *4 Maccabees,* esp. 71 and 118; van Henten, *Maccabean Martyrs;* Tessa Rajak, "Dying for the Law," esp. 56–57; Robin Darling Young, "The 'Woman with the Soul of Abraham,'" 67–81.

10. D'Angelo, *"Eusebeia"*; Haber, "Living and Dying for the Law," 84–89; Rajak, "Dying for the Law," 56–57; van Henten, *Maccabean Martyrs,* 232–34, and "The *Passio Perpetuae* and Jewish Martyrdom"; Young, "The 'Woman with the Soul of Abraham,'" 76.

11. I am indebted to Susan Haber's essay for the connection between the broader questions that animate this book and the relevance of the Maccabean mother to them. Her essay "Living and Dying for the Law" anticipates the kind of comparative work I am doing in this chapter. I hope to build upon her initial observations to provide a robust account of the social, cultural, and rhetorical stakes embedded within the mother's appeal to breast-feeding and nurturance.

12. See, e.g., 2 Macc. 7.20–21 and 4 Macc. 15.23.

13. Van Henten, "The *Passio Perpetuae* and Jewish Martyrdom," 127, and *Maccabean Martyrs,* 232–34.

14. Young, "The 'Woman with the Soul of Abraham,'" 73.

15. D'Angelo, *"Eusebeia,"* 150.

16. I have consulted the Rahlfs edition of the Septuagint and the translations found in the NRSV.

17. Haber, "Living and Dying for the Law," 83.

18. Homer, *The Iliad* 2.22.78–90. The phrase translated as "care-banishing breast" appears in Clement of Alexandria's *Paedagogus* 1.6, a passage that will be explored at length in the following chapter.

19. In a different context (a papyrus from the mid-first century CE: O.Berenike.2.129 [50–75 CE]), a mother chastises her son for failing to send her a letter with an update on his life. She rebukes him: "Was it for this that I carried you for ten months and nursed you for three years, so that you would be incapable of remembering me by letter?"

20. Haber, "Living and Dying for the Law," 86.

21. On the idea that God implanted, formed, and fed the boys, see also Rajak, "Dying for the Law," 57, and van Henten, "Maccabean Martyrs," 175–76. In a study on later rabbinic traditions, Gwynn Kessler has helpfully analyzed the ways in which the rabbis emphasized God's prenatal and postnatal care of children as a theological resource for understanding God's care of Israel writ large (though there is less discussion of how breast-feeding and nourishment function within this tradition). See Kessler, *Conceiving Israel,* esp. 72–77.

22. Haber, "Living and Dying for the Law," 86.

23. Young, "The 'Woman with the Soul of Abraham,'" 76.

24. Jordan Rosenblum has analyzed the symbolic power of food within rabbinic constructions of Jewish identity: "Concomitant with this notion that certain foods serve as a metonym for 'Us' is the conception that eating metonymic food is a practice of embodiment. By the term embodiment, I mean to suggest that tannaitic food regulations create both individual and communal bodies (i.e., identities). What is on the plate and the manner in which one consumes that food is a kind of 'social digestion': breaking down and reassembling the building blocks of society." Rosenblum, *Food and Identity,* 45.

25. See Martha Himmelfarb, "The Mother of the Seven Sons," 327.

26. As quoted in Galit Hasan-Rokem, *Web of Life,* 117. The connection between breast-feeding, the Song of Songs, and formation will be drawn out at even greater length in the analysis of Gregory of Nyssa.

27. In oration 15 on the Maccabean martyrs, Gregory of Nazianzus also pauses on the scene in which the mother bares her breasts. So captivated by her bravery, Gregory refers to her as a mother true to her noble birth, even calling her (and not her sons) a mighty and great-souled nursling. See Martha Vinson's translation in *St. Gregory of Nazianzus,* 75, 79.

28. D'Angelo, "Gender and Geopolitics," 64–65.

29. Maren Niehoff, *Philo on Jewish Identity and Culture*, 163.

30. *On Flight* 137 (LCL 275:82).

31. *On Flight* 137 (LCL 275:82).

32. Rosenblum, *Food and Identity*, 61–62.

33. For more on the Logos in Philo, see also Cristina Termini, "Philo's Thought within the Context of Middle Judaism," 98–99, and Daniel Boyarin, *Border Lines*, 92–115. In *On Flight* 112 (LCL 275:71), Philo refers to God's Logos as "the bond of all existence" that "holds and knits together all the parts, preventing them from being dissolved and separated." The Logos is a formative, binding force, mediating between God and creation. The manna is a material manifestation of God's mediation into the created world. In this way, Philo posits the Logos as a meal.

34. For a general introduction to "the family" in Philo, see Adele Reinhartz, "Parents and Children," 61–88.

35. *Who Is the Heir of Divine Things?* 294–300 (LCL 261:435–37).

36. On the pervasive use of this theme in ancient educational theory, see Susan Holman, "Molded as Wax."

37. *Who Is the Heir of Divine Things?* 265 (LCL 261:436).

38. This is echoed in *On the Special Laws* 2.228–30 (LCL 341:449), where Philo also emphasizes the crucial role that parents play as teachers: "First, [the parents] have brought [the children] out of non-existence; then, again, they have held them worthy of nourishment along with education of body and soul so that they may have not only life but a good life." See also *On the Virtues (Virt.)* 178–79 for more on the danger of poor instruction by parents and nurses.

39. *Virt.* 130 (LCL 341:242).

40. *Virt.* 128 (LCL 341:240).

41. *On Drunkenness* 33 (LCL 247:335).

42. *On Drunkenness* 34–35 (LCL 247:337). Along with the previous, this passage exemplifies Sharon Lea Mattila's assertion that "One can conceive . . . of a kind of gender gradient underlying much of Philo's thought, whose positive ('male') and negative ('female') poles are consistently defined, and whose predominant feature is hierarchy." See Mattila, "Wisdom, Sense Perception, Nature," 106.

43. For a discussion of *enkyklios paideia* as a form of socialization, see Teresa Morgan, "Ethos," 512–16. Morgan suggests that this general course of education "socialized learners mainly in three ways. It gave them the skills of literacy and numeracy in Greek. It transmitted at least a little Greek culture to all learners, and a great deal to those who could afford to pursue it for several years. And it taught Greek ethics: the diverse, diffuse, elusive but culturally definitive

assumptions about the nature of the world and human life that help to define the mindset of a society" (512).

44. *On Mating* 9 (LCL 261:463). See also *On Mating* 73 for further description of Hagar as *enkyklios paideia,* the handmaid to wisdom.

45. *On Mating* 19 (LCL 261:467).

46. For a brief analysis of the *enkyklios paideia* as it appears in Philo's work, see especially Peder Borgen, *Bread from Heaven,* 100–115. Borgen draws especially on the connection between manna (*trophe*), virtue (*arête*), and education (*paideia*) in Philo's *On the Changes of Names* (*Mut.*) 258. Borgen concludes, "The concept of manna in Mut. 255–263 has then been interpreted within this context of Greek educational ideas. Manna itself is interpreted as the 'virtue' and 'wisdom' of philosophy in contrast to encyclical education. This 'manna' of philosophy is sufficient and perfect, because it is associated with the selftaught by nature" (105). However, this conclusion is not supported by the shift in emphasis found in *On Mating* 9 or 19, in which *paideia* becomes a necessary first step en route to wisdom—indeed it is the milk that makes one strong enough for the "manna of philosophy."

47. In *On the Confusion of Tongues* 13.49 (LCL 261:37), Philo refers to Wisdom as the nurse and mother of the wise man.

48. *On Dreams* 2.10 (LCL 275:447). In chap. 5, I will show how Gregory of Nyssa presents a similar account of his brother Basil in the *Encomium for Saint Basil.* With both Philo and Gregory, being self-fed indicates the intellectual prowess of one who is also self-taught.

49. Mattila, "Wisdom, Sense Perception, Nature," 109.

50. Exod. 2:7 (referring to the Septuagint [LXX]): "Then the sister of Moses said to the daughter of the Pharaoh, 'Do you want me to summon a nursing woman from among the Hebrews who will suckle the infant for you?'"

51. Philo, *On the Life of Moses* (*Mos.*) 1.17 (LCL 289:285).

52. The LSJ entry on *gnesios* reveals the word's complex function for demarcating insiders and outsiders, whether politically, familialy, or ethnically. The word is used to identify "true Greeks," "lawful members of the city," as well as wives and children whose status is legitimate in a legal sense within the *genos.*

53. *Mos.* 1.18 (LCL 289:285).

54. *Mos.* 1.18 (LCL 289:285). The word *galaktotrophia* also appears in 4 Macc. 16.7, analyzed previously.

55. Patricia Cox Miller, *Biography in Late Antiquity,* 22.

56. *Mos.* 1.19 (LCL 289:285). In Exod. 2:2 (LXX), Moses is described as "refined" (*asteios*) from the time of his birth. Philo is clearly extending this characteristic into the growth of Moses under his mother's care.

57. *Mos.* 1.20 (LCL 289:285).

58. *Mos.* 1.23 (LCL 289:288–89).

59. For more on Philo's discussion of Greek *paideia* within *On the Life of Moses*, see especially René Bloch, "Alexandria in Pharaonic Egypt," 69–84. Bloch concludes, "Philo is consistently trying to situate Jewish tradition in the context of contemporary philosophy and science: he attempts to make sense of the paradoxes in Jewish tradition, while at the same time participating in Jewish and non-Jewish discourses" (82–83).

60. E. A. Judge, "St Paul and Socrates," 670–83 (essay originally published in 1973).

61. Ibid., 675.

62. Troels Engberg-Pedersen, *Paul Beyond the Judaism/Hellenism Divide*, "Introduction," 4. For a selection of recent book-length scholarship on Paul in this vein (with emphasis on 1 Cor.), see also Troels Engberg-Pedersen, *Cosmology and Self*; Michelle V. Lee, *Paul, the Stoics, and the Body of Christ*; Robert S. Dutch, *The Educated Elite*; L. L. Welborn, *Paul the Fool of Christ*; L. L. Welborn, *Politics and Rhetoric*; Bruce W. Winter, *Philo and Paul among the Sophists*; Dale Martin, *The Corinthian Body*; Daniel Boyarin, *A Radical Jew*; Duane Liftin, *St. Paul's Theology of Proclamation*; Margaret M. Mitchell, *Paul and the Rhetoric of Reconciliation*.

63. There are other texts from the New Testament (especially 1 Thess. 2:7, 1 Pet. 2:2, and Heb. 5:11–14) that engage the milk-and-solid-food motif. I have focused on 1 Cor. 3 because it is, as the following chapters will make clear, the passage that garnered the most attention from ancient interpreters—the others being used mostly to supplement commentary on that text. On these and other texts, see also Jennifer Houston McNeel, *Paul as Infant and Nursing Mother*; Alicia D. Myers, "In the Father's Bosom"; and Philip L. Tite, "Nurslings, Milk and Moral Development." Drawing primarily upon the "cognitive metaphor theory" of Lakoff and Johnson, McNeel's work on 1 Thessalonians shares a similar analytical starting point to what I am proposing here. However, I have found the linguistic theory of Bourdieu (as well as Derrida and Butler), outlined in the introduction to this book, to be more useful in the broader examination of how social reality shapes and is shaped by language. Since my work here is not isolated to the scriptural text itself—as is the case in McNeel's study—but rather seeks to widen the historical lens in order to survey the traditions behind, within, and produced by that text, a robust appraisal of nourishment as a conjuncture of social realities and rhetorical conventions proved more fruitful than the cognitive model provided by Lakoff and Johnson in their oft-cited book *Metaphors We Live By*.

64. I follow the work of Engberg-Pedersen here on the dual nature of *pneuma*—a "material" with both physical and cognitive aspects: "[T]here is absolutely no inconsistency in understanding [*pneuma*] as a physical entity and as a cognitive power that generates understanding. At least, that is exactly the picture one gets in the Stoic understanding of the *pneuma*, which is both a material entity and a cognitive one" (Engberg-Pedersen, *Cosmology and Self*, 65).

65. The reference to "noble birth" (*eugeneia*) is crucial for two reasons. First, it evokes the belief that nobility of birth was not merely something innate but was directly connected to nurture and nourishment. Second, it also indicates the importance of social status in Corinth and the divisions this caused in Paul's community there. This point has been explored by Dale Martin, *The Corinthian Body*, 56, and most thoroughly by L. L. Welborn in "On the Discord in Corinth," 85–111.

66. Welborn's essay ("On the Discord in Corinth") remains the classic study of Paul's political rhetoric in response to the Corinthian factionalism. See also Mitchell, *Paul and the Rhetoric of Reconciliation*, 65–110.

67. I follow Judith Kovacs in rendering the word *psychikoi* as "soulish." There will be more discussion on this terminology in the next chapter.

68. On this distinction, see Engberg-Pedersen, *Cosmology and Self*, 104–5—in which the "psychic man" is characterized as "a person of flesh and blood . . . who has not received a portion of God's pneuma" (104). Also see Richard A. Horsley, "Pneumatikos vs. Psychikos," 269–88, in which *psychikos* refers to those "who have not attained this substantial relationship with Sophia . . . and are mortal insofar as they are still subject to the corruptible bodily and earthly influences" (287). Horsley's emphasis on Sophia misses the deeper and more fundamental role played by the *pneuma* in this distinction. Paul seems primarily concerned with the fact that, although the Corinthians have received God's *pneuma* from his preaching (1 Cor. 1:17) and from baptism (1 Cor. 12:13), they are nevertheless behaving as though they are without *pneuma*. As a result, he must speak to them *as if* they were *pneuma*-less. That is, as if they were *psychikoi*. Their spiritual atrophy reveals a critical depletion of *pneuma*. Paul pivots away from an emphasis on *sophia* toward *pneuma* in order to demonstrate that the Corinthians are more concerned with human conventions than with the vital essence that animates life in Christ.

69. Engberg-Pedersen, *Cosmology and Self*, 203.

70. Ibid., 207.

71. It is worth noting here that we can trace strands of this connection between oral-epistolary instruction and material nourishment to the rabbinic sources as well. Martin Jaffee has convincingly argued for a "sacramental" approach to

rabbinic instruction, in which the teaching of the rabbis "brought into the body something that came from outside; something that had to be mediated by a person already sanctified to his task." See Jaffee, "Oral Transmission of Knowledge as Rabbinic Sacrament," 78.

72. Hans Conzelmann, *1 Corinthians*, 71–72.

73. Charles A. Wannamaker, "A Rhetoric of Power," 130.

74. Richard B. Hays, *First Corinthians*, 48.

75. Liftin, *St. Paul's Theology of Proclamation*, 223.

76. Pheme Perkins, *First Corinthians*, 72–73. Similarly, Robert Dutch concludes that 1 Cor. 3 demonstrates that "Feeding is not solely associated with well-being but, in antiquity, with social well-being and character formation. Instead of the Corinthians developing as they should from Paul's correct feeding they had failed to mature in their characters." See Dutch, *The Educated Elite*, 253.

77. James Francis, "As Babes in Christ."

78. Beverly Roberts Gaventa, *Our Mother Saint Paul*, 42.

79. On Paul's use of "infants" as a category for Christian identity, see Walter Grundmann, "Die *NEPIOI* in der urchristlichen Paränese."

80. Hays, *First Corinthians*, 49.

81. It is commonplace for interpreters of this text to note that Paul's appeal to milk and solid food, while generally similar, stands in contrast to that which is found in Philo's *On Husbandry* 9 or in Epictetus's *Discourses* 2.16.39—both of which use different foods to express different levels of pedagogical content. Scholars such as Francis ("As Babes in Christ," 56) have argued against the idea that Paul is suggesting a Christian curriculum with content portioned differently for beginners and for advanced students. Likewise, Hays cautions that Paul does not advocate for a kind of social stratification in the church through his use of milk and solid food. As we will see throughout the following chapters, for many of Paul's interpreters, such connections and connotations were inevitable— even as they shared the apostle's concern for division and stratification within the Christian community. For even as Paul railed against discord at Corinth, he did so by invoking categorical distinctions of identity and maturity and applying those categories to his correspondents.

82. It is notable that Paul does not identify himself as a "pedagogue" but rather identifies Apollos in this role (1 Cor. 4:15). Welborn has convincingly and exhaustively demonstrated how this can only be viewed as "a gesture of contempt" (*Paul the Fool of Christ*, 109). The pedagogue, unlike the wet nurse, was thought to contribute very little of positive substance to the rearing of the child. At best, he could "do no harm" in his guardianship. See also Norman H. Young, "Paidagogos," 150–76. Note also the clear dynamics of social status at

work in Paul's identification with mother and father in 1 Corinthians and his designation of Apollos with the role of a slave.

83. See especially Elizabeth Castelli, *Imitating Paul*.

84. In this way, Paul claims for himself both the fathering and mothering of the Corinthians as a strategy for producing the kind of individual and collective character he desires from that community. Paul in fact reflects the expectations of Roman parents outlined in the speech of Augustus to the senate recorded in Dio Cassius, in which the highest good of being a mother and a father was the formation of a child endowed with your "physical and spiritual image." While I find Gaventa's analysis of the "Greco-Roman gender dynamics" at play in Paul's appropriation of a maternal role compelling, I do not agree that Paul "concedes the culturally predisposed battle for his masculinity" by appropriating the symbol of breast milk (Gaventa, *Our Mother Saint Paul*, 48). He is manipulating the key ideological symbols of Roman family values to his own strategic advantage in locating himself in a place of authority over the Corinthians.

85. On Paul's Corinthian paternity, see Trevor J. Burke, "Paul's Role as 'Father,'" 95-114, and Eva Maria Lassen, "The Use of the Father Image," 127-36.

86. Margaret M. Mitchell, *Paul, the Corinthians, and the Birth of Christian Hermeneutics*, 4.

87. Ibid., 12.

Chapter 3. Ruminating on Paul's Food in the Second Century

1. Aristotle, *Politics* 1.1.7 (LCL 264:6–8).

2. In Longus, *Daphnis and Chloe* 4.9.3 (LCL 69:161), a text generally dated to the late second century CE, Longus also evokes this idea of being raised on the same milk (*homogalaktes*): "Being fond of Daphnis, [Eudromus] advised them to admit everything to the young master beforehand and promised to help them personally, since he had influence as having been nursed at the same breast [as the young master]." Longus indicates here that Eudromus's mother had also breast-fed the son of her master (the "young master" who is now on his way to speak with the protagonists Daphnis and Chloe). The shared milk implies a unique bond of kinship and, in this case, a warrant for frank speech with a social superior on behalf of others.

3. See *New Testament Apocrypha: Volume Two*, 262–63. As Karen King has observed, genealogy was a crucial metaphor in the debates of early Christianity: "Identity was often articulated in terms of origin, and common identity in terms of common origin." Karen L. King, *What Is Gnosticism?* 32 and 37. In a striking passage from the *Second Apocalypse of James*, there is a brief passage

that evokes the *homogalaktes* motif: "As I raised my face to look at [Jesus], my mother said to me: 'Do not be afraid, my son, because he said to you "My brother." For you were both nourished with the same milk—that is why he calls me "My mother." For he is no stranger to us.'" Here, the power of milk to establish kinship is on display once again. Only this time it is not Paul but James whose legacy is at stake. See *New Testament Apocrypha: Volume One,* 335.

4. On this history, see David Brakke, *The Gnostics,* 118, and Elaine Pagels, *The Gnostic Paul,* 1–6.

5. Margaret M. Mitchell, *Paul, the Corinthians, and the Birth of Christian Hermeneutics,* 43.

6. Judith Kovacs helpfully summarizes: Origen "expands Clement's exegesis by connecting these [food] images with other symbolic foods from Scripture, arranged in a hierarchical sequence, thus portraying the Christian life as consisting not of two, but of three or more levels." See her essay "Echoes of Valentinian Exegesis," 329. Origen's contribution will be analyzed at length in the following chapter.

7. John Behr, *Asceticism and Anthropology,* 17.

8. "Soulish" is Judith Kovacs's phrase, which beautifully captures the ambiguity of Paul's categories. See Kovacs, "Grace and Works," 195.

9. I am not particularly invested in the moniker "Gnostic" (much less the category "Gnosticism") as reflecting actual historical figures or schools of thought. I recognize that some scholars, such as Karen King, would have us do away with Gnostic/Gnosticism entirely as a useful category, while others, such as David Brakke, seek a more specific retrieval of the term "Gnostic" for a particular strand of ancient thought identified with "Sethians." Although I find aspects of both arguments compelling, it is outside the scope of this project to offer a more exhaustive engagement in this complex debate. However, as the texts in question regularly refer to people as "Gnostics," I have tried to analyze the role that this term plays within exegesis of 1 Cor. 3 during the second century— especially when it attaches to other categories such as milk/solid food and infant/perfect. For the sake of clarity, when referring to specific people or groups of people that are criticized for their incorrect emphasis on *gnosis,* I have used the capitalized version "Gnostic." When referring to Clement's more general and positive use of the term in his *Stromateis* for intellectually advanced Christians, I have used "gnostic."

10. The intriguing points of convergence and divergence that can be traced between Irenaeus, Clement, and their opponents are, in large part, due to their shared intellectual pedigree within the high literary culture of the Roman Empire. This shared *paideia* provided a common lexicon, a common set of

analytical tools, and common philosophical comportment despite, in some cases, quite drastic disagreement on scriptural interpretation. I eagerly anticipate Lewis Ayres's forthcoming project on this theme. See his essay "Irenaeus vs the Valentinians."

11. Walter Schmithals, *Gnosticism in Corinth,* 151.

12. Ibid., 152.

13. Ibid.

14. On this point, Christoph Markschies observes, "Of course Christians ... strove for 'gnosis'; they were interested in what philosophers were seeking and what other religious groups promised. The letter of Paul to the Christian community at Corinth ... documents in the middle of the first century the fact that the members of the Christian community in the port were proud of certain higher insights into revelation." It should also be kept in mind, as 2 Cor. 12 makes clear, that Paul himself was not above making claims to "certain higher insights into revelation." See Markschies, *Gnosis,* 16.

15. For exegesis among the Gnostics, see Louis Painchaud, "The Use of Scripture in Gnostic Literature." Especially helpful is Painchaud's emphasis on allusion as a typical Gnostic exegetical strategy, precisely because this strategy can so readily be observed at use in the champions against the Gnostics examined to come, as well.

16. Origen, *Commentary on John* 5.8 (translation Ronald E. Heine, *Origen: Commentary on the Gospel According to John: Books 1–10,* 166). Origen will be examined in greater detail in the chapter that follows.

17. John Hick, *Evil and the God of Love.*

18. Behr, *Asceticism and Anthropology,* 49.

19. Ibid., 43. For more on this theme in Irenaeus, see also Behr, *Irenaeus of Lyons,* 192–95; M. C. Steenberg, "Children in Paradise"; Eric Osborn, *Irenaeus of Lyons;* Richard A. Norris, "Irenaeus' Use of Paul," 91; Rolf Noormann, *Irenäus als Paulusinterpret,* esp. 260–62.

20. Irenaeus, *Demonstration of Apostolic Preaching,* 1.1.8–12 (SC 406:94 & 100): *sed omnino omnium (sumpantes) Altor-et-Nutritor (tropheus). . . . Homo vero puer erat nondum perfectum habens consilium (boule).* The *Sources Chrétiennes* edition of this text is derived from a Latin translation of an Armenian manuscript tradition (itself based on a Greek original). I have consulted John Behr's English translation of the Armenian. For a helpful overview of the manuscript tradition, see the introductory material in Behr's edition of *On the Apostolic Preaching,* 27–38.

21. For the theme of being rendered into the likeness of God in Irenaeus, see Behr, *Asceticism and Anthropology,* 114.

22. Irenaeus, *Against Heresies* (*Her.*), 4.Pr.4 (SC 100:388–90).

23. *Her.,* 4.Pr.4 (SC 100:390).

24. This point has been persuasively demonstrated by Steenberg in "Children in Paradise," 20: "There is an ontological, even a physical, component to his being that promulgates his lack of understanding just as there is such a physiological limitation in any human infant upon its capabilities for rational thought; but this want in Adam cannot be conversely equated with his actual nature as *nepios* any more than a two-year-old infant's lack of adult, cognitive capabilities can be understood as the source of her being a child. . . . Man's materiality is, in this sense, a preventative limitation: it is materiality that binds him to time and time that restricts the capabilities of his knowledge and receptivity of his body. Growth, maturation, and accustomization are requirements not only of man's 'newness' as a creature (see again the angels, newly created yet fully 'mature') but also of his materiality." See also Ysbel de Andia, *Homo Vivens.*

25. See especially Steenberg's argument that "The intention of Irenaeus' entire polemic is patently literalistic." "Children in Paradise," 9.

26. *Her.,* 2.19.3.

27. On Irenaeus's avoidance of "seed" language, see Behr, *Asceticism and Anthropology,* 123: "The creative activity of God effects and matches the growth of man. When speaking of growth, Irenaeus emphatically distances himself from the idea of 'spiritual development' found in various representatives of Gnosticism, the idea that a 'divine seed' was deposited in men as in a womb, to grow therein until it is ready for perfect gnosis. Irenaeus does not even speak of man as possessing a 'seed' of the Spirit which grows within him until he receives the fullness thereof." At the same time, an emphasis on "milk" over and against "seed" does not necessarily preclude notions of insemination. In some cases, milk was viewed to have precisely this effect. See Edward Engelbrecht, "God's Milk," 514–16.

28. I am building here upon Robert Grant's claim that "Irenaeus' basic approach was genetic." See his *Irenaeus of Lyons,* 12.

29. *Her.,* 4.9.3 (SC 100:488).

30. *Her.,* 4.9.3 (SC 100:486–88).

31. *Her.,* 4.37.7 (SC 100:942).

32. Steenberg, "Children in Paradise," 7–10.

33. *Her.,* 4.38.1 (SC 100:944–46).

34. *Her.,* 4.38.1 (SC 100:946).

35. *Her.,* 4.38.2 (SC 100:948–50).

36. *Her.,* 4.38.2 (SC 100:950).

37. *Her.,* 4.38.3 (SC 100: 954–56).

38. *Her.,* 4.38.4 (SC 100:956). On this section, see Noormann, *Irenäus als Paulusinterpret,* 470–71.

39. See also Norris, "Irenaeus' Use of Paul," 91: "Irenaeus thinks that the spelling-out of humanity's creation and salvation in time is implied not only by Paul's insistence that the race moves from the 'psychic' to the 'spiritual' (1 Cor. 15:46) but also by his statement 'I fed you with milk, not solid food; for you were not ready for it' (1 Cor. 3:2). Irenaeus is very conscious, then, that Paul sees God's dealings with humanity to be susceptible of analysis in terms of 'befores' and 'afters.'" My contention is that according to his reading of human infancy, Irenaeus views the human species as still existing in a period marked primarily as "before"—that is, before maturity, before perfection, before the capacity to consume solid food and thus a period of inescapable infancy.

40. "The dominant note in Clement's writings is, as we shall see, that of *paideia.*" John Behr, *Asceticism and Anthropology,* 134.

41. Brakke, *The Gnostics,* 33.

42. On this issue, see also Judith L. Kovacs, "Divine Pedagogy," 7: "[Clement] adapts his teaching to the capabilities of various students. . . . Those who are not eager learners—the hard of heart—he treats as 'servants,' teaching them through the elementary method of disciplinary punishment. More receptive students, called 'faithful servants,' are motivated through teaching about eschatological rewards. The most mature students receive gnosis, or instruction in the mysteries. Because of their intimacy with the divine Teacher, they are called his 'friends.'" While I speak in this chapter about Clement as "catechist" or about his "curriculum," I avoid the murkier debate about the actual structure and day-to-day life of the so-called catechetical school of Alexandria. For an excellent analysis of the sources and scholarship on this, see Annewies van den Hoek, "The 'Catechetical' School of Alexandria."

43. Clement of Alexandria, *Paedagogus* (*Paed.*) 1.6.35 (*VCSup* 61:23). A point of clarification is needed on this quote: Simon P. Wood's translation renders the final word as "figure"—i.e., "A considerable difficulty arises from the figure used in these passages." The sense is correct enough, but the translation is not quite precise. The Greek word is "joining" or "coming together" (*sumbole*) rather than "figure" or "symbol" (*sumbolon*). The point Clement is making has to do not only with the difficulty of the words found within 1 Cor. 3 but also with his attempt to read those words in light of other passages from scripture. It is not at all wrong to speak of the "great difficulty" as referring to such scriptural symbols as milk and solid food, but this is a problem that Clement frames specifically within his attempt to make sense of 1 Cor. 3 by joining it with Exod. 3. See Wood's translation in *Clement of Alexandria: Christ the Educator,* 34.

44. Eric Osborn, *Clement of Alexandria*. John Ferguson dated the writing of these three works sequentially: ca. 195, *Protrepticus;* ca. 197, *Paedagogus;* ca. 199–203, *Stromateis.* See Ferguson, *Clement of Alexandria,* 17. It is both logical and convenient if this order of publication is correct. However, it is not crucial for the argument I seek to make here. My point in what follows is not so much that Clement's reading of 1 Cor. 3 changed over time but rather that he was willing to offer quite different—often antithetical—interpretations when the occasion and intended audience warranted it.

45. Denise Kimber Buell, *Making Christians,* 120: "Clement draws upon and reshuffles the cultural norms of *paideia* to create a specifically Christian *paideia.* He not only presents Christianity as consistent with traditional *paideia* but positions Christianity as its pinnacle—above the expected summit of philosophy."

46. John Behr helpfully unpacks how Irenaeus and Clement diverge: "These two very different elaborations of asceticism and anthropology clearly correspond to two different narratives inscribing man. The narrative for Irenaeus is the economy unfolded in Scripture . . . as the pattern for the whole human race and for each human being. . . . For Clement, on the other hand, the narrative into which man is inscribed is a paideia, which, through progressive training and instruction, leads beyond salvation, to the heights of gnostic Perfection." Behr, *Asceticism and Anthropology,* 214–15.

47. One crucial example of how Clement mimics his opponents is his emphasis on "spiritual seed" passed between teacher and student. As I have shown, Irenaeus refused such language. For more on this, see especially Osborn, *Clement of Alexandria,* 12; Alain Le Boulluec, "Pour qui, pourquoi, comment?" 23–36; Buell, *Making Christians,* 50–68. More on this to follow.

48. Clement of Alexandria, *Protrepticus (Prot.)* 2.14 (LCL 92:32). Clement's tell-all of ritual intrigue can, I think, be read as part of a long-standing genre of literature exposing beliefs and practices of secretive groups. The rites performed by others behind closed doors have long been a source of scandal, speculation, and caution. Christ-followers, after all, were once accused of eating babies. In writing the *Protrepticus,* Clement joins a literary tradition that continues to this day. For a contemporary example, consider Lawrence Wright's *Going Clear.*

49. *Prot.* 2.16 (LCL 92:34).

50. *Prot.* 10.108 (LCL 92:232). Throughout the *Protrepticus,* custom (*sunetheia*) is used by Clement as a catchall term for any practice or intellectual system that he is calling on his readers to abandon. See, e.g., the use of "custom" at the opening of *Prot.* 12 (LCL 92:250).

51. *Prot.* 10 (LCL 92:234). The phrase "good nursing-mother" is borrowed from a reference to Ithaca in Homer (*Odyssey* 9.27).

52. At the opening of *Prot.* 11 (LCL 92:236), Clement observes that the "first man, being free, played like a child in paradise—because he was a child of God. But . . . the child became a man by means of disobedience." This, it seems, forms the basis of Clement's understanding of why Christians must be "born again." To reverse a disobedient and ill-wrought maturity, each person must return to the freedom and innocence of infancy. Though Clement's elaboration of this point is deferred to the *Paedagogus,* the passage here is strikingly similar to the anthropology offered by Irenaeus in *Her.* 4.38.

53. *Prot.* 9 (LCL 92:185).

54. The LSJ entry on this term is striking in its range of connotations for kinship, including "belonging to the race," "lawfully begotten," and more generally "lawful" or "genuine" or "legitimate." For Philo, the milk of Moses's biological mother is described as being a "legitimate" source—her milk carrying to the infant the essential material of his family's ethnic and religious lineage. For more on the relationship between Philo and Clement, see especially Annewies van den Hoek, *Clement of Alexandria and His Use of Philo.*

55. Milk, as Denise Kimber Buell has pointed out, becomes for Clement the "material bond" linking Christians together. See her *Making Christians,* 150. My work in this chapter (and in this project as a whole) has been deeply informed and inspired by Buell's masterful study. It was in response to reading her book as a graduate student that I began to wonder about the relationship between kinship and nourishment as a pervasive and complex rhetorical strategy in early Christian thought.

56. Clement of Alexandria, *Paed.* 1.5.19 (*VCSup* 61:13).

57. For a few examples, see Dawn LaValle, "Divine Breastfeeding," 322–36; Matthew J. Chalmers, "Seeking as Suckling," 59–73; Kovacs, "Divine Pedagogy"; Behr, *Asceticism and Anthropology,* 185–86; Buell, *Making Christians;* Verna E. F. Harrison, "The Care-Banishing Breast of the Father," 401–5; John Ferguson, *Clement of Alexandria,* 74–76.

58. Ferguson, *Clement of Alexandria,* 75–76.

59. It is worth noting that Galatians 3:28 has its own complicated exegetical history, precisely on the issue of how this text and its interpreters purport to resolve the problems associated with human difference "in Christ." For more on this, see especially Benjamin H. Dunning, *Specters of Paul.*

60. *Paed.* 1.6.31 (*VCSup* 61:20).

61. *Paed.* 1.5.21 (*VCSup* 61:14).

62. *Paed.* 1.6.34 (*VCSup* 61:22).

63. *Paed.* 1.6.35–36 (*VCSup* 61:23).

64. *Paed.* 1.6.36 (*VCSup* 61:23).
65. *Paed.* 1.6.36 (*VCSup* 61:24).
66. *Paed.* 1.6.37 (*VCSup* 61:24).
67. LaValle, "Divine Breastfeeding," 335.
68. Edward J. Kilmartin, "The Baptismal Cups," 252. See also Annewies van de Bunt, "Milk and Honey," 27–39. The connection between 1 Cor. 3, Exod. 3, and early Christian milk rites is attested in a variety of sources (such as Jerome, *Against the Luciferians* 8, to name only one).
69. Andrew McGowan, *Ascetic Eucharists*, 108.
70. *Paed.* 1.6.40 (*VCSup* 61:26).
71. I am persuaded by Dawn LaValle's approach to the *pneuma*-centric framework of Clement's physiological and medical theory of milk. LaValle demonstrates how, as opposed to Aristotelian arguments that suggest blood turns to milk when heat is applied, Clement is drawing upon Diogenes of Apollonia, who asserted the importance of pneuma in his account of human milk and semen production. For more discussion on the physiological and medical resonances within this passage, see the excellent recent essay by Matthew Chalmers, "Seeking as Suckling." In contrast to Buell's *Making Christians,* which downplays the interaction between Clement and the medical traditions of his day, Chalmers wants a more robust appreciation of the cultural specificity that attends Clement's biological theorizing.
72. *Paed.* 1.6.41 (*VCSup* 61:27).
73. *Paed.* 1.6.42 (*VCSup* 61:27).
74. *Paed.* 1.6.43 (*VCSup* 61:28; translation, Wood, *Clement of Alexandria: Christ the Educator,* 41). The phrase "care-banishing breast" is derived from a climactic scene in *The Iliad* (22.83)—discussed already in chapter 2—in which Hector's parents plead with him not to face Achilles in combat. Hecuba, Hector's mother, pulls aside her robe and, weeping uncontrollably, bears her breast to her son. Pointing to the breast, she implores Hector by reminding him that it was from this breast that he received nourishment and comfort and pity as a child. And it is because of this breast, she argues, that he should heed her warnings now and not seek death on the battlefield. It is a striking reference for Clement to associate with God's nurturing care.
75. *Paed.* 1.6.45 (*VCSup* 61:28–29).
76. *Paed.* 1.7.54 (*VCSup* 61:34). For reasons of scope, I have not considered in this chapter the evocative "Hymn to Christ the Educator" appended to the manuscript tradition of the *Paedagogus*. Potentially one of the earliest recorded hymns in Christian literature, it ends with a praise of the "breasts of the Word." The difficulties surrounding this hymn (its authorship, date, liturgical setting)

only add to its intrigue. See the annotated translation by Annewies van den Hoek in "Hymn of the Holy Clement," 296–303.

77. This, of course, is not to deny the role that polemics play in Clement's writing more broadly. On this issue, see especially Everett Procter, *Christian Controversy in Alexandria.*

78. Kovacs, "Echoes of Valentinian Exegesis," 323–24. Behr describes it like this: "Whereas the primary contrast in the *Paedagogus* was between the maturity of the new children of God and the immaturity of those outside Christ, one of the main themes of the *Stromateis* is the maturity of the true Gnostic compared with the immaturity of the simple believer. The milk of faith, which appeared as inedible meat to those outside the Church, is now seen to be only milk compared with the Gnostic 'meat.'" Behr, *Asceticism and Anthropology,* 185–86.

79. Kovacs, "Echoes of Valentinian Exegesis," 328.

80. For the place of the *Stromateis* in Clement's writing, and the theme of deeper wisdom within it, see especially Andrew Itter, *Esoteric Teaching.*

81. Clement's widespread use of "gnostic" to identify the advanced Christian produces some interpretive problems. The most prominent English translation of the *Stromateis,* in an attempt to avoid confusing readers between Clement's good and bad versions of "gnostic," uses phrases like "Christian Gnostic" and "true Gnostic." (See Ferguson, *Stromateis: Books One to Three,* 11.) But such phrasing is nowhere to be found in Clement's text, and the difficulty of parsing good and bad gnostics is one of the more intriguing and vexing legacies of a writer who is largely counted among the first champions of "orthodoxy" against Gnostic writing.

82. Clement of Alexandria, *Stromateis (Strom.)* 2.19.97.1 (SC 38:109).

83. *Strom.* 4.3.9.2 (SC 463:70).

84. *Strom.* 4.21.130.4 (SC 463:270).

85. *Strom.* 2.19.98.3 (SC 38:110) and *Strom.* 2.19.100.1 (SC 38:110).

86. *Strom.* 2.20.104.2 (SC 38:114). Having described the ascetic discipline of the *gnostikos* in the previous section, Clement here draws heavily on the language of kinship to articulate the salvific effect of *gnosis.* Such a Christian becomes a "fellow-inhabitant" (*sunoikos*), a "sharer of hearth and home" (*sunestios*), and a "familiar friend" (*oaristes*) to the Lord.

87. *Strom.* 1.1.1.3–1.1.2.1 (SC 30:45). First demonstrating that teachers, through their instruction, deposit seed within the souls of their students, Clement then recounts his own education as a proof for patrilineal legitimacy: "[My teachers] preserved the true tradition of the blessed teachings in direct line from Peter, James, John, and Paul, the holy apostles, child inheriting from father (only a few are like their fathers) and came with God's help to plant in us the seeds of

their apostolic parentage." *Strom.* 1.11.3 (SC 30:52). Buell helpfully accents the "self-authorizing" nature of this passage (*Making Christians,* 83–86). From a general argument about legitimate procreative lines derived from Christian instruction, Clement pivots to his own education as a specific example of a son who is like his father—one who is an heir to that apostolic family. For other discussions of patrilineal legitimacy, see also Taylor G. Petrey, "Semen Stains," 343–72, and Richard Valantasis, *Spiritual Guides of the Third Century.*

88. On Clement's appropriation of the long-standing tradition linking insemination, childbirth, and education, see Buell, *Making Christians,* 52: "The Christian teacher serves as the progenitor of and model for other Christians. . . . [T]he primary function of the teacher is to transmit tradition, by preparing for the next generation to take over as teachers themselves, who model the truth of God's word." And again: "In this metaphoric construction of the educational process, the student's soul is symbolically feminine, cast in a maternal role as the earth. The intellectual offspring thus has the teacher as its father and the learner as its mother. . . . While teachings are the offspring of a teacher's soul, which gestate in the soul of the learner, Clement also consistently identifies the students as the teacher's offspring" (Buell, *Making Christians,* 61).

89. *Strom.* 1.1.7.2–3 (SC 30:48).

90. *Paed.* 1.6.38 (*VCSup* 61:25).

91. *Strom.* 1.11.53.2 (SC 30:87).

92. *Strom.* 1.11.53.3 (SC 30:87).

93. *Paed.* 1.6.39 (*VCSup* 61:26).

94. *Strom.* 5.10.62.3 (SC 278:128).

95. *Strom.* 5.10.66.2–3 (SC 278:134).

96. *Strom.* 5.10.66.2 (SC 278:134).

97. *Strom.* 5.11.70.1–2 (SC 278:140).

98. Buell, *Making Christians,* 150 and 159.

99. Alain Le Boulluec, "The Bible in Use," 215.

Chapter 4. Animal, Vegetable, Milk

1. For the section in question, see the Oxford World Classics edition of Milton, *Paradise Lost,* 115–41.

2. *Dialogue with Heraclides* (*Dial.*) 13.19–20 (SC 67:84). This passage was a central component of Peter Brown's reading of Origen in his landmark book *The Body and Society*—and even served as the title for that chapter. See chap. 8, pp. 60–77.

3. *Dial.* 16.11 (SC 67:88).

4. *Dial.* 16.12–14.

5. On this reading of Origen and the *nous,* I am following the work of Eric Osborn, "Philo and Clement," 108–24, and, especially, Blossom Stefaniw, *Mind, Text, and Commentary.* This term is meant to expand, not restrict, the methodology present in early Christian exegesis beyond an allegorical/literal binary. It is, for Stefaniw, "an attempt to reflect the relevant exegetes' belief that the higher interpretation of the text required the application of the *nous* to the text in order to perceive the intelligible truths contained within it" (29). Finally, noetic exegesis is a practice that "relates to and is born up by the larger culture which gives it its meaning, since interpretive assumptions are located in the (cultural) community reading the text" (42). This connection between Origen's exegetical method and the larger culture that informs him is fundamental for my understanding of the broader, more complex dynamics at play in his widespread usage of symbolic language drawn from nourishment to discuss the formation of the *nous.*

6. Stefaniw, *Mind, Text, and Commentary,* 28.

7. Alexandra Kleeman, "Hylomorphosis," 295.

8. As Judith Kovacs has aptly observed, Origen's "comments on 1 Cor. 3 . . . are not polemical, as Clement's are, but hortatory and pedagogic." See Kovacs, "Servant of Christ," 162.

9. Peter Martens, *Origen and Scripture,* 98.

10. Origen, *On First Principles (Prin.)* 3.6.7 (SC 252:250; translation, Butterworth, 253). In contrast to previous generations, there is now general agreement among scholars regarding the trustworthiness of the Latin versions of Origen's work. I will not rehearse the arguments here, but see especially Ronald Heine, *Origen: Homilies on Genesis and Exodus,* 27–39; Joseph T. Lienhard, S.J., *Homilies on Luke,* xxxii–xxxvi; Martens, *Origen and Scripture,* 21 n. 64.

11. This is consistent with Origen's commentary on the creation of man in the image of God found in his *Homilies on Genesis and Exodus (Hom. Gen. Ex.).* Only the "inner man, invisible, incorporeal, incorruptible, and immortal," is made in God's image. The outer man—visible, corruptible, and mortal—was not *made.* According to Origen, he was *formed. Hom. Gen. Ex.* 1.13 (see p. 63 in Heine's translation). For further discussion of how Origen interprets the "making" (*poieo*) of man in Gen. 1:26 and the "forming" (*plasso*) of man in Gen. 2:7, see Henri Crouzel, *Théologie de l'image de Dieu,* 147–79, and Anders Lund Jacobsen, "Genesis 1–3 as Source for the Anthropology of Origen."

12. *Prin.* 2.1.4 (SC 252:240).

13. *Prin.* 2.1.4 (SC 252:240; translation, Butterworth, 79). Here is a provocative parallel between Origen and Raphael in Milton's *Paradise Lost:* both suggest

that, in being eaten, food is transformed into the proper substance of the one who consumes it.

14. *Prin.* 2.2.2 (SC 252:248).

15. Hal Koch, *Pronoia und Paideusis,* 37. Koch goes on to note that the potential "goodness" of corporality resides not in materiality itself but rather in its function as a "trial, a necessary mechanism for divine guidance, instruction, in which the soul regains its purity" (41).

16. For a variety of perspectives on Origen's anthropology, see Benjamin P. Blosser, *Become Like the Angels,* 38–59; Peter Martens, *Origen and Scripture,* 94–101; Christopher A. Beeley, *The Unity of Christ,* 3–48; David Robertson, *Word and Meaning in Ancient Alexandria,* 47–48; Jacobsen, "Genesis 1–3 as Source," 213–32; Christoph Markschies, *Origenes und sein Erbe,* 98–103; Anders Lund Jacobsen, "The Constitution of Man," 78–89; Stephen Thomas, "Anthropology," 54–55; Mark J. Edwards, *Origen Against Plato;* Mark J. Edwards, "Origen, No Gnostic," 23–37; Padraig O'Cleirigh, "The Dualism of Origen," 346–50; Rowan A. Greer's translation of *Origen: An Exhortation to Martyrdom,* 24. It seems to me that Benjamin Blosser's account oversimplifies the issue in too tidy a manner: "As a Platonist, Origen could and would occasionally feel the lure of dualism; yet as a Christian, Origen was an unflinching defender of the goodness of the material order." Blosser, *Become Like the Angels,* 44. Mark Edwards provides a more nuanced defense of Origen's approach to materiality by recognizing the dualistic aspects of his thought while accounting for his inability to "disown the salvation of the body." Edwards, "Origen, No Gnostic," 37.

17. Jacobsen, "Constitution of Man," 81–82, and "Genesis 1–3 as Source," 216–23. Jacobsen's primary interest is in Origen's exegesis of the two creation accounts in Gen. 1:26 and 2:7. Whether we categorize Origen's anthropology "tripartite"—composed of body, soul, and spirit—or "dipartite"—composed of an outer corporality and an inner spirituality—need not detain us here. The two are not exclusive models for Origen, and he finds them both useful for thinking about the composition of the human person.

18. Jacobsen, "Constitution of Man," 81.

19. Ibid., 82.

20. Ibid., 83.

21. Anders Lund Jacobsen, "Origen on the Human Body," 656.

22. Jacobsen, "Genesis 1–3 as Source," 225.

23. Ibid., 232 (emphasis added).

24. *Prin.* 1.1.6 (SC 252:102).

25. *Prin.* 3.4.2 (SC 268:206).

26. *Prin.* 1.1.6 (SC 252:102–4; translation, Butterworth, 11).

27. *Prin.* 1.1.7 (SC 252:104–6).

28. *Prin.* 1.1.7 (SC 252:106). See the brief discussion on this in Martens, *Origen and Scripture,* 94–95.

29. Indeed, this entire section of *On First Principles* considers the immateriality of the mind and its "nearness to God" as an "intellectual image."

30. *Prin.* 1.1.9 (SC 252:110; translation, Butterworth, 14).

31. *Prin.* 2.10.1 (SC 252:376).

32. *Prin.* 2.10.3. (SC 252:380). I have left it untranslated here to retain its wide and complicated semantic range.

33. *Prin.* 2.10.3 (SC 252:380).

34. *Prin.* 2.11.2 (SC 252:396). For discussion of Origen's distinction between "body" and "flesh," see especially Henri Crouzel, "L'anthropolgie d'Origène," 377–84; Jacques Dupuis, S.J., *"L'esprit de l'homme,"* 60–61; and Cécile Blanc, "L'attitude d'Origène," 843–58.

35. *Prin.* 2.11.3 (SC 252:398–400).

36. *Prin.* 2.11.6 (SC 252:408; translation, Butterworth, 152).

37. *Prin.* 2.11.7 (SC 252:412; translation, Butterworth, 153–54). Origen also refers to this spiritual growth as a diet derived from "the problems of the meaning of things and the nature of their causes."

38. In *Prin.* 3.4.2, Origen explains how the embodied soul of creaturely life fluctuates between flesh and spirit, bending toward "whichever it has chosen to obey." In the resurrection, Origen argues that the substance of the flesh "certainly persists," "is restored to life," and "advances to the glory of a spiritual body." *Prin.* 3.6.5 (SC 268:246). Crucially, the transformation of the flesh occurs not all at once but rather "gradually and by degrees" (*paulatim et per partes*)—to the extent that the body serves the soul, it "progresses into a spiritual condition" (*qualitatemque proficiat spiritalem*). The flesh is, therefore, not simply a passive vehicle or tool for the progress of the soul that will be discarded but, rather, is a precondition of its formation, reformation, and passage to God. *Prin.* 3.6.6 (SC 268:246–50). This spiritual progress of the flesh discussed in book 3 calls into question some of the more dramatic distinctions made between flesh and body, earthly and spiritual life in scholarship on Origen (see, e.g., Blanc, "L'attitude d'Origène," 850–53). The material substance of the flesh, no matter how opposed it may become to the spirit in this life, is nevertheless an integral component of the raising and transforming of the embodied soul.

39. *Prin.* 2.11.6 (SC 252:412; translation, Butterworth, 152).

40. On the Logos as food, as a divine discourse that nourishes Christians, see especially Derek Krueger, *Writing and Holiness,* 141–49.

41. *Prin.* 4.2.4 (SC 268:312).

42. *Prin.* 4.2.4 (SC 268:312).

43. Henri de Lubac, *Histoire et Esprit,* 86.

44. Jean Daniélou, *Origène,* 59.

45. Henri Crouzel, *Origène et la "Connaissance Mystique,"* 183, and Crouzel, *Origène,* 175. The passage in question is nearly identical in both texts.

46. Crouzel, *Origène et la "Connaissance Mystique,"* 173: "Chacun doit accepter la nourriture à lui destinée et ne pas blâmer celui qui en prend une autre."

47. Karen Jo Torjesen, *Hermeneutical Procedure,* 13.

48. Ibid., 123.

49. Kovacs, "Servant of Christ," 169. Though Kovacs also recognizes the basic division, Origen seems to perceive among those in his audience. Elsewhere, she has noted how "the contrasts between 'milk' and 'meat' and between 'babes' and 'perfect ones' suggest to Origen that there are two distinct groups in the church in Corinth, and he interprets the whole letter in light of this dual audience, reading it as an exhortation to beginners in the faith to make moral and spiritual progress and thus join the more perfect ones." (Judith Kovacs, "Echoes of Valentinian Exegesis," 327.) Kovacs's insightful work attests to this tension throughout Origen's writing.

50. A similar position is articulated in Elizabeth Ann Dively Lauro's *The Soul and Spirit of Scripture:* "The 'perfect,' then, are not 'completed,' but are the more advanced among spiritual journeyers. They have become able to receive edification from all three senses [of scripture], and they now have the privilege to receive more edification as well as the duty to help other souls also to progress in understanding Scripture's edifying truths" (85). See also Virginia L. Noel, "Nourishment in Origen's *On Prayer,*" 482–85.

51. R. P. C. Hanson, *Allegory and Event,* 213–14 (emphasis added). See also Hanson, *Origen's Doctrine of Tradition,* 74–88.

52. Gunnar af Hällström's thorough examination of the "simple" Christians in Origen further nuances Hanson's argument. The problem with the *simpliciores,* for Hällström, is that they must be fed by a mediator and cannot receive nourishment directly from the Logos. This establishes a division between two kinds of Christians within the community from the very outset: those who eat and those who are fed by others. Hällström suggests that, despite Origen's desire for it to be otherwise, Christianity ever runs the risk of being divided along these lines. Hällström does offer a helpful correction of Hanson, however, in noting that the milk diet of simple faith is not, for Origen, a compulsory stage for all Christians. See Hällström, *Fides Simpliciorum,* esp. 94–95.

53. Origen, *Commentary on 1 Corinthians (Comm. Cor.)* XII.2 (*JTS* 9 [1908]: 241).

54. *Comm. Cor.* XII.8–10 (*JTS* 9 [1908]: 241). See also Kovacs, "Servant of Christ," 163, esp. n62. I have paraphrased because, as Kovacs rightly identifies, it is unclear in the fragment of this passage just how Origen distinguishes these various designations. Thus, in line 8, he mentions the Pauline *broma* in conjunction with various other terms, such as *broseos alethines, stereas trophes,* and *sarkos tou logou.* It is possible that these were all interchangeable for Origen, but, beyond the milk and the vegetables, there is little indication of how the various "solid" foods are related to one another.

55. *Comm. Cor.* XII.12 (*JTS* 9 [1908]: 241).

56. *Comm. Cor.* XII.6 (*JTS* 9 [1908]: 241). Origen draws upon the language of being "trained" or "exercised"(*gymnazo*) found in Heb. 5:12–14. He appeals to this passage from Hebrews regularly, especially to draw out the idea of "training the senses" and its connection to the "perfect" ones who eat solid food. Here, however, he uses it to describe the limitations of those who are unable to consume the noetic lessons of scripture.

57. *Comm. Cor.* XII.15–18. (*JTS* 9 [1908]: 242). It is worth noting that Origen also makes the connection between martyrdom and the Pauline "solid food" in the opening lines of his *Exhortation to Martyrdom.*

58. Kovacs, "Servant of Christ," 165.

59. *Comm. Cor.* XII.5, 13 (*JTS* 9 [1908]: 241).

60. In the previous analysis of *Prin.* 2.1.4, Origen's understanding of the relationship between the outward, creaturely body and the inward, spiritual body hinges on the assumption that both undergo transformation according to the process of ingestion, digestion, and transubstantiation of food appropriate to each. In his *Commentary on 1 Corinthians,* Origen is indicating a broader program of noetic nourishment and formation.

61. The motif of nourishment in Origen's thought has been most explicitly examined by Henri Crouzel and Cécile Blanc. Both Crouzel and Blanc emphasize Origen's association of Pauline food categories with corresponding "ages" or levels of maturity in the soul. See Crouzel, *Origène et la "Connaissance Mystique,"* 166–84, and Blanc, "Les nourritures spirituelles," 12–13.

62. Blanc, "Les nourritures spirituelles," 12.

63. Origen, *On Prayer (Pray.)* 27.2 (GCS 3:364; translation, Greer, 138). Virginia Noel notes that "Origen relates our bodily need for physical food to our soul's need for spiritual nourishment. . . . The physical metaphor of eating thus carries the spiritual meaning; physical metaphors are the means for sensing the inner spiritual realm." Noel, "Nourishment in Origen's *On Prayer,*" 482. Noel helpfully situates the relationship between the physical and the spiritual forms of nourishment in Origen but does not push the analysis beyond the notion

that they function metaphorically as part of Origen's commitment to "three stages of the spiritual life: purification, illumination, and union" (485). In drawing upon her insights, I am also trying to broaden the frame of reference for how this "metaphor" functions and why it would have been a powerful interpretive strategy for Origen in the first place.

64. *Pray.* 27.4 (GCS 3:365).
65. *Pray.* 27.4 (GCS 3:365).
66. *Pray.* 27.4 (GCS 3:365).
67. *Pray.* 27.4 (GCS 3:365).
68. *Pray.* 27.5 (GCS 3:366).
69. *Pray.* 27.6 (GCS 3:366).
70. The conspicuous absence of an explicit and extensive discussion of the Eucharist is notable here. In the precise place where Origen could have drawn a close connection between the shadowy power of material food to the spiritual sustenance of the Word, he pivots from the ritual context almost immediately. This ambiguous relationship between Eucharistic elements and noetic food is also reflected in Origen's highly symbolic connection of nourishment to the soul's "passage" back to God in *On Pascha*—a text that, as Ruth Anne Clements has noted, "contains no references to Christian celebration of Easter" and its Eucharistic connotations can only be derived by inference (see Clements, "τέλειος ἄμωμος," 286n3). Origen's discussion of the body and blood of Christ does not, in the extant literature, provide a robust account of how Eucharistic nourishment might aid in the transformation of flesh and soul into spirit. Thus Dragos Andrei Giulea goes too far in his reading of *Pascha* when he notes that "reference to Christ's Eucharistic body and blood is an obvious feature" and "Origen places the mystery of Pascha within a Eucharistic context." Giulea, *Pre-Nicene Christology,* 116, 166. Origen's interpretation of Christ's body and blood is more cautious, and his connection of Pauline nourishment to Eucharistic practice remains suggestive more than systematic. In this way, Origen follows the precedent of Clement before him in creating a "space of play" for the symbol of nourishment to slide between figural and literal senses.
71. *Pray.* 27.7 (GCS 3:367). Christoph Markschies has explored the background and meaning of Origen's use of *ousia* in *On Prayer,* with particular attention to how he navigates the platonic definition (= incorporeal) with the stoic definition (= corporeal). See Markschies, *Origenes und sein Erbe,* 173–87.
72. *Pray.* 27.8 (GCS 3:367–68).
73. *Pray.* 27.9 (GCS 3:369).
74. *Pray.* 27.9 (GCS 3:369; translation, Greer, 141–42).

75. Origen, *Hom. Gen. Ex.* 7.8 (SC 321:232–39), which begins, "Do not be surprised that the Word of God is called flesh, bread, milk, and vegetable—and is called different things according to the capacity of those believing or according to the strength of those accepting it." In the same section, Origen concludes that the nourishment of the Word "delivers to your mouth whatever taste you desire." Elsewhere, he describes the priest as a teacher who can discern the proper food to be offered on the altar of each individual soul. See G. W. Barkley's translation of Origen's *Homilies on Leviticus*, 35–36.

76. Origen, *Against Celsus* (*Ag. Cel.*) 4.18 (*VCSup* 54:231; translation, Chadwick, 195–96).

77. Origen, *Homilies on Numbers* (*Hom. Num.*) 27.1 (SC 461:270–78).

78. *Hom. Num.* 27.1.1 (SC 461:270; translation, Greer, 245).

79. *Hom. Num.* 27.1.2 (translation, Greer, 246).

80. A similar discussion of how different foods are apportioned to different animals can be found in Sextus Empiricus's *Outlines of Skepticism* 1.55–58.

81. *Hom. Num.* 27.1 (translation, Greer, 247).

82. Origen, *Homilies on Judges* (*Hom. Jud.*) 5.6 (SC 389:144). See the translation in Elizabeth Ann Dively Lauro's *Origen: Homilies on Judges*, 85–86.

83. *Hom. Jud.* 5.6 (SC 389:144).

84. *Hom. Jud.* 6.2 (SC 389:154).

85. *Ag. Cel.* 3.52 (*VCSup* 54:194).

86. *Ag. Cel.* 3.54 (*VCSup* 54:195).

87. In *Ag. Cel.* prologue, 6, Origen describes those whom the treatise was intended to help by a reference to Romans 14 (i.e., the "weak" vegetable-eaters). For additional discussion of the frame and setting of the text, see Michael Frede, "Origen's Treatise *Against Celsus*," 131–55.

88. Origen, *Commentary on Romans* (*Comm. Rom.*) 8.9.5 (SC 543:544): *infirmos holere*.

89. *Comm. Rom.* 9.36.1 (SC 555:204). Toward the end of this passage, Origen makes a provocative (and sarcastic) side comment: "Are we to be so inept as to think the apostle . . . carried milk with him to give to the Corinthians?" This sensitivity to an overly literal rendering of Paul's symbolic language is all the more interesting given that Origen is trying to develop an account of the "sense" of the soul—that is, of the ways in which the soul grows in its ability to accept and digest the Word of God. He dismisses the "literal" notion that Paul fed the Corinthians "actual" milk, while intensifying the very logic of formation from which the Pauline trope acquires it symbolic power.

90. *Comm. Rom.* 9.36.2 (SC 555:206): *nec gulae et gurgitis est magister*. Here I follow the translation of Scheck and take *gutturis* to be more likely than *gurgitis*.

See the translation in Thomas P. Scheck's *Commentary on the Epistle to the Romans, Books 6–10*, 235.

91. *Comm. Rom.* 9.36.3 (SC 555:206).

92. *Comm. Rom.* 9.36.3 (SC 555:208). The point here seems to be that the weaker Christians would be harmed by stronger food: what is meant to fortify and promote growth in the perfect would harm the imperfect and make them sick. Thus the weak should not despise those who eat other foods. At the same time, the perfect are not harmed by eating foods designated for those less perfect. So, likewise, they should not be critical of those who must eat less hearty food either. On the harm of strong food when eaten by the weak, see Blanc, "Les nourritures spirituelles," 12.

93. *Ag. Cel.* 7.59 (*VCSup* 54:510).

94. I use the idea of "class" with reservation. I have preferred to speak of Origen's division of food types as a mechanism for *classifying* or *categorizing* different noetic capacities within the Christian community. But in the context of *Against Celsus*, the terminology Origen uses in response to Celsus reflects strata of groups within the broader societal structure. That is, these designations are not derived from Origen's exegetical conceit but rather are culled from the ambient landscape composed of quite different levels of social, intellectual, and economic status. Indeed, Origen is responding to the notion that Christians allow "lower class" people into their mystery—something that scandalized Celsus. Nevertheless, I use the concept cautiously and only in a general sense.

95. *Ag. Cel.* 7.59 (*VCSup* 54:510).

96. *Ag. Cel.* 7.60 (*VCSup* 54:511).

97. The passage uses cognates of the verb "to prepare" (*skeuazo*) five times—amplifying the force of the link between nourishment, its power, and the taxonomy of souls according to their digestive capacities.

98. It is important to note here that the effect of nourishment is said to be identical regardless of the status of the one who eats it. The food of Christian teaching promotes good health and vigor (*hygieia kai eueksias*) from the peasant to the philosopher—but it does not seem to promote progress from simple to more luxurious food. The yokel is not, in being fed by the simpler power of the Word, on his way to becoming a member of the wealthy. The power of the Word, it seems, changes according to the capacity of the one eating it. But neither the varying capacities nor the social statuses inscribed at the level of biology seem to change as a result. For more on the function of social status distinctions in early Christianity, see also David I. Rankin, "Class Distinction as a Way of Doing Church."

99. As should be clear, I take Origen's usage of *agroikoi* throughout *Against Celsus* as a metonym for those to whom he refers elsewhere as "drinking milk" or "eating vegetables."

100. Epiphanius of Salamis, *Panarion* 64.72.9 (GCS 31:523).

Chapter 5. Gregory of Nyssa at the Breast of the Bridegroom

1. Gregory of Nyssa, *Homilies on the Song of Songs* (*Hom. Song*) 15. I refer throughout to the recent edition edited by Richard A. Norris, Jr., in the WGRW series, with volume, page, and line numbers provided in parentheses. The Greek text found there is the same as that in Langerbeck's 1960 edition for Brill's *Gregorii Nysseni Opera* series. Norris provides page references to Langerbeck's edition to the right of the Greek on each page. Unless otherwise indicated, all translations are my own.

2. Virginia Burrus, *"Begotten Not Made,"* 5–6.

3. This is best articulated in *On the Soul and Resurrection,* where Gregory explicitly describes how the soul permeates all the elements of the body without diminishing in its own integrity. See especially Catherine P. Roth's translation in *On the Soul and Resurrection,* 47–48. Gregory's description of humanity as a mixture of intellectual and corporeal natures is strikingly similar to Galen's argument explored previously in chapter 1.

4. Basil of Caesarea, *Letters* 37 (LCL 190:192–95).

5. *Letters* 37 (LCL 190:192–94).

6. *Letters* 37 (LCL 190:194).

7. *Letters* 37 (LCL 190:194).

8. The discussion of Basil's "brother in milk" (*suntrophos*) evokes the Maccabean mother of 4 Macc. 13:19–22, whose sons were formed according to a "common nourishment" (*suntrophias*). See the discussion in chapter 2 of this book. In *Education of Children* 3, Plutarch observes that "feeding together [*suntrophia*] results in a bond of goodwill" (LCL 197:15).

9. Gregory of Nyssa, *Encomium on Saint Basil* (*En. Bas.*) 24 (Stein, 50).

10. *En. Bas.* 24–25 (Stein, 55–57). For a classic example of encomiastic conventions, see Plato's *Menexenus* 237A-B, in which the speaker proceeds from the subject's noble birth, to their nurture and training (*trophe kai paideia*), and concludes with the issue of their deeds. In the *Encomium*, Gregory has opted only to narrate the last of these, even though he, of all people, would have been capable of a full encomium for his brother.

11. As we have already seen in Philo's discussion of Isaac, the "self-fed" man was a topos used to emphasize the exceptional intellect of a person who did not require the food of another for his own formation.

12. *En. Bas.* 16 (Stein, 34).
13. *En. Bas.* 16 (Stein, 34).
14. *En. Bas.* 20 (Stein, 40–42).
15. I will return to this point.
16. The *Encomium* is usually dated to 380 (Stein, xxxi) or 381 (Lucas Francisco Mateo-Seco and Giulio Maspero, *The Brill Dictionary of Gregory of Nyssa,* 93). Gregory's *Life of Moses,* despite some difficulty, is usually dated to the final period of his literary output in the early 390s. See either Mateo-Seco and Maspero, *Dictionary of Gregory of Nyssa,* 788, or the translation by Abraham J. Malherbe and Everett Ferguson of *Gregory of Nyssa: The Life of Moses,* "Introduction," 1. This was also the period in which Gregory produced his *Homilies on the Song of Songs.*
17. In Gregory of Nyssa, *Life of Moses* 1.2–3, Gregory explicitly states that the treatise was written to provide "counsel in the perfect life" in response to a request from an acquaintance for an essay on that topic. Citations are from the Daniélou edition, SC 1:44–326, which corresponds with the section numbers in the English version of Malherbe and Ferguson's *Gregory of Nyssa: The Life of Moses.* I have provided the page references to the Classics of Western Spirituality (CWS) edition for ease of reference.
18. *Life of Moses* (*Mos.*) 1.5 (SC 1:3; translation, CWS, 30). See Heine, *Perfection in the Virtuous Life,* 60: "Continual transformation to the better, while being movement, is nevertheless real stability for it does not involve a falling and slipping backward. The latter, which is also movement, is unstable, for lacking progress it is a continual alternation between good and bad." In addition, Gregory uses the verb *choreo* to discuss the unceasing motion and forward progress that perfects human nature: *Mos.* 1.10 (SC 1:4).
19. Philo, *On the Life of Moses* 1.17 (LCL 289:285).
20. See especially D'Angelo, "Gender and Geopolitics."
21. For more on Gregory and Philo, see Albert C. Geljon, *Philonic Exegesis.*
22. *Mos.* 1.17 (SC 1:8; CWS, 33). The source of the sage's nurture and nourishment as an infant was a prominent strategy for demonstrating the divine character of the person in question from childhood. See Cox, *Biography in Late Antiquity.*
23. *Mos.* 1.17 (SC 1:8; CWS, 33).
24. Gregory follows Philo's terminology (using *epinoia*) in describing how Moses came back to his own mother. For Gregory, it was through family members. For Philo, however, it was ordained by God.
25. *Mos.* 1.18 (SC 1:8–9; CWS, 34). While I think a case can be made for the translation of "pagan learning" offered by Malherbe and Ferguson (on the grounds that this is the sense Gregory will give it in the second section of the *Life of Moses*), I nonetheless maintain that the translation "culture of foreigners" is

more appropriate insofar as it clarifies the symmetrical structure between kin and foreigners so crucial for the force of Gregory's framing at the opening of his historical interpretation. Gregory applies the boundaries of belonging and otherness to the sources of Moses's nourishment as much as to the content of his education. In fact, nourishment and education are folded together into a single process of formation.

26. Literally, "mixed back into his kin."

27. I follow Rebecca Krawiec here, who has aptly noted that "Gregory does not present the asceticized household as in conflict with itself, but rather as a new coexistence of 'family' and family." This blending of *literal* (or biological) family with *rhetorical* family had already been taking place in the expanding web of social relations found in the Roman household of the early Empire. So the slippage between "family" and family in Christian discourse can be understood as a further development of the ways in which ancient kinship bonds were flexible enough to be transferred to nonbiological relationships while retaining the same rhetorical force. See Krawiec, "From the Womb of the Church," 301. For the link between "real" and "rhetorical" families in early Christianity, see especially Andrew Jacobs and Rebecca Krawiec, "Fathers Know Best?" 261-62.

28. *Mos.* 2.1 (SC 1:32; CWS, 55).

29. *Mos.* 2.3 (SC 1:32; CWS, 56).

30. *Mos.* 2.6 (SC 1:33; CWS, 56).

31. *Mos.* 2.5 (SC 1:33; CWS, 56).

32. *Mos.* 2.12 (SC 1:35): φύσις μήτηρ.

33. *Mos.* 2.12 (SC 1:35; CWS, 56).

34. See especially *Mos.* 2.238-39 (SC 1:108-9; CWS, 116) for Gregory's discussion of *epektasis* at the conclusion of the *Life*. When viewed in relation to his discussion of how material food changes to suit the capacities of the one eating, *epektasis* takes on a new dimension of meaning, in which certain kinds of noetic food instigate the intellectual expansion and the stretching ever outward toward the divine by people of varying capacities.

35. Gregory is standing squarely within Origen's exegetical method here, while nevertheless utilizing that method toward his own ends. Indeed, the result of Gregory's work on the Song of Songs is, despite methodological debts to Origen, wholly his own. For more discussion of the relationship between Origen and Gregory on this text's history of interpretation, see Elizabeth A. Clark, "Origen, the Jews, and the Song of Songs," 274-93; Mark W. Elliot, *The Song of Songs and Christology;* Andrew Louth, "Eros and Mysticism," 241-54; Richard A. Norris, "The Soul Takes Flight," 517-32.

36. *Hom. Song*, Preface (WGRW 13:2.9-10).

37. *Hom. Song,* Preface (WGRW 13:2).

38. *Akatergastos*—literally, undigested and indigestible.

39. On the need to purify Solomon's text for "more carnal" Christians, see especially Andrew S. Jacobs, "Solomon's Salacious Song," 23: "Reading and interpreting powerful texts is a way of wielding power, and the particular power
wielded by Origen and Gregory was that of defining the true Christian subject.
Describing the nature of the true 'author' was for them a means of constructing
not only the true 'meaning,' but also the true 'reader,' and of erecting cultural
boundaries essential to the articulation of early Christian identity."

40. It is worth noting that the *Homilies* were first delivered as a Lenten sermon
series. But these were later revised and expanded before Gregory sent them to
Olympias.

41. Gregory's *Homilies on the Song of Songs* has received increasing attention from
scholars, and the recent publication of a new English edition by the late Richard
Norris will surely expand this interest. And while the themes of pedagogy, eros,
and spiritual transformation have all received scholarly comment, Gregory's emphasis on nourishment throughout has not. For scholarship on the *Homilies,* see
Hans Boersma, *Embodiment and Virtue;* Hans Boersma, "Saving Bodies"; Richard T. Lawson III, "Gregory of Nyssa's *Homilies on the Song of Songs*"; Martin
Laird, "The Fountain of His Lips"; Martin Laird, *Gregory of Nyssa and the Grasp
of Faith;* Martin Laird, "Under Solomon's Tutelage"; Jacobs, "Solomon's Salacious Song"; Norris, "The Soul Takes Flight"; Franz Dunzl, *Braut und Bräutigam;* Verna E. F. Harrison, "A Gender Reversal," 34–38; Ronald E. Heine,
"Gregory of Nyssa's Apology for Allegory"; J. B. Cahill, "Date and Setting."

42. In the prologue to Origen's *Commentary on the Song of Songs,* the Greeks are
said to have derived their entire curriculum of education from Solomon. See
also Heine, *Gregory of Nyssa's Treatise on the Inscriptions of the Psalms,* 75.
Heine observes that Gregory's *Homilies* begin "by speaking of the soul already
'united to God'" whereas his treatise on the Psalms "embraces the whole spectrum of those seeking God." This is not quite right. The later homilies do address the more advanced. But the prologue and the first two homilies are
offered as a remedial course to the more fleshly people in the audience, who
must be properly fed on the text's larger purpose before they can access its
deeper, more substantial meaning.

43. *Hom. Song* 1 (WGRW 13:14 and 26).

44. *Hom. Song* 1 (WGRW 13:14 and 26).

45. *Hom. Song* 1 (WGRW 13:22).

46. *Hom. Song* 1 (WGRW 13:18). On this theme, see Susan R. Holman, "Molded
as Wax."

47. *Hom. Song* 1 (WGRW 13:30).

48. *Hom. Song* 1 (WGRW 13:32).

49. Gregory even dismisses debates about what such a method of reading should be called—anagogical? tropological? allegorical?—and argues instead that it is only the effect of reading that matters, not the method. See *Hom. Song,* Preface (WGRW 13:2–4).

50. *Hom. Song* 1 (WGRW 13:34).

51. *Hom. Song* 1 (WGRW 13:34).

52. Michel Barnes has helpfully unpacked the complexity of this theme in Gregory's writing. See Barnes, *The Power of God.* For more on this, see also n. 19 in Norris's edition of *Hom. Song* 1 (WGRW 13:35); Lewis Ayres, "On Not Three People"; Verna E. F. Harrison, *Grace and Human Freedom,* 44–55.

53. Origen also emphasizes the nourishment provided by the bridegroom's breasts throughout book 1 of his *Commentary on the Song of Songs,* though it is less developed than what we find in Gregory. Whereas Origen largely uses food to construct categories of identity for different kinds of Christians, for Gregory the emphasis is on food's transformative power and how this aids an individual's progress toward perfection.

54. This is not to say that the erotic content of the song is erased or negated. As with the figure of Tellus depicted on the Ara Pacis (discussed in chapter 1), maternity and sexuality are by no means exclusive in the ideological construction of milk's transformative power. For more on this theme in general, see Stephen Moore, "The Song of Songs in the History of Sexuality."

55. *Hom. Song* 1 (WGRW 13:36.2–3).

56. *Hom. Song* 1 (WGRW 13:36.21).

57. *Hom. Song* 1 (WGRW 13:36.17–20).

58. See, e.g., Norris, "The Soul Takes Flight," 526; Harrison, "A Gender Reversal," 37; Laird, *Gregory of Nyssa and the Grasp of Faith,* 152.

59. *Hom. Song* 1 (WGRW 13.40.15–16).

60. *Hom. Song* 1 (WGRW 13.42.5). Once again, Gregory employs the verb *epekteino* to describe the growth of the maidens. They are stretched and expanded so that they might be reformed into the likeness of the bride.

61. As I have argued throughout, infancy and maternity functioned in the ancient world as prominent and anxiously regulated sites for the work of cultural construction, wherein the values and concerns of particular social groups were worked out especially upon the bodies and behaviors of women and children. While infants were largely viewed as plastic and malleable by nature, Gregory's positive framing of infancy as a state of dispassionate potential is not totally consistent with broader Greco-Roman theories of childhood and education, in

which children are described as unruly and irrational. If anything, the plasticity of the infant soul tended to be viewed as a fundamentally precarious state in which the child is too readily shaped by bad behaviors of others.

62. *Hom. Song* 1 (WGRW 13:42.9). On the bride's perfection, see Norris, "The Soul Takes Flight," 530: "Origen occasionally describes the Bride of the Song as 'perfect,' taking her to represent the mature Christian, but Gregory, with Paul's words in mind, invariably refuses this epithet and characterizes the Bride rather as 'more perfect'; for in a sense, as he understands it, the proper Christian is always immature, since the goal is precisely never to arrive but always to respond to the 'upward call of God.'" Norris is correct that Origen speaks of perfection in more emphatic terms than Gregory does. However, I see no example in which the "more perfect" bride is characterized as also somehow immature.

63. *Hom. Song* 1 (WGRW 13:42–44).

64. *Hom. Song* 1 (WGRW 13:44.3).

65. *Hom. Song* 2 (WGRW 13:50.1–2).

66. *Hom. Song* 2 (WGRW 13:50.4): τὴν ἐκ τῶν λογικῶν αὐτῆς μαζῶν ἀπορρέουσαν χάριν.

67. *Hom. Song* 2 (WGRW 13:50.15–20). Here Gregory draws explicitly on Pauline language of mimesis from Galatians and 1 Corinthians. The bride is a new Paul, offering milk to little ones so that they may grow into her likeness.

68. *Hom. Song* 3 (WGRW 13:78.21–25).

69. *Hom. Song* 3 (WGRW 13:78.30–80.1).

70. *Hom. Song* 6 (WGRW 13:188.2–6): μεταξὺ τῶν λογικῶν μαζῶν, ὅθεν βρύει τὰ θεῖα διδάγματα.

71. *Hom. Song* 6 (WGRW 13:199.5–16).

72. *Hom. Song* 7 (WGRW 13:226.25–28).

73. E.g., in response to Song 4.5 ("Your breasts are like two twin fawns"), Gregory offers an anthropological consideration: "[T]here are two human beings to be observed in each person: one is bodily and visible, the other spiritual and imperceptible. Yet the birth of either is always twofold, because they are brought into life together. For the soul does not exist before the body, nor is the body prepared before the soul. Both come into being simultaneously. And the nourishment that is natural to these is purity and fragrance and all such things produced by the virtues" (*Hom. Song* 7 [WGRW 13:250.25–30]). The purpose of each body part is derived from this twofold nature, and Gregory's discussion of the parts' various functions resonates with medical and social values that were widely applied to the body—especially to the female body—in his day.

74. *Hom. Song* 7 (WGRW 13:252.3–13).

75. *Hom. Song* 9 (WGRW 13:278.1–3).

76. *Hom. Song* 9 (WGRW 13:278.10).

77. *Hom. Song* 9 (WGRW 13:278.13–20). Gregory's reference to the bride's breasts as "fountains of good doctrine" has a parallel in his *On the Soul and Resurrection:* "[T]he person who is nourished always grows and never ceases from growth. Since the fountains of good things flows unfailingly, the nature of the participants who use all the influx to add to their own magnitude (because nothing of what is received is superfluous or useless) becomes at the same time more capable of attracting the better and more able to contain it. Each adds to the other: the one who is nourished gains greater power from the abundance of good things, and the nourishing supply rises in flood to match the increase of the one who is growing." See the translation in Roth, *On the Soul and Resurrection,* 87.

78. *Hom. Song* 9 (WGRW 13:294.9–10).

79. *Hom. Song* 14 (WGRW 13:438.21–22).

80. *Hom. Song* 15 (WGRW 13:468.9–10).

81. Werner Jaeger, *Early Christianity and Greek Paideia,* 87.

82. John Henry Newman, *Historical Sketches,* vol. 2, 17.

83. Franz Dunzl aptly observed that individual Christian formation, for Gregory, is not an isolated process. Rather, the church is the space in which all are fed together (zusammenzuführen). See Dunzl, *Braut und Bräutigam,* 243.

84. Gregory's eclectic depiction of his sister's character has received significant scholarly discussion. See, e.g., Ellen Muehlberger, "Salvage," 273–97; Philip Rousseau, "The Pious Household and the Virgin Chorus," 165–86; Virginia Burrus, "Is Macrina a Woman?" 249–64; J. Warren Smith, "A Just and Reasonable Grief," 37–60; Rebecca Krawiec, "From the Womb of the Church," 283–307. Virginia Burrus has offered a convincing analysis of the constantly shifting bonds of kinship that connect Gregory, his sister, and the whole cast of characters that appear in the *Life of Macrina:* "Macrina is at once the child who never left her mother's womb and all the husband her mother could want, her mother her own nursemaid, and she both her mother's maidservant and her brother's father. Conjunctions, displacements, and reversals of parent-child, husband-wife, and master-slave relations thus accumulate, intensifying and complicating the intimacy that envelops a family now reconfigured as a feminine community of pedagogical formation." See Burrus, "Gender, Eros, and Pedagogy," 175. The image of Christian formation found in the *Homilies on the Song of Songs* that I have been presenting replicates this "feminine community of pedagogical formation" with its similar emphasis on shifting relations of kinship in which the mother-child/nurse-infant model serves as foundation.

85. Gregory of Nyssa, *Life of Macrina* 3 (SC 178:149).

86. *Life of Macrina* 12 (SC 178:182). Gregory's identification of Macrina as "father, teacher, pedagogue, [and] mother" is nearly identical to Clement of Alexandria's description of the Logos as "father, mother, pedagogue, and nurse" in the *Paedagogus* (*VCSup* 61:27) discussed in chapter 3. Gregory seems to borrow this litany of roles ascribed to the Word by Clement in order to accentuate his sister's virtuosity as mediator of that same Word to others.

87. *Life of Macrina* 12 (SC 178:182).

88. *Life of Macrina* 26 (SC 178:232). I take this to mean that one group of women under Macrina's care were abandoned infants at the time of their rescue, requiring someone to provide lifesaving sustenance and care.

89. *Life of Macrina* 22 (SC 178:214).

90. Michel Foucault, *Security,* 1.

91. Ibid., 126.

92. Ibid., 126–27.

93. In his discussion of Gregory the Wonderworker's oration for Origen, Richard Valantasis highlights Gregory's claim that Origen had "planted a spark" in him. This language, Valantasis notes, has maternal resonances in the medical literature. However, Valantasis prefers the paternal and masculine sense with respect to Gregory the Wonderworker and Origen. See Valantasis, *Spiritual Guides,* 28–30. Denise Kimber Buell's *Making Christians* also provides a thoroughgoing discussion of teaching as a kind of insemination.

94. As Cristina L. H. Traina has recently observed, acknowledging the reality of a maternal eroticism "furnishes a language and a logic for dealing more adequately with the ethics of parent-child relations in general, children's sexuality, and the erotic dimensions of, e.g., teacher-student . . . relations." See Traina, *Erotic Attunement,* 4. For other critical interventions into the eroticism of nurturance, see also Noelle Oxenhandler, *The Eros of Parenthood,* and Alison Bartlett, *Breastwork.* I am grateful to Mara Benjamin for her conversation on this point and for referring me to this literature.

95. Burrus, "Gender, Eros, and Pedagogy," 168.

Chapter 6. Milk Without Growth

1. For debates on the dating of the *Saturnalia,* see especially Alan Cameron, *The Last Pagans of Rome,* 254, and Robert Kaster's discussion in the introduction to Macrobius's *Saturnalia* (*Sat.*) (LCL 510:xiv). The *Saturnalia* is traditionally dated ca. 395. Cameron has argued convincingly that this cannot be the case, pushing for a date closer to 430.

2. Cameron, *Last Pagans of Rome,* 231.

3. It is outside the scope of this essay to offer a more robust discussion about Macrobius's position vis-à-vis paganism and Christianity. I find Cameron's circumspection about the *Saturnalia* having a "pagan agenda" convincing. Ibid., 255–71. In what follows, the specific content of Macrobius's antiquarianism is more important than his own personal investment in it. See also Elaine Fantham, *Roman Literary Culture,* 282–87.

4. Macrobius, *Sat.* 5.11.15–17 (LCL 511:328). Macrobius seems to be drawing directly from Aulus Gellius's *Attic Nights* 12.1 (a passage discussed already in chapter 1).

5. H. I. Marrou, *A History of Education,* 314.

6. Marrou offered the following conclusion regarding the collapse of the Roman education system: "It seems fairly certain that the generation that came after Ausonius (d. c. 395) was the last to be familiar with the normal system of Roman education, with its three stages—*magister ludi,* grammarian, rhetor. This system must have disappeared with the great invasion and the catastrophes that marked the beginning of the fifth century." Ibid., 344. The timing here is crucial for our purposes, for Augustine (like Macrobius) was reflecting upon and reconfiguring this system precisely during its twilight.

7. Kate Cooper, *The Fall of the Roman Household,* ix. For a general survey of the Roman family in the later empire, see Geoffrey S. Nathan, *The Family in Late Antiquity.*

8. For more on this transformation, see especially Kristina Sessa's masterful study on episcopal authority within the domestic sphere in late antiquity, *The Formation of Papal Authority.* Sessa's interest is primarily in the transformation of papal reach within household affairs of the fifth and sixth centuries. Even in the late fourth and early fifth centuries there are discernable traces of this transformation already under way. Indeed, Sessa suggests as much when she concludes, "[T]he line between domus and ecclesia was never firmly drawn, and Rome's prelates viewed the breaching of the boundary as an opportunity for intervention in domestic matters" (274).

9. This is not to say that Augustine is representative of Christian approaches to family or nourishment on the whole. Nevertheless, Augustine's legacy was not predicated upon him being representative of a majority view.

10. Augustine, *Letters* 33.5.

11. Augustine, *Expositions of the Psalms* 98.1.

12. Here I am following the work of Richard Saller, who observes, "When a Roman spoke of the pleasures of his *domus,* it is often impossible to discover whether he meant his physical house or the family and servants in it over whom he exercised

potestas or *dominium.* Or again, when pride is expressed in a *domus,* it could be pride in a physical *domus* or the household establishment or the wider circle of kin who derived from a single household. Further, the distinction between *domus* as the living extended family and *domus* as the descent group is often not worth making." See Saller, "*Familia, Domus,* and the Roman Conception of the Family," 347–48. For more on this dynamic in Christianity, see Cooper, *The Fall of the Roman Household,* 101–11, and Sessa, *The Formation of Papal Authority.* For a thoroughgoing analysis of Augustine in light of the social history of the Roman family, see Brent D. Shaw, "The Family in Late Antiquity."

13. For more on the "milk of Mother Church" replacing the authority of flesh and blood teachers, see the brief discussion in Philip Cary, *Outward Signs,* 119.

14. D. B. Capelle, "Le progrès," 410–19.

15. Ibid., 413.

16. Ibid., 414.

17. Ibid., 415. Capelle's argument has most recently been advanced (with a slight modification) in Guy Stroumsa's *Hidden Wisdom,* 132–46. In a chapter titled "Milk and Meat: Augustine and the End of Ancient Esotericism," Stroumsa analyzes Augustine's homilies 96, 97, and 98 on the Gospel of John and finds "a strong opposition to the cultivation of esoteric attitudes" (134). For Stroumsa, Augustine most fully embodies the "demoticization" of religion in antiquity—a process in which instruction once done in private and reserved for the elite was offered publicly for mass consumption (145). I have some reservations about this argument put forth by Capelle and Stroumsa, insofar as it too tidily avoids the places in Augustine's writing where the trope of milk and solid food does acquire an esoteric resonance. One prime example is the catechetical program laid out in *On Instructing the Beginners* (ca. 399), which, in successive chapters, suggests different methods of instruction for one who is unlearned (*rudis*), one who has been developed in the liberal arts (*liberalibus doctrinus excultus*), and those coming from the grammarian's or the rhetor's school (*Sunt item quidam de scholis usitatissimis grammaticorum oratorumque venientes*). In his discussion of this third group, Augustine explicitly describes how "the usefulness of [scripture's] hidden meanings whereby they are called 'mysteries' . . . are dug out [for such educated people] by a certain allegorical explanation" (*deque ipsa utilitate secreti, unde etiam mysteria vocantur . . . enodatione allegoriae alicujus eruitur*). See *On Instructing the Beginners* 9. I agree that such descriptions of Christian teaching as "inaccessible" or "hidden" fade in Augustine's writing; this text indicates that he never fully reconciled the fact that the church contains people of vastly different intellectual capacities—and that this dynamic resulted in an ongoing struggle to account for the varying levels of meaning

within scripture. In *Institutes of Oratory* 1.2.20, Quintilian observes that initiation into educational instruction has the same force as initiation into sacred mysteries. This similarity no doubt vexed Augustine throughout his later career, in which his focus was directed almost exclusively toward the uneducated—the *indocti*—within the church. In the last analysis, "stages of understanding" versus "stages of doctrine" seems like a false distinction with little functional difference between the two.

18. Tarsicius van Bavel, "L'humanitè du Christ," 245–81. For a related study on the "mothering of God" in Augustine's thought, see Robert J. O'Connell, S.J., "Isaiah's Mothering God," 199–206.

19. According to van Bavel, "L'humanitè du Christ," 253, this is a cornerstone of Augustine's thought from as early as the 390s. Like Capelle before him (and Stroumsa after), van Bavel also concludes that there is "no need to talk of esotericism in Augustine" (264).

20. Ibid., 255. O'Connell, in a different register, also observed that, for Augustine, "God suckles us as infants, but gradually weans us for the 'grown-up' food 'spiritual' adults alone may eat and digest. But even that accession to the food of grown-ups takes the form of suckling." See O'Connell, "Isaiah's Mothering God," 196.

21. Margaret Miles, in "Infancy, Parenting, and Nourishment," has utilized psychoanalysis to investigate the therapeutic or cathartic effect of "infantile experience" upon Augustine's psyche. Marsha L. Dutton, in "When I Was a Child," 113–14, explores the ways in which infancy and maternity function as guiding metaphors within Augustine's theology of spiritual development. She concludes that the Pauline distinction between milk and solid food in 1 Cor. 3 governs Augustine's reading of the nursing breast as a location where infantile faith begins as well as that which must be disavowed in the fullness of maturity. Last, Felecia McDuffie, in "Augustine's Rhetoric of the Feminine," 97–118, convincingly demonstrates the ways in which women, both real and symbolic, haunt the landscape of Augustine's theological imagination. Despite abandoning female particularity in his eschatological framework, McDuffie concludes that Augustine's broader theology of Christian formation never fully transcends the milky diet of faith. See, e.g.: "Although he sometimes speaks of the Christian moving beyond the infant state and on to the 'solid food' of difficult doctrine, Augustine's depiction of his own life implies an end in a state of union and ease like that of a baby at the breast. This state is far removed from the world of separation, language, and 'difficult doctrine.' Augustine associates maturity with an all-consuming sexual desire, and he suggests a solution in the return to a 'childhood' of relative innocence and dependence on God as Mother" (112).

22. Peter Brown, *Augustine*, 139–50.

23. Carol Harrison, *Augustine*, 28–29, and *Rethinking Augustine's Early Theology*.

24. Catherine Conybeare, *The Irrational Augustine*, 1.

25. Ibid., 7.

26. Augustine, *Contra Academicos* 3.20.43–45 (CCSL 29:60–61). In his *De Ordine*, 2.5.16 (CCSL 29:115), Augustine refers to authority and reason as the "two ways we should follow when the unintelligibility of things disturbs us." Throughout this chapter, I will refer to "reason" or "rational understanding" as interchangeable translations of the Latin *ratio*. Both are meant to indicate not simple analytical functions of the mind, but rather an independent form of intellectual judgment not dependent upon outside structures of authority. On the meaning of *ratio* and its relation to authority, I have followed the thorough study provided by Frederick van Fleteren in "Authority and Reason," 43–45. See also Harrison, *Augustine*, 3–25.

27. On the overarching aim of Augustine's early dialogues, see Ryan N. S. Topping, *Happiness and Wisdom*.

28. Van Fleteren, "Authority and Reason," 56. Later in the essay, van Fleteren unpacks the decentering of reason that takes place in Augustine's writings once he has become a bishop: "During his mature period, Augustine tends to discuss faith in relation to vision, the former being a prelude to the latter. Finally, from after his conversion until his death, Augustine thinks that reason has a priority as the object of man's pursuit, but that faith in authority must have temporal priority" (71). One of the primary aims of this chapter is to suggest that Augustine's later emphasis on the temporal priority of faith in authority nearly eclipses any positive role that *ratio* holds within the formation of the Christian. For Augustine, independent reason and the faith induced by the authority of the church come to play a zero-sum game—especially when analyzed through his shifting use of milk and solid food. In contrast to the constancy and humility of milk, the solid food of *ratio* is an unreliable source of nourishment that can easily lead the faithful astray.

29. Augustine, *On the Catholic Way of Life (Cath.)* 1.2.3 (PL 32:1311–12).

30. *Cath.* 1.10.17 (PL 32:1318; modified from Roland Teske's translation in Augustine's *The Manichean Debate*, 39.).

31. As Conybeare has suggested, in the wake of his Manichaean experience, *ratio* becomes for Augustine a marker of pride. In order to salvage reason from Manichaean arrogance, Augustine must draw it closer and closer to authority. Thus, Conybeare provocatively concludes, "The way, then, really is 'twofold' (*duplex*), not forked; there are not two different routes by which one arrives at the same place, but one route with two aspects, each of which depends in some

way on the other. Ultimately, all that elaborate process of philosophical enquiry can teach the eager student is how to accept the mystery of divinity. Authority is the way for the less educated, but such people are dependent at the very least upon *ratio communis*—the organization of elementary communication—and on their own capacity as rational human beings (*homines rationales*), even if the more exalted, philosophical notions of ratio (in the traditional formulations) are not available to them. . . . The miracle of the incarnation leads Augustine to reflect on the gulf between any human interpretation or grasp of *ratio* and the divine principles at work in the universe. Against that gulf, the distinction between human ratio and human authority becomes functionally almost non-existent." Conybeare, *Irrational Augustine*, 154.

32. In Augustine, *Confessions* (*Conf.*) 3.5.9–6.10, Augustine explicitly frames his experience among the Manichaeans as a grasping at food that was not suitable to the capacity of his soul. He explains how he sought out the esoteric sect because he was unsatisfied with the infantile language of scripture. Puffed up with pride in his own intellect, Augustine "refused to be an infant (*sed ego dedignabar esse parvulus*)" (CCSL 27:31). The language of the Manichaeans, by contrast, was complex, inscrutable, and thus seemed closer to the solid food of truth.

33. Augustine, *On the Greatness of the Soul* 32.69 (PL 32:1073).

34. *On the Greatness of the Soul* 33.70–76.

35. *On the Greatness of the Soul* 33.76 (PL 32:1076).

36. *On the Greatness of the Soul* 33.76 (PL 32:1076; modified from Joseph M. Colleran's translation in *St. Augustine: The Greatness of the Soul/The Teacher*, 105).

37. Augustine, *On True Religion* (*True Rel.*) 26.48 (CCSL 32:217).

38. *True Rel.* 26.49 (CCSL 32:218). Note here the parallel between the natural and the spiritual ages at the outset: each depicts the human person as first dependent on the nourishment of milk.

39. *True Rel.* 26.49 (CCSL 32:218).

40. *True Rel.* 26.49 (CCSL 32:218).

41. *True Rel.* 26.49 (CCSL 32:218).

42. *True Rel.* 26.49 (CCSL 32:219).

43. In Augustine, *Sermons* (*Serm.*) 216.7 (PL 38:1080)—composed at roughly the same time as *True Religion* (ca. 391)—Augustine cautions his audience to be patient while they are within the womb of the church, not to become restless with their infantile status, so that they are "born healthy, not savagely aborted (*enitere ut salubriter pariaris, ne feraliter abortiaris*)." In this gestational period, Augustine continues, "because you are being breastfed, praise God. Because you are being suckled, praise. Because you are being nourished, advance in wisdom and age (*Quia lactaris, lauda: quia aleris, lauda: quia nutriris, pro-*

fice sapientia et aetate)." Augustine bolsters his exhortation of patience in being a nursling of the church by appealing once again to the notion of spiritual ages, in contrast to ages of those born from earthly parents. Those who have God as father and church as mother, he argues, do not grow toward death like those with natural parents. Rather, they grow toward the "white hairs of wisdom" and "everlasting peace." *Serm.* 216.8. The paradigm for Christian formation at this point in Augustine's thought presumes that, while it is necessary for Christian infants to drink the milk of the church, they will nevertheless grow out of this phase.

44. *True Rel.* 28.50 (CCSL 32:220; modified from John H. S. Burleigh's translation in *Augustine: Earlier Writings*, 250–51).

45. Roland Teske has examined the concept of the "spiritual man"—which I take to be closely related to the *virum perfectum*—in Augustine's thought, with specific attention to the *Confessions*. He concludes that "to be a spiritual in Augustine's sense involves at least two necessary conditions: first, that one is in the church and, second, that one is adept at Neoplatonic spiritualism." See Teske, " 'Homo Spiritualis' in the *Confessions*," 70.

46. See Jason David BeDuhn, *The Manichaean Body*, 126–208, and BeDhun, *Augustine's Manichaean Dilemma*, vol. 1, esp. 58–59.

47. Elizabeth A. Clark, "Vitiated Seeds," 325.

48. Johannes van Oort, "The Young Augustine's Knowledge of Manichaeism," 465.

49. *Conf.* 3.6.10.

50. BeDuhn, *Augustine's Manichaean Dilemma*, vol. 1, 59.

51. BeDuhn, *The Manichaean Body*, 167.

52. *Conf.* 3.1.1 (CCSL 27:27): *eram sine desiderio alimentorum incorruptibilium.*

53. *Conf.* 3.6.10 (CCSL 27:31): *apponebantur adhuc mihi in illis ferculis phantasmata splendida.*

54. *Conf.* 1.6.7 (CCSL 27:4).

55. *Conf.* 1.6.7 (CCSL 27:4). The divine origin of human breast milk described by Augustine echoes a similar claim made by Philo in his *On the Life of Moses*. (See the previous discussions of this in chapters 2 and 5.)

56. Unlike Jerome, who replicates the more conservative strand of imperial family values in his warning against the corruptive influence of nurses and other child attendants (see *Letters* 107 and 128), Augustine does not moralize the influence of his own nurses. This is a departure from the embodied politic of the Roman *familia*, which sought to secure legitimate heirs through strict regulation of child-minders—often to the explicit exclusion of wet nurses. Though he does not elaborate on his nurses, the tenor of this passage suggests that, like Basil,

Augustine viewed his nurses with affection and appreciation. I am grateful to Sophie Lunn-Rockliffe for her conversation on this point. For more on Augustine and his nutrix, see Shaw, "Family in Late Antiquity," 41–42.

57. *Conf.* 3.4.8 (CCSL 27:30): *quod nomen Christi non erat ibi, quoniam hoc nomen secundum misericordiam tuam, domine, hoc nomen salvatoris mei, filii tui, in ipso adhuc lacte matris tenerum cor meum pie biberat et alte retinebat.*

58. *Conf.* 3.4.8 (CCSL 27:30): *et quiquid sine hoc nomine fuisset, quamvis litteratum et expolitum et veridicum, non me totum rapiebat.*

59. *Conf.* 4.1.1 (CCSL 27:40).

60. For more on the erotics of nourishment, see Laura Moncion, "Erotic Food Metaphors," and Gilbert Meilaender, "Sweet Necessities."

61. This is perhaps the most direct connection made between the discourse of nourishment and the Pauline trope of milk and solid food within the *Confessions*. Augustine develops this equivalence of John's prologue to Paul's *cibus* further in other writings.

62. *Conf.* 7.18.24 (CCSL 27:108).

63. This point is nicely articulated by Felecia McDuffie in "Augustine's Rhetoric of the Feminine," 112. In the *Confessions,* the maturity of adulthood is increasingly associated with the sins of sexual incontinence, intellectual hubris, and professional ambition. In this way, a reversion to infancy and a stasis in that "age" replaces Augustine's earlier stage-by-stage schematic for progressive steps (*gradus*) of Christian formation. See, e.g., *On the Greatness of the Soul* 33.70–76).

64. *Conf.* 2.8.16 (CCSL 27:25). As early as *De Magistro* 11.38, Augustine had already undermined the necessity of teachers with his notion of the "inner Teacher" (i.e., Christ) who resides within each person and makes instruction unnecessary for those who can listen. For an excellent account of Augustine's thinking on interior instruction, see Brian Stock, *Augustine's Inner Dialogue,* esp. 11–14, on how this theme relates to "progressive knowledge."

65. This theme is analyzed at length by Lewis Ayres in "Into the Poem," esp. 278–79. This is a theme that reemerges with particular force in Augustine's later homiletic and exegetical writings. For more on *imitatio* and *exempla,* see also Cooper, *The Fall of the Roman Household,* 217–19.

66. *On Christian Teaching* 1.11.11 (CCSL 32:12).

67. Mark Jordan, "The Word, His Body" (in Virginia Burrus, Mark Jordan, and Karmen MacKendrick, *Seducing Augustine*, 52–53).

68. Ibid., 58–59.

69. On Augustine's reluctance to speak of himself or of Christian peers as an example, see Ayres, "Into the Poem," 279.

70. See Brian Stock, *Augustine the Reader,* 148: "In Augustine's view, overcoming the difficulties (in the verbal exchange of signs) requires a type of instruction that does not originate in external sounds but silently enlightens us from within. Ultimately, this enlightenment arises through a nonhuman source and requires an intermediary that is accessible to human senses and minds, such as speech, images, or texts."

71. *On Christian Teaching* 2.12.17 (CCSL 32:43).

72. *Conf.* 7.10.16 (CCSL 27:103–4).

73. Paulinus of Nola, *Letters* 8.1 (CSEL 29:45–46).

74. Found in Augustine, *Letters* 109.1 (CCSL 31B:85).

75. Augustine, *Homilies on the Gospel of John* (*Hom. Gosp. John*) 7.23 (CCSL 36:80).

76. *Hom. Gosp. John* 7.23 (CCSL 36:81).

77. The dating of these homilies is somewhat difficult, though most scholars agree that they belong to a late period in Augustine's career (perhaps ca. 419). This trio of homilies has received much attention for its "anti-esoteric" agenda. Scholars have long seen it as the best resource for understanding how the motif of milk and solid food functions in Augustine's approach to pastoral care. I have offered only a cursory glance here in order to shift the focus to the *Expositions of the Psalms,* which I've highlighted. For the history of scholarship on this series, see van Bavel, "L'humanitè du Christ," 273; M. F. Berrouard, "Saint Augustin et la ministere de la predication," 463–65; Stroumsa, *Hidden Wisdom,* 132–46; Paul Kolbet, *Augustine and the Cure of Souls,* 175–78.

78. *Hom. Gosp. John* 96.1 (CCSL 36:569).

79. *Hom. Gosp. John* 96.2–3.

80. *Hom. Gosp. John* 97.2 (CCSL 36:574).

81. In fact, at one point in the opening of homily 97, Augustine asks a flurry of rhetorical questions directed at the limitations of human knowledge and understanding. He concludes by asking his audience, "And who among men understands the Trinity as the angels do?" See *Hom. Gosp. John* 97.1 (CCSL 36:573). The whole homily is explicitly addressed to the *parvuli* in 97.2, suggesting once again that Augustine's primary concern remained the protection of the Christian infants rather than their progress from milk to solid food. In his mature writings, Augustine refers to Christians who are newly baptized as *infantes* and more broadly refers to all Christians as *parvuli.*

82. *Hom. Gosp. John* 98.2 (CSL 36:577).

83. *Hom. Gosp. John* 98.4 (CSL 36:578).

84. *On Teaching the Uninstructed* (*Teach. Un.*) is perhaps the most fascinating—and disappointingly brief—consideration of catechesis for Christians of different

intellectual capacities. Augustine does not employ the milk-and-solid-food trope in that text, nor does he describe any of these groups as "perfect." However, in *Teach. Un.* 4.8, he does mention the difference between carnal people and spiritual people as part of a broader typology that views the Old Testament as a veil for the New. This typology supports his later discussion in *Teach. Un.* 9.13, of scripture's hidden mysteries that the more learned Christians may approach via allegory. As in *Hom. Gosp. John* 98, Augustine seems compelled to discuss such distinctions only because he is prompted to do so by scripture. His center of gravity is always tethered to the infants, the milk-drinking Christians.

85. *Hom. Gosp. John* 98.6 (CCSL 36:579–80). Augustine not only presumes that the majority of his audience will fall among the *parvuli in Christo* (as he states clearly in *Hom. Gosp. John* 98.7), but also that the "solid food" of the perfect has most often been flaunted by seducers (*seductores*) who lead others away from the sustaining milk of faith. See *Hom. Gosp. John* 98.7 (CCSL 36:580). And so, while I agree that the general strategy of homilies 96–98 is to refute esoteric tendencies within the church, Augustine achieves this by reserving the maturity of solid food to those rare few who become teachers. Yet he undermines this by warning that the weaning of infants from milk to solid food has often been the tactic of heretics and schismatics. After all, the three major polemical opponents of Augustine's career—the Manichaeans, the Donatists, and the Pelagians—each imagined a community of perfectible people in different ways. Augustine's primary concern is that the infants of the church not be pulled from their milk. The broader implication, as we will see, is a connection between clerics and solid food.

86. Augustine, *Homilies on the First Epistle of John* (*Hom. First. Ep.*) 3.1 (BA 76:148).

87. *Hom. First. Ep.* 3.1 (BA 76:148–50).

88. There has been a renaissance of scholarship on the *Expositions of the Psalms* (*Ex. Ps.*), particularly in light of the new English translation found in the Works of Saint Augustine series. The work of Michael McCarthy, S.J., Michael Cameron, Jason Byassee, and Michael Fiedrowicz (among others) has helped to reorient scholarship on Augustine toward this rich collection. As Michael Fiedrowicz has noted, the *Expositions* are notoriously difficult to date. In this section, I will primarily look at *Ex. Ps.* 8; 30(2–3) and 130. With the exception of *Ex. Ps.* 8, all of the other passages come from texts identified as a *sermo ad plebem* (sermon to the people) and are reflective of Augustine's later (ca. 407 and following) views on formation and the progress from milk to solid food. In addition, it is worth noting that Psalms 30 and 130 in Augustine's text refer to Psalms 31 and 131 in modern Bibles. For an introduction to the major textual

issues within the *Expositions,* see Michael Fiedrowicz's introduction to Augustine's *Expositions of the Psalms 1–32,* 13–66; Fiedrowicz, *Psalmus Vox Totius Christi,* 11–50; and Allan D. Fitzgerald's introduction to Augustine's *Homilies on the Gospel of John 1–40,* 29–31.

89. *Ex. Ps.* 8.5 (CCSL 38:50): *ex ore infantium et lactantium perfecisti laudem.*

90. *Ex. Ps.* 8.5 (CCSL 38:51).

91. *Ex. Ps.* 8.5 (CCSL 38:50): *Sunt enim in ecclesiis etiam hi qui non iam lacte potantur, sed vescuntur cibo.*

92. Augustine's optimism here regarding the existence of solid-food-eating youths within the church—or of the potential for maturity from milk to solid food in general—is a stark contrast to his approach to milk and solid food in the other *Expositions* from a later date and registers the rupture in his thought between the earlier and later periods of writing within a single commentary set. His attention shifts away from human potential for growth toward the deleterious effects of maturity—a view consistent with what we find developing within and after the *Confessions.* Here, however, perfection is discussed without hesitation. Thus it seems probable that this *Exposition* was written in the liminal space between his Cassiciacum dialogues and his *Confessions* while he was still tinkering with his understanding of the nature of Christian formation.

93. *Ex. Ps.* 8.5 (CCSL 38:51). Augustine goes on to describe the "breast milk of faith in temporal history": "This history, following from the time of the patriarchs and prophets, was done for our salvation by the most excellent power and wisdom of God—now undertaken in the sacrament of man being administered, in whom resides the salvation of all those who believe. It was done in order that each person awoken by [Christ's] authority and obedient to his commands would be made pure, rooted on a foundation of love, and able to run with the saints. This person is not an infant drinking milk but rather a youth eating solid food, able to grasp the breadth, length, height, and depth, and to know the love of Christ that is above all knowledge." Here, the solid-food-eating youth runs with the saints outside the bounds of temporal history.

94. *Ex. Ps.* 30(2).9 (CCSL 38:197).

95. *Ex. Ps.* 30(2).9 (CCSL 38:197): *Ergo corpus Christi loquitur: et enutries me.*

96. *Ex. Ps.* 30(3).6 (CCSL 38:206).

97. *Ex. Ps.* 30(3).6 (CCSL 38:207): *Istis itaque talibus cum sint plenae ecclesiae.*

98. *Ex. Ps.* 30(3).12 (CCSL 38:210).

99. *Ex. Ps.* 30(3).12 (CCSL 38:210).

100. *Mammothreptus* is a combination of the Greek word *threptos* (meaning either "a slave born and raised in the house of its master" or, alternatively, "an adopted foundling") and the Latin word *mamma* (meaning "breast").

101. *Ex. Ps.* 30(3).12 (CCSL 38:210). Augustine has in mind here all those led astray by Donatus and Caecilian. As in the *Confessions,* Augustine's suspicion of human authority stems from his polemics against bad Christians who create division and gain followers to their name rather than the name of Christ. Thus, he echoes Paul's rebuke of the Corinthians who created a division between followers of himself and Apollo: "I am not walking under the name of a man. I hold only the name of Christ [*Non ad hominis nomen ambulo, Christi nomen teneo*]."

102. In *Ex. Ps.* 98.1 Augustine addresses his audience as "children of the church, educated in the school of Christ through the writings of our ancient fathers" (CCSL 39:1378): *filiis ecclesiae, et eruditis in schola Christi per omnes litteras antiquorum partum nostrorum.* This education does not necessarily indicate a progressive development of the children. Augustine does not describe the instruction of the *schola Christi* as weaning from milk to solid food. Contrast this to the perspective given in Marjorie O'Rourke Boyle, "Augustine in the Garden of Zeus," 139.

103. NRSV. In modern bibles this would be Psalm 131:1–2.

104. *Ex. Ps.* 130.9 (CCSL 40:1905).

105. *Ex. Ps.* 130.11 (CCSL 40:1907).

106. Note also that the link between contemplation of the Trinity and the trope of milk and solid food is made explicit in Augustine's *On the Trinity.* See *Trin.* 1.1.3 (CCSL 50:30).

107. *Ex. Ps.* 130.12 (CCSL 40:1907).

108. Hilary of Poitiers, *Commentary on the Psalms* 130.4–5 (CSEL 22:658–59): *tenendus ergo humilitatis et altitudinis modus est.* Drawing on the text of the same Psalm, Hilary distinguishes a negative exaltation of the heart (which is akin to sinful pride) from a praiseworthy exaltation of the soul (which demonstrates that proper weaning and spiritual growth have occurred). See his *Commentary on the Psalms* 130.4 (CSEL 22:658).

109. Hilary, *Commentary on the Psalms* 130.4 (CSEL 22:659): *ergo profectus maximus est, iam lacte non indigere.*

110. *Ex. Ps.* 130.12 (CCSL 40:1907).

111. *Ex. Ps.* 130.12 (CCSL 40:1907).

112. *Ex. Ps.* 130.12 (CCSL 40:1908): *Lactare, ut nutriaris; sic nutrire, ut crescas; sic cresce, ut panem manduces. Cum enim coeperis panem manducare, ablactaberis, id est, iam tibi non opus erit lac, sed solidus cibus.*

113. *Ex. Ps.* 130.12 (CCSL 40:1908): *si non mente, sed malitia parvulus fui.* The thrust of this second reading of *Ex. Ps.* 130.2 seems to resonate with Augustine's earlier use of *mammothreptus* in *Ex. Ps.* 30(3). However, in that text,

Augustine was chiefly concerned with Christians attached to other Christians for their nourishment and formation rather than being attached to the church. In this passage, the concern is simply directed toward those Christians who refuse to be weaned even though they are being properly nourished in the church. In either case, Augustine has little interest in the notion that the church's milk should be thought of as insufficient for any member of the Christian community.

114. *Ex. Ps.* 130.13 (CCSL 40:1909).

115. Ibid.

116. Ibid.

117. *Ex. Ps.* 130.13–14 (CCSL 40:1909–10).

118. *Serm.* 119.1 (PL 38:673). See also the English translation of this sermon, with notes on dating, by Edmund Hill, O.P., Augustine, *Sermons (94A–147A) on the New Testament,* 227–30.

119. *Serm.* 119.4.

120. Tertullian, *On the Crown* 3. Jerome also mentions the rite: "[A]fter leaving [the baptismal water], there is a foretaste of milk and honey according to the symbol of infancy" (*deinde egressos, lactis et mellis praegustare concordiam ad infantiae significationem*). See Jerome, *Against the Luciferians* 8 (PL 23:0164A). This reference is of particular interest because it explicitly presents Christian milk rites as evoking both the Promised Land of Exodus 3 as well as infancy—a link between exegesis and liturgy we have already seen in Clement of Alexandria. *The Apostolic Tradition* 21.24–38 stipulates a similar practice, also emphasizing the infantile status of those who drink. There is yet to be a thoroughgoing account of milk in early Christian ritual. In a future project, I intend to explore this in more detail. For discussions of the rite, see Andrew B. McGowan, *Ancient Christian Worship,* 160–63; McGowan, *Ascetic Eucharists,* 107–14; Edward J. Kilmartin, "Baptismal Cups," 249–67.

121. Shaw, "Family in Late Antiquity," 41–42.

122. Cooper, *The Fall of the Roman Household,* 99. Cooper describes this process as being "the result of social engineering, yet another instance of the cooperation of episcopal authority with the state."

123. Charles Norris Cochrane, *Christianity and Classical Culture,* 498–99: "The doctrine of sin and grace marks, in its most acute form, the breach between Classicism and Christianity. . . . Thus, for [Augustine], the classical ideal of perfectibility through knowledge or enlightenment was wholly illusory; and, for the aberrations of humanity, he saw no remedy through education."

124. Brown, *Augustine of Hippo,* 150. For an excellent comparison of Brown and Marrou, see Mark Vessey, "The Demise of the Christian Writer."

125. Robert Markus, *The End of Ancient Christianity*, 50.
126. Stroumsa, *Hidden Wisdom*, 132–46.
127. Neil McLynn, "Disciplines of Discipleship," 41.

Conclusion

1. Eusebius, *Ecclesiastical History* 4.23 (LCL 153:380).
2. Judith Butler, *Senses of the Subject*, 21.
3. As Patricia Cox Miller has observed, "While it is certainly true that the human body and its sensorium became a locus for religious epistemology, this does not mean that . . . Christians embraced the body and its senses without reserve." See Patricia Cox Miller, *The Corporeal Imagination*, 4.
4. Elizabeth A. Clark, "Antifamilial Tendencies," 380.
5. See Caroline Walker Bynum's classic study, *Jesus as Mother*. The current project was prompted in part by Bynum's groundbreaking work.
6. Avner Giladi, *Infants, Parents, and Wet Nurses*, 28.
7. Ibid., 79–81.
8. Meredith Martin, *Dairy Queens*, 246–57.
9. Joan B. Wolf, *Is Breast Best?* 4.
10. Jerome, *Letters* 82.2 (PL 22:737): *Nos nec Ecclesiam scindimus, neque a patrum communione dividimur: sed ab ipsis, ut ita dicam, incunabulis catholico sumus lacte nutriti. Nemo namque magis Ecclesiasticus est, quam qui nunquam haereticus fuit.*
11. Catherine Keller, "Seeking and Sucking," 77.
12. Donna J. Haraway, "Parting Bites," 294: "The surrogate remains a creature that nourishes indigestion, that is, a kind of dyspepsia with regard to proper place and function that queer theory is really all about. The surrogate is nothing if not the mutter/matter of gestation out of place, a necessary if not sufficient cut into the female defining function called reproduction."
13. Though it was published late in my own research, Sharon Jacob's book *Reading Mary Alongside Indian Mother Surrogates* offers an important and incisive comparative analysis.
14. Judith Butler, *Excitable Speech*, 156–59.
15. Throughout my work on this project, a quote by Adrienne Rich was often in the back of my mind: "There is nothing revolutionary whatsoever about the control of women's bodies by men. The woman's body is the terrain on which patriarchy is erected." See Rich, *Of Woman Born*, 55.

Bibliography

Ancient Texts and Translations

ARISTOTLE

On the Soul. Edited by W. S. Hett. *Aristotle,* vol. 8, 2–203. LCL 288. Cambridge, MA: Harvard University Press, 1986.

Parts of Animals. Edited by A. L. Peck. *Aristotle,* vol. 12, 52–431. LCL 323. Cambridge, MA: Harvard University Press, 1937.

Politics. Edited by H. Rackham. *Aristotle: Politics.* LCL 264. Cambridge, MA: Harvard University Press, 1932.

ARTEMIDORUS

Interpretation of Dreams. Edited by R. A. Pack. *Artemidori Daldiani Onirocriticon Libri V.* Leipzig, Germany: Teubner, 1963.

The Interpretation of Dreams: The Oneirocritica of Artemidorus. Translated by Robert J. White. Park Ridge, NJ: Noyes Press, 1975.

AUGUSTINE OF HIPPO

Augustine: Earlier Writings. Translated by John H. S. Burleigh. LCC. Philadelphia: Westminster Press, 1953.

Confessions. Edited by L. Verheijen. *Augustinus: Confessionum Libri XIII.* CCSL 27. Turnhout, Belgium: Brepols, 1981.

Contra Academicos, De Ordine, and *De Magistro.* Edited by W. M. Green and K. D. Daur. *Augustinus: Contra Academicos, De Beata Vita, De Ordine, De Magistro, De Libero Arbitrio.* CCSL 29. Turnhout, Belgium: Brepols, 1970.

Expositions of the Psalms. Edited by E. Dekkers and J. Fraipont. *Augustinus: Enarrationes in Psalmos I-CL.* CCSL 38–40. 2nd ed. Turnhout, Belgium: Brepols, 1990.

Expositions of the Psalms 1–32. Translated by Maria Boulding, O.S.B. WSA III/15. Hyde Park, NY: New City Press, 2000.

Homilies on the First Epistle of John. Edited by J. W. Mountain. *Augustin d'Hippone, Homélies sur la première Épître de saint Jean: In Iohannis epistulam ad Parthos tractatus decem.* BA 76. Turnhout, Belgium: Brepols, 2008.

————. Translated by Boniface Ramsey. *Homilies on the First Epistle of John.* WSA III/14. Hyde Park, NY: New City Press, 2008.

Homilies on the Gospel of John. Edited by R. Willems. *Augustinus: In Iohannis Evangelium Tractatus CXXIV.* CCSL 36. 2nd ed. Turnhout, Belgium: Brepols, 1990.

————. Translated by Edmund Hill, O.P. *Homilies on the Gospel of John 1–40.* WSA III/12. Hyde Park, NY: New City Press, 2009.

Letters. Edited by K. D. Daur. *Augustinus: Epistulae CI-CXXXIX.* CCSL 31B. Turnhout, Belgium: Brepols, 2009.

The Manichean Debate. Translated by Roland Teske, S.J. WSA I/19. Hyde Park, NY: New City Press, 2006.

On the Catholic Way of Life. Edited by J. P. Migne. *De Moribus Ecclesiae et Manichaeorum.* PL 32. Paris, 1877.

On the Greatness of the Soul. Edited by J. P. Migne. *De Quantitate Animae.* PL 32. Paris, 1877.

On Instructing the Beginners. Edited by J. B. Bauer. *De Catechizandis Rudibus.* CCSL 46. Turnhout: Brepols, 1969.

On the Trinity. Edited by W. J. Mountain. *De Trinitate.* CCSL 50. Turnhout, Belgium: Brepols, 1970.

On True Religion and *On Christian Teaching.* Edited by K. D. Daur and J. Martin. *Augustinus: De Doctrina Christiana, De Vera Religione.* CCSL 32. Reprint, Turnhout, Belgium: Brepols, 1996.

Sermons. Edited by J. P. Migne. *Sermones ad Populum. Classis I. De Scripturis.* PL 38. Paris, 1882.

Sermons (94A–147A) on the New Testament. Translated by Edmund Hill, O.P. WSA III/4. Brooklyn, NY: New City Press, 1992.

St. Augustine: The Greatness of the Soul/The Teacher. Translated by Joseph M. Colleran. ACW 9. Westminster, MD: Newman Press, 1950.

AUGUSTUS CAESAR

Res Gestae. Edited by Alison E. Cooley. *Res Gestae Divi Augusti: Text, Translation, and Commentary.* Cambridge: Cambridge University Press, 2009.

AULUS GELLIUS

Attic Nights. Edited by J. C. Rolfe. *Aulus Gellius: Attic Nights,* vol. 2, books 6–13. LCL 200. Cambridge, MA: Harvard University Press, 1927.

BASIL OF CAESAREA

Letters. Edited by Roy J. Deferrari, *Basil: The Letters,* vol. 1. LCL 190. Cambridge, MA: Harvard University Press, 1926.

CICERO

Tusculan Disputations. Edited by E. King. *Cicero: Tusculan Disputations.* LCL 141. Cambridge, MA: Harvard University Press, 1927.

CLEMENT OF ALEXANDRIA

Paedagogus. Edited by M. Marcovich. *Clementis Alexandrini Paedagogus. VCSup* 61. Leiden: Brill, 2002.

———. Translated by Simon P. Wood. *Clement of Alexandria: Christ the Educator.* FOC 23. Washington, DC: Catholic University of America Press, 1954.

Protrepticus. Edited by G. W. Butterworth. *Clement of Alexandria: Exhortation to the Greeks; The Rich Man's Salvation; To the Newly Baptized.* LCL 92. Cambridge, MA: Harvard University Press, 1919.

Stromateis. Edited by Claude Mondésert and Marcel Caster. *Clément D'Alexandrie: Les Stromates: Stromate I.* SC 30. Paris: Éditions du Cerf, 1954.

———. Edited by P. Th. Camelot and Claude Mondésert. *Clément D'Alexandrie: Les Stromates: Stromate II.* SC 38. Paris: Éditions du Cerf, 1954.

———. Edited by Annewies van den Hoek and Claude Mondésert. *Clément D'Alexandrie: Les Stromates: Stromate IV.* SC 463. Paris: Éditions du Cerf, 2001.

———. Edited by Alain Le Boulluec and Pierre Voulet. *Clément D'Alexandrie: Les Stromates: Stromate V, Tome I.* SC 278. Paris: Éditions du Cerf, 2006.

———. Translated by John Ferguson. *Clement of Alexandria: Stromateis: Books One to Three.* FOC 85. Washington, DC: Catholic University of America Press, 1991.

DIO CASSIUS

Roman History. Edited by Earnest Cary. *Dio Cassius: Roman History,* vol. 7, books 56–60. LCL 175. Cambridge, MA: Harvard University Press, 1921.

EPICTETUS

Encheiridion. Edited by Jeffrey Henderson. *Epictetus: The Discourses, Books 3–4; Fragments; Encheiridion.* LCL 218. Cambridge, MA: Harvard University Press, 1928.

EPIPHANIUS OF SALAMIS

Panarion. Edited by K. Holl. *Epiphanius, Bände 1–3: Ancoratus und Panarion.* GCS 31. Leipzig, Germany: Hinrichs, 1922.

EUSEBIUS OF CAESAREA

Ecclesiastical History. Edited by Kirsopp Lake. *Eusebius: The Ecclesiastical History,* vol. 1. LCL 153. Cambridge, MA: Harvard University Press, 1965.

GALEN

Galen: Selected Works. Translated by Peter Singer. Oxford World Classics. New York: Oxford University Press, 1997.
On the Properties of Foodstuffs. Edited by C. G. Kuhn. *Claudii Galeni Opera Omnia 6.* Hildesheim, Germany: Georg Olms, 1964–1965.
The Capacities of the Soul Depend on the Mixtures of the Body. Edited by C. G. Kuhn. *Quod animi mores corporis temperamenta sequantur.* Claudii Galeni Opera Omnia 4. Hildesheim, Germany: Georg Olms, 1964–1965.

GREGORY OF NAZIANZUS

St. Gregory of Nazianzus: Select Orations. Translated by Martha Vinson. FOC 107. Washington, DC: Catholic University of America Press, 2003.

GREGORY OF NYSSA

Encomium on Saint Basil. Edited by Sr. James Aloysius Stein. *Encomium of Saint Gregory Bishop of Nyssa on his Brother Saint Basil.* Catholic University of America Patristic Studies 17. Washington, DC: Catholic University of America Press, 1928.
Homilies on the Song of Songs. Edited by Richard A. Norris Jr. *Gregory of Nyssa: Homilies on the Song of Songs.* WGRW 13. Atlanta: Society of Biblical Literature, 2012.

Life of Macrina. Edited by P. Maraval, *Grégoire de Nysse. Vie de sainte Macrine.* SC 178. Paris: Éditions du Cerf, 1971.

Life of Moses. Edited by Jean Daniélou. *Grégoire de Nysse. La vie de Moïse.* 3rd ed. SC 1. Paris: Éditions du Cerf, 1968.

———. Translated by Abraham J. Malherbe and Everett Ferguson. *Gregory of Nyssa: The Life of Moses.* CWS. Mahwah, NJ: Paulist Press, 1978.

On the Soul and Resurrection. Translated by Catherine P. Roth. *On the Soul and Resurrection.* Popular Patristics 12. Crestwood, NY: St Vladimir's Seminary Press, 1992.

HILARY OF POITIERS

Commentary on the Psalms. Edited by A. Zingerle. *Tractatus super Psalmos.* CSEL 22. Vienna, 1891.

HIPPOCRATES

On the Nature of the Child. Edited by Paul Potter. *Hippocrates,* vol. 10. LCL 520. Cambridge, MA: Harvard University Press, 2012.

On Nutriment. Edited by W. H. S. Jones. *Hippocrates,* vol. 1. LCL 147. Cambridge, MA: Harvard University Press, 1962.

Regimen. Edited by W. H. S. Jones. *Hippocrates,* vol. 4. LCL 150. Cambridge, MA: Harvard University Press, 1962.

HOMER

The Iliad. Translated by Robert Fagles. New York: Penguin, 1990.

IRENAEUS OF LYONS

Against Heresies. Edited by Adelin Rousseau. *Irénée de Lyon: Contre les hérésies.* Livre IV. SC 100. Paris: Éditions du Cerf, 1965.

Demonstration of Apostolic Preaching. Edited by Adelin Rousseau. *Irénée de Lyon: Démonstration de la prédeication apostolique.* SC 406. Paris: Éditions du Cerf, 1995.

On the Apostolic Preaching. Translated by John Behr. Popular Patristics 17. Crestwood, NY: St Vladimir's Seminary Press, 1997.

JEROME

Against the Luciferians and *Against Jovinian.* Edited by J. P. Migne. *Hieronymi Operum Tomus II: Contra Luciferianos, Adversus Jovinianum.* PL 23. Paris: 1845.
Letters. Edited by J. P. Migne. *Hieronymus: Epistulae.* PL 22. Paris: 1854.

LONGUS

Daphnis and Chloe. Edited by Jeffrey Henderson. *Longus: Daphnis and Chloe; Xenephon of Ephesus: Anthia and Habrocomes.* LCL 69. Cambridge, MA: Harvard University Press, 2009.

MACROBIUS

Saturnalia. Edited by Robert A. Kaster. *Macrobius: Saturnalia: Books 1–2.* LCL 510. Cambridge, MA: Harvard University Press, 2011.

NEW TESTAMENT APOCRYPHA

New Testament Apocrypha: Volume One: Gospels and Related Writings. Edited by Wilhelm Schneemelcher. Translated by R. McL. Wilson. Rev. ed. Louisville, KY: Westminster John Knox Press, 2003.
New Testament Apocrypha: Volume Two: Writings Related to the Apostles, Apocalypses, and Related Subjects. Edited by Wilhelm Schneemelcher. Translated by R. McL. Wilson. Rev. ed. Louisville, KY: Westminster John Knox Press, 2003.

ORIGEN

Against Celsus. Edited by M. Marcovich. *Origenes: Contra Celsum III. VCSup* 54. Leiden: Brill, 2001.
——. Translated by Henry Chadwick. *Origen: Contra Celsum.* Cambridge: Cambridge University Press, 1953.
Commentary on 1 Corinthians. Edited by Claude Jenkins. "Origen on 1 Corinthians." *JTS* 9 (1907–1908): 231–47; 353–72; 500–514.
Commentary on John. Translated by Ronald E. Heine. *Origen: Commentary on the Gospel According to John: Books 1–10.* FOC 80. Washington DC: Catholic University of America Press, 1989.

Commentary on Romans. Edited by L. Brésard and M. Fédou. *Origène: Commentaire sur l'Épître aux Romains.* SC 543–555. Paris: Éditions du Cerf, 2011–2012.

———. Translated by Thomas P. Scheck. *Commentary on the Epistle to the Romans, Books 6–10.* FOC 104. Washington DC: Catholic University of America Press, 2002.

Commentary on the Song of Songs. Translated by R. P. Lawson. *Origen: The Song of Songs: Commentary and Homilies.* ACW 26. New York: Newman Press, 1957.

Dialogue with Heraclides. Edited by J. Scherer. *Entretien d'Origène avec Héraclide.* SC 67. Paris: Éditions du Cerf, 1960.

Homilies on Genesis and Exodus. Edited by M. Borret. *Origène: Homélies sur l'Exode.* SC 321. Paris: Éditions du Cerf, 1985.

———. Translated by Ronal Heine. *Origen: Homilies on Genesis and Exodus.* FOC 71. Washington, DC: Catholic University of America Press, 1982.

Homilies on Judges. Edited by P. Messié. *Origène: Homélies sur les Juges.* SC 389. Paris: Éditions du Cerf, 1993.

———. Translated by Elizabeth Ann Dively Lauro. *Origen: Homilies on Judges.* FOC 119. Washington, DC: Catholic University of America Press, 2010.

Homilies on Leviticus. Translated by G. W. Barkley. *Homilies on Leviticus.* FOC 83. Washington, DC: Catholic University of America Press, 1990.

Homilies on Luke. Translated by Joseph T. Lienhard. *Origen: Homilies on Luke.* FOC 94. Washington, DC: Catholic University of America Press, 1996.

Homilies on Numbers. Edited by L. Doutreleau. *Origène: Homélies sur les Nombres XX–XXIII, Tome 3.* SC 461. Paris: Éditions du Cerf, 2001.

On First Principles. Edited by Henri Crouzel and M. Simonetti. *Traité des Principes.* SC 253, 268, 269, 312. Paris: Éditions du Cerf, 1978–84.

———. Translated by G. W. Butterworth. *Origen: On First Principles.* Gloucester, MA: Peter Smith, 1973.

On Prayer. Edited by P. Koetschau. *De Oratione,* Origenes Werke, vol. 2. GCS 3. Leipzig, Germany: Hinrichs, 1899.

Origen: An Exhortation to Martyrdom, Prayer, and Selected Works. Translated by Rowan A. Greer. CWS. Mahwah, NJ: Paulist Press, 1979.

PAULINUS OF NOLA

Letters. Edited by W. Hartel. *Paulinus of Nola: Epistolae.* CSEL 29. Vienna, 1894.

PHILO

On Drunkenness. Edited by F. H. Colson and G. H. Whitaker, *Philo,* vol. 3. LCL
   247. Cambridge, MA: Harvard University Press, 1930.

On Flight and *On Dreams.* Edited by F. H. Colson and G. H. Whitaker. *Philo,* vol.
   5. LCL 275. Cambridge, MA: Harvard University Press, 1934.

On Mating with Preliminary Studies. Edited by F. H. Colson and G. H. Whitaker,
   Philo, vol. 4. LCL 261. Cambridge, MA: Harvard University Press, 1932.

On the Confusion of Tongues. Edited by F. H. Colson and G. H. Whitaker, *Philo,*
   vol. 4. LCL 261. Cambridge, MA: Harvard University Press, 1935.

On the Life of Moses. Edited by F. H. Colson and G. H. Whitaker, *Philo,* vol. 6. LCL
   289. Cambridge, MA: Harvard University Press, 1935.

On the Special Laws and *On the Virtues.* Edited by F. H. Colson and G. H. Whitaker. *Philo,* vol. 8. LCL 341. Cambridge, MA: Harvard University Press, 1939.

Who Is the Heir of Divine Things? Edited by F. H. Colson and G. H. Whitaker.
   Philo, vol. 4. LCL 261. Cambridge, MA: Harvard University Press, 1932.

PLATO

Laws. Edited by R. G. Bury. *Plato,* vols. 10–11. LCL 187 and 192. Cambridge, MA:
   Harvard University Press, 1977.

Republic. Edited by Paul Shorey. *Plato,* vols. 5–6. LCL 237 and 276. Cambridge,
   MA: Harvard University Press, 1977.

Timaeus. Edited by R. G. Bury. *Plato,* vol. 9. LCL 234. Cambridge, MA: Harvard
   University Press, 1977.

PLINY THE ELDER

Natural History. Edited by H. Rackham. *Pliny: Natural History,* vol. 4. LCL 370.
   Cambridge, MA: Harvard University Press, 1967.

PLUTARCH

Education of Children. Edited by Frank Cole Babbitt. *Plutarch: Moralia,* vol. 1,
   3–71. LCL 197. Cambridge, MA: Harvard University Press, 1927.

Fragments. Edited by F. H. Sandbach. *Plutarch: Moralia,* vol. 15. LCL 429. Cambridge, MA: Harvard University Press, 1969.

Lives. Edited by Bernadotte Perrin. *Plutarch's Lives,* vol. 1. LCL 46. Cambridge,
   MA: Harvard University Press, 1959.

QUINTILIAN

Institutes of Oratory. Edited by H. E. Butler. *The Institutio Oratoria of Quintilian.* LCL 124–127, 494. Cambridge, MA: Harvard University Press, 1985.

SEXTUS EMPIRICUS

Outlines of Skepticism. Edited by Julia Annas and Jonathan Barnes. *Sextus Empiricus: Outlines of Scepticism.* Cambridge Texts in the History of Philosophy. Cambridge: Cambridge University Press, 2000.

SOPHOCLES

Antigone. Edited by G. P. Goold. *Sophocles,* vol. 1. LCL 20. Cambridge, MA: Harvard University Press, 1981.

SORANUS

Gynecology. Edited by Johannes Ilberg. *Sorani: Gynaeciorum Libri IV.* Corpus Medicorum Graecorum 4. Leipzig, Germany: Teubner, 1926.
———. Translated by Owsei Temkin. *Soranus's Gynecology.* Baltimore: Johns Hopkins University Press, 1956.

TACITUS

Dialogue on Oratory. Edited by M. Hutton et al. *Tacitus,* vol. 1: *Agricola; Germanica; Dialogus.* LCL 35. Cambridge, MA: Harvard University Press, 1914.

TERTULLIAN

On Monogamy. Edited by V. Bulhart. *De Monogamia.* CSEL 76. Vienna, 1957.
To Scapula. Edited by Emil Dekkers. CCSL 2. Turnhout, Belgium: Brepols, 1954.

VIRGIL

Aeneid. Edited by H. R. Fairclough and G. P. Goold. *Virgil: Eclogues, Georgics, Aeneid: Books 1–6.* LCL 63. Cambridge, MA: Harvard University Press, 1916.

Secondary Texts

Allen, Pauline. "Some Aspects of Hellenism in Early Greek Church Historians." *Traditio* 43 (1987): 368–81.

Ando, Clifford. *Imperial Ideology and Provincial Loyalty in the Roman Empire.* Classics in Contemporary Thought 6. Berkeley: University of California Press, 2000.

Arjava, Antti. *Women and Law in Late Antiquity.* New York: Oxford University Press, 1996.

Atwood, Margaret. *The Handmaid's Tale.* Everyman's Library 301. New York: Alfred A. Knopf, 2006.

Austin, J. L. *How to Do Things with Words.* Cambridge, MA: Harvard University Press, 1975.

Ayres, Lewis. "Into the Poem of the Universe: Exempla, Conversion, and Church in Augustine's *Confessions.*" *Zeitschrift fur Antikes Christentum* 13 (2009): 263–81.

———. "Irenaeus vs the Valentinians: Toward a Rethinking of Patristic Exegetical Origins." *JECS* 23.2 (2015): 153–87.

———. "On Not Three People: The Fundamental Themes of Gregory of Nyssa's Trinitarian Theology as Seen in *To Ablabius: On Not Three Gods.*" In *Rethinking Gregory of Nyssa,* edited by Sarah Coakley. Malden, MA: Blackwell Publishing, 2004.

Barnes, Michel. *The Power of God: DYNAMIS in Gregory of Nyssa's Trinitarian Theology.* Washington, DC: Catholic University of America Press, 1998.

Barthes, Roland. *How to Live Together: Novelistic Simulations of Some Everyday Spaces.* New York: Columbia University Press, 2012.

Bartlett, Alison. *Breastwork: Rethinking Breastfeeding.* Sydney, Australia: University of New South Wales Press, 2005.

BeDuhn, Jason David. *Augustine's Manichaean Dilemma.* Vol. 1: *Conversion and Apostasy.* Divinations: Rereading Late Ancient Religion. Philadelphia: University of Pennsylvania Press, 2010.

———. *The Manichaean Body in Discipline and Ritual.* Baltimore: Johns Hopkins University Press, 2000.

Beeley, Christopher A. *The Unity of Christ: Continuity and Conflict in Patristic Tradition.* New Haven, CT: Yale University Press, 2012.

Behr, John. *Asceticism and Anthropology in Irenaeus and Clement.* Oxford Early Christian Studies. New York: Oxford University Press, 2000.

———. *Irenaeus of Lyons: Identifying Christianity.* Christian Theology in Context. New York: Oxford University Press, 2013.

Berrouard, M. F. "Saint Augustin et la ministère de la predication." *Recherches augustiniennes* 2 (1962): 447–501.

Bjorklund, David F. "Mother Knows Best: Epigenetic Inheritance, Maternal Effects, and the Evolution of Human Intelligence." *Developmental Review* 26 (2006): 213–42.

Blanc, Cécile. "L'attitude d'Origène a l'égard du corps et de la chair." *Studia Patristica* 17 (1982): 843–58.

———. "Les nourritures spirituelles d'après Origène," *Didaskalia* 6 (1976): 3–19.

Bloch, René. "Alexandria in Pharaonic Egypt: Projections in *De Vita Mosis.*" *Studia Philonica* 24 (2014): 69–84.

Bloomer, W. Martin. *The School of Rome: Latin Studies and the Origins of Liberal Education.* Berkeley: University of California Press, 2011.

Blosser, Benjamin P. *Become Like the Angels: Origen's Doctrine of the Soul.* Washington, DC: Catholic University of America Press, 2012.

Boersma, Hans. *Embodiment and Virtue in Gregory of Nyssa: An Anagogical Approach.* Oxford Early Christian Studies. New York: Oxford University Press, 2013.

———. "Saving Bodies: Anagogical Transposition in St. Gregory of Nyssa's *Commentary on the Song of Songs.*" *Ex Auditu* 26 (2010): 168–200.

Bonner, Stanley. *Education in Ancient Rome: From the Elder Cato to the Younger Pliny.* Berkeley: University of California Press, 1977.

Borg, Barbara, ed. *Paideia: The World of the Second Sophistic.* Berlin: Walter de Gruyter, 2004.

Borgen, Peder. *Bread from Heaven: An Exegetical Study of the Concept of Manna in the Gospel of John and the Writings of Philo.* Supplements to Novum Testamentum 10. Leiden: Brill, 1981.

Bosanquet, Bernard. *The Education of the Young in the Republic of Plato.* Cambridge: Cambridge University Press, 1917.

Bourdieu, Pierre. *Language and Symbolic Power.* Cambridge, MA: Harvard University Press, 1999.

———. *The Logic of Practice.* Stanford, CA: Stanford University Press, 1980.

Bourdieu, Pierre, and Loïc J. D. Wacquant. *An Invitation to Reflexive Sociology.* Chicago: University of Chicago Press, 1992.

Bowersock, G. W. *Greek Sophists in the Roman Empire.* Oxford: Oxford University Press, 1969.

———. *Julian the Apostate.* Cambridge, MA: Harvard University Press, 1997.

Boyarin, Daniel. *Border Lines: The Partition of Judaeo-Christianity.* Divinations: Rereading Late Ancient Religion. Philadelphia: University of Pennsylvania Press, 2004.

———. *A Radical Jew: Paul and the Politics of Identity.* Contraversions: Critical Studies in Jewish Literature, Culture, and Society 1. Berkeley: University of California Press, 1994.

Boyle, Marjorie O'Rourke. "Augustine in the Garden of Zeus: Lust, Love, and Language." *HTR* 83.2 (1990): 117–39.

Bradley, Keith R. *Discovering the Roman Family: Studies in Roman Social History.* New York: Oxford University Press, 1991.

———. "The Roman Child in Sickness and in Health." In *Roman Family in the Empire: Rome, Italy, and Beyond,* edited by George Michele, 67–92. New York: Oxford University Press, 2005.

———. "Sexual Regulations in Wet-Nursing Contracts from Roman Egypt." *Klio* 62 (1980): 321–25.

———. "Wet-Nursing at Rome: A Study in Social Relations." In *The Family in Ancient Rome: New Perspectives,* edited by Beryl Rawson, 201–29. Ithaca, NY: Cornell University Press, 1986.

Brakke, David. *The Gnostics: Myth, Ritual, and Diversity in Early Christianity.* Cambridge, MA: Harvard University Press, 2010.

Brown, Peter. *Augustine of Hippo: A Biography.* Rev. ed. Berkeley: University of California Press, 2000.

———. *The Body and Society: Men, Women, and Sexual Renunciation in Early Christianity.* New York: Columbia University Press, 1988.

———. *Power and Persuasion in Late Antiquity: Towards a Christian Empire.* Madison: University of Wisconsin Press, 1992.

Buell, Denise Kimber. *Making Christians: Clement of Alexandria and the Rhetoric of Legitimacy.* Princeton, NJ: Princeton University Press, 1999.

Burke, Trevor J. "Paul's Role as 'Father' to His Corinthian 'Children' in Socio-Historical Context (1 Corinthians 4:14–21)." In *Paul and the Corinthians: Studies on a Community in Conflict: Essays in Honour of Margaret Thrall,* edited by Trevor J. Burke and J. Keith Elliott, 95–114. Supplements to Novum Testamentum 109. Leiden: Brill, 2004.

Burrus, Virginia. *"Begotten Not Made": Conceiving Manhood in Late Antiquity.* Figurae: Reading Medieval Culture. Stanford, CA: Stanford University Press, 2000.

———. "Gender, Eros, and Pedagogy: Macrina's Pious Household." In *Ascetic Culture: Essays in Honor of Philip Rousseau,* edited by Blake Leyerle and Robin Darling Young. Notre Dame, IN: University of Notre Dame Press, 2013.

———. "Is Macrina a Woman? Gregory of Nyssa's *Dialogue on the Soul and Resurrection.*" In *The Blackwell Companion to Postmodern Theology,* ed. Graham Ward, 249–64. Malden, MA: Blackwell Publishers, 2004.

Burrus, Virginia, Mark Jordan, and Karmen MacKendrick. *Seducing Augustine: Bodies, Desires, Confessions.* New York: Fordham University Press, 2010.

Butler, Judith. *Bodies That Matter: On the Discursive Limits of Sex.* New York: Routledge, 1993.

———. *Excitable Speech: A Politics of the Performative.* New York: Routledge, 1997.

———. *Senses of the Subject.* Bronx, NY: Fordham University Press, 2015.

Bynum, Caroline Walker. *Jesus as Mother: Studies in the Spirituality of the High Middle Ages.* Berkeley: University of California Press, 1982.

Cahill, J. B. "Date and Setting of Nyssa's Commentary on Song of Songs." *JTS* 32.1 (1981): 447–60.

Cameron, Alan. *The Last Pagans of Rome.* New York: Oxford University Press, 2010.

Cameron, Averil. *Christianity and the Rhetoric of Empire: The Development of a Christian Discourse.* Sather Classical Lectures. Berkeley: University of California Press, 1994.

Capelle, D. B. "Le progrès de la connaissance religieuse d'après s. Augustin." *Recherches de thèologie ancienne et mèdièval* 2 (1930): 410–19.

Carcopino, Jerome. *Daily Life in Ancient Rome.* New Haven, CT: Yale University Press, 1940.

Cary, Philip. *Outward Signs: The Powerlessness of External Things in Augustine's Thought.* New York: Oxford University Press, 2008.

Castelli, Elizabeth. *Imitating Paul: A Discourse of Power.* Louisville, KY: Westminster John Knox Press, 1991.

Chalmers, Matthew J. "Seeking as Suckling: The Milk of the Father in Clement of Alexandria's Paedagogus I, 6." *Studia Patristica* 72 (2014): 59–73.

Cherno, Melvin. "Feuerbach's 'Man Is What He Eats': A Rectification." *Journal of the History of Ideas* 24.3 (1963): 397–406.

Chin, Catherine. *Grammar and Christianity in the Late Roman Empire.* Divinations: Rereading Late Ancient Religion. Philadelphia: University of Pennsylvania Press, 2007.

Clark, Donald Lemen. *Rhetoric in Greco-Roman Education.* New York: Columbia University Press, 1957.

Clark, Elizabeth A. "Antifamilial Tendencies in Ancient Christianity." *Journal of the History of Sexuality* 5.3 (1995): 356–80.

———. "Origen, the Jews, and the Song of Songs." In *Perspectives on the Song of Songs,* edited by Anselm C. Hagerdorn, 274–93. Berlin: Walter de Gruyter, 2011.

———. "Vitiated Seeds and Holy Vessels: Augustine's Manichaean Past." In *Ascetic Piety and Women's Faith: Essays on Late Ancient Christianity,* edited by Elizabeth A. Clark, New York: Edwin Mellen Press, 1986.

Clark, Gillian. *Christianity and Roman Society.* Key Themes in Ancient History. Cambridge: Cambridge University Press, 2004.

Clarke, M. L. *Higher Education in the Ancient World.* London: Routledge Press, 1971.

Clements, Ruth Ann. "τέλειος ἄμωμος: The Influence of Palestinian Jewish Exegesis on the Interpretation of Exodus 12.5 in Origen's *Peri Pascha.*" In *The Function of Scripture in Early Jewish and Christian Tradition,* edited by Craig A. Evans and James A. Sanders. Library of New Testament Studies 154. Sheffield, UK: Sheffield Academic Press, 1998.

Cochrane, Charles Norris. *Christianity and Classical Culture: A Study of Thought and Action from Augustus to Augustine.* Indianapolis, IN: Liberty Press, 2003 (originally 1940).

Conybeare, Catherine. *The Irrational Augustine.* New York: Oxford University Press, 2006.

Conzelmann, Hans. *1 Corinthians: A Commentary on the First Epistle to the Corinthians.* Hermeneia. Philadelphia: Fortress Press, 1975.

Cooper, Kate. *The Fall of the Roman Household.* Cambridge: Cambridge University Press, 2011.

Cribiore, Raffaella. *Gymnastics of the Mind: Greek Education in Roman and Hellenistic Egypt.* Princeton, NJ: Princeton University Press, 2005.

——. *Libanius the Sophist: Rhetoric, Reality, and Religion in the Fourth Century.* Cornell Studies in Classical Philology. Ithaca, NY: Cornell University Press, 2013.

——. *The School of Libanius in Late Antique Antioch.* Princeton, NJ: Princeton University Press, 2007.

Crouzel, Henri. "L'anthropologie d'Origène dans la perspective du combat spirituel." *Revue d'ascétique et de mystique* 124 (1955): 377–84.

——. *Origène.* Paris: Lethielleux, 1985.

——. *Origène et la "Connaissance Mystique."* Paris: Desclée de Brouwer, 1961.

——. *Théologie de l'image de Dieu chez Origène.* Théologie 34. Paris: Aubier, 1956.

D'Ambra, Eve. *Roman Women.* Cambridge: Cambridge University Press, 2007.

D'Angelo, Mary Rose. "Early Christian Sexual Politics and Roman Imperial Family Values: Rereading Christ and Culture." In *The Papers of the Henry Luce III Fellows in Theology,* edited by Christopher I. Wilkins, vol. 6, 23–48. Pittsburgh: Association of Theological Schools, 2003.

——. "*Eusebeia:* Roman Imperial Family Values and the Sexual Politics of 4 Maccabees and the Pastorals." *Biblical Interpretation* 11.2 (2003): 139–65.

——. "Gender and Geopolitics in the Work of Philo of Alexandria: Jewish Piety and Imperial Family Values." In *Mapping Gender in Ancient Religious Dis-*

courses, edited by Todd Penner and Caroline Vander Stichele, 63–88. Leiden: Brill, 2007.

Daniélou, Jean. *Origène.* Paris: La Table Ronde, 1948.

Dasen, Véronique. "Childbirth and Infancy in Greek and Roman Antiquity." In *A Companion to Families in the Greek and Roman Worlds,* edited by Beryl Rawson, 291–314. Malden, MA: Blackwell Publishing, 2011.

———. "Des nourrices grecques à Rome?" *Pedagogica Historica* 46.6 (2010): 699–713.

Dasen, Véronique, and Thomas Späth, eds. *Children, Memory, and Family Identity in Roman Culture.* New York: Oxford University Press, 2010.

de Andia, Ysbel. *Homo Vivens: Incorruptibilité et divinisation de l'homme selon Irénée de Lyon.* Paris: Etudes Augustiniennes, 1986.

Dean-Jones, Lesley Ann. *Women's Bodies in Classical Greek Science.* New York: Oxford University Press, 1994.

de Lubac, Henri. *Histoire et Esprit: L'intelligence de l'Écriture d'après Origène.* Théologie 16. Paris: Aubier, 1950.

Derrida, Jacques. "'Eating Well,' or the Calculation of the Subject." In *Points,* edited by Elisabeth Weber, translated by Peggy Kamuf et al., 255–87. Stanford, CA: Stanford University Press, 1995.

———. "Signature, Event, Context." In *Limited, Inc,* translated by Samuel Weber, 1–24. Evanston, IL: Northwestern University Press, 1988.

———. "White Mythology: Metaphor in the Text of Philosophy." *New Literary History* 6.1 (1974): 5–74.

———. *Writing and Difference.* Translated by Alan Bass. Chicago: University of Chicago Press, 1978.

de Saussure, Ferdinand. *Course in General Linguistics.* Translated by Wade Baskin. New York: Columbia University Press, 2011.

deSilva, David A. *4 Maccabees.* Guides to the Apocrypha and Pseudepigrapha. Sheffield, UK: Sheffield Academic Press, 1998.

de Wet, Chris L. *Preaching Bondage: John Chrysostom and the Discourse of Slavery.* Berkeley: University of California Press, 2015.

Dimoula, Kiki. *The Brazen Plagiarist.* Translated by Cecile Inglessis Margellos and Rika Lesser. New Haven, CT: Yale University Press, 2012.

Dingel, Joachim. *Scholastica materia: Untersuchungen zu den Declamationes minores und der Institutio oratoria Quintilians.* Berlin: Walter de Gruyter, 1988.

Dixon, Suzanne. *The Roman Family.* Baltimore: Johns Hopkins University Press, 1992.

Doran, Robert. *2 Maccabees: A Critical Commentary,* Hermeneia. Minneapolis, MN: Fortress Press, 2012.

Douglas, Mary. *Purity and Danger: An Analysis of the Concepts of Purity and Taboo*. Routledge Classics. New York: Routledge, 2002.

Ducat, Jean. *Spartan Education: Youth and Society in the Classical Period*. Swansea, UK: Classical Press of Wales, 2006.

Dunn, Geoffrey D. "Rhetorical Structure in Tertullian's 'Ad Scapulam.'" *VC* 56.1 (2002): 47–55.

Dunning, Benjamin H. *Aliens and Sojourners: Self as Other in Early Christianity*. Divinations: Rereading Late Ancient Religion. Philadelphia: University of Pennsylvania Press, 2009.

———. *Specters of Paul: Sexual Difference in Early Christian Thought*. Divinations: Rereading Late Ancient Religion. Philadelphia: University of Pennsylvania Press, 2011.

Dunzl, Franz. *Braut und Bräutigam: Die Auslegung des Canticum durch Gregor von Nyssa*. Beiträge zur Geschichte der Biblischen Exegese 32. Tübingen, Germany: Mohr Siebeck, 1993.

Dupuis, S.J., Jacques. *"L'esprit de l'homme": Étude sur l'anthropologie religieuse d'Origène*. Museum Lessianum section théologique 62. Paris: Desclée de Brouwer, 1967.

Dutch, Robert S. *The Educated Elite in 1 Corinthians: Education and Community in Conflict in Graeco-Roman Context*. London: T&T Clark, 2005.

Dutton, Marsha L. "'When I Was a Child': Spiritual Infancy and God's Maternity in Augustine's *Confessiones*." In *Collactanea Augustiniana*, edited by Joseph C. Schnaubelt and Frederick van Fleteren, 113–40. New York: Lang, 1990.

Edwards, Mark J. *Origen Against Plato*. Ashgate Studies in Philosophy and Theology in Late Antiquity. Aldershot, UK: Ashgate, 2002.

———. "Origen, No Gnostic, or, On the Corporeality of Man." *JTS* 43.1 (1992): 23–37.

Elliot, Mark W. *The Song of Songs and Christology in the Early Church*. Studies and Texts in Antiquity and Christianity 7. Tübingen, Germany: Mohr Siebeck, 2000.

Elm, Susanna. *Sons of Hellenism, Fathers of the Church: Emperor Julian, Gregory of Nazianzus, and the Vision of Rome*. Transformation of the Classical Heritage 49. Berkeley: University of California Press, 2012.

Engberg-Pedersen, Troels. *Cosmology and Self in the Apostle Paul: The Material Spirit*. New York: Oxford University Press, 2010.

———. *Paul Beyond the Judaism/Hellenism Divide*. Louisville, KY: Westminster John Knox Press, 2001.

Engelbrecht, Edward. "God's Milk: An Orthodox Confession of the Eucharist." *JECS* 7.4 (1999): 509–26.

Eyben, Emiel. *Restless Youth in Ancient Rome*. New York: Routledge, 1993.

Fantham, Elaine. *Roman Literary Culture: From Plautus to Macrobius*. 2nd ed. Baltimore: Johns Hopkins University Press, 2013.

Ferguson, John. *Clement of Alexandria*. Twayne's World Authors Series 289. New York: Twayne Publishers, 1974.

Feuerbach, Ludwig. "Das Geheimnis des Opfers oder Der Mensch ist, was er isst" [The Mystery of Sacrifice or Man Is What He Eats]. Edited by Wilhelm Bolin and Friedrich Jodl, Sämtliche Werke, vol. 10, 41–67. Stuttgart: Frommann, 1960.

———. "Die Naturwissenschaft und die Revolution" [Natural Science and the Revolution]. Edited by Wilhelm Bolin and Friedrich Jodl. Sämtliche Werke, vol. 10, 3–24. Stuttgart: Frommann, 1960.

Fiedrowicz, Michael. *Psalmus Vox Totius Christi: Studien zu Augustins* Enarrationes in Psalmos. Freiburg, Germany: Herder, 1997.

Fildes, Valerie. *Wet-Nursing: A History from Antiquity to the Present*. London: Blackwell Publishers, 1988.

Flemming, Rebecca. "Demiurge and Emperor in Galen's World of Knowledge." In *Galen and the World of Knowledge*, edited by Christopher Gill et al., 59–84. Cambridge: Cambridge University Press, 2009.

———. *Medicine and the Making of Roman Women: Gender, Nature, and Authority from Celsus to Galen*. New York: Oxford University Press, 2000.

Foucault, Michel. *The History of Sexuality: Volume 1: An Introduction*. New York: Vintage Books, 1990.

———. *Security, Territory, Population: Lectures at the College de France, 1977–1978*. New York: Palgrave Macmillan, 2007.

Francis, James. *Adults as Children: Images of Childhood in the Ancient World and the New Testament*. Religions and Discourse 17. Bern, Switzerland: Peter Lang, 2006.

———. "As Babes in Christ—Some Proposals Regarding 1 Corinthians 3:1–3." *Journal for the Study of the New Testament* 7 (1980): 41–60.

Frede, Michael. "Origen's Treatise *Against Celsus*." In *Apologetics in the Roman Empire: Pagans, Jews, and Christians*, edited by Mark J. Edwards et al., 131–55. New York: Oxford University Press, 1999.

Galinsky, Karl. *Augustan Culture*. Princeton, NJ: Princeton University Press, 1995.

Gardner, Jane F. *Family and* Familia *in Roman Law and Life*. New York: Oxford University Press, 1998.

Garnsey, Peter. *Cities, Peasants, and Food in Classical Antiquity*. Cambridge: Cambridge University Press, 1998.

———. "Child Rearing in Ancient Italy." In *The Family in Italy: From Antiquity to the Present*, edited by David Kertzer and Richard Saller, 48–65. New Haven, CT: Yale University Press, 1991.

———. *Food and Society in Classical Antiquity.* Key Themes in Ancient History. Cambridge: Cambridge University Press, 1999.

Gaventa, Beverly Roberts. *Our Mother Saint Paul.* Louisville, KY: Westminster John Knox Press, 2007.

Geljon, Albert C. *Philonic Exegesis in Gregory of Nyssa's* De Vita Moysis. Brown Judaic Studies 333, Studia Philonica Monographs 5. Providence, RI: Brown University, 2002.

Giladi, Avner. *Infants, Parents, and Wet Nurses: Medieval Islamic Views on Breast-feeding and Their Social Implications.* Islamic History and Civilization: Studies and Texts 25. Leiden: Brill, 1999.

Giulea, Dragos Andrei. *Pre-Nicene Christology in Paschal Contexts: The Case of the Divine Noetic Anthropos.* VCSup 123. Leiden: Brill, 2014.

Glancy, Jennifer A. *Corporal Knowledge: Early Christian Bodies.* Oxford: Oxford University Press, 2010.

Gleason, Maud W. *Making Men: Sophists and Self-Presentation in Ancient Rome.* Princeton, NJ: Princeton University Press, 1995.

Goodenough, Erwin. *Jewish Symbols in the Greco-Roman Period.* Vol. 6: *Fish, Bread, and Wine II.* New York: Pantheon Books, 1958.

Grant, Robert M. *Irenaeus of Lyons.* The Early Church Fathers. New York: Routledge, 1997.

Grubbs, Judith Evans, and Tim Parkin. *The Oxford Handbook of Childhood and Education in the Classical World.* New York: Oxford University Press, 2013.

Grundmann, Walter. "Die *NEPIOI* in der urchristlichen Paränese." *New Testament Studies* 5 (1958–1959): 188–205.

Gunderson, Erik. *Nox Philologiae: Aulus Gellius and the Fantasy of the Roman Library.* Wisconsin Studies in Classics. Madison: University of Wisconsin Press, 2009.

Gwynn, Aubrey. *Roman Education from Cicero to Quintilian.* New York: Teachers College Press, 1966.

Haber, Susan. "Living and Dying for the Law: The Mother-Martyrs of 2 Maccabees." In Susan Haber, *They Shall Purify Themselves: Essays on Purity in Early Judaism,* edited by Adele Reinhartz. Early Judaism and Its Literature 24, 75–92. Atlanta: Society of Biblical Literature, 2008.

Hällström, Gunnar af. *Fides Simpliciorum According to Origen of Alexandria.* Commentationes Humanarum Litterarum 76. Helsinki: Societas Scientiarum Fennica/Finnish Society of Sciences and Letters, 1984.

Hankinson, R. J. "Philosophy of Nature." In *The Cambridge Companion to Galen*, edited by R. J. Hankinson, 210–41. Cambridge: Cambridge University Press, 2009.

Hanson, Ann Ellis. "The Medical Writer's Woman." In *Before Sexuality: The Construction of Erotic Experience in the Ancient World*, edited by David M. Halperin et al., 309–38. Princeton, NJ: Princeton University Press, 1990.

Hanson, R. P. C. *Allegory and Event: A Study of the Sources and Significance of Origen's Interpretation of Scripture*. Richmond, VA: Westminster John Knox Press, 1959.

———. *Origen's Doctrine of Tradition*. London: SPCK, 1954.

Haraway, Donna J. "Parting Bites: Nourishing Indigestion." In *When Species Meet*, edited by Donna J. Haraway, 285–302. Minneapolis: University of Minnesota Press, 2008.

Harrison, Carol. *Augustine: Christian Truth and Fractured Humanity*. Cambridge: Cambridge University Press, 2000.

———. *Rethinking Augustine's Early Theology: An Argument for Continuity*. New York: Oxford University Press, 2006.

Harrison, Verna E. F. "The Care-Banishing Breast of the Father: Feminine Images of the Divine in Clement of Alexandria's Paedagogus 1." *Studia Patristica* 31 (1997): 401–5.

———. "A Gender Reversal in Gregory of Nyssa's *First Homily on the Song of Songs*." *Studia Patristica* 27 (1991): 34–38.

———. *Grace and Human Freedom According to St. Gregory of Nyssa*. Studies in the Bible and Early Christianity 30. Lewiston, NY: Edwin Mellen Press, 1992.

Hasan-Rokem, Galit. *Web of Life: Folklore and Midrash in Rabbinic Literature*. Contraversions: Jews and Other Differences. Stanford, CA: Stanford University Press, 2000.

Hays, Richard B. *First Corinthians*. Interpretation. Louisville: Westminster John Knox Press, 1997.

Heine, Ronald E. "Gregory of Nyssa's Apology for Allegory." *VC* 38 (1984): 360–70.

———. *Gregory of Nyssa's Treatise on the Inscriptions of the Psalms: Introduction, Translation, and Notes*. Oxford Early Christian Studies. New York: Oxford University Press, 1995.

———. *Perfection in the Virtuous Life: A Study in the Relationship Between Edification and Polemical Theology in Gregory of Nyssa's De Vita Moysis*. Cambridge, MA: Philadelphia Patristic Foundation, 1975.

Hick, John. *Evil and the God of Love*. New York: Palgrave Macmillan, 2007 (originally 1966).

Himmelfarb, Martha. "The Mother of the Seven Sons in Lamentations Rabbah and the Virgin Mary." *Jewish Studies Quarterly* 22 (2015): 325–51.

Hinde, Katie. "Motherhood." In *Emerging Trends in the Social and Behavioral Sciences: An Interdisciplinary, Searchable, and Linkable Resource,* edited by Robert Scott and Stephan Kosslyn, 1–16. John Wiley & Sons, 2015.

Hirshman, Marc. *The Stabilization of Rabbinic Culture, 100 CE–300 CE: Texts on Education in Their Late Antique Context.* New York: Oxford University Press, 2009.

Hodgson, Geraldine. *Primitive Christian Education.* Edinburgh: T&T Clark, 1906.

Holford-Strevens, Leofranc. *Aulus Gellius: An Antonine Scholar and His Achievement.* Rev. ed. New York: Oxford University Press, 2003.

Hollywood, Amy. "Performativity, Citationality, Ritualization." *History of Religions* 42.2 (2002): 93–115.

Holman, Susan R. "Molded as Wax: Formation and Feeding of the Ancient Newborn." *Helios* 24 (1997): 77–95.

Horsley, Richard A. "Pneumatikos vs. Psychikos: Distinctions of Spiritual Status among the Corinthians." *HTR* 69.3–4 (1976): 269–88.

Husserl, Edmund. "Vom Ursprung der Geometrie" [The Origin of Geometry]. In *Husserliana*, VI, Beilage III, 365–86. The Hague: Martinus Nijhoff, 1954.

Itter, Andrew. *Esoteric Teaching in the Stromateis of Clement of Alexandria. VCSup* 97. Leiden: Brill, 2010.

Jacob, Sharon. *Reading Mary Alongside Indian Surrogate Mothers: Violent Love, Oppressive Liberation, and Infancy Narratives.* The Bible and Cultural Studies. New York: Palgrave Macmillan, 2015.

Jacobs, Andrew. "Solomon's Salacious Song: Foucault's Author Function and the Early Christian Interpretation of the *Canticum Canticorum.*" *Medieval Encounters* 4 (1998): 1–23.

Jacobs, Andrew, and Rebecca Krawiec. "Fathers Know Best? Christian Families in the Age of Asceticism." *JECS* 11.3 (2003): 257–73.

Jacobsen, Anders Lund. "The Constitution of Man According to Irenaeus and Origen." In *Körper und Seele; Aspekte spätantiker Anthropologie,* edited by Barbara Feichtinger et al. Leipzig, Germany: K. G. Saur, 2006.

———. "Genesis 1–3 as Source for the Anthropology of Origen." *VC* 62 (2008): 213–32.

———. "Origen on the Human Body." In *Origeniana Octava,* edited by L. Perrone, 649–56. Leuven, Belgium: Peeters, 2004.

Jaeger, Werner. *Early Christianity and Greek Paideia.* Cambridge, MA: Belknap Press of Harvard University Press, 1961.

———. *Paideia: The Ideals of Greek Culture.* 3 vols. Oxford: Oxford University Press, 1986.

Jaffee, Martin S. "Oral Transmission of Knowledge as Rabbinic Sacrament: An Overlooked Aspect of Discipleship in Oral Torah." In *Study and Knowledge in Jewish Thought,* edited by Howard Kriesel, 65–79. Beer Sheva, Israel: Ben Gurion University of the Negev Press, 2006.

———. *Torah in the Mouth: Writing and Oral Tradition in Palestinian Judaism, 200 BCE–400 CE.* New York: Oxford University Press, 2001.

Johann, Horst-Theodor. *Erziehung und Bildung in der heidnischen und christlichen Antike.* Darmstadt, Germany: Wissenschaftliche Buchgesellschaft, 1976.

Johansen, Thomas Kjeller. *The Powers of Aristotle's Soul.* Oxford Aristotle Studies. New York: Oxford University Press, 2012.

Johnson, W. A. *Readers and Reading Culture in the High Roman Empire: A Study of Elite Communities.* New York: Oxford University Press, 2010.

Joshel, Sandra R. "Nurturing the Master's Child: Slavery and the Roman Child-Nurse." *Signs* 12.1 (1986): 3–22.

———. *Slavery in the Roman World.* Cambridge Introduction to Roman Civilization. Cambridge: Cambridge University Press, 2010.

Joshel, Sandra, and Sheila Murnaghan. *Women and Slaves in Greco-Roman Culture: Differential Equations.* London: Routledge, 2001.

Jouanna, Jacques. "Does Galen Have a Programme for Intellectuals and the Faculties of the Intellect?" In *Galen and the World of Knowledge,* edited by Christopher Gill et al., 190–205. Cambridge: Cambridge University Press, 2009.

———. *Greek Medicine from Hippocrates to Galen: Selected Papers.* Edited by Philip Van Der Eijk. Translated by Neil Allies. Leiden: Brill, 2012.

Judge, E. A. "The Interaction of Biblical and Classical Education in the Fourth Century." *Journal of Christian Education* (1983): 31–37.

———. "Reaction Against Classical Education in the New Testament." *Evangelical Review of Theology* (1985), 166–74.

———. "St Paul and Socrates." In *The First Christians in the Roman World: Augustan and New Testament Essays.* Wissenschaftliche Untersuchungen zum Neuen Testament 229. Tübingen, Germany: Mohr Siebeck, 2008 (originally 1973).

Kaster, Robert A. *Guardians of Language: The Grammarian and Society in Late Antiquity.* Transformation of the Classical Heritage 11. Berkeley, CA: University of California Press, 1988.

Keller, Catherine. "Seeking and Sucking: On Relation and Essence in Feminist Theology." In *Horizons in Feminist Theology: Identity, Tradition, and*

Norms, edited by Rebecca S. Chopp and Sheila Greeve Devaney, 54–78. Minneapolis, MN: Fortress Press, 1997.

Kennedy, George A. *Classical Rhetoric and Its Christian and Secular Tradition from Ancient to Modern Times.* Chapel Hill: University of North Carolina Press, 1999.

———. *A New History of Classical Rhetoric.* Princeton, NJ: Princeton University Press, 1994.

Kertzer, David, and Richard Saller. *The Family in Italy: From Antiquity to the Present.* New Haven, CT: Yale University Press, 1993.

Kessler, Gwynn. *Conceiving Israel: The Fetus in Rabbinic Narratives.* Divinations: Rereading Late Ancient Religion. Philadelphia: University of Pennsylvania Press, 2009.

Kilmartin, Edward J. "The Baptismal Cups: Revisited." In *Eulogema: Studies in Honor of Robert Taft, S.J.,* edited by E. Carr et al., 249–67. Rome: S. Anselmo, 1993.

King, Helen. *Hippocrates' Woman: Reading the Female Body in Ancient Greece.* New York: Routledge, 1998.

King, Karen L. *What Is Gnosticism?* Cambridge, MA: Harvard University Press, 2003.

Kleeman, Alexandra. "Hylomorphosis." *Conjunctions* 59 (2012): 292–97.

Klinghardt, Matthias. *Gemeinschaftsmahl und Mahlgemeinschaft: Soziologie und Liturgie frühchristlicher Mahlfeiern.* Texte und Arbeiten zum neutestamentlichen Zeitalter 13. Tübingen, Germany, and Basel, Switzerland: Francke, 1996.

Koch, Hal. *Pronoia und Paideusis: Studien Über Origenes und Sein Verhältnis zum Platonismus.* Arbeiten Zur Kirchengeschichte 22. Berlin: Walter de Gruyter, 1932.

Kolbet, Paul. *Augustine and the Cure of Souls: Revising a Classical Ideal.* Christianity and Judaism in Antiquity 17. South Bend, IN: University of Notre Dame Press, 2010.

König, Jason. *Saints and Symposiasts: The Literature of Food and the Symposium in Greco-Roman and Early Christian Culture.* Greek Culture in the Roman World. Cambridge: Cambridge University Press, 2012.

Kotrosits, Maia. *Rethinking Early Christian Identity: Affect, Violence, and Belonging.* Minneapolis, MN: Fortress Press, 2015.

Kovacs, Judith. "Divine Pedagogy and the Gnostic Teaching according to Clement of Alexandria." *JECS* 9.1 (2001): 3–25.

———. "Echoes of Valentinian Exegesis in Clement of Alexandria and Origen: The Interpretation of 1 Cor 3.1–3." In *Origeniana Octava,* edited by L. Perrone, 317–29. Leuven, Belgium: Peeters, 2004.

———. "Grace and Works: Clement of Alexandria's Response to Valentinian Exegesis of Paul." In *Ancient Perspectives on Paul,* edited by Andreas Merkt, et al. Novum Testamentum et Orbis Antiquus/Studien Zur Umwelt Des Neuen Testaments 102. Göttingen: Vandenhoeck & Ruprecht: 2013.

———. "Servant of Christ and Steward of the Mysteries of God: The Purpose of a Pauline Letter According to Origen's Homilies on 1 Corinthians." In *In Dominico Eloquio (In Lordly Eloquence): Essays on Patristic Exegesis in Honor of Robert Louis Wilken,* edited by Paul Blowers et al. Grand Rapids, MI: Eerdmans Publishing, 2002.

Krawiec, Rebecca. "From the Womb of the Church: Monastic Families." *JECS* 11.3 (2003): 283–307.

Kristeva, Julia. *Powers of Horror: An Essay on Abjection.* Translated by Leon S. Roudiez. New York: Columbia University Press, 1982.

Krueger, Derek. *Writing and Holiness: The Practice of Authorship in the Early Christian East.* Divinations: Rereading Late Ancient Religions. Philadelphia: University of Pennsylvania Press, 2004.

Laird, Martin. "The Fountain of His Lips: Desire and Divine Union in Gregory of Nyssa's *Homilies on the Song of Songs.*" *Spiritus* 7 (2007): 40–57.

———. *Gregory of Nyssa and the Grasp of Faith: Union, Knowledge, and Divine Presence.* Oxford Early Christian Studies. New York: Oxford University Press, 2004.

———. "Under Solomon's Tutelage: The Education of Desire in the *Homilies on the Song of Songs.*" *Modern Theology* 18.4 (2002): 507–25.

Lakoff, George, and Mark Johnson. *Metaphors We Live By.* Chicago: University of Chicago Press, 1980.

Lassen, Eva Maria. "The Use of the Father Image in Imperial Propaganda and 1 Corinthians 4:14–21." *Tyndale Bulletin* 42.1 (1991): 127–36.

Lauro, Elizabeth Ann Dively. *The Soul and Spirit of Scripture within Origen's Exegesis.* The Bible in Ancient Christianity 3. Leiden: Brill Publishers, 2005.

LaValle, Dawn. "Divine Breastfeeding: Milk, Blood, and *Pneuma* in Clement of Alexandria's *Paedagogus.*" *Journal of Late Antiquity* 8.2 (2015): 322–36.

Lawson III, Richard T. "Gregory of Nyssa's *Homilies on the Song of Songs:* Is the Erotic Left Behind?" *Sewanee Theological Review* 54.1 (2010): 29–40.

Le Boulluec, Alain. "The Bible in Use among the Marginally Orthodox in the Second and Third Centuries." In *The Bible in Greek Christian Antiquity,* edited by Paul Blowers. South Bend, IN: University of Notre Dame Press, 1997.

———. "Pour qui, pourquoi, comment? Les 'Stromateis' de Clément d'Alexandrie." In *Entrer en matière: Les prologues,* 23–36, edited by J. D. Dubois and B. Roussel. Paris: Cerf, 1998.

Lee, Michelle V. *Paul, the Stoics, and the Body of Christ.* Society for New Testament Studies Monograph Series 137. Cambridge: Cambridge University Press, 2006.

Leitao, David. *The Pregnant Male as Myth and Metaphor in Classical Greek Literature.* Cambridge: Cambridge University Press, 2012.

Liftin, Duane. *St. Paul's Theology of Proclamation: 1 Corinthians 1–4 and Greco-Roman Rhetoric.* Society for New Testament Studies Monograph Series 79. Cambridge: Cambridge University Press, 1994.

Lively, Genevieve. "*Mater Amoris:* Mothers and Lovers in Augustan Rome." In *Mothering and Motherhood in Ancient Greece and Rome,* edited by Lauren Hackworth Petersen and Patricia Salzman-Mitchell, 185–202. Austin: University of Texas Press, 2012.

Lofton, Kathryn. "Religion and the Authority in American Parenting." *Journal of the American Academy of Religion* 84.1 (2016): 1–36.

Lord, Carnes. *Education and Culture in the Political Thought of Aristotle.* Ithaca, NY: Cornell University Press, 1982.

Lorenz, Hendrik. *The Brute Within: Appetitive Desire in Plato and Aristotle.* Oxford Philosophical Monographs. New York: Oxford University Press, 2006.

Louth, Andrew. "Eros and Mysticism: Early Christian Interpretation of the Song of Songs." In *Jung and the Monotheisms: Judaism, Christianity, and Islam,* edited by Joel Ryce-Menuhin, 241–54. London: Routledge, 1994.

Lynch, J. P. *Aristotle's School: A Study of a Greek Educational Institution.* Berkeley: University of California Press, 1972.

Markschies, Christoph. *Gnosis: An Introduction.* London: T&T Clark, 2003.

———. *Origenes und sein Erbe: Gesammelte Studien.* Text und Untersuchungen zur Geschichte der altchristlichen Literatur 160. Berlin: Walter de Gruyter, 2007.

Markus, Robert. *The End of Ancient Christianity.* Cambridge: Cambridge University Press, 1990.

Marrou, H. I. *Histoire de l'éducation dans l'Antiquité.* Paris: Le Seuil, 1948.

———. *A History of Education in Antiquity.* Translated by George Lamb. Madison: University of Wisconsin Press, 1956.

Martens, Peter. *Origen and Scripture: The Contours of the Exegetical Life.* New York: Oxford University Press, 2012.

Martin, Dale B. *The Corinthian Body.* New Haven, CT: Yale University Press, 1995.

Martin, Meredith. *Dairy Queens: The Politics of Pastoral Architecture from Catherine de Medici to Marie-Antoinette.* Harvard Historical Studies 176. Cambridge, MA: Harvard University Press, 2011.

Mateo-Seco, Lucas Francisco, and Giulio Maspero, eds. *The Brill Dictionary of Gregory of Nyssa. VCSup* 99. Leiden: Brill, 2010.

Mattern, Susan. *Galen and the Rhetoric of Healing.* Baltimore: Johns Hopkins University Press, 2008.

———. *The Prince of Medicine: Galen in the Roman Empire.* New York: Oxford University Press, 2013.

Mattila, Sharon Lea. "Wisdom, Sense Perception, Nature, and Philo's Gender Gradient." *HTR* 89.2 (1996): 103–29.

McDuffie, Felecia. "Augustine's Rhetoric of the Feminine in the *Confessions:* Woman as Mother, Woman as Other." *Feminist Interpretations of Augustine,* edited by Judith Chelius Stark, 97–118. University Park: Pennsylvania State University Press, 2007.

McGowan, Andrew. *Ancient Christian Worship: Early Church Practices in Social, Historical, and Theological Perspective.* Grand Rapids, MI: Baker Academic, 2014.

———. *Ascetic Eucharists: Food and Drink in Early Christian Ritual Meals.* Oxford Early Christian Studies. New York: Oxford University Press, 1999.

McLynn, Neil. "Disciplines of Discipleship in Late Antique Education: Augustine and Gregory Nazianzen." In *Augustine and the Disciplines: From Cassiciacum to Confessions,* edited by Karla Pollmann and Mark Vessey. New York: Oxford, 2005.

McNeel, Jennifer Houston. *Paul as Infant and Nursing Mother: Metaphor, Rhetoric, and Identity in 1 Thessalonians 2:5–8.* Early Christianity and Its Literature 12. Atlanta: Society of Biblical Literature Press, 2014.

McWilliam, Janet. "The Socialization of Roman Children." In *The Oxford Handbook of Childhood and Education in the Classical World,* edited by Judith Evans Grubbs and Tim Parkin, 264–85. New York: Oxford University Press, 2013.

Meilaender, Gilbert. "Sweet Necessities: Food, Sex, and Saint Augustine." *Journal of Religious Ethics* 29.1 (2001): 3–18.

Mendelson, Alan. *Secular Education in Philo of Alexandria.* Cincinnati, OH: Hebrew Union College Press, 1982.

Miles, Margaret. "Infancy, Parenting, and Nourishment in Augustine's *Confessions." Journal of the American Academy of Religion* 50.3 (1982): 349–64.

Miller, Patricia Cox. *Biography in Late Antiquity: A Quest for the Holy Man.* Transformation of the Classical Heritage 5. Berkeley: University of California Press, 1983.

———. *The Corporeal Imagination: Signifying the Holy in Late Ancient Christianity.* Divinations: Rereading Late Ancient Religion. Philadelphia: University of Pennsylvania Press, 2009.

Milnor, Kristina. *Gender, Domesticity, and the Age of Augustus.* New York: Oxford University Press, 2005.

Milton, John. *Paradise Lost.* Edited by Stephen Orgel and Jonathan Goldberg. Oxford World Classics. New York: Oxford University Press, 2004.

Mitchell, Margaret M. *Paul and the Rhetoric of Reconciliation: An Exegetical Investigation of the Language and Composition of 1 Corinthians.* Louisville, KY: Westminster John Knox Press, 1993.

———. *Paul, the Corinthians, and the Birth of Christian Hermeneutics.* Cambridge: Cambridge University Press, 2010.

Moncion, Laura. "Erotic Food Metaphors in Augustine's Confessions." *Heythrop Journal* 57.4 (2016): 653–58.

Moore, Stephen D. "The Song of Songs in the History of Sexuality." *Church History* 69.2 (2000): 328–49.

Moore, Stephen D., and Janice Capel Anderson. "Taking It Like a Man: Masculinity in 4 Maccabees." *JBL* 117.2 (1998): 249–73.

Morgan, Teresa. "Ethos: The Socialization of Children in Education and Beyond." In *A Companion to Families in the Greek and Roman Worlds,* edited by Beryl Rawson, 504–20. Malden, MA: Blackwell Publishing, 2011.

———. *Literate Education in the Hellenistic and Roman Worlds.* Cambridge: Cambridge University Press, 1997.

Muehlberger, Ellen. *Angels in Late Ancient Christianity.* New York: Oxford University Press, 2013.

———. "Salvage: Macrina and the Christian Project of Cultural Reclamation." *Church History* 81:2 (2012): 273–97.

Myers, Alicia D. "In the Father's Bosom: Breastfeeding and Identity Formation in John's Gospel." *Catholic Biblical Quarterly* 76.3 (2014): 481–97.

Nasrallah, Laura. *Christian Responses to Art and Architecture: The Second-Century Church amid the Spaces of Empire.* Cambridge: Cambridge University Press, 2010.

Nathan, Geoffrey S. *The Family in Late Antiquity: The Rise of Christianity and the Endurance of Tradition.* London: Routledge, 2000.

Newman, John Henry. *Historical Sketches.* Vol. 2. New York: Longman's, Green, 1906.

Niehoff, Maren. *Philo on Jewish Identity and Culture.* Texts and Studies in Ancient Judaism 86. Tübingen, Germany: Mohr Siebeck, 2001.

Nietzsche, Friedrich. *Die fröhliche Wissenschaft [The Gay Science].* In Nietzsche Werke: Kritische Gesamtausgabe 5.2, edited by Giorgio Colli and Mazzino Montinari. Berlin: Walter de Gruyter, 1973.

Noel, Virginia L. "Nourishment in Origen's *On Prayer.*" In *Origeniana Quinta,* edited by Robert J. Daly, 482–85. Leuven, Belgium: Peeters, 1992.

Noormann, Rolf. *Irenäus als Paulusinterpret: Zur Rezeption und Wirkung der paulinischen und deuteropaulinischen Briefe im Werk des Irenäus von Lyon.* Wissenschftliche Untersuchungen zum Neuen Testament 2.66. Tübingen, Germany: Mohr Siebeck, 1994.

Norris, Richard A. "Irenaeus' Use of Paul in His Polemic Against the Gnostics." In *Paul and the Legacies of Paul,* edited by William Babcock. Dallas, TX: Southern Methodist University Press, 1990.

———. "The Soul Takes Flight: Gregory of Nyssa and the Song of Songs," *Anglican Theological Review* 80.4 (1998): 517–32.

O'Cleirigh, Padraig. "The Dualism of Origen." In *Origeniana Quinta,* edited by Robert J. Daly, 346–50. Leuven, Belgium: Peeters, 1992.

O'Connell, S.J., Robert J. "Isaiah's Mothering God in St. Augustine's *Confessions.*" *Thought* 58 (1983): 199–206.

Osborn, Eric. *Clement of Alexandria.* Cambridge: Cambridge University Press, 2005.

———. *Irenaeus of Lyons.* Cambridge: Cambridge University Press, 2001.

———. "Philo and Clement: Quiet Conversion and Noetic Exegesis." *Studia Philonica* 10 (1998): 108–24.

Oxenhandler, Noelle. *The Eros of Parenthood: Explorations in Light and Dark.* New York: St. Martin's Press, 2001.

Paffenroth, Kim, and Kevin L. Hughes, eds. *Augustine and Liberal Education.* Burlington, VT: Ashgate Publishing, 2000.

Pagels, Elaine. *The Gnostic Paul: Gnostic Exegesis of the Pauline Letters.* London: Continuum, 1992.

Painchaud, Louis. "The Use of Scripture in Gnostic Literature." *JECS* 4.2 (1996): 129–46.

Parkin, Tim. "The Demography of Infancy and Early Childhood in the Ancient World." In *The Oxford Handbook of Childhood and Education in the Classical World,* edited by Judith Evans Grubbs and Tim Parkin, 40–61. New York: Oxford University Press, 2013.

Pelikan, Jaroslav. *Christianity and Classical Culture: The Metamorphosis of Natural Theology in the Christian Encounter with Hellenism.* New Haven, CT: Yale University Press, 1995.

Penniman, John David. "Fed to Perfection: Mother's Milk, Roman Family Values, and the Transformation of the Soul in Gregory of Nyssa." *Church History* 84.3 (2015): 495–530.

Perkins, Pheme. *First Corinthians.* Paideia: Commentaries on the New Testament. Grand Rapids, MI: Baker Academic, 2012.

Petrey, Taylor G. "Semen Stains: Seminal Procreation and the Patrilineal Genealogy of Salvation in Tertullian." *JECS* 22.3 (2014): 343–72.

Phillips, Adam. *The Beast in the Nursery*. New York: Pantheon Books, 1998.

Pomeroy, Sarah. *Families in Classical and Hellenistic Greece*. New York: Oxford University Press, 1997.

Procter, Everett. *Christian Controversy in Alexandria: Clement's Polemics against the Basilideans and Valentinians*. American University Studies Series 7: Theology and Religion 172. New York: Peter Lang, 1995.

Rajak, Tessa. "Dying for the Law: The Martyr's Portrait in Jewish-Greek Literature." In *Portraits: Biographical Representation in Greek and Latin Literature of the Roman Empire*, edited by M. J. Edwards and Simon Swain, 39–68. New York: Oxford University Press, 1997.

Rankin, David I. "Class Distinction as a Way of Doing Church: The Early Fathers and the Christian Plebs." *VC* 58 (2004): 298–315.

Rawson, Beryl. *A Companion to Families in the Greek and Roman Worlds*. Malden, MA: Blackwell Publishing, 2011.

———. *The Family in Ancient Rome: New Perspectives*. Ithaca, NY: Cornell University Press, 1986.

———. "Iconography of Roman Childhood." In *The Roman Family in Italy: Status, Sentiment, Space*, edited by Beryl Rawson et al., 205–32. New York: Oxford University Press, 1997.

Rawson, Beryl, and Paul Weaver. *The Roman Family in Italy: Status, Sentiment, Space*. New York: Oxford University Press, 1997.

Reinhartz, Adele. "Parents and Children: A Philonic Perspective." In *The Jewish Family in Antiquity*, Brown Judaic Studies 289, edited by Shaye J. D. Cohen, 61–88. Atlanta: Scholars Press, 1993.

Rich, Adrienne. *Of Woman Born: Motherhood as Experience and Institution*. New York: W. W. Norton, 1986.

Robb, Kevin. *Literacy and Paideia in Ancient Greece*. Oxford: Oxford University Press, 1994.

Robertson, David. *Word and Meaning in Ancient Alexandria: Theories of Language from Philo to Plotinus*. Aldershot, UK: Ashgate, 2008.

Rosenblum, Jordan D. *Food and Identity in Early Rabbinic Judaism*. Cambridge: Cambridge University Press, 2010.

Rousseau, Philip. "The Pious Household and the Virgin Chorus: Reflections on Gregory of Nyssa's *Life of Macrina*." *JECS* 13:2 (2005): 165–86.

Rutledge, Steven H. "Tacitus' *Dialogus de Oratoribus*: A Socio-Cultural History." In *A Companion to Tacitus*, edited by Victoria Emma Pagan, 62–83. Malden, MA: Blackwell Publishing, 2012.

Saller, Richard. "Familia, Domus, and the Roman Conception of the Family." *Phoenix* 38.4 (1984): 336–55.

———. "Family Values in Ancient Rome." Fathom Archive. University of Chicago Library Digital Archive, 2001. http://fathom.lib.uchicago.edu/1/777777121908/. Accessed February 2015.

———. *Patriarchy, Property and Death in the Roman Family*. Cambridge: Cambridge University Press, 1994.

———. "The Roman Family as Productive Unit." In *A Companion to Families in the Greek and Roman Worlds*, edited by Beryl Rawson, 116–28. Malden, MA: Blackwell Publishing, 2011.

Salzman-Mitchell, Patricia. "Tenderness or Taboo: Images of Breast-Feeding Mothers in Greek and Latin Literature." In *Mothering and Motherhood in Ancient Greece and Rome*, edited by Lauren Hackworth Petersen and Patricia Salzman-Mitchell, 141–64. Austin: University of Texas Press, 2012.

Schmemann, Alexander. *For the Life of the World: Sacraments and Orthodoxy*. Crestwood, NY: St Vladimir's Seminary Press, 1973.

Schmithals, Walter. *Gnosticism in Corinth*. Nashville, TN: Abingdon Press, 1971.

Scholten, C. "Die alexandrinische Katencheteschule." *Jahrbuch für Antike Christentum* 38 (1995): 16–37.

Secord, Jared. "Medicine and Sophistry in Hippolytus' *Refutatio*." *Studia Patristica* 65 (2013): 217–24.

Sessa, Kristina. *The Formation of Papal Authority in Late Antique Italy: Roman Bishops and the Domestic Sphere*. Cambridge: Cambridge University Press, 2011.

Severy, Beth. *Augustus and the Family at the Birth of the Roman Empire*. New York: Routledge, 2003.

Shaw, Brent D. "The Family in Late Antiquity: The Experience of Augustine." *Past and Present* 115 (1987): 3–51.

Smith, Dennis E. *From Symposium to Eucharist: The Banquet in the Early Christian World*. Minneapolis, MN: Fortress Press, 2003.

Smith, Dennis E., and Hal Taussig, eds. *Meals in the Early Christian World: Social Formation, Experimentation, and Conflict at the Table*. New York: Palgrave Macmillan, 2012.

Smith, J. Warren. "A Just and Reasonable Grief: The Death and Function of a Holy Woman in Gregory of Nyssa's *Life of Macrina*." *JECS* 12:1 (2004): 37–60.

Steenberg, M. C. "Children in Paradise: Adam and Eve as 'Infants' in Irenaeus of Lyons." *JECS* 12.1 (2004): 1–22.

Stefaniw, Blossom. *Mind, Text, and Commentary: Noetic Exegesis in Origen of Alexandria, Didymus the Blind, and Evagrius Ponticus*. Early Christianity in the Context of Antiquity 6. Berlin: Peter Lang, 2010.

Stern, Sacha. *Jewish Identity in Early Rabbinic Writings*. Arbeiten zur Geschichte des Antiken Judentums und des Urchristentums 23. Leiden: Brill, 1994.

Stock, Brian. *Augustine's Inner Dialogue: The Philosophical Soliloquy in Late Antiquity.* Cambridge: Cambridge University Press, 2010.

———. *Augustine the Reader: Meditation, Self-Knowledge, and the Ethics of Interpretation.* Cambridge, MA: Harvard University Press, 1996.

Stroumsa, Guy. *Hidden Wisdom: Esoteric Traditions and the Roots of Christian Mysticism.* Leiden: Brill, 1996.

Swain, Simon. *Hellenism and Empire: Language, Classicism, and Power in the Greek World.* Oxford: Oxford University Press, 1996.

Syme, Ronald. *The Roman Revolution.* Rev. ed. New York: Oxford University Press, 2002.

Taussig, Hal. *In the Beginning Was the Meal: Social Experimentation and Early Christian Identity.* Minneapolis, MN: Fortress Press, 2009.

Teloh, Henry. *Socratic Education in Plato's Early Dialogues.* South Bend, IN: University of Notre Dame, 1986.

Termini, Cristina. "Philo's Thought within the Context of Middle Judaism." In *The Cambridge Companion to Philo,* edited by Adam Kamesar, 95–123. Cambridge: Cambridge University Press, 2009.

Teske, Roland. "'Homo Spiritualis' in the *Confessions* of Augustine." In *Augustine: From Rhetor to Theologian,* edited by Joanne McWilliam. Ontario: Wilfred Laurier University Press, 1992.

Thomas, Stephen. "Anthropology." In *The Westminster Handbook to Origen,* edited by John Anthony McGuckin. Louisville, KY: Westminster John Knox Press, 2004.

Tieleman, Teun. "Galen and the Stoics, or: the Art of Not Naming." In *Galen and the World of Knowledge,* edited by Christopher Gill et al., 282–99. Cambridge: Cambridge University Press, 2009.

Tite, Philip L. "Nurslings, Milk and Moral Development in the Greco-Roman Context: A Reappraisal of the Paraenetic Utilization of Metaphor in 1 Peter 2.1–3." *Journal for the Study of the New Testament* 31 (2009): 371–400.

Too, Yun Lee, ed. *Education in Greek and Roman Antiquity.* Leiden: Brill, 2001.

Topping, Ryan N. S. *Happiness and Wisdom: Augustine's Early Theology of Education.* Washington, DC: Catholic University of America Press, 2012.

Torjesen, Karen Jo. *Hermeneutical Procedure and Theological Method in Origen's Exegesis.* Patristische Texte und Studien 28. Berlin: Walter de Gruyter, 1986.

Traina, Cristina L. H. *Erotic Attunement: Parenthood and the Ethics of Sexuality among Unequals.* Chicago: University of Chicago, 2011.

Trigg, J. W. "God's Marvelous *Oikonomia:* Reflections of Origen's Understanding of Divine and Human Pedagogy in the *Address* Ascribed to Gregory Thaumaturgus." *JECS* 9 (2001): 27–52.

Valantasis, Richard. *Spiritual Guides of the Third Century: A Semiotic Study of the Guide-Disciple Relationship in Christianity, Neoplatonism, Hermetism, and Gnosticism.* Harvard Dissertations in Religion. Philadelphia: Fortress Press, 1991.

van Bavel, Tarsicius. "L'humanitè du Christ comme lac parvulorum et comme via dans la spiritualitè de saint Augustin." *Augustiniana* 7 (1987), 245–81.

van de Bunt, Annewies. "Milk and Honey in the Theology of Clement of Alexandria." In *Fides Sacramenti, Sacramentum Fidei: Studies in Honor of Pieter Smulders,* edited by Hans Jörg Auf der Maur et al., 27–39. Assen, the Netherlands: Van Gorcum, 1981.

van den Berg, R. M. "The Christian 'School' of Alexandria in the Second and Third Centuries." In *Centres of Learning: Learning and Location in Pre-Modern Europe and the Near East,* edited by J. W. Drijvers and A. M. MacDonald, 39–47. Leiden: Brill, 1995.

van den Hoek, Annewies. "The 'Catechetical' School of Early Christian Alexandria and Its Philonic Heritage." *HTR* 90 (1997): 59–87.

———. *Clement of Alexandria and His Use of Philo in the* Stromateis: *An Early Christian Reshaping of a Jewish Model. VCSup* 3. Leiden: Brill, 1988.

———. "Hymn of the Holy Clement to Christ the Saviour." In *Prayer from Alexander to Constantine: A Critical Anthology,* edited by Mark Kiley, 296–303. London: Routledge, 1997.

van der Eijk, Philip J. " 'Aristotle! What a Thing for You to Say!' Galen's Engagement with Aristotle and Aristotelians." In *Galen and the World of Knowledge,* edited by Christopher Gill et al., 261–81. Cambridge: Cambridge University Press, 2009.

van Fleteren, Frederick. "Authority and Reason, Belief and Understanding in the Thought of St. Augustine." *Augustinian Studies* 4 (1973): 33–71.

van Henten, Jan Willem. "Datierung und Herknuft des Vierten Makkabäerbuches." In *Tradition and Reinterpretation in Jewish and Early Christian Literature: Essays in Honor of Jürgen C. H. Lebram,* edited by J. van Henten, et al., 137–45. Leiden: Brill, 1986.

———. *The Maccabean Martyrs as Saviours of the Jewish People: A Study of 2 and 4 Maccabees.* Supplements for the Journal of the Study of Judaism 57. Leiden: Brill, 1997.

———. "The *Passio Perpetuae* and Jewish Martyrdom: The Motif of Motherly Love." In *Perpetua's Passions: Multidisciplinary Approaches to the* Passio Perpetuae et Felicitatis, edited by Jan N. Bremmer and Marco Formisano, 118–33. New York: Oxford University Press, 2012.

Van Hoof, Lieve. "Performing Paideia: Greek Culture as an Instrument for Social Promotion in the Fourth Century AD." *Classical Quarterly* 63.1 (2013): 387–406.

van Oort, Johannes. "The Young Augustine's Knowledge of Manichaeism: An Analysis of the Confessiones and Some Other Relevant Texts." *VC* 62 (2008): 441–66.

van Unnik, W. C. *Tarsus or Jerusalem: The City of Paul's Youth.* Translated by George Ogg. London: Eppworth Press, 1962.

Vessey, Mark. "The Demise of the Christian Writer and the Remaking of 'Late Antiquity': From H.-I. Marrou's Saint Augustine (1938) to Peter Brown's Holy Man (1983)." *JECS* 6.3 (1998): 377–411.

Vössing, Konrad. *Schule und Bildung im Nordafrika der Römischen Kaiserzeit.* Brussels: Latomus, 1997.

Wannamaker, Charles A. "A Rhetoric of Power: Ideology and 1 Corinthians 1–4." In *Paul and the Corinthians: Studies on a Community in Conflict: Essays in Honour of Margaret Thrall,* edited by Trevor J. Burke and J. Keith Elliott. Supplements to Novum Testamentum 109. Leiden: Brill, 2004.

Watts, Edward. *City and School in Late Antique Athens and Alexandria.* Transformation of the Classical Heritage 41. Berkeley: University of California Press, 2006.

Welborn, L. L. "On the Discord in Corinth: 1 Corinthians 1–4 and Ancient Politics." *JBL* 106.1 (1987): 85–111.

———. *Paul the Fool of Christ: A Study of 1 Corinthians 1–4 in the Comic-Philosophic Traditions.* Journal for the Study of the New Testament Supplement Series 293. London: T&T Clark, 2005.

———. *Politics and Rhetoric in the Corinthian Epistles.* Macon, GA: Mercer University Press, 1997.

Whitmarsh, Tim. *The Second Sophistic.* New Surveys in the Classics 35. Oxford: Oxford University Press, 2006.

Wiedemann, Thomas. *Adults and Children in the Roman Empire.* New Haven, CT: Yale University Press, 1989.

Winter, Bruce W. *Philo and Paul among the Sophists.* Society for New Testament Studies Monograph Series 96. Cambridge: Cambridge University Press, 1997.

Wolf, Joan B. *Is Breast Best? Taking on the Breastfeeding Experts and the New High Stakes of Motherhood.* Biopolitics. New York: New York University Press, 2011.

Wright, Lawrence. *Going Clear: Scientology, Hollywood, and the Prison of Belief.* New York: Vintage, 2013.

Yalom, Marilyn. *A History of the Breast.* New York: Ballantine Books, 1997.

Yoshiko Reed, Annette, and Natalie B. Dohrmann, *Jews, Christians, and the Roman Empire: The Poetics of Power in Late Antiquity.* Philadelphia: University of Pennsylvania Press, 2013.

Young, Frances M. "Paideia and the Myth of Static Dogma." In *The Making and Remaking of Christian Doctrine: Essays in Honour of Maurice Wiles,* edited by Sarah Coakley and David A. Pailin, 265–83. New York: Oxford University Press, 1993.

Young, Norman H. "Paidagogos: The Social Setting of a Pauline Metaphor." *Novum Testamentum* 29.2 (1987): 150–76.

Young, Robin Darling. "The 'Woman with the Soul of Abraham': Traditions about the Mother of the Maccabean Martyrs." In *"Women Like This": New Perspectives on Jewish Women in the Greco-Roman World,* edited by Amy-Jill Levine, 67–81. Early Judaism and Its Literature 1. Atlanta: Scholars Press, 1991.

Index of Subjects

Abraham, 65, 66

Achilles, 57, 247n74

Adam, 86, 109, 110, 135, 136

Aeneas, 165, 166

Ambrose of Milan, 85, 181–82

angels, 109–10

Antiochus IV Epiphanes, 55, 57

Antony, 182

Ara Pacis, 37–38, 204

Aristotle, 31–33, 34, 80, 100, 204

asceticism, 162, 163, 203–4

Augustine of Hippo, 19, 21, 86, 137, 168–99, 208, 268n21

Augustus Caesar, 36, 37–38, 39, 40, 41, 44, 204, 224n55. *See also* Rome

Aulus Gellius, 47, 49, 167

authority, 172–75, 181, 191, 269n26, 276n101

Basil of Caesarea, 140–42, 144–48, 157, 158, 159–60, 163, 236n84

BeDuhn, Jason, 177

Behr, John, 82

bio-power, 161, 163, 174, 203

Bjorklund, David F., 215n31

Blanc, Cécile, 124

Bloomer, W. Martin, 11

body: breast milk, 49; female, 155, 161, 170, 227n79; and mind, 116–17; mother's, 58, 180; nature, 113–14; and nourishment, 28, 30, 31, 34–35; resurrected, 117–19, 135; and soul, 25–26, 29, 30, 34, 114–16, 118; spiritual, 117–19, 131, 155. *See also* soul

Bonner, Stanley, 10

Borgen, Peder, 236n46

Boulluec, Alain Le, 106

Bourdieu, Pierre, 14–17, 18, 23, 203, 217n48, 217n50

Bradley, Keith, 228nn88–89, 230n111

Brakke, David, 92

bread, 124–27

breast-feeding: biological, 67, 155, 159, 163; bond, 57–58, 61; culture, 18, 43; eroticism, 12, 265n94; essence, 2–3, 5, 32, 197–98; God, 94, 95, 99; identity, 170; in Judaism, 63, 76; males, 203; maturity, 79; Moses, 142, 146; scripture, 111; spiritual, 155; symbolic, 5, 11, 19, 21, 43, 50, 71. *See also* milk

Brown, Peter, 171, 199

Buell, Denise Kimber, 102, 105, 216n39, 249n87

Burrus, Virginia, 138, 163, 254n84

Butler, Judith, 202, 209, 218nn57–58

Capelle, D. B., 169, 267n17

Caracalla (Antoninus), 9

Cassiciacum, 172–73, 200

Castelli, Elizabeth, 215n39

Celsus, 129, 131, 133, 134

children: divine origin, 56–57; family, 36–37, 44, 81; formation, 64; innocence, 94; nobility, 46; nourishment/nurture, 8–9, 10–11, 26–28, 29, 39, 41, 44, 46, 48, 59, 75–76, 214n21; perfection 97; plastic, 45; wisdom, 69. *See also* infants

Christianity: catechesis, 93; classes, 122–23, 128–29, 130, 131, 133, 257n92, 257n94; culture, 54, 158, 204; education, 167; family, 18, 163; food, 3–4, 7; growth, 103; household of God,

Christianity (*continued*)
102–3, 105, 167, 168, 198, 204, 209;
identity, 3, 20; instruction, 100;
knowledge, 13; mature, 154, 170; milk,
6, 9, 17, 83, 90, 91, 96–97, 107, 154,
189–90; nourishment, 77, 91, 92, 107,
157, 158, 161; pastoral care, 161–62,
273n77; perfection, 90, 121; second-
century, 80–81, 83, 106, 136; solid food,
6, 17, 189; stages, 121; weaning, 195
church: breast, 142, 146–47, 159–60, 197;
diversity, 130, 131, 133; formation, 148,
173–74; nourishment, 21, 88, 91, 95,
145, 156–57, 174, 160, 189, 190, 200,
270n43, 277n113; Rome, 167, 174
Clark, Elizabeth, 177, 203
Clement of Alexandria, 20, 82, 83, 85,
91–106, 107, 108, 135, 169, 247n71
Cochrane, Charles Norris, 199
Conybeare, Catherine, 172
Conzelmann, Hans, 13–14, 74, 217n50
Cooper, Kate, 167, 198
Corinth, Corinthians, 5, 51, 66, 71, 72,
73–76, 77, 83, 84, 85, 87, 90, 96–97,
204, 238n68, 240n84. *See also*
pneumatics/*pneumatikoi*
Coriolanus, 49–50
Council of Carthage, 197
Cribiore, Raffaella, 11
Crouzel, Henri, 121

D'Angelo, Mary Rose, 56, 58, 62
Daniélou, Jean, 121, 122
Dean-Jones, Leslie, 32, 222n33
de Lubac, Henri, 121, 122
Derrida, Jacques, 13, 201, 208; 218n58
Dido, 165, 166
Dio Cassius, 39, 44, 52, 53
Dionysius of Corinth, 201
divine sense, 116–17, 119, 130–31
divinization, 121
Dunn, Geoffrey, 9

Dunning, Benjamin H., 246n59
Dutton, Marsha, 170

Early Christianity and Greek Paideia, 7–8
eating well, 5–6, 9, 21, 53, 202, 206–8, 209,
210
education: Christian, 9; classical, 7–8, 199;
culture, 12, 65; feminine, 67; imitation,
216n40; liberal arts, 172–73; nature, 10,
11, 45, 46; nobility, 46; nourishment, 11,
24, 29, 30, 46, 65, 143; nurture, 10, 11,
45, 46; reason, 46; Roman, 10, 36, 168,
266n6; wisdom, 70. See also *paideia;*
teacher
Eleazar, 55
Elijah, 141
Engberg-Pedersen, Troels, 73, 238n64
Enlightenment, 205
epektasis, 139, 260n34
Epiphanius of Salamis, 134
Eucharist, 2–3, 103, 104, 105, 125, 126, 186,
188, 195, 200, 255n70
Eusebius, 201
Eve, 86, 109, 110, 135, 136
example (*exemplum*), 183, 191

faith, 184, 194, 196
family, 59–60, 140, 145, 197, 204, 208. *See
also under* Rome
father, 65, 75–76. *See also* Rome:
paterfamilias
Faustus, 181
Favorinus, 47–49, 52, 73, 99, 144, 147, 152,
230n118, 231nn124–25
femininity, 26, 67, 138, 162–63, 249n88,
264n84
Feuerbach, Ludwig, 1–3, 4
Fiedrowicz, Michael, 274n88
firstborn, 94–95, 105
Flemming, Rebecca, 42
food: classes, 112, 120, 131–33; culture, 1, 5,
18, 21, 62, 70; digestion, 109, 110, 203;

divinizing, 118; essence, 2, 18, 21, 28, 33, 62, 64, 68, 127–28, 139, 203; family, 140–41; formation, 47, 60; gods, 2; heavenly, 109; human nature, 4, 33; identity, 1, 17, 23, 203; intellect/mind, 31, 32, 70; likeness, 28; manna, 99; material, 4, 12, 113–14, 124, 158, 160, 179, 212n9; perfection, 3, 146; power, 131; rational, 132–33, 177; ritual, 2–3, 178–79, 188; sacrifice, 2; scripture, 149; social, 17, 23, 112; solid, 66, 68, 70, 92, 93, 97, 100, 103, 121, 122, 123, 130, 132, 169, 170–71, 186, 187, 191, 195; soul, 26, 34, 63, 135, 180; spiritual, 109–10, 149, 157, 158, 179; stages, 112, 120; symbolic, 4, 6, 8, 19, 112, 179, 207; transformation, 148; vegetables, 125, 128, 130, 131. *See also* bread; milk; nourishment/nurturance
formation: Christian, 99, 168, 171, 175–76, 190; church, 147; growth, 175–76; human, 5, 6–7, 19, 23, 24, 25, 32, 42, 72, 169; identity, 13, 17; imitation, 182–84; intellectual, 4, 7, 31, 33, 66, 67, 70, 74, 125, 158; and nourishment, 23, 121, 162, 173; order, 173; perfection, 147; persecution, 60; progressive, 122; rational, 130; scripture, 65; soul, 34, 64; spiritual, 10, 74
Foucault, Michel, 161, 203
France, supposed moral decline of, 205
Francis, James, 239n81

Galen of Pergamum, 33–36, 42, 53, 223nn42–43
Galinksy, Karl, 39
Gardner, Jane, 40, 226n66
Gaventa, Beverly, 74
Gleason, Maud, 11, 231n124
gnosis, Gnosticism, 83, 84–85, 87–88, 91, 92, 96, 101–3, 104, 105, 106, 241n9, 248n81. *See also under* Paul, apostle

God: activity (*energeia*), 151; breasts/breast milk, 94, 95, 100, 107, 151–53, 156, 179, 181; food, 63, 103, 178–80; image and likeness, 90, 118, 156, 250n11; nourishment, 86–87, 88–89; *Paradise Lost,* 109; power (*dynamis*), 151; source, 59; wisdom, 184
Gregory of Nyssa, 7, 21, 137, 138, 141, 142–64, 189, 200, 236n48, 260n35
Gregory the Wonderworker, 265n93
Gunderson, Erik, 48

Haber, Susan, 57, 58
Hagar, 65, 68
Hällström, Gunnar af, 253n52
Hanson, Ann Ellis, 43
Hanson, R. P. C., 122, 130, 136
Haraway, Donna 209
Harrison, Carol, 171–72
Hays, Richard, 239n81
Hector, 57, 247n74
Hecuba, 57, 247n74
Heracleon, 85, 108, 136
heretics, 192–94
Hick, John, 86
Hierius, 181
Hilary of Poitiers, 193, 194, 200
Himmelfarb, Martha, 61
Hippocrates/Hippocratics, 25, 28, 33, 34, 35, 72–73
History of Sexuality, 161
Hodgson, Geraldine, 9–10
Holy Spirit, 89–90, 91, 192–93
Homer, 48, 99
humanity: flesh, 150, 252n38; food, 23; infancy, 86–87, 88–92; perfection, 11, 89–90; purification, 150; two natures, 110, 113, 114–15, 148, 264n73
humility, 170, 183, 188, 196
Husserl, Edmund, 217n55

identity, 13–14

infants: Christians, 96, 102–3, 131;
    Corinthians, 87; essence, 52, 100, 191;
    food, 139, 179, 180–81; growth, 87,
    193–94, 200; identity, 147; initiation,
    105, 196–97; nourishment, 36, 42, 44,
    48; nurture, 43, 151; perfection, 89, 104;
    plastic, 47, 51, 64, 262n61; scripture,
    111; temptation, 187–88;
    transformation, 145; weaning, 46.
    See also children

intellect, 27, 34–35, 49, 67–68, 175

Irenaeus of Lyons, 20, 82, 85, 86–91, 92,
    106, 107, 135

Isaac, 66, 67, 69

Jacobs, Andrew, 18, 261n39

Jacobsen, Anders, 114

Jaeger, Werner, 7, 10, 11–12, 158,
    212n16

Jaffee, Martin, 239n71

Jesus Christ, 89, 94, 125, 127, 132, 170, 183.
    See also Logos

Jordan, Mark, 183

Jouanna, Jacques, 28, 34

Judaism, 19–20, 24; assimilation, 55;
    culture, 53, 63; essence, 54, 63, 70;
    family, 55; food, 54; Greek *paideia*, 53;
    Law, 55, 57, 58; milk, 76, 232n1;
    morality, 62; mother, 53; provincial, 53;
    Roman rule, 52, 53; wisdom, 66;
    worldview, 62

Judge, E. A., 70–71

Keller, Catherine, 207

Kilmartin, Edward, 98

kinship, 80, 94–95, 100, 105–6, 145, 152,
    167, 246n54

Kleeman, Alexandra, 111

Koch, Hal 114

Kovacs, Judith, 101, 121, 123, 253n49

Krawiec, Rebecca, 17–18, 260n27

language, 15–18, 23, 201, 202, 218n57

LaValle, Dawn, 98, 99, 247n71

Leitao, David D., 222n33

Libanius, 11

Lively, Genevieve, 225n60

Logos, 63, 66, 93, 96, 99, 102, 103, 125, 147,
    150; Philo, 235n33

Lord's Prayer, 125

Lorenz, Hendrik 33

Maccabeans, 54, 63, 70, 76, 141. *See also*
    martyr

Macrina, 142, 159–60, 162, 163, 208,
    264n84

Macrobius, 165–67, 180

magister. See teacher

Manichaeism, 171, 173, 174, 177–79, 184,
    189, 197, 199, 269n31, 270n32

manna, 63

Markus, Robert, 199

Marrou, H. I, 12, 167, 198, 266n6

Martens, Peter, 112

Martin, Dale, 26

martyr, 54, 55, 56, 61, 70, 76, 233n7. *See
    also* Maccabeans

masculinity, 26, 68, 138, 163,
    231n124

matrona. See mother

Mattern, Susan, 33

Mattila, Sharon Lea, 67, 68

McDuffie, Felecia, 179, 268n21

McGowan, Andrew, 98

McLynn, Neil, 199

metaphor, 9, 12, 13, 14, 16, 202, 217n48,
    237n63

Milan, 172

Miles, Margaret, 170, 268n21

milk: authority, 174; blood, 166; bond, 87;
    character, 166, 168; Christian, 142;
    culture, 156; essence, 35–36, 180; faith,
    184, 193, 268n21, 275n93; flesh, 99;
    formation, 174; God, 95, 150, 153;

growth, 196; humility, 170, 191; identity, 50, 168; imitation, 12, 75; infants, 124, 274n85; instruction, 129–30; intellect, 156; kinship, 100; mother's/breast, 47, 48–49, 52, 53–54, 56, 57, 58, 59–60, 61, 62, 64, 70, 75, 76, 144, 145, 159, 166; nature, 167; perfection, 97, 98, 104, 147, 163, 174; political, 79–80; preaching, 102; ritual, 98, 103–4, 197, 219n62; Rome, 37, 50; scripture, 128, 196–97; shared, 80; and solid food, 66, 68, 70, 92, 93, 97, 100, 121, 122, 123, 130, 169, 170–71, 186, 187, 193–94, 200; symbolic, 43–44, 107; transformation, 139; weaning, 186, 188–89, 194; wisdom, 147. *See also* breast-feeding

Miller, Patricia Cox, 69, 278n3

Milton, John, 109–10, 112, 136

mind, 115–19. *See also* intellect; *nous, noetic*

Mitchell, Margaret, 77, 78, 81–82

Monica, 172, 180, 182, 184–85, 199–200

Morgan, Teresa, 10

morphosis, 7, 31, 158

Moses, 68–70, 73, 140, 141–46, 147, 157, 159

mother: affection, 60; androcentric, 56; formation, 49, 58, 170; and infant, 43–44, 47, 64, 70; influence, 57, 65; Maccabean, 54–62, 73, 76, 141; nature, 48; and nurse, 45; as nurse, 69; nurture, 59, 61, 76, 151, 159; reasoning, 60; wisdom, 67

Muhammad, 205

mystagogy, 149–50

mystery cults, 93–94, 149–50

Nasrallah, Laura, 225n61

Newman, John Henry, 158

Niehoff, Maren 62–63

Noel, Virginia, 254n63

nourishment/nurturance: anthropology, 112; authority, 173; belief, 146; biology, 3, 140–41, 142, 143–45, 210; body, 29, 113–14, 155; bride, 154–56; Christianity, 9, 158, 205; church, 189; culture, 3, 17; education, 11, 24, 30, 143; erotics of, 162; essence, 198; family, 140–41; God, 86–87, 100, 107; growth, 33; heavenly, 68; humanity, 1, 42, 72, 86, 138; identity, 147; for intellect, 35, 67–68; kinship, 105–6; knowledge of gods, 1; likeness, 31, 32, 47; material, 68, 143–44; mimetic, 139; and nature/essence, 2; and nobility, 72, 76; and nurture, 31, 58, 64, 214n25; and offspring, 27; perfection, 150; physical, 7, 8–9, 24, 25; power, 31, 33, 35, 49, 50, 73, 202–3, 204; social, 69, 107–8, 257; and soul, 25, 28, 31–32, 35, 36, 67, 102, 138, 151; spiritual, 11–12, 117, 123, 126, 160; symbolic, 24, 60, 121, 138–39, 160, 177, 204, 207, 210; wisdom, 67; Word, 124–25, 127–29. *See also* food; milk

nous, noetic, 110–11, 116, 120, 126, 131, 135, 250n5

nurse, 43, 44–46, 47–48, 52, 64

Olympias, 148, 149, 154, 160, 162

Origen of Alexandria, 20, 21, 85, 108, 110–37, 149, 169, 250n11, 250n17, 260n35, 262n35, 265n93

Osborn, Eric, 93

paideia: classical, 53, 172; education, 12, 29–31; Greek, 6–8, 54, 66, 62, 63, 67, 142, 146, 158–59, 167; mother's, 58, 65; Origen, 129, 134; Paul, 13, 74; Solomon, 149, 157, 159. *See also* education

Paideia: The Ideals of Greek Culture, 8

pangenesis, 27–28

Paradise Lost, 109–10, 135

Paul, apostle, 4, 18, 20; anthropology, 111;
    epistolary practice, 73; flesh, 148–49;
    food, 53, 66, 76, 107, 119–23, 131;
    formation, 54, 66, 107; and Gnosticism,
    84; infant, 89–90; interpretation of, 87,
    88–89, 92, 93, 97, 99, 134, 136; legacy,
    80–82, 83, 106; martyrdom, 81; milk,
    4–5, 13–14, 15, 17, 20, 21, 24, 54, 71, 72,
    73–76, 77–78, 81, 85, 89–90, 97, 98,
    125, 130, 135–36; nourishment, 71;
    pedagogy, 91–92; philosophy, 70–71;
    preacher, 186; solid food, 5, 13–14, 17,
    20, 21, 24, 71, 73–74, 77–78, 85, 97, 130,
    135–36; wisdom, 71–72, 74, 84, 87
Paulinus of Nola, 185
perfection, 148, 152, 154, 158, 163–64, 174,
    189, 190, 200, 275n92
Peter (brother of Macrina), 160
Pharaoh, 69–70
Philo of Alexandria, 54, 62–70, 71, 76, 107,
    143–44, 235n33, 236n48
Pinytos of Knossos, 201
Plato, 28–30, 33, 34, 132, 222n33
Plutarch, 11, 46–47, 53, 72, 73, 167, 230n118
pneuma, 26, 71, 72–73, 77, 99, 220n5,
    238n64, 238n68
pneumatics/pneumatikoi, 72, 84, 87, 88,
    90, 96. See also Corinth, Corinthians
Pomeroy, Sarah, 41
Ponticianus, 182
Promised Land, 98, 104

Quintilian, 11, 45–46, 49, 73, 167

rabbinic tradition, 61–62, 239n71
Raphael, 109–10, 112, 119, 134, 136
Rawson, Beryl, 37
reason (ratio), 65, 172–75, 187, 269n26,
    269n28
Remus, 165, 224n56
reproduction, 36
resurrection, 117–19, 135

rhetorical analysis, 17–18
Rome, 19; children, 40–42, 152, 165;
    domus, 38, 40, 75, 168; family, 40, 41,
    43, 58–59, 61, 73, 80, 145, 152, 167,
    226n66, 271n56; family values, 23, 36,
    37, 38–39, 49, 50, 52, 53, 54, 62, 63, 68,
    75, 76, 107, 143, 159, 161, 162, 163,
    167–68, 173, 198, 208, 224n53, 225n62,
    228n79; gender, 41, 42; imperium/
    imperial ideology, 36–38, 40, 41, 47, 50,
    54, 58–59, 162; law, 38–39, 226–27n70;
    male heirs, 37, 39; marriage, 38–40, 45;
    medicine, 42; mother, 39, 40, 42–43, 52,
    68; nourishment, 42, 225n62; nurse, 41,
    42–43, 229n90; paterfamilias, 39–40,
    168; slavery, 43; souls, 169; women, 40,
    228n79
Romulus, 37, 165, 224n56
Rosenblum, Jordan D., 63

Sabazios, cult of, 93–94
salvation, 93, 101, 139, 164
Sarah (of scripture), 65, 66, 68
Schmemann, Alexander, 212n9
Schmithals, Walter, 84
scripture: and identity, 76; interpretation,
    20, 111, 119, 125; milk, 184;
    nourishment, 63, 65, 112, 120, 121, 123,
    124, 128, 149, 150; spiritual, 156
Second Sophistic, 33–34
seed (semen), 27–28, 32, 102, 205;
    insemination, 105, 162, 243n27, 265n93
Sessa, Kristina, 225n63, 266n8, 267n12
Severus, 185
Shakespeare, William, 49
Shaw, Brent, 197–98
Simplicianus, 182
slavery, 10, 43, 45, 48, 140, 208, 227n79
social history, 17–18
solid food. See under food
Solomon, 149, 150, 155, 159, 261n39,
    261n42

Sophocles, 9

Soranus, 43–44, 52, 53, 167

soul: appetitive, 33, 34; and body, 26, 28, 112, 114–17, 118, 134; classifying, 111, 119–21, 126, 128–30, 132–33, 134, 136–37; development, 35, 143, 188; education, 30–31; greatness, 174–75; health, 36; milk, 130; nourishment, 25, 27, 28–29, 34, 157; perfection, 121, 138; progress, 120; purified, 150; rational, 34, 156–57; spiritual, 34, 119, 148; stages, 174–75; transformation, 139; wax, 64; weaning, 150. *See also* body

Steenberg, M. C., 88

Stefaniw, Blossom, 111

Stoics, 34

Strousma, Guy, 199, 267n17

Tacitus, pearl-clutching of, 45

Taussig, Hal, 3

teacher, 46, 50, 181, 184–85, 199, 272n64

Tellus, 37–38, 204

telos, 140, 143, 163, 168, 170

Tertullian, 9, 206

Teske, Roland, 271n45

Theudas, 81

Torah, 61, 63, 73. *See also* Judaism: Law

Torjesen, Karen Jo, 121

transformation: bride, 152–53; education, 209; food, 112, 124, 133, 148, 209, 254n60; free choice, 146; imitation, 182; maternal, 152; milk, 139; rational, 113, Solomonic, 159; spiritual, 109–10, 134, 136, 148

trophe, 29–30, 31, 46, 140, 141, 142, 143

Unnik, W. C. van, 221n32

Valantasis, Richard, 249n87, 265n93

Valentinus, Valentinians, 81, 83, 84–85, 92, 101, 108, 136

Van Bavel, Tarsicius, 170

van Fleteren, Frederick, 173, 268n28

van Henten, Willem, 56, 233n7

Virgil, 48, 165

Volumnia, 49–50, 51, 57

weaning, 46, 69, 187, 188, 190, 194, 195, 197, 199

wet nurse. *See* nurse; Rome: nurse

wisdom, 65–66, 67, 72, 74, 184, 186–87

Wolf, Joan B., 205

Word (of God), 21, 89, 97, 103–4, 120, 124–26, 127–28, 129, 131, 133, 135, 154, 184, 188, 195, 256n75. *See also* Logos

Young, Robin Darling, 56

Index of Ancient Texts

Old Testament

Gen.

1:26	250n11, 250n17
2:7	250n11, 250n17
2:18	66
15:16	63
28	186

Exod. 143

2:2 (LXX)	236n56
2:7 (LXX)	69, 236n05
2:7–10	68
2:10	69
3	98, 244n43, 247n68, 277n120
3:8	97
16	63

Num.

2:6–9 123	

Ps.

30	190–91, 274n88
130	195, 274n88
130:1–2	192
131:1–2	276n103

Prov.

2:5	116

Song, 138, 149–50, 152, 153, 154, 155, 157, 158, 160, 162, 163

3:7–8	154
4:5	263n73
4:10	156
4:11	61

5:13	156
6:2–3	157

Isa.

7:9	184

Lam.

1:16	62

New Testament

Matt.

21:16	189

Luke

11:7	154

John, 95, 180, 187, 197

1:1	196
3	94
6:51–57	125
16:12–13	187

Rom.

14	111, 125, 256n87
14:2	130

1 Cor., 53, 81, 84, 87, 100, 107, 152

1–2	71
1–4	20, 75
1:17	71, 238n68
1:21	84
1:26	71
2–3	73, 96
2:6	190
2:13	72
2:14–15	72

2:16	72
3	4, 16, 66, 70, 72, 75, 76, 77, 79, 84, 89, 91, 92, 95, 96, 97, 98, 100, 103, 104, 106, 111, 123, 130, 136, 169, 186, 239n76, 241n9, 244n43, 245n44, 247n68
3:1–3	4, 6, 14, 18, 71, 74, 122, 123, 187
3:2	101
4	75
4:15	239n82
4:16	75
8	4
8:8	4
12	155, 242n14
12:13	238n68
15	117

2 Cor.

12	186

Gal.

3:28	96, 246n59

Eph.

2:19	167
4:22–24	175

Phil.

3:13	143

Col.

1:15	94

1 Thess.

2:7	237n63

Heb.

5:11–14	237n63

5:12–14	187, 254n56
5:14	130
12:23	94

1 Pet.

2:2	237n63

1 John

2:18	188

Apocrypha

2 Macc., 54, 55, 56, 57, 59, 60, 62, 71

4:11	233n5
6–7	54, 55
7:20–22	56

4 Macc. 54, 55, 56, 58–59, 60–62, 71, 233n6

13:19–22	59, 258n8
14:13	60
15:23	60
16:5–8	60
16:7	236n54
18:1	61
18:3	61

Philo of Alexandria

Conf.

13.49	236n47

Dreams, 67, 69

2.10	66

Drunkenness

33	65
34–35	65

Flight

112	235n33
137	63

Husbandry, 239n81

Mating, 66, 67, 68, 70

9	65, 236n46
19	65, 236n46
73	236n44

Mos., 68, 271n55

1.17	69, 143
1.18	69
1.19	69
1.20	70
1.23	70

Spec. Laws

2.228–30	235n38

Virt., 67

128	64
130	64
178–79	235n38

Heir?

265	64
294–300	64

Rabbinic Works

Lam. Rabbah, 61

Nag Hammadi Codices

2 Apoc. Jas, 240n3

Early Christian Literature

Augustine of Hippo
Acad.

3.20.43–45	172

Catech.

9	267n17

Cath.

1.2.3	173
1.10.17	173

Conf., 183, 190, 200, 275n92

1.6.7	179, 180
2.8.16	181
3.1.1	178
3.4.8	180
3.5.9–6.10	270n32
3.6.10	177, 179
4.1.1	180
7	180
7.10.16	184
7.18.24	181
8	182

Doct. chr., 183, 184, 199

1.11.11	183
2.12.17	184

Ex. Ps., 274n88, 275n92

8	189, 190, 274n88
8.5	189, 190
30(2–3)	274n88
30(2).6	191
30(2).9	190, 191
30(2).12	191
98.1	168, 192, 276n102
130	192, 274n88
130.2	277n113
130.9	192
130.11	193
130.12	193, 194
130.13	194, 195
130.13–14	195

Hom. First. Ep

3.1	188, 274n86

Hom. Gosp. John

7	186
7.23	186

96	187
96–98	187, 267n17, 274n85
96.1	187
96.2–3	187
97	273n81
97.1	273n81
97.2	187, 273n81
98	187, 274n84
98.2	187
98.4	187
98.6	187
98.7	274n85

Letters

33.5	168
109.1	185

Mag., 184

11.38	272n64

Ord.

2.5.16	269n26

Quant. an.

32.69	174
33.70–76	174
33.76	174

Serm.

119.1	196
119.4	197
216.7	270n43
216.8	271n43

Simpl., 171

Teach. Un.

4.8	274n84

Trin.

1.1.3	276n106

True Rel.

26.48	175
26.49	175
28.50	176, 186

Basil of Caesarea

Letters

37	140, 147

Clement of Alexandria

Paed., 92, 93, 100, 101, 104, 105, 107

1.5.19	95
1.6	95, 98, 101, 103, 127, 234n18
1.6.31	96
1.6.34	97
1.6.35	92
1.6.35–36	97
1.6.36	97
1.6.37	97
1.6.38	102
1.6.39	103
1.6.40	99
1.6.41	99
1.6.42	99
1.6.43	99
1.6.45	100
1.7.54	100
1.36.5–6	98

Prot., 93, 94–95, 96, 105

2.16	94
9	94
10	94
10.108	94
11	246n52
12	245n50

Strom., 93, 100, 101, 104

1.1.1.3–1.1.2.1	102
1.1.7.2–3	102
1.11.3	249n87

Clement of Alexandria, *Strom. (continued)*

1.11.53.2	102
1.11.53.3	103
2.19.97.1	102
2.19.98.3	102
2.19.100.1	248n85
2.20.104.2	102
4.3.9.2	102
4.21.130.4	102
5	101, 103
5.10.62.3	103
5.10.66.2	104
5.10.66.2–3	103
5.11.70.1–2	104

Epiphanius of Salamis
Pan.

64.72.9	134

Eusebius of Caesarea
Hist. eccl.

4.23	201

Gregory of Nazianzus
Or.

15	234n27

Gregory of Nyssa
En. Bas., 139, 141, 142, 144, 145, 146–47, 159

16	141
20	142
24	141
24–25	141

Hom. Song, 139, 148, 149, 154, 156, 158, 160, 264n84

Preface	148
1	149, 150, 151, 152, 153
2	153, 155
3	154
6	154, 155
7	155, 263n73
7–10	155

9	156
14	157
15	138, 157

Mos., 139, 142–43, 145, 146–47

1.2–3	259n17
1.5	143
1.17	143, 144
1.18	144
2.1	146
2.3	146
2.5	146
2.6	146
2.12	146
2.238–38	260n34

Soul, 258n3

Vit. Macr., 159, 264n84

3	159
12	160
22	160
26	160

Hilary of Poitiers
Comm. Ps.

130.4	193, 276n108
130.4–5	193

Hippolytus
Trad. ap.

21.24–38	277n120

Irenaeus
Dem.

1.1.8–12	86

Her., 86, 90, 91, 92

4	89
4.Pr.4	86–87
4.9.3	88
4.37.7	88

4.38.1	89, 246n52
4.38.2	89
4.38.3	89, 90
4.38.4	90

Jerome
Jov., 219n61

Letters

82.2	206
107	271n56
122.4	219n61
128	271n56

Lucif.

| 8 | 277n120 |

Origen of Alexandria
Ag. Cel.

Prol.6	129
3.52	129
4.18	127
7.59	131, 132
7.60	132

Comm. Cor., 124, 133, 254n60

12	122–23
12.2	123
12.5	124
12.6	123
12.8–10	123
12.12	123
12.13	124
12.15–18	123

Comm. Jo.

| 5.8 | 85 |

Comm. Rom., 133

8.9.5	130
9.36.1	130
9.36.2	131
9.36.3	131

Comm. Song

| 1 | 262n53 |

Dial.

13.19–20	110
16.11	110
16.12–14	110

Hom. Gen. Ex.

| 1.13 | 250n11 |
| 7.8 | 127 |

Hom. Jud.

| 5.6 | 129 |
| 6.2 | 129 |

Hom. Num.

27.1	128
27.1.1	128
27.12	128

Pasch., 255n70

Pray., 133

27.2	124
27.4	124, 125
27.5	125
27.6	126
27.7	126
27.8	126
27.9	126

Princ., 130

1.1.6	115
1.1.7	116
1.1.9	116
2.1.4	114, 124
2.2.2	115
2.10.1	117
2.10.3	117
2.11.2	117
2.11.3	118

Origen of Alexandria, *Princ.* (*continued*)

2.11.6	118, 119
2.11.7	119
3	113
3.4.2	115, 119
3.6.5	252n38
3.6.6	252n38
4.2.4	120

Paulinus of Nola

Letters

8.1	185

Tertullian

Cor.

3	197

Mon.

11.9	214n24, 219n61

Scap., 206

IV.5	9

Greco-Roman Literature

Aristotle

De An.

415a	31

Part. An.

672b8–23	31

Pol.

1.1.7	79–80

Artemidorus

Interp.

1.16	231n127

Augustus Caesar

Lex Julia de Adulteriis, 39

Lex Julia de Maritandis Ordinibus, 39

Lex Papia Poppaea, 39

Res Gestae

8.5	224n5
8.67	224n55

Aulus Gellius

Attic Nights, 47, 48, 144

12.1.9	47, 266n4
12.1.14	47
12.1.17–18	48
12.1.20–24	48

Cicero

Tusc.

3.1–3	230n106

Epictetus

Disc.

2.16.39	239n81

Ench.

46	216n46

Galen of Pergamum

Cap.

1	34
2	34

Properties, 35

Hippocratic texts

Nature, 221n19

Nut., 26, 36, 48, 99

2	25
7	25
22	26

Reg., 28

26–28	26
28	26, 27
35	26, 27

Homer
Il.
  22.78–90   57
  22.83   247n74

Od.
  9.27   245n51

Longus
Daphn.
  4.9.3   240n2

Macrobius
Sat., 265n1
  5.11.15–17   166

Plato
Laws
  643c–d   30
  788c   30
  807d   30, 221n31

Menex.
  237A–B   258n10

Prot.
  313c–d   30

Rep.
  376e–377c   30
  441a   30

Soph.
  230c–d   30

Tim.
  43a   29
  44a–b   29
  44b–c   29
  47d   29

Plutarch
Lives, 224n56
On Ed.

  1   46
  2   46
  3   46, 47, 258n8

Quintilian
Inst.
  1.1.2   45
  1.1.4–5   45
  1.1.21   214n25
  1.2.20   268n17
  2.4.5   46
  10.2.13   216n40

Sextus Empiricus
Outlines
  1.55–58   256n80

Sophocles
Ant., 9

Soranus
Gyn., 45
  2.18.4   43
  2.19   44
  2.19.15   44
  2.20   44
  2.46–48   46
  2.47.2   46

Tacitus
Ann.
  13.15   214n28
Dial.
  28.3   45
  29   45

Theodosian Code
  9.24.1.1   221n27

Virgil
Aen., 165, 198

Papyri

O. Berenike
  2.129   234n19

Islamic Literature

Hadith, 205

Quran
  Sura 4:32   204–5